SHI'ISM

SHI^CISM

Doctrines, Thought, and Spirituality

Edited, Annotated, and with
an Introduction by

SEYYED HOSSEIN NASR

HAMID DABASHI

SEYYED VALI REZA NASR

State University of New York Press

Published by
State University of New York Press, Albany

©1988   State University of New York

Printed in the United States of America

For information, address State University of New York
Press, State University Plaza, Albany, N.Y., 12246

Library of Congress Cataloging-in-Publication Data
Shiᶜism : doctrines, thought and spirituality.

   Includes index.
   1. Shiᶜah.   I. Nasr, Seyyed Hossein.   II. Dabashi,
Hamid, 1951–   .   III. Nasr, Seyyed Vali Reza,
1960–   .
BP1935.S527   1988   297'.82   87-10258
ISBN 0-88706-689-5
ISBN 0-88706-690-9

              10   9   8   7   6   5   4   3   2

To the blessed memory of our revered teachers

Sayyid Abu'l-Hasan Rafiᶜi Qazwini
Sayyid Muhammad Kazim 'Assar
Sayyid Muhammad Husayn Tabataba'i

May God's Mercy be upon their souls

Contents

I. Origins

II. The Shi^ci Position vs. Other Divisions Within Islam

III. Shi^ci Doctrines and Beliefs

IV. Shi^ci Spirituality and Piety

V. The Intellectual and Artistic Life

VI. Shi^ci Thought in the Twentieth Century

Preface

Recent political events in the Middle East have drawn a picture of Shiᶜism in the collective Western mind that rests solely on the immediate experience of the West with the Islamic world and that reflects misconceptions born of a primarily political confrontation. Therefore, Shiᶜism is often seen not only as an essentially political phenomenon but also as a creed of violence. This book is an effort to dispel this common view. It has been our objective to supercede this politically fabricated notion and to present Shiᶜism in its most essential nature—in its doctrinal, intellectual, and spiritual dimensions. Understanding Shiᶜism in its total reality will not only do justice to a religious tradition, rich and thriving in the course of its historical unfolding, but it also will be instrumental in promoting a more balanced approach to issues of primarily political significance.

This volume is a collection of the most significant works already extant on the doctrinal, intellectual, and spiritual dimensions of Shiᶜism. It is our belief that the impediment to the genuine understanding of Shiᶜism, and the intellectual lacunae in the more recent works done on the subject, does not lie in the inadequacy of new research, but in the excessive attention paid to only one aspect of Shiᶜism—political—at the expense of others. In selecting the material that appears in this volume, we looked primarily for works, by Shiᶜi and non-Shiᶜi scholars, that attempted to foster an interpretative understanding of Shiᶜism in its dogmatic and cognitive aspects. Therefore, although this volume is not oblivious to the political manifestations of Shiᶜism, it views its main contribution in bringing to the fore equally important and often neglected religious and spiritual beliefs and practices of a world community.

S.H.N.
H.D.
S.V.R.N.

Note To The Reader

In this volume we have used the standard rules of transliteration prevalent in academia. Most words are transliterated according to their Arabic pronounciation. However, for those words where the Persian form is more common to Shi^ci studies, transliteration follows the Persian pronounciation. For instance, we have used *marja^c-i taqlid* rather than *marja^c al-taqlid*. Moreover, in the case of words for which there exist widely used standardized forms in English such as Allah, Qur'an, Muhammad, Imam, Ayatollah, Shi^ci, or names of dynasties such as Safavid, Qajar and Pahlavi, no transliteration will appear in the text.

So far as titles such as *Hadrat*, Imam, Ayatollah, or ^cAllamah are concerned, they appear in this volume in the exact form in which they were presented in the original texts which we have reprinted. In our preface, introduction, and explanatory paragraphs, title of various personages reflect the standard form of reference to that person in Western academic works. Hence, we have used Imam Husayn, ^cAllamah Tabataba'i, or Ayatollah Taliqani. The usage of title in no way reflects a judgement on behalf of the editors concerning the political, religious, or spiritual status of the personage in question.

In preparing this volume we have changed the transliteration system of the sources we have used in order to present a single transliteration system for this volume.

Acknowledgments

Grateful acknowledgment is made to the following for permission to reprint from previously published works in this volume:

Cambridge University Press: Excerpt from *Literary History of Persia* by E.G. Browne, copyrighted © 1953 Cambridge University Press, Cambridge, U.K. Reprinted by permission.

Center for Middle East Studies, Harvard University: Excerpt from *Arabic and Islamic Studies in Honor of Hamilton A.R. Gibb*, edited by George Makdisi, copyrighted © 1965 Harvard University Press, Cambridge, U.S. Reprinted by permission.

Edinburgh University Press: Excerpt from *Islamic Philosophy and Theology*. by W. Montgomery Watt, copyrighted © 1962 Edinburgh University Press, Edinburgh, U.K. Reprinted by permission.

George Allen & Unwin: Excerpt from *Sufi Essays*, by Seyyed Hossein Nasr, copyrighted © 1972 George Allen & Unwin, London, U.K. Reprinted by permission.

Iranian Studies: Excerpt from "Color in Safavid Architecture: the Poetic Diffusion of Light", by Nader Ardalan, Copyrighted © 1974 Iranian Studies, New York, U.S. Reprinted by permission.

Kegan Paul International: Excerpt from *Muslim Sects and Divisions, the section on Muslim sects in Kitab al-milal wa'l-nihal of Muhammad ibn ᶜAbd al-Karim Shahrastani,* translated by A.K. Kazi and J.G. Glynn, copyrighted © 1984 Kegan Paul International, London, U.K. Reprinted by permission.

Khaneghah and Maktab of Maleknia Naseralishah: Excerpt from *The Excellent Sayings of the Prophet Muhammad and Hazrat Ali,* copyrighted © 1978 Khaneghah and Maktab of Maleknia Naseralishah, New York, U.S. Reprinted by permission.

Luzac & Co.: Excerpts from *Al-Babu al-Hadi ᶜAshar*, by ᶜAllamah al-Hilli, copyrighted © 1958 Luzac & Co., U.K. Reprinted by permission.

and

Excerpt from The *Shiᶜite Religion*, by Dwight Donaldson, copyrighted © 1933 Luzacs & Co. London, U.K. Reprinted by permission.

Middle East Center, University of Utah: Excerpt from *Islamic Philosophy in Contemporary Persia: A Survey of Activity During the Past Two Decades*, by Seyyed Hossein Nasr, copyrighted © 1972, Middle East Center, University of Utah, Salt Lake City, U.S. Reprinted by permission.

Mouton Publications: Excerpt from *Redemptive Suffering in Islam: A Study of the Devotional Aspects of ᶜAshura in Twelver Shiᶜism*, by Mahmud Ayoub, copyrighted © 1978 Mouton Publications, Berlin, West Germany. Reprinted by permission.

Muhammadi Trust: Excerpts from *Alserat, Selection of Articles (1975–1983)*, copyrighted ©1983 Muhammadi Trust, London, U.K. Reprinted by permission.

and

Alserat, Imam Husayn Conference Number, copyrighted © 1986 Muhammadi Trust, London, U.K. Reprinted by permission.

and

Amir al-Mu'minin Supplications, translated by William Chittick, copyrighted © nd. Muhammadi Trust, London, U.K. Reprinted by permission.

and

Kitab al-Irshad by Shaykh al-Mufid, copyrighted © 1981 Muhammadi Trust, London, U.K. Reprinted by permission.

and

Falsafaduna, by Muhammad Baqir Sadr, translated by Shams Inati, unpublished manuscript. Reprinted by permission.

Princeton University Press: Excerpt from *Spiritual Body and Celestial Earth, From Mazdean Iran to Shiᶜi Iran*, by Henry Corbin, translated by Nancy Pearson, copyrighted © 1977 Princeton University Press, Princeton, U.S. Reprinted by permission.

Ronald Press Co.: Excerpt from *Islam: The Straight Path; Islam Interpreted by Muslims*, edited by Kenneth Morgan, copyrighted © 1958 Ronald Press Co., New York, U.S. Reprinted by permission.

Simon and Shuster: Excerpt from *Mantle of the Prophet; Religion and Politics in Iran*, by Roy Mottahedeh, copyrighted © 1985 Simon and Shuster, New York, U.S. Reprinted by permission.

Studies in Comparative Religion: Excerpt from "The Force of Traditional Philosophy in Iran Today", by Henry Corbin, copyrighted © 1968 Studies in Comparative Religion, U.K. Reprinted by permission.

State University of New York Press: Excerpts from *Shi͏ci Anthology*, by William Chittick, copyrighted © 1981 SUNY Press, Albany, U.S. Reprinted by permission.

and

Shi͏ci Islam, by ͏cAllamah Sayyid Muhammad Husayn Tabataba'i, translated by Seyyed Hossein Nasr, copyrighted © 1975 SUNY Press, Albany, U.S. Reprinted by permission.

Syracuse University Press: Excerpt from *Mysticism and Dissent: Socio-Religious Thought in Qajar Iran*, by Mangol Bayat, copyrighted 1982 Syracuse University Press, Syracuse, U.S. Reprinted by permission.

University of Chicago Press: Excerpt from *Venture of Islam*, by Marshall Hodgson, copyrighted © 1966 Universityt of Chicago Press, Chicago, U.S. Reprinted by permission.

University of Texas Press: Excerpt from *Modern Islamic Political Thought*, by Hamid Enayat, copyrighted © 1982 University of Texas Press, Austin, U.S. Reprinted by permission.

List of Abbreviations

In preparing this volume we have used the following sources. They have been cited here, alphabetically, according to the abbreviations with which they have been referred to in the text. This list provides information regarding the exact title, author, translator, place and time of publication, and name of publisher of each source.

ALSERAT *Alserat, Selection of Articles (1975–1983).* London: Muhammadi Trust, nd.

AMS *Amir al-Mu'minin Supplications.* Translated and edited by William Chittick. London; Muhammadi Trust, nd.

ASIHCN *Alserat, Imam Husayn Conference Number.* Vol. XII, No. 1 (Spring 1986).

BHA ᶜAllamah al-Hilli. *Al-Babu al-Hadi ᶜAshar.* London: Luzac and Co., 1958.

CSA Nader Ardalan. "Color in Safavid Architecture: The Poetic Diffusion of Light." *Iranian Studies.* Vol. VII, Nos. 1–2. (Winter–Spring 1974).

ESPHEMA *The Excellent Sayings of the Prophet Muhammad and Hazrat Ali.* New York: Khaneghah and Maktab of Maleknia Naseralishah, 1978.

IICD Seyyed Hossein Nasr. *Introduction to Islamic Cosmological Doctrines.* Boulder, Colo.: Shambala, 1978.

IPCP Seyyed Hossein Nasr. *Islamic Philosophy in Contempo-*

rary Persia: A Survey of Activity During the Past Two Decades. Salt Lake City: Middle East Center, University of Utah, 1972.

IPT W. Montgomery Watt. *Islamic Philosophy and Theology.* Edinburgh: Edinburgh University Press, 1962.

KI Shaykh al-Mufid. *Kitab al-Irshad.* London: Muhammadi Trust, 1981.

LHP Edward G. Browne: *Literary History of Persia.* 4 vols. Cambridge: Cambridge University Press, 1953.

MDSTQI Mangol Bayat. *Mysticism and Dissent; Socio-Religious Thought in Qajar Iran.* Syracuse, N.Y.: Syracuse University Press, 1982.

MIPT Hamid Enayat. *Modern Islamic Political Thought.* Austin: University of Texas Press, 1982.

MP Roy Mottahedeh. *Mantle of the Prophet; Religion and Politics in Iran.* New York: Simon and Shuster, 1985.

MSCV *Mulla Sadra Commemoration Volume.* Tehran: Faculty of Theology of Tehran University, 1960–1961.

MSD A. K. Kazi and J. G. Flynn (trans.) *Muslim Sects and Divisions. The section on Muslim sects in Kitab al-milal Wa'l-nihal of Muhammad ibn ᶜAbd al-Karim Shahrastani (d.1153).* London: Kegan Paul International, 1984.

PCIP Murtada Mutahhari. "The Problem of Contradiction in Islamic Philosophy" Shahriyar Saᶜadat (trans.). *Al-Tawhid,* Vol. 1, No. 1. (Muharram 1404).

POI Leonard Binder. "The Proofs of Islam: Religion and Politics In Iran." In George Makdisi, ed., *Arabic and Islamic Studies in Honor of Hamilton A. R. Gibb.* Cambridge, Mass, Harvard University Press, 1965.

RSISD   Mahmud Ayoub. *Redemptive Suffering in Islam: A Study of the Devotional Aspects of ^cAshura in Twelver Shi^cism.* The Hague, Netherlands: Mouton Publications, 1978.

SA   William Chittick (ed. and trans.). *A Shi^cite Anthology.* Selected by ^cAllamah Tabataba'i, with an introduction by Seyyed Hossein Nasr. Albany, N.Y.: SUNY Press, 1981.

SAPC   Seyyed Hossein Nasr. *Sacred Art in Persian Culture.* Ipswich: Golgonza Press, 1971. Reprinted in *Islamic Art and Spirituality.* Albany: N.Y.: SUNY Press, 1986.

SBCE   Henry Corbin. *Spiritual Body and Celestial Earth, From Mazdean Iran to Shi^ci Iran,* Nancy Pearson, trans. Princeton, N.J.: Princeton University Press, 1977.

SE   Seyyed Hossein Nasr. *Sufi Essays.* London: George Allen and Unwin, 1972.

SH   Mahmud Shahabi. "Shi'a". In Kenneth Morgan, ed. *Islam: The Straight Path; Islam Interpreted by Muslims.* New York: The Ronald Press Company, 1958.

SI   ^cAllmah Sayyid Muhammad Husayn Tabataba'i. *Shi^cite Islam,* Seyyed Hossein Nasr, trans., ed. and with an introduction. Albany, N.Y.: SUNY Press, 1975.

SR   Dwight Donaldson. *The Shi^cite Religion.* London: Luzac and Co.: 1933.

SSJ   Seyyed Hossein Nasr. "The Spiritual Significance of *Jihad*". *Parabola.* Vol. VII, No. 4. (Fall 1982).

UUQ   Murtada Mutahhari. "Understanding the Uniqueness of the Qur'an" Mahliqa Qard'i (trans.) *Al-Tawhid* Vol 1, No. 1 (Muharram 1404).

VI   Marshall Hodgson. *Venture of Islam.* 3v. Chicago: University of Chicago Press, 1966.

Introduction

The events of the past decade certainly have drawn the attention of the West to Twelve-Imam Shiᶜism, but they have done little to bring about a greater depth in understanding Shiᶜism as a religious tradition within Islam. Although the name of Shiᶜism is heard almost every day in relation to this or that political event, the works that have flooded the market in the last few years, for the most part, have either catered to present day prejudices and fears or tried to normalize in the eyes of the West a very exceptional period of the history of Shiᶜism. By presenting Shiᶜism as if it always were a volatile and disruptive force, these works ignore all the theology, piety, and spirituality that characterize this and every integral, authentic religion.

Despite the appearance of so many works on Shiᶜism in the past few year, therefore, even more than before, it is necessary to present the integral Shiᶜi tradition as a major branch of Islam: its doctrines, intellectual life, religious practices, and spirituality; and to contrast it with the other branch of Islamic orthodoxy, namely Sunnism. Shiᶜism has had its periods of social and political activism, but it also has experienced centuries of peace and tranquility, during which it has cultivated its intellectual and theological teachings. Shiᶜism has been concerned with the oppressed and the downtrodden, but for many centuries it also has been the religion of the majority and the ruling powers in several parts of the Islamic world. Shiᶜism has produced its martyrs, but so has Sunnism, and in many periods of Shiᶜism's most creative and productive history, very few martyrs were produced. Nearly every cliché that the Western mass media, and even much of official Western scholarship, has been presented to the public recently concerning Shiᶜism fails to reveal an in-depth understanding of this tradition of Islamic religion. One must first comprehend the Shiᶜi tradition in its totality to see why, in certain historical circumstances, certain parts of the Shiᶜi world have acted or act as they do.

This volume and its sequel seek to remedy the lamentable state of present-day knowledge of Shiᶜism in the West by making available an extensive anthology of writings dealing with nearly every aspect of the religion. This volume deals with the doctrines, intellectual activity, piety, religious life, and spiritual aspects of Shiʿism; a second volume examines the manifestations of Shiʿism in history and human society. The selections are from either the writings of eminent Shiʿi authorities or of reputable scholars of various aspects of Shiʿism. The anthology therefore is a mosaic in which one can read the words of both Shiʿi thinkers and the scholars that study them and their thought.

Shiʿism, an integral part of Islam, has its origins in the beginning of the religion itself. During fourteen centuries of history, it has developed its own sciences of Qur'anic exegesis and *Hadith*, of metaphysics and theology, of law and its principles — all based on the Qur'an and the teachings of the Prophet and the Imams. For Twelve-Imam Shiʿism, which is the subject of this anthology, the Imams begin with ʿAli ibn Abu Talib and end with Muhammad al-Mahdi. The latter, who is the Twelfth Iman, continues as a living reality who rules over the world and whose full appearance on the stage of history will inaugurate the eschatological events leading to the second coming of the Messiah.

Shiʿism also has developed its own religious practices based upon the Qur'an and the *Sunnah* of the Prophet, with particular features related to the life and teachings of the Imams. Over the centuries, it created and has sustained its own educational system, nurtured the growth of several schools of philosophy, made possible the appearance of a rich literature in several languages, and has had a living relationship with several forms of art. Moreover, Shiʿi thought, as well as popular religion, has continued to live as a vibrant tradition to the present day, reacting in different ways to the challenges of modernism.

The anthology begins with a part on origins. Here, the Shiʿi view of religion in general and Shiʿism in particular is presented in the words of one of the most eminent Shiʿi scholars of this century, the late ʿAllamah Sayyid Muhammad Husayn Tabataba'i, and the relationship between Shiʿism and the Islamic revelation is discussed by the late Mahmud Shahabi, another eminent contemporary Shiʿi scholar. Shiʿism has developed an extensive set of sciences of the Qur'an, which make possible the understanding of both its outward and inner meaning. The most extensive Shiʿi commentary of this century, *al-Mizan*, was written by ʿAllamah Tabataba'i. Through his words and those of his most famous student, the late Murtada Mutahhari, translated by Iranian scholar, Mahlaqa Qard'i, the Shiʿi view of this basic religion discipline is presented.

In Shiʿism, *Hadith* includes not only the sayings of the Prophet, as one finds in Sunni Islam, but also those of the Twelve Imams, although a clear distinction is made between the two. Again, through the writings of ʿAllamah Tabataba'i as well as those of the contemporary Pakistani Shiʿi scholar, S. M. Waris Hasan, the Shiʿi view on *Hadith*, as understood traditionally, is presented. In a separate section, S. H. M. Jafri, another Pakistani Shi^ci scholar, deals with the *Nahj al-balaghah* of ^cAli ibn Abu Talib, a work whose significance for Shi^ci thought hardly can be overemphasized. Selections from Jafri's writings also deal with the teachings of the Imams, although a selection also is provided of the actual words of ^cAli. In the last section of the first part of the book, ^cAllamah Tabataba'i explains the doctrinal divisions within Shi^cism, that separate Twelve-Imam Shi^cism from Isma^cilism and Zaydism.

To understand Shi^cism fully, it is necessary to "situate" it within the Islamic tradition and in relation to the other branches and schools in Islam. Hamid Enayat, the late Iranian scholar of Islamic political thought, deals with the complex question of the relation between Shi^cism and Sunnism, which is followed by the vast majority of Muslims. Around 85 to 87 percent of Muslims are Sunnis and 13 to 15 percent Shi^cis and Kharijites, the latter constituting a very small number. It therefore is imperative to clarify the position of Shi^cism vis-a-vis Sunnism as a whole.

It also is necessary to understand the relationship among various branches of Shi^cism. Although usually, in referring to Shi^cism, one means Twelve-Imam Shi^cism, which includes by far the largest number of Shi^cis, there are other branches of Shi^cism, the Isma^cili and the Zaydi. In earlier periods of Islamic history, both of these branches played an important role, especially Isma^cilism, which created in the form of the Fatimid caliphate, a major political dominion stretching from North Africa to Syria and threatening the Sunni ^cAbbasid caliphate itself. Moreover, these forms of Shi^cism have survived to this day. There are schools, furthermore, that grew out of Twelve-Imam Shi^cism, the most important being the Shaykhi movement of the nineteenth century. Selections of writings by ^cAllamah Tabataba^ci; the classical Muslim authority on religious schools and sects al-Shahrastani, translated by A.K. Kazi and J.G. Flynn; the American historian Marshall Hodgson; and the contemporary Iranian historian Mangol Bayat cast light upon these complicated relationships and deal more fully with each of these schools.

Finally, in the last section of this part, S. H. Nasr discusses the important and complicated issue of the relationship between Shi^cism and Sufism. The Imams of Shi^cism, especially up to the eighth Imam, also provided the foundation of Sufism and appear in the chain of transmission (*silsilah*) of nearly all the Sufi orders. Moreover, Sufism and Shi^cism share such basic doctrines as the significance of esoteric knowledge and the process of hermeneutic interpretation (*ta'wil*), which makes the attainment of such knowledge possible. Yet, in certain eras of their history such as the late Safavid period in Persia, official Shi^cism became strongly opposed to Sufism. This complicated theological relationship and interwined destiny, on the one hand, and external opposition, on the other, is analyzed mostly with Persia in mind rather than India.

The third part of this anthology is concerned with what lies at the heart of Shiᶜism, as that of any religion, namely, doctrines and beliefs. As an orthodox branch of Islam, Shiᶜism emphasizes the doctrine of the Unity of God (*al-tawhid*) as the central axis of all religious belief. ᶜAllamah Tabataba'i examines this doctrine, bringing out the particular Shiᶜi interpretations of the-meaning of *al-tawhid* as well as the question of the multiple Names and Qualities of Allah in relation to His Oneness. Some sayings of Shiᶜis Imams on this subject are added in William Chittick's translation. Next to *al-tawhid, al-nubuwwah*, or prophecy; constitutes the second major pillar in the Shiᶜi conception of the principles of religion (*usul al-din*). Works of both the contemporary authority, ᶜAllamah Tabatabaᶜi and eighth/fourteenth century Shiᶜi authority, ᶜAllamah al-Hilli (in the translation of the British scholar I. K. A. Howard), and S. M. Waris Hasan are quoted to explain the way Shiᶜis envisage the meaning of revelation, the nature of prophecy and the prophets, and the finality of the prophethood of the Prophet of Islam.

The two principles of *al-tawhid* and *al-nubuwwah* are shared by Shiᶜis and Sunnis. Such is not the case of *al-imamah*, or Imamate, which distinguishes Shiᶜism from Sunnism and is central to the understanding of the Shiᶜi ethos. ᶜAllamah Tabataba'i discusses the traditional Shiᶜi doctrine of the Imamate, whereas Henry Corbin, the French scholar who was the foremost Western interpretor of Shiᶜism, investigates the same subject with great sympathy and understanding, especially its more esoteric dimensions.

One of the functions of the Imam is to interpret the inner meaning of the Qur'an, which is the unaltered Word of God for all Muslims; and the Shiᶜi sciences of the Qur'an, both exoteric (*tafsir*) and esoteric (*ta'wil*), are directly related to the teachings of the Imams. Corbin's in-depth philosophical study of Shiᶜi hermeneutics, brings out its importance, not only for the understanding of Shiᶜism but for religious thought in general.

Certain beliefs and practices particular to Shiᶜism also are not found in Sunni Islam. One of them is *taqiyyah*, or dissimulation, according to which, when in danger, a Shiᶜi can dissimulate his specifically Shiᶜi beliefs. Corbin concentrates on the spiritual significance of this practice, and Hamid Enayat looks at the social and political significance of this specifically Shiᶜi practice. This section is followed by one on the Shiᶜi practice of temporary marriage. ᶜAllamah Tabataba'i and S. H. Nasr explain the traditional foundations of this practice at the time of the Prophet, its human and social effects, and reasons why it is accepted by Shiᶜi law.

The Shiᶜis also share with Sunnism *al-maᶜad*, or eschatology, although with some differences, such as the role of the Imams as intercessor. The complicated doctrines of eschatology are summarized by ᶜAllamah Tabataba'i to complete the basic doctrinal teachings of Shiᶜism. Finally, a section presents certain Shiᶜi legal doctrines that are of the utmost importance for understanding its social and political teachings. These are the *ijtihad*, which has the power of giving fresh views in matters of jurisprudence, and the *marjaᶜiyyat*, which scrutinizes the question of following and emulating a living authority in matters of the Sacred Law. These questions, which lie at the heart of the power and function of Shiᶜi religious scholars, or *ᶜulama'*, are examined by the Iranian scholar of religion the late Mahmud Ramyar and the American political scientist Leonard Binder.

Shiᶜism, as an integral part of the Islamic religion, of course, provides means for living a life of piety and spirituality at the highest level. Although these are none other than Islamic spirituality and piety, in Shiᶜism they have a particular flavor of their own. In studying and experiencing Shiᶜi spirituality and piety, one becomes aware immediately of their genuinely Islamic character without relinquishing their particular Shiᶜi quality. In the first section of this part, S. H. Nasr looks at various religious rites, as well as prayers and supplications. The rites are nearly the same as those of Sunni Islam, with minor differences that, for the most part, vary no more than those among various Sunni schools. The prayers and supplications differ in that, in addition to the reading of the Qur'an, the Shiᶜis often recite extensive prayers originally composed by various Shiᶜi Imams. A sample of some prayers is provided in the translation by William Chittick. These prayers hold a key for the understanding of Shiᶜi religious attitudes and of the tapestry of the soul of the Shiᶜi faithful.

A number of religious practices also are prevalent among Shiᶜis. These range from processions and the passion play (*taᶜziyyah*) during the month of Muharram to religious sermons related to the tragedy of Karbala', also practiced mostly during Muharram but also Safar, and pilgrimage to the tomb of local saints. Selections are by Ayatullah Khu'i, one of the leading Shiᶜi authorities today; Mahmud Ayoud, a Lebanese Shiᶜi scholar; Edward G. Browne, the famous British scholar of Iran; Peter Chelkowski, the leading American authority on the passion play; and Dwight Donaldson, one of the well-known American students of Iran of the early part of this century. They all present the rich, diversified panorama of popular Shiᶜi religious practices. Most of the material concerns Iran but the practices described also are practiced in the Arab world and the Indo-Pakistani subcontinent.

Few concepts have been as misconstrued and distorted as the concept of *jihad* in recent years in the West. Translated as "holy war," *jihad* means exertion in the path of God rather than war, as it is usually understood. Only rarely does this exertion become external war, as when the life or the borders of Islam are threatened. The concept is found both in Sunni and Shiᶜi Islam. In fact, during most of Islamic history and especially in Twelve-Imam Shiᶜism, which distanced itself from political entanglement during most of its history, *jihad* has been understood as exertion in the field of religious sciences and an inner struggle to establish equilibrium among the various forces that surround the human soul and prevent it from experiencing peace. To counterbalance the sensationalist interpretations that are made of it in the Western press today, S. H. Nasr deals with the inner meaning of *jihad* and its centrality to the religious life.

The fifth part of the anthology turns to the intellectual and artistic life of Shiᶜism. The role of Shiᶜism has been immense in the cultivation of the arts and sciences and philosophy in the history of Islam. The Shiᶜi educational system produced some of the foremost Islamic thinkers over the centuries. Following the Mongol invasion and its aftermath, Shiᶜi Persia became the main center for the intellectual sciences, and especially philosophy, in the Islamic world. Likewise, in India, the cultivation of the sciences was closely associated with Shiᶜism.

In the first section, Roy Mottahedeh, an American historian of Iranian origin, discusses the Shiᶜi educational system, which has drawn a great deal of attention since the recent rise of the political power of the Iranian ᶜulama', who are products of this system. This educational system has been the refuge for the Shiᶜi sciences, both the juridical which will be treated in the second volume, and the theological. Shiᶜi theology (*Kalam*) constitutes a distinct school for Islamic theology. In contrast to Sunni and Ismaᶜili theology, it was not systematized until the later centuries of Islamic history, long after the legal and philosophical schools had been established. W. Montgomery Watt, the well-known British Islamicist, summarizes Shiᶜi theology, and selections are provided of the writings of two of the leading classical Shiᶜi theologians, Nasir al-Din Tusi and ᶜAllamah al-Hilli, both translated by I. K. A. Howard.

As for philosophy and the intellectual sciences, once again the words of ᶜAllamah Tabataba'i are cited to clarify the Shiᶜi attitude to these disciplines. This author belongs to the long chain of the Islamic philosophical tradition extending from Ibn Sina to Nasir al-Din Tusi, Ibn Turkah Isfahani, Mir Damad, Mulla Sadra, Sabziwari, and to the present generation. ᶜAllamah Tabataba'i considers this tradition from its philosophical, as well as its religious, significance. In order to understand Shiᶜism, it is important to note that although Islamic philosophy more or less perished as a distinct school in the Arab world after Ibn Rushd, it survived in Persia more and more under the protection and patronage of Shiᶜism. This later tradition of Islamic philosophy, which reached its peak with Mulla sadra and also played an important role in the intellectual life of India, is central to the understanding of Shi^ci religious thought as well as philosophy. To provide a taste of this later philosophico-theological school, Corbin has chosen two selections from the writings of Mulla Sadra's most famous students, Lahiji and Kashani, who were even more popular and widely accepted religious and theological authorities than their master.

Although most of the famous Persian poets such as Rumi and ^cAttar were Sunnis, Persian literature also has produced notable works of a distinctly Shi^ci character. The same holds true for literature in Arabic, Turkish, Gujrati, Urdu, and Swahili. Such works either deal with specifically Shi^ci religious motifs, such as the martyrdom of Husayn in Karbala', or the more general themes of suffering and redemption found in Shi^ci piety. Selections by Mahmud Ayoub, E. G. Browne, and Peter Chelkowski examine various facets of this specifically Shi^ci literature in a scholarly manner, and a selection from the fourth/tenth century Shi^ci scholar and theologian, Shaykh al-Mufid, provides a primary example of classical Shi^ci literature.

Under the patronage of the Shi^ci Safavids, some of the greatest masterpieces of Islamic art were produced in Isfahan, Tabriz, and other Persian cities. Likewise, the Shi^ci dynasties in India were instrumental in the flowering of the arts. Nader Ardalan, an Iranian architect and scholar of Persian architecture, and S. H. Nasr investigate the relationship of art of Shi^cism and the characteristics of the Islamic art produced in the climate of Shi^cism and embued with its spirit and ethos.

In the last section of Part V, S. H. Nasr considers the relation of Shi^cism to the mathematical and natural sciences. As a result of a more open espousal of the intellectual sciences in Shi^cism than in Ash^carism, usually supported by the Caliphate, during Shi^ci dynasties, greater attention was paid to the mathematical and natural sciences. This question and the attitude of Shi^cism to these sciences is examined to bring out the role of Shi^cism in the history of Islamic science.

Finally, in the last part of this volume, attention is focused upon this century. Until the political events of the last decade turned the interest of Western observers to Shi^cism, few were aware of the living Shi^ci intellectual tradition that has continued to this day. The Western categories of medieval and modern have hardly any meaning when applied to Islamic history, especially in the intellectual field. This made it difficult to understand the living nature of a thought that seemed "medieval" and yet was very much alive. S. H. Nasr brings out the traits of this contemporary intellectual tradition, based to a large extent upon the teachings of Sadr al-Din Shirazi. This is followed by selections from the writings of four of the most famous Shi^ci religious scholars of this age, translated by S. H. Nasr, Shahriyar Sa^cadat, an Iranian scholar; and Shams Inati, a Lebanese scholar. Sayyid Muhammad Baqir Sadr is an Iraqi Shi^ci thinker, whereas the other contemporary figures presented here are Iranian.

It is hoped that, through this anthology, the reader will gain an awareness of Shiʿism as a religious and cultural tradition with a long history and its own distinct educational system, theological and philosophical thought, piety, and religious practices. It is hoped that Shiʿism will be seen as an integral part of the Islamic tradition, in dynamic relationship with the Sunni majority and a major facet of Islamic history. This volume should provide evidence, much of it from primary Shiʿi sources, of the character of Shiʿism — not as a violent minority in the state of constant protest but as a major interpretation of the Islamic religion. Through fourteen centuries of history, Shiʿism has been witness, like any other religious group, to periods of peace as well as war, of felicity as well as oppression, of victory as well as humility. The words of the followers of this tradition, as well as its most perceptive Western interpretors, should provide an antidote to sensationalism and shallow journalism that have distorted the image of Shiʿism in the West during the past few years, even though the actions of certain Shiʿi have helped to fan this fire of animosity and enmity. Those actions can be understood in depth only in the light of the manifestation of Shiʿism in human history, which will be explored in the second volume of this anthology.

My two collaborators in the composition of these volumes, Seyyed Vali Reza Nasr and Hamid Dabashi, join me in thanking all the publishers and editors who have given us permission to reproduce sections from works published by them. In preparing this volume we are indebted to the contributions of Roy Mottahedeh and Charles Adams. We also thank Sarolyn Joseph for helping with the preparation of the manuscript.

Wa ma tawfiqi illa bi'Llah

Seyyed Hossein Nasr

Part I

Origins

Chapter One

Shiᶜi View of Religion in General and Shiᶜism in Particular

To the ordinary adherents of a religion, that religion is seen as being the religion, although from the universal point of view it is one among many. So it is with Islam, whose common followers usually view it as the ultimate manifestation of the Divine Will and as the religion. Likewise, within the Islamic framework, Shiᶜi Islam views itself not as a particular aspect of Islam or a "sect" but as the embodiment of the Qur'anic revelation. In the following short passage, ᶜAllamah Tabataba'i provides a universal definition of religion and then locates a definition of Shiᶜism within it. The passage is taken from SI, *pages 31–33.*

ʿAllamah Tabatabaʾi

There is no doubt that each member of the human race is naturally drawn to his fellow-men and that in his life in society he acts in ways which are interrelated and interconnected. His eating, drinking, sleeping, keeping awake, talking, listening, sitting, walking, his social intercourse and meetings, at the same time that they are formally and externally distinct, are invariably connected with each other. One cannot perform just any act in any place or after any other act. There is an order which must be observed.

There is, therefore, an order which governs the actions man performs in the journey of this life, an order against which his actions cannot rebel. In reality, these acts all originate from a distinct source. That source is man's desire to possess a felicitous life, a life in which he can reach to the greatest extent possible the objects of his desire, and be gratified. Or, one could say that man wishes to provide in a more complete way for his needs in order to continue his existence.

This is why man continually conforms his actions to rules and laws either devised by himself or accepted from others, and why he selects a particular way of life for himself among all the other existing possibilities. He works in order to provide for his means of livelihood and expects his activities to be guided by laws and regulations that must be followed. In order to satisfy his sense of taste and overcome hunger and thirst, he eats and drinks, for he considers eating and drinking necessary for the continuation of his own happy existence. This rule could be multiplied by many other instances.

The rules and laws that govern human existence depend for their acceptance on the basic beliefs that man has concerning the nature of universal existence, of which he himself is a part, and also upon his judgment and evaluation of that existence. That the principles governing man's actions depend on his conception of being as a whole becomes clear if one meditates a moment on the different conceptions that people hold as to the nature of the world and of man.

Those who consider the Universe to be confined only to this material, sensible world, and man himself to be completely material and therefore subject to annihilation when the breath of life leaves him at the moment of death, follow a way of life designed to provide for their material desires and transient mundane pleasures. They strive solely on this path, seeking to bring under their control the natural conditions and factors of life.

Similarly, there are those who, like the common people among idol-worshipers, consider the world of nature to be created by a god above nature who has created the world specially for man and provided it with multiple bounties so that man may benefit from his goodness. Such men organize their lives so as to attract the pleasure of the god and not invite his anger. They believe that if they please the god he will multiply his bounty and make it lasting and if they anger him he will take his bounty away from them.

On the other hand, such men as Zoroastrians, Jews, Christians, and Muslims follow the "high path" in this life for they believe in God and in man's eternal life, and consider man to be responsible for his good and evil acts. As a result they accept as proven the existence of a day of judgment (*qiyamah*) and follow a path that leads to felicity in both this world and the next.

The totality of these fundamental beliefs concerning the nature of man and the Universe, and regulations in conformity with them which are applied to human life, is called religion (*din*). If there are divergences in these fundamental beliefs and regulations, they are called schools such as the Sunni and Shi'i schools in Islam and the Nestorian in Christianity. We can therefore say that man, even if he does not believe in the Deity, can never be without religion if we recognize religion as a program for life based on firm belief.

Religion can never be separated from life and is not simply a matter of ceremonial acts.

The Holy Qur'an asserts that man has no choice but to follow religion, which is a path that God has placed before man so that by treading it man can reach Him. However, those who have accepted the religion of the truth (Islam) march in all sincerity upon the path of God, while those who have not accepted the religion of the truth have been diverted from the divine path and have followed the wrong road.

Islam etymologically means surrender and obedience. The Holy Qur'an calls the religion which invites men toward this end "Islam" since its general purpose is the surrender of man to the laws governing the Universe and men, with the result that through this surrender he worships only the One God and obeys only His commands. As the Holy Qur'an informs us, the first person who called this religion "Islam" and its followers "Muslims" was the Prophet Abraham, upon whom be peace.

Shi'i, which means literally partisan or follower, refers to those who consider the succession to the Prophet — may God's peace and benediction be upon him — to be the special right of the family of the Prophet and who in the field of the Islamic sciences and culture follow the school of the House-hold of the Prophet.

Chapter Two

The Roots of Shiʿism in Early Islamic History

Shiʿism sees itself as the true continuity of the Muhammadan message, not a heterodoxy apart from orthodoxy. Justification of this centrality obviously is rooted in the Shiʿi self-understanding based on the Islamic revelation. In the following passage, Mahmud Shahabi provides a descriptive analysis of the role of the Qur'an, Prophet Muhammad, and ʿAli in Shiʿism, in which that faith's foundation in Islamic revelatory tradition is expounded. The passage is taken from SH, *pages 180, 188–197.*

Mahmud Shahabi

The word *Shiʿi*, meaning follower, has come to be accepted as the designation for those Muslims who are followers of ʿAli—who was seconded only to Muhammad. They are followers of God's revelation in the Qur'an, of Muhammad who was the last of the prophets, and of ʿAli who was the Prophet's choice for his successor.

The Prophet had a daughter, Fatimah, by his wife Khadijah. Because he loved and honored her very much he married her to ʿAli, his most trusted disciple. Muhammad was also very fond of their two children, his grandchildren Hasan and Husayn. He used to honor them on every occasion, at the mosque and at home, and called them his children and the best youth of Heaven. To hurt Hasan or Husayn, or Fatimah their mother, or ʿAli their father, was considered a defiance of God and of Muhammad.

The Prophet recommended his family to people in private and in public. For instance, at the Ghadir-Khumm meeting he said as guidance to the people, "Oh people, I will die, but I leave two things for you so that if you follow them you will never be misled—they are the Holy Book, the Qur'an, and my family [*Itrat*]." On the day of Ghadir, as we mentioned previously—and it is mentioned by both Shiʿi and Sunni—he indicated that ʿAli should be his successor and he named him as the master of the people. This was an indication that ʿAli should be the next Caliph, that is, Successor to Muhammad.

*   *   *

ʿAli, Muhammad's cousin, had been brought up by the Prophet, was the husband of the Prophet's beloved daughter, and was the closest person to Muhammad. From his early childhood until the day the Prophet died, day and night, on journeys and in the cities, in mountains and on the plains, in battle and in peace, on strenuous days and on calm ones, in public appearances and in hiding—ʿAli was with the Prophet. He wholeheartedly adopted Muhammad's way of life; he learned about his aims and his methods of instruction so that he understood Muhammad's teachings better than anyone else.

On many occasions ʿAli made personal sacrifices for the sake of the Prophet and for the sake of Islam. His bravery, which was motivated by his great faith, accounts for the early progress of Islam. In every good quality — in virtues, in knowledge, in bravery, in faithfulness, in generosity and reliability — ᶜAli was superior to others; he was second only to Muhammad.

The Prophet both explicitly and implicitly affirmed ᶜAli's eminent position, mentioning ᶜAli's superiority over the others a number of times. We have seen that Ghadir-Khumm was a significant event in ᶜAli's honor, for there Muhammad explicitly named himself as the master of the people and ᶜAli next to him, in relation to God. On the day that he invited the Christian leaders for *Mubahilah* (to pray to God to damn a person and his family if he knowingly misrepresents religious facts and lies willfully), he had his daughter Fatimah, his grandchildren Hasan and Husayn, and ᶜAli sit with him; it was on this occasion that he referred to ᶜAli as his soul. In this way he paid tribute to the greatness of ᶜAli. These events, and other similar ones, made Muhammad's choice of his successor quite evident. All the evidence pointed to the fact that Muhammad wished ᶜAli to succeed him with complete authority to guide the people. ᶜAli was justly fitted to lead the Muslims and to head the affairs of Islam.

Consequently, after the death of Muhammad, ᶜAli, who felt assured of his position and was greatly saddened by Muhammad's death, went on to fulfill Muhammad's wishes for his funeral. Meanwhile a few followers, who apparently were driven by selfishness, ambition, and a great desire for power, gathered their followers to decide for themselves the question of the succession. Abu Bakr, ᶜUmar, and Abu ᶜUbaydah, with glib tongues and skillful speeches, weakened the position of their rivals. Some of the delegates followed them through hope, some through fear, and some made no commitment at all. With the support of ᶜUmar and Abu ᶜUbaydah, Abu Bakr was named Caliph. This choice led to conflict between the supporters of Abu Bakr and the other Muslims, but they recognized that if the conflict continued Islam would be so weakened that it might even lead to its destruction. Furthermore, the followers of Abu Bakr would make trouble for those who did not express an opinion in his favor. Therefore, for the sake of Islam, the people gradually took the oath of allegiance to Abu Bakr as Caliph and showed no opposition when he assumed office.

At the same time, there were people who knew that the position of Caliph should have been given to ᶜAli, and they recognized him as the leader of Islam. It was these people who were to follow ᶜAli and to believe in him, and they eventually became the sect known as Shiᶜism. They believed that Muhammad's successor should have been appointed by God and the Prophet himself, and that the Caliph should not have been chosen on the basis of men's capricious will and temptation. Many of them took the oath of allegiance reluctantly, and ᶜAli himself did not give his approval until six months later.

Abu Bakr, who was Caliph for about two years, nominated ᶜUmar as his successor. ᶜUmar was a man of will, a ruthless administrator, and a man who abstained from worldly pleasures. As Caliph he decided to extend the borders of Islam and conquered Iran and some of the Roman territories, organizing a widespread empire.

While ᶜUmar was Caliph, ᶜAli's position was supreme; for ᶜUmar had to recognize his high position in Islam and ascertain his views on important matters. At times ᶜUmar acted on his suggestions and at other times ᶜAli pointed out the Caliph's mistakes. ᶜUmar admitted his errors, and once said, "If it were not for ᶜAli I should have perished."

When ᶜUmar's warriors vanquished Iran they captured the daughters of Yazdigird, the king of Iran, and brought them to ᶜUmar. He was going to sell them like any other slaves but ᶜAli advised him that this would be an unjust treament for princesses and the religion forbade it. As a result the women were allowed to choose their own husbands, and one of them was married to ᶜAli's son Husayn and the other to Abu Bakr's son Muhammad. On another occasion ᶜUmar was going to execute Hurmuzan, a captured Iranian prince, but ᶜAli persuaded the prince to become a Muslim and his life was spared. During his life he honored ᶜAli.

For ten years ᶜUmar served as Caliph and made great conquests for the glory of Islam. Before he died he made plans for the choice of his successor. Although he knew that ᶜAli was well qualified to replace him, he would not consider ᶜAli as his successor. Instead of making ᶜAli the next Caliph, ᶜUmar appointed six persons, including ᶜAli and ᶜUthman, to select one person from among themselves as the next Caliph and spiritual leader of the believers. When the six men were assembled to reach a decision, they were surrounded by fifty brave armed men who were ordered to watch the election committee. If after three days they could not select a successor to the Caliph, they were all to be killed on the spot; if they selected someone but could not agree unanimously, the minority should be killed. If three persons selected one Caliph and three selected another, then the group in which ᶜAbd al-Rahman ibn ᶜAwf was a member would have the deciding vote and the other three must agree or be killed. This was ᶜUmar's plan, which was to be carried out after his death. This plan was set up so that ᶜUthman would become Caliph, because ᶜAbd al-Rahman ibn ᶜAwf was his relative and supporter.

At the meeting of the committee, ᶜAbd al-Rahman ibn ᶜAwf asked ᶜAli "If you are selected will you act according to the Qur'an, the *Sunnah*, and the policies of the two previous Caliphs?" ᶜAli replied that he would act according to the Qur'an and the *Sunnah*, but he would not follow the opinions of others. After that, the original plan was followed and ᶜUthman was chosen.

As Caliph, ^cUthman acted against the principles of the previous Caliphs. He made his own corrupt relatives governors; he used the treasury to further his own interests by giving gold and silver to relatives and friends. Democracy, freedom, justice, and equality, which had more or less prevailed under ^cUmar, were silenced by ^cUthman's rule. Therefore the people became disappointed in him and rose up against him.... . He was attacked and killed in his own home in the thirty-fifth year of the Hijrah, twelve years after he became Caliph.

After ^cUthman's death the representatives of Islamic cities who were in Medina asked ^cAli to become their Caliph. From that day, ^cAli's friends and followers freely and openly expressed their devotion to ^cAli, and they were proud of it. They all vowed their belief in Shi^cism and honored it.

When, before his death, ^cUthman saw that he was surrounded by Muslims who disapproved of his policies, he asked help from Mu^cawiyah, who was a relative in the Umayyid family, the governor of Syria (Sham), and a man who would be called a politician today.... .

Mu^cawiyah knew that ^cAli had a strong faith and that the majority of his followers were sincere believers. Therefore, after he had done all he could to deceive the followers whose religious beliefs were weak, he started a war against ^cAli with a large army made up of people from Syria. The fighting continued for some time and several thousand people were killed on both sides. Just when victory was close at hand for ^cAli's side, Mu^cawiyah turned the battle by means of a devilish trick. He asked ^cAli to stop fighting so they could arrange a truce, and ^cAli unwillingly accepted the offer for negotiations. Mu^cawiyah appointed ^cAmr ibn al-^cAs, a tricky, clever man, while ^cAli's group selected Abu Musa Ash^cari, a weak, ambitious man, to represent them. ^cAmr ibn al-^cAs took advantage of Abu Musa Ash^cari's selfishness and stupidity to deceive him, just as Mu^cawiyah had planned.

When they saw how the negotiations were going, the same people who had urged ^cAli to accept the truce started to critize him for starting the negotiations and for sending as a delegate the man whom they had chosen to represent them. They said that ^cAli had committed an error and he should either repent or be killed. ^cAli defended himself by giving them evidence from the Qur'an and citing the reasons for the action, but they were not convinced. Over ten thousand of ^cAli's men, all Shi^cis, left his army.

It is one of the puzzles of history that a group of people who believed in ^cAli and had made great sacrifices for his sake, who knew him to be right and his enemy wrong, and who had even risked their lives by going into battle for him should desert him and even take up their swords against him. A group of soldiers who were good Shi^ci and who had believed in ^cAli just a few days previously now suddenly left ^cAli's camp and became his enemies. It was truly a strange happening.

The men who deserted ^cAli and abandoned their faith became famous in history as unbelievers and were known as Kharijites—the people who have forsaken their faith. Twelve thousand of these Kharijites formed an army which tried to kill ^cAli. Therefore it was necessary for ^cAli to deal with them before he could turn to Mu^cawiyah. With only four thousand men ^cAli approached the Kharijites; he heard their protest and answered them, and as a result of his preaching eight thousand Kharijites changed their minds; but four thousand remained as bitter enemies. When the eight thousand had left the battlefield, ^cAli spoke to his men in the name of Allah, saying, "Our loss will not be more than their survivors, and in neither case will the number be more than ten." After the battle, just as ^cAli had miraculously predicted, nine of the enemy remained and nine of ^cAli's men were dead. Although ^cAli was victorious, that battle did not eliminate the Kharijites.

During the five years that ^cAli ruled as Caliph he was busy with emergencies at home which prevented him from returning to the conflict with Mu^cawiyah. On the nineteenth of Ramadan in the year 40 of the Hijrah, while ^cAli was praying in the mosque at Kufa he was struck down with a poisoned sword by Ibn Muljam, a Kharijite.

In the last hours while he lay on his death bed, ^cAli besought the people to act with self-sacrifice, rectitude, and gentleness, to serve the poor, the orphans, and the weak, and to follow religion. He said to them, 'O people, we are from God and we will go back to Him. Therefore try to know Him, worship Him, be virtuous and do good. In this short time that you are in the world prepare yourself for the life to come." As a man who revered and worshiped God, ^cAli wished death to come. He said repeatedly, "By God, ^cAli is more acquainted with death than a child with his mother's breast!" When he was attacked in the mosque he had said, "I have my wish and I join my God." Before he died he showed again his magnanimous spirit by saying concerning his murderer, "As long as I am alive, do not hurt him, but tolerate him. If I do not die and I remain, I will know what to do. If I die never attack him with more than a stroke for he hit only once." Thus just before he died he protected his murderer from torture.

In writing about ^cAli's sublime qualities and counting his virtues, one can argue with what is said by one of his followers, "To describe your qualities, it would not suffice to wet the finger with all the water of the seas in order to leaf through your book of virtues." Once when the Sunni authority Muhammad ibn Idris al-Shafi^ci was asked to talk about ^cAli he said, "What should be said about him when his virtues are concealed by his friends because they are afraid, and by his foes because of jealousy? Yet in spite of this his virtuous character was revealed and has been made known to us... ."

Chapter Three

The Shi⁣ᶜi Interpretation
of the Qur'an

For all Muslims the Qur'an is the Word of God. It is the sacred and irre-
vocably valid foundation of the Islamic community (ummah). As such,
the Sacred Text has been subject to interpretations (tafsir),
hermeneutics (ta'wil), and mystical exegisis (istinbat) throughout Islamic
history. The Shiᶜi understanding of the Qur'an is founded on the doc-
trinal belief that the Shiᶜi Imams possess the hidden, esoteric (batin)
knowledge of the Qur'anic verses. In the following two passages,
ᶜAllamah Tabataba'i and Murtaza Mutahhari provide specific Shiᶜi
views concerning Islamic Sacred Scripture. The passages are taken from
SI, pages 94–101 and UUQ, pages 9–24, respectively.

^c*Allamah Tabataba'i*

The Book of God, the Holy Qur'an, is the principal source of every form of Islamic thought. It is the Qur'an which gives religious validity and authority to every other religious source in Islam. Therefore, it must be comprehensible to all. Moreover, the Qur'an describes itself as the light which illuminates all things. Also it challenges men and requests them to ponder over its verses and observe that there are no disparities or contradictions in them. It invites them to compose a similar work, if they can, to replace it. It is clear that if the Holy Qur'an were not comprehensible to all there would be no place for such assertions.

To say that the Qur'an is in itself comprehensible to all is not in any way contradictory to the previous assertion that the Prophet and his Household are religious authorities in the Islamic sciences, which sciences in reality are only elaborations of the content of the Qur'an. For instance, in the part of the Islamic sciences which comprises the injunctions and laws of the *Shari^cah*, the Qur'an contains only the general principles. The clarification and elaboration of their details, such as the manner of accomplishing the daily prayers, fasting, exchanging merchandise, and in fact all acts of worship (*^cibadat*) and transactions (*mu^camalat*), can be achieved only by referring to the traditions of the Holy Prophet and his Household.

As for the other part of Islamic sciences dealing with doctrines and ethical methods and practices, although their content and details can be comprehended by all, the understanding of their full meaning depends on accepting the method of the Household of the Prophet. Also each verse of the Qur'an must be explained and interpreted by means of other Qur'anic verses, not by views which have become acceptable and familiar to us only through habit and custom.

^cAli has said: "Some part of the Qur'an speak with other parts of it revealing to us their meaning and some parts attest to the meaning of others." And also: "Whosoever interprets the Qur'an according to his own opinion has made a place for himself in the fire."

As a simple example of the commentary of the Qur'an throught the Qur'an may be cited the story of the torture of the people of Lot about whom in one place God says, "And we rained on them a rain," and in another place He has changed this phrase to, "Lo! We sent a storm of stones upon them (all)." By relating the second verse to the first it becomes clear that by "rain" is meant "stones" from heaven. Whoever has studied with care the *hadiths* of the Household of the Prophet, and the outstanding companions who were the followers of the Prophet, will have no doubt that that commentary of the Qur'an through the Qur'an is the sole method of Qur'anic commentary taught by the Household of the Prophet.

The Outward and Inward Aspects of the Qur'an

It has been explained that the Holy Qur'an elucidates religious aims through its own words and gives commands to mankind in matters of doctrine and action. But the meaning of the Qur'an is not limited to this level. Rather, behind these same expressions and within these same meanings there are deeper and wider levels of meaning which only the spiritual elite who possess pure hearts can comprehend.

The Prophet, who is the divinely appointed teacher of the Qur'an, says: "The Qur'an has a beautiful exterior and a profound interior." He has also said, "The Qur'an has an inner dimension, and that inner dimension has an inner dimension up to seven inner dimensions." Also, in the sayings of the Imams there are numerous references to the inner aspects of the Qur'an.

The main support of these assertions is a symbol which God has mentioned in Chapter XIII, verse 17, of the Qur'an. In this verse divine gifts are symbolized by rain that falls from heaven and upon which depends the life of the earth and its inhabitants. With the coming of the rain, floods begin to flow and each river bed accepts a certain amount of the flood, depending on its capacity. As it flows, the flood is covered with foam, but beneath the foam there is that same water which is life-giving and beneficial to mankind... .

It is at this point that through earthly and heavenly signs, signs upon the horizons and within the souls of men, they "observe" in a spiritual vision the Infinite Light of the Majesty and Glory of God. Their hearts become completely enamored with the longing to reach an understanding of the secret symbols of creation. Instead of being imprisoned in the dark and narrow well of personal gain and selfishness they begin to fly in the unlimited space of the world of eternity and advance ever onwards toward the zenith of the spiritual world.

When they hear that God has forbidden the worship of idols, which outwardly means bowing down before an idol, they understand this command to mean that they should not obey other than God, for to obey means to bow down before someone and to serve him. Beyond that meaning they understand that they should not have hope or fear of other than God; beyond that, they should not surrender to the demands of their selfish appetites; and beyond that, they should not concentrate on anything except God, May His Name be Glorified.

Likewise when they hear from the Qur'an that they should pray, the external meaning of which is to perform the particular rites of prayers, through its inner meaning they comprehend that they must worship and obey God with all their hearts and souls. Beyond that they comprehend that before God they must consider themselves as nothing, must forget themselves and remember only God... .

From this discussion the meaning of the outward and inward aspects of the Qur'an has become clear. It has also become evident that the inner meaning of the Qur'an does not eradicate or invalidate its outward meaning. Rather, it is like the soul which gives life to the body. Islam, which is a universal and eternal religion and places the greatest emphasis upon the "reformation" of mankind, can never dispense with its external laws which are for the benefit of society, nor with its simple doctrines which are the guardians and preservers of these laws.

How can a society, on the pretense that religion is only a matter of the heart, that man's heart should be pure and that there is no value to actions, live in disorder and yet attain happiness? How can impure deeds and words cause the cultivation of a pure heart? Or how can impure words emanate from a pure heart? God says in His Book, "Vile women are for vile men, and vile men for vile women. Good women are for good men, and good men for good women." (Qur'an, XXIV, 26) He also says, "As for the good land, its vegetation cometh forth by permission of its Lord; while as for that which is bad, only evil cometh forth (from it)." (Qur'an, VII, 58) Thus it becomes evident that the Holy Qur'an has an outward and inward aspect and the inward aspect itself has different levels of meaning. The *hadith* literature, which explains the content of the Qur'an, also contains these various aspects.

The Principles of Interpretation of the Qur'an

At the beginning of Islam it was commonly believed by some Sunnis that if there was sufficient reason one could ignore the outward meaning of Qur'anic verses and ascribe to them a contrary meaning. Usually the meaning which opposed the outward, literal meaning was called *ta'wil*, and what is called "*ta'wil* of the Qur'an" in Sunni Islam is usually understood in this sense.

In the religious works of Sunni scholars, as well as in the controversies that have been recorded as taking place between different schools, one often observes that if a particular point of doctrine (that has been established through the consensus of the ⁼ulama' of a school or through some other means) is opposed to the outward meaning of a verse of the Qur'an, that verse is interpreted by *ta'wil* to have a meaning contrary to its apparent meaning. Sometimes two contending sides support two opposing views and present Qur'anic verses in proof of their contentions. Each side interprets the verses presented by the other side through *ta'wil*. This method has also penetrated more or less into Shicism and can be seen in some Shici theological words.

Yet, sufficient deliberation upon Qur'anic verses and the *hadith* of the Household of the Prophet demonstrates clearly that the Holy Qur'an with its attractive language and eloquent and lucid expression never uses enigmatic or puzzling methods of exposition and always expounds any subject in a language suitable for the subject. What has been rightly called *ta'wil*, or hermeneutic interpretation, of the Holy Qur'an is not concerned with certain truths and realities that transcend the comprehension of the common run of men; yet it is from these truths and realities that the principles of doctrines and the practical injunctions of the Qur'an issue forth.

The whole of the Qur'an possesses the sense of *ta'wil*, of esoteric meaning, which cannot be comprehended directly through human thought alone. Only the prophets and the pure among the saints of God who are free from the dross of human imperfection can contemplate these meanings while living on the present plane of existence. On the Day of Resurrection the *ta'wil* of the Qur'an will be revealed to everyone.

This assertion can be explained by pointing to the fact that what forces man to use speech, create words and make use of expressions is nothing other than his social and material needs. In his social life man is forced to try to make his fellow-men understand his thoughts and intentions and the feelings which exist within his soul. To accomplish this end he makes use of sounds and hearing. Occasionally also he uses to a degree his eyes and gestures. That is why between the mute and the blind there can never be any mutual comprehension, for whatever the blind man says the deaf cannot hear, and whatever the mute makes understood through gestures of blind man cannot see.

The creation of words and the naming of objects have been accomplished mostly with a material end in view. Expressions have been created for those objects, states, and conditions which are material and available to the senses or near to the sensible world. As can be seen in those cases where the person addressed lacks one of the physical senses, if we wish to speak of matters which can be comprehended through the missing sense we employ a kind of allegory and similitude. For example, if we wish to describe light or color to one who is born blind, or the pleasures of sex to a child that has not reached the age of adolescence, we seek to achieve our purpose through comparison and allegory and through providing appropriate examples.

Therefore, if we accept the hypothesis that in the scale of Universal Existence there are immense levels of reality which are independent of the world of matter (and this is in reality the case), and that in each generation there are among mankind but a handful who have the capability of comprehending and having a vision of these realities, then questions pertaining to these higher worlds cannot be understood through common verbal expressions and modes of thought. They cannot be referred to except by allusion and through symbolism. Since religious realities are of this kind, the expression of the Qur'an in such matters must of necessity be symbolic.

God says in his book, "Lo! We have appointed it a Lecture in Arabic that haply ye may understand. And Lo! in the Source of Decrees, which We possess, it is indeed sublime, decisive." (Common comprehension cannot understand it or penetrate into it.) (Qur'an, XLIII, 3–4) He also says, "That (this) is indeed a noble Qur'an, In a book kept hidden, Which none toucheth save the purified" (Qur'an, LVI, 77–79). Concerning the Prophet and his Household he says, "Allah's wish is but to remove uncleanness far from you, O Folk of the Household, and cleanse you with a thorough cleansing" (Qur'an, XXXIII, 33).

As proved by these verses, the Holy Qur'an emanates from sources beyond the comprehension of common man. No one can have a full comprehension of the Qur'an save those servants of God whom He has chosen to purify. And the Household of the Prophet are among those pure beings.

In another place God says, "Nay, but they denied that (the Qur'an), the knowledge whereof they could not compass, and whereof the interpretation (in events) [*ta'wil*] hath not yet come into them" (Qur'an, X, 40) (meaning the day of Resurrection when the truth of things will become known). And again he says, "On the day (the Day of Resurrection) when the fulfillment [*ta'wil*] thereof (of the whole Qur'an) cometh, those who were before forgetful thereof will say: The messengers of our Lord did bring the Truth!" (Qur'an, VII, 53)

Murtaza Mutahhari

The Three Distinguishing Characteristics of the Qur'an

Our study of the Qur'an acquaints us with three distinguishing characteristics of this holy book. The first distinguishing characteristic is the absolute authenticity of its source. That is, without the slightest need of any comparison between the oldest manuscripts, it is evident that what we recite as the verses of the Holy Qur'an, are exactly the same words presented before the world by Muhammad ibn ᶜAbdullah (S). The second characteristic feature of the Qur'an is the quality of its contents: its teachings are genuinely original and have not been adopted or plagiarized. It is the duty of an analytical study to prove this fact. The third characteristic of the Qur'an is its Divine identity: its teachings have been delivered to the Prophet from a world that transcends his thought and mind. The Prophet (S) was only a recepient of this revelation and message. This is the result that we obtain from the study of the sources and roots of the Qur'an.

But the study of the sources of the Qur'an, and confirmation of its originality, depend upon the analytical study. So I resolve to open this discussion with the analytical study of the Qur'an. We shall first see what is the subject matter of the Qur'an, what kind of problems are discussed in it, what type of problems have been given priority, and in what manner those subjects are presented in it. If we are successful in our critical analysis, and acquire a sufficient understanding of the Qur'anic teachings, it will bring us to an acknowledgement of its principle aspect, which is the Divine aspect of the Qur'an, the quality of its being a Divine miracle.

Conditions Necessary for the Study of the Qur'an

The understanding of the Qur'an requires certain preliminaries which are briefly described here. The first essential condition necessary for the study of the Qur'an, is the knowledge of the Arabic language, such as for the understanding of Hafiz and Saᶜdi, it is impossible to get anywhere without the knowledge of the Persian language. In the same way, to acquaint oneself with the Qur'an without knowing the Arabic language is impossible. The other essential condition is the knowledge of the history of Islam; since, unlike the Bible and the Torah, this book was revealed gradually during a long period of twenty-three years of the Prophet's life, a tumultous time in the history of Islam. It is on this account that every verse of the Qur'an is related to certain specific historical incident called *sha'n-i nuzul*. The *sha'n-i nuzul*, by itself does not restrict the meaning of the verses, but the knowledge of the particulars of revelation throws more light on the subject of the verses in an effective way.

The third condition essential for the understanding of the Qur'an, is the correct knowledge of the sayings of the Prophet (S). He was, according to the Qur'an itself, the interpreter of the Qur'an par excellence. The Qur'an says:

We have been revealed to you the Reminder that you may make clear to men what has been revealed to them. . . . (XVI,44)

The Qur'an also says:

It is He who has sent among the illiterate a Messenger from among them, to recite His songs to them, and to purify them and to teach them the Book and the Wisdom. (LXII, 2)

According to the Qur'an, the Prophet (S) himself is the exegetist and the interpreter of the Qur'anic text. Whatever has reached us from the Prophet, is of great help in our understanding of the Qur'an. For the Shi^cis, who believe in the infallible Imams (A) also, and believe that the Prophet (S) has transmitted everything he obtained from God to his spiritual successors (*awsaya'*), those genuine *riwayat* (narrations about the Prophet (S)) that have reached us through the Imams, possess the same degree of authenticity as those obtained direclty from the Prophet (S). Accordingly, the authentic *riwayat* of the Imams are of great heal to us in our understanding of the Qur'an.

A very important point to remember during the initial stages of study, is that we should try to understand the Qur'an with the help of the Qur'an itself; because, the verses of the Qur'an constitute a completely united integral whole, a coherent unified structure. If we single out any verse from the Qur'an and try to understand it in isolation from the rest of the Book, it would not be a correct method. However, it is possible that we may happen to understand it, but the method is not recommended by caution, as certain verses of the Qur'an are explanatory for certain other verses. All great commentators of the Qur'an have affirmed this method; the infalliable Imams also had approved of this manner of interpretation of the Qur'anic verses. The Qur'an has its own specific mode of discussing various problems. There are instances where if a solitary verse is studied without placing it in its proper context, it gives quite a different sense than when it is seen under the light of the verses dealing with a similar subject.

For instance, the specific mode and style of the Qur'an may be noticed from the distinction drawn between *al-ayat al-muhkamat* (the firm verses) and *al-ayat al-mutashabihat* (the ambiguous verses). There is a prevalent view regarding the *muhkamat* and the *mutashabihat*. Some people imagine that *al-ayat al-muhkamat* are such verses as whose meaning is quite simple and clear, whereas the meaning of *al-ayat al-mutashabihat* is cryptic, enigmatic and puzzling. According to this notion, men are only permitted to cogitate upon the meaning of *al-ayat al-muhkamat*, and *al-ayat al-mutashabihat* are basically-inscrutable and beyond their understanding. Here, the question arises, what is the philosophy underlying *al-ayat al-mutashabihat*? Why has the Qur'an put forward such verses that are incomprehensible? A brief answer to this question is that neither *muhkam* means "simple" and "clear", nor *mutashabih* means "ambiguous", "cryptic" and "enigmatic". "Ambiguous" and "enigmatic" are adjectives applicable to sentences that do not convey the meaning in a direct and simple manner, as are sometimes met in the writings of various authors. For example, when Sultan Mahmud rewarded the poetic efforts of Firdowsi with a reward of an insignificant and humiliating amount of money, Firdowsi did not accept it, and instead he accused Sultan Mahmud of the trait of parsimony in his versified lampoons. Some of them were quite clear and obvious whereas the others were not devoid of ambiguity and a lot of enigma. Firdowsi is quite direct when he says:

> *Had the king's mother been an honourable lady,*
> *He would have rewarded me with knee-high gold and silver.*

However, when he remarks:

> *The palm of king Mahmud, the conquerer of lands,*
> *Was nine times nine and three times four,*

what does he intend to say? Here Firdowsi has made use of an enigmatic technique. Those who are interested would like to know the solution: $9 \times 9 = 81$, $3 \times 4 = 12$, and 81 plus 12 add up to 93. Firdowsi says, the Sultan's palm was just like 93. It means that the fist of the Sultan was so tightly closed that only his thumb was free, and this thumb along with the index finger (which acquires the shape of 9) and other three fingers makes 93. Through this obscure statement Firdowsi wants to emphatically report the miserliness of the Sultan.

We shall see whether there are actually any enigmatic and abstruse verses in the Qur'an. Such an assumption contradicts with the text of the Qur'an which unequivocally states that it is a clear and comprehensible book whose verses provide guidance and shed light. The core of the problem is that some of the issues dealt with in the Qur'an are related to metaphysical matters and the transcendental world, which cannot be expressed in ordinary language. In the words of Shaykh Shabistari:

> *The word fails to encompass meaning,*
> *The ocean cannot be poured into a pot.*

Since the language of the Qur'an is the same as used by men, inevitably, the same diction is used for the most sublime and spiritual themes as we human beings use for earthly subjects. But in order to prevent any misunderstanding about certain problems, some verses have been deviced in such a way that they need to be explained with the help of other verses. There is no way except this. For example, the Qur'an wanted to point out to a truth namely, seeing God through the heart; that is, to witness the presence of God by means of one's heart. This idea has been expressed in the following terms:

(Some) faces on the Day shall be bright,
looking towards their Lord. (LXXV, 22–23)

The Qur'an makes use of the verb 'looking', and no other word more suitable could be available for the expression of the desired sense. But to avert the possibility of any doubt, the Qur'an explains in other place:

Vision perceives Him, not, and He perceives all vision (VI, 104).

The second verse makes the reader distinguish between two different meanings conveyed by the same word. In order to avoid any possibility of ambiguity in its exalted themes, the Qur'an asks us to check the *mutashabihat* against the *muhkamat*:

He sent down upon thee the Book, wherein are verses firm (ayat muhkamat) that are the essence of the Book. (III, 6)

Thereby, the Qur'an means that there are certain verses whose firmness cannot be denied and other meanings cannot be derived from them, except their real ones. Such verses are the 'mother' of the Book (*umm al-kitab*). In the same way as a mother is the refuge to her child, or a cosmopolitan city (*umm al-qura*) is the center of small cities, *al-ayat al-muhkamat* are also regarded as the axes of the *mutashabihat*. *Al-ayat al-mutashabihat* are, of course, to be cogitated upon and understood, but they are to be pondered upon with the help of *al-ayat al-muhkamat*. Any inference drawn without the help of *al-ayat al-muhkamat*. Any inference drawn without the help of the mother-verses would not be correct and reliable.

Is the Qur'an Understandable?

During the analysis and study of the Qur'an, the first question that arises is whether the Qur'an can be studied and understood. Has this book been introduced for the purpose of studying and understanding it, or whether it is just for reading and reciting and obtaining reward and blessing? The reader, possibly, may wonder at raising of such a question. To him it may appear beyond doubt that the Qur'an is meant for the purpose of knowing and understanding it. Nevertheless, in view of various undesirable currents, which due to numerous reasons came into existence in the Muslim world regarding the question of understanding of the Qur'an, and which had an important role in bringing about the decline of Muslims, we shall discuss this matter in brief. Regrettably, the roots of those degenerate and dangerous notions still persist in our societies. So I consider it necessary to elaborate on this topic.

Among the Shi'i scholars of three or four centuries ago, there appeared a group which believed that the Qur'an is not a *hujjah* ("proof", meaning a legal source usable for vindication). Among the four sources of *fiqh* that have been regarded as the criteria and standard for the understanding of the Islamic problems by Muslim scholars, i.e. the Qur'an, the *sunnah* (tradition), '*aql* (reason) and *ijma'* (consensus of opinion), they did not recognize three of them. Regarding *ijma'*, they said that it belongs to the Sunni tradition and they could not follow it. Concerning reason, they maintained that reason can also err, and reliance on reason is not legitimate. About the Qur'an they respectfully asserted that the Qur'an is greater in station than being subject to study and comprehension by us humble human creatures. It is only that privilege of the Prophet and the Imams to ponder over the verses of the Holy Qur'an. We ordinary human beings have only the right to read and recite them. This group was that of the Akhbariyyun or Akhbaris.

The Akhbaris regarded *hadith* and chronicles as the only permissible sources of *fiqh* (Islamic jurisprudence). One may be astounded to learn that in some of the Qur'anic exegeses written by these people, they mentioned only those verses about which the tradition existed, and refrained from mentioning other verses as if they are not a part of the Qur'an.

Such a kind of practice was an injustice to the Qur'an. This shows that a society that could neglect and alienate their own heavenly book and that too of the standard and stature of the Qur'an, is not at all up to the Qur'anic standards. Besides the Akhbaris there were other groups who also regarded the Qur'an as inaccessible to the ordinary human intellect. Among them the Ash'arites can be named, who believed that the knowledge of the Qur'an does not necessarily mean that its verses should be pondered over, but the real meanings are the same as that the words literally communicate. According to them, whatever we understand from the outward meaning, we have to be satisfied with it. We should not be concerned with the secret and inner meanings. It was quite natural that this sort of thinking regarding the Qur'an, very rapidly, gave rise to serious deviations and grave misunderstandings. Since they were forced on the one hand to the task of interpretation of the meaning of the Qur'anic verses, and, on the other hand, banished reason also from the realm of religious learning, as a result, they were forced to adopt merely vulgar and superficial interpretations of the Qur'anic verses. On account of their faulty way of thinking, they deviated from the regular course of correct thinking, and thus gave way to distorted and faulty religious vision. As the result of this type of religious thinking, heretic beliefs like the personification of God the Almighty, and numerous other distorted ideas like the possibility of visual perception of God, His possession of physical characteristics etc., came into existence.

Opposing the group which abandoned the Qur'an, another group came into existence which used the Qur'an as the means to fulfill their selfish aims. They gave the Qur'anic verses such interpretations as were favourable to their selfish interests, and wrongfully attributed certain ideas to the Qur'anic text that were not at all in agreement with the spirit of the Qur'an. In answer to every objection that was made against them, they said that none except themselves could understand the esoteric and secret meaning of the Qur'anic verses, and whatever they stated was based on the understanding and knowledge of the esoteric meaning of the verses.

The champions of this movement in the history of Islam consist of two groups: the first group are the Ismaᶜilis, who are also known as the Batinis (secret sect), and the other are the Sufis. Most of the Ismaᶜilis are found in India and some of them are in Iran. They had formed an empire in Egypt known as the Fatimid caliphate. The Ismaᶜilis are so-called Shiᶜis who believe in six Imams. But all the Twelve Imami Shiᶜi scholars are unanimous in the opinion that in spite of their belief in six Imams, the Ismaᶜilis stand at a greater distance from the Shiᶜi faith than the non-Shiᶜi sects. The Sunnis, who do not believe in any of the Imams in the same sense as the Shiᶜi do, nevertheless are nearer to the Shiᶜi than these 'Six Imami Shiᶜis'. The Ismaᶜilis, on account of ther *batini* beliefs and secretive practices have played a treacherous role in the history of Islam and have had a big hand in causing serious deviations in the realm of Islam.

Besides the Ismaᶜilis, the Sufis are also charged with distortion of the Qur'anic verses and had a long hand in interpreting them according to their personal beliefs. Here I present a specimen of their exegesis so that the extent and method of their misinterpretation may be known:

The anecdotes of Ibrahim (A) and his son Ismaᶜil is described by the Qur'an as follows: It occurred to Ibrahim (A) in his dream that he has to sacrifice his son for the sake of God. At first he is perplexed regarding such an instruction; but as he repeatedly has the dream reiterating the same theme, he becomes certain of the Will of God and decides to obey the Divine command. He puts the whole matter before his son, who also faithfully accepts his father's proposal of executing the Divine command:

> *"My son, I see in a dream that I shall sacrifice thee; consider what thinkest thou?" He said, "My father, do as thou art bidden; thou shalt find me, God willing, one of the steadfast." (XXXVII, 102)*

Here the aim is the expression of total submission and resignation towards the Divine decree. For the same reason the father and son are ready to execute the Divine command with whole-hearted purity and sincerity, but the execution of the command was stopped by the Will of God. But the same incident is interpreted by the Sufis in this fashion: Ibrahim here represents intellect and reason (*^caql*) and Isma^cil represents the self (*nafs*); the Qur'anic anecdote is an allegory that hints at the attempt of reason to murder the human self (*nafs*).

It is obvious that such interpretation of the Qur'an is like wanton treatment of it, and presents a distorted perspective of its teachings. It is in the context of such deviate interpretations of the Qur'an based upon personal or sectarian bias and interests that the Prophet has said:

> One who interprets the Qur'an according to his wish, should be certain of his place in hell.

This kind of frivolous attitude towards the verses of the Qur'an amounts to the betrayal of the Qur'an and that too of a grievous degree. The Qur'an itself strikes a middle course between the stagnant and narrow-minded attitude of the Akhbaris and the unwarranted and deviate interpretations of the Batinis. It recommends a course of sincere, disinterested study and asks for unbiased and unprejudiced meditation over its meanings. Not only the believers and the faithful, but even the infidels are invited by it to contemplate over its verses. The Qur'an demands that its verses should be first contemplated over, before forming any adverse opinion against them. Addressing the opponents, it says, why they don't ponder over the Qur'an, what sort of hearts they possess, they are as if shut close and sealed:

> *What, do they not ponder the Qur'an? Or is it that there are locks upon their hearts? (XLVII, 24)*

The Qur'an also says in one of its verses:

> *(This is) a Book We have revealed to you abounding in good, that they may ponder the verses*

That is, We have not sent the Qur'an to be kissed, embraced and put on the niche to gather dust, but for men to read and to contemplate about its contents:

> *. . . that those endowed with understanding may ponder its signs and so remember. (XXXVIII, 29)*

The above verse and scores of other such verses emphasize the importance of contemplation in the Qur'an and interpretation of the Qur'anic verses, although not an interpretation based on personal caprices and bias, but a just, truthful and balanced interpretation free of all traces of selfish interests. If we try to comprehend the Qur'an in an honest and unbiased way, it is not at all necessary to solve all problems that we find in it. In this regard the Qur'an is similar to Nature. In Nature, too, a number of mysteries have neither been solved yet, nor can they be solved in present conditions, yet are likely to be solved in the future. Moreover, in studying and understanding nature, man has to tailor his ideas in accordance with Nature itself. He is forced to interpret Nature in accordance with its reality. He canot define Nature in terms of his own caprices and inclinations. The Qur'an, like the book of Nature, is a book that has not been sent for a specific age and time. Had it been otherwise, all the secrets of the Qur'an would have been discovered in the past; this heavenly Book would not have preserved its charm, freshness and vitality. But we see that the possibility of contemplation, reflection and discovery of new dimensions is inexhaustible in the case of this Holy Book. This is a point that has amply been emphasized and clarified by the Prophet and the Imams. In a tradition, it is related from the Prophet (S) that the Qur'an, like the sun and the moon, will preserve its movement and continuity; that is, the Qur'an is not static or monotonous. In some other place the Prophet has said that outwardly the Qur'an is beautiful and inwardly it is deep and unfathomable. . . .In *ᶜUyun akhbar al-Rida*, from the Imam al-Rida (A), it is quoted that Imam Jaᶜfar al-Sadiq (A) was asked about the secret of it that as the time passes and the more it is read and recited, the Qur'an increases in its novelty and freshness day by day. The Imam al-Sadiq (A) answered:

> Because the Qur'an is not for an exclusive age or for an exclusive people.

The Qur'an has been sent for all ages and for all human beings. It is so composed that in spite of changes in knowledge, outlook and approach through various times and ages, it surpasses all learning and knowledge in all ages. While it encompasses mysteries and abstruce intricacies for the reader of every age, at the same time it presents a great feast of meanings and ideas that can satiate the needs of every time in accordance with the capacity of that particular age.

Chapter Four

The Shi*c*i Interpretation of Hadith *Literature*

For all Muslims Muhammad is both the messenger of Allah, through whose agency the Word of God and ethical principles mandated by Him were communicated to the Islamic community (**ummah**)*, and the archetypal figure of perfection and authority (*al-Insan al-Kamil*). In this latter function, Muhammad has established, in his normative behavior, permanent modalities of conduct for all Muslims. Like all other Muslims, Shicis consider Muhammad's conducts exemplary, and the ethical principles emenating from them complementary to those rooted in the Qur'an. In the following two passages cAllamah Tabataba'i and S. M. Waris Hasan discuss the centrality of prophetic tradition (*Hadith and Sunnah*) in the Shici community. (*Hadith refers to the words and Sunnah to the deeds of the Prophet). The passages are taken from* SI, *pages 101–103 and* Alserat, *pages 41–47, respectively.*

ʿAllamah Tabataba'i

The principle that the *hadith* possesses validity, as attested by the Qur'an, is not all disputed among Shiʿis, or in fact among all Muslims. But because of the failure of some of the early rulers of Islam in preserving and guarding the *hadith*, and the excesses of a group among the companions and followers of the Prophet in propagating *hadith* literature, the corpus of *hadith* came to face a certain number of difficulties.

On the one hand the caliphs of the time prevented the writing down and recording of the *hadith* and ordered any pages containing texts of *hadith* to be burned. Sometimes also any increase in activity in the transmission and study of *hadith* was forbidden. In this way a certain number of *hadiths* were forgotten or lost and a few were even transmitted with a different or distorted meaning. On the other hand another tendency also prevailed among another group of the companions of the Holy Prophet who had had the honor of seeing his presence and actually hearing his words. This group, which was respected by the caliphs and the Muslim community, began an intense effort to propagate the *hadith*. This was carried to such an extent that sometimes *hadith* overruled the Qur'an and the injunction of a Qur'anic verse was even considered abrogated by some people through a *hadith*. Often the transmitters of *hadith* would travel many miles and bear all the difficulties of traveling in order to hear a single saying.

A group of outsiders who had worn the dress of Islam and also some of the enemies within the ranks of Islam began to change and distort some of the *hadith* and thus diminished the reliability and validity of the *hadith* that was then heard and known. For this very reason Islamic scholars began to think of a solution. They created the sciences concerned with the biography of learned men and chains of transmission of *hadith* in order to be able to discriminate between true and false *hadith*... .

* * *

Shiʿism, in addition to seeking to authenticate the chain of transmission of *hadith*, considers the correlation of the text of the *hadith* with the Qur'an as a necessary condition for its validity. In Shiʿi sources there are many *hadiths* of the Prophet and the Imams with authentic chains of transmission which themselves assert that a *hadith* contrary to the Qur'an has no value.

Only that *hadith* can be considered valid which is in agreement with the Qur'an.

Basing itself on these *hadiths*, Shiʿism does not act upon those *hadiths* which are contrary to the text of the Qur'an. As for *hadiths* whose agreement or disagreement cannot be established, according to instructions received from the Imams they are passed by in silence without being accepted or rejected. Needless to say there are also within Shiʿism those who, like a group among the Sunnis, act on any *hadith* whatsoever which they happen to find in different traditional sources... .

*   *   *

A *hadith* heard directly from the mouth of the Prophet or one of the Imams is accepted as in the Qur'an. As for *hadiths* received through intermediaries, the majority of Shiʿis act upon them if their chain of transmission is established at every step or if there exists definite proof concerning their truth, and, if they are concerned with principles of doctrine which require knowledge and certainty, according to the text of the Qur'an. Other than these two kinds of *hadith*, no other *hadith* has any validity concerning principles of doctrine, the invalid *hadith* being called "tradition with a single transmiter" (*khabar wahid*). However, in establishing the injunctions of the *Shariʿah*, because of reasons that have been given, Shiʿis act also on a tradition which is generally accepted as reliable. Therefore it can be said that for Shiʿism a certain and definitely established *hadith* is absolutely binding and must be followed, while a *hadith* which is not absolutely established but which is generally considered as reliable is utilized only in the elaboration of the injunctions of the *Shariʿah*... .

S. M. Waris Hasan

....On the positive side, the "term" *Sunnah* was defined, the qualifications of a *rawi* (transmiter) discussed and the accepted *turuq* (routes) of the authorities in *ʿIlm al-Hadith* were noted. The examination of the essential features of the subject would remain incomplete if the "classes" of *al-Hadith* were not pointed out.

The prime category of *al-Hadith* is called *al-Sahih*. This category has been defined as: a tradition which is transmitted by person or persons.

a. of the specified qualifications (see part one of this article.).

b. the tradition has been *heard* by the *rawi* from his transmiter and that transmiter heard from his source and so on.

c. the tradition is not in direct contravention of another accepted and acknowledged tradition.

The second category is called *al-Hassan*. This category has been defined as a tradition whose *rijal* (narrators) and the source are well known.

The third category is called *al-Muᶜallaq*. This category has been defined as a tradition of which one, or more, link or links are missing. For example, Imam Shafiᶜi's narration from Nafiᶜ ibn ᶜUmar. Here it is assumed that he must have missed out Imam Malik.

The fourth category is called *al-Mursal*. This category has been defined as: a tradition from which the Companion has been omitted. For example, a chain of *rawis* ending up with Saᶜid ibn al-Musayyib (who was a *tabiᶜ*) who, in turn, quoted the Prophet having said something or done something.

The fifth category is called *al-daᶜif*. This category has been defined as: a tradition which fails to conform to one or more conditions specified in *al-Sahih* category mentioned above.

The sixth category is called *al-Muwathathaq*. This kind is exclusive to the Shiᶜis. It has been defined as: a tradition which has been transmitted by a person who is not of the Shiᶜi faith but who, however, is of dependable character and is regarded as truthful... .

The sheer number and variations of the classes of *hadith* bear witness to the seriousness with which Muslims took the *Sunnah* of their Prophet. Another proud feature of *al-Hadith* is that all the classical works were complete within three hundred years of the death of the Prophet. (Imam Malik ibn Anas 95–179 A.H., Imam Ahmad ibn Hanbal 164–241 A.H., Imam Muhammad ibn Ismaᶜil al-Bukhari 194–256 A.H., Imam Muslim ibn al-Hajjaj 206–261 A.H., Abu Dawud Sulayman ibn Ashᶜath 202–275. A.H. Muhammad ibn ᶜIsa al-Tirmidhi 209–279 A.H. and Ahmad ibn Shuᶜayb al-Nasa'i 225–303 A.H.).

I chose to contribute on the subject (i.e. *Sunnah*) in the present series on Imam ᶜAli ibn Abu Talib because although much has been written on the subject of *al-Hadith* and *Sunnah* by the old masters as well as by the contemporary scholars one area which I propose to touch upon has not perhaps, been fully investigated. And that is: what sort of *Sunnah* may have survived in view of the policies adapted by the Umayyids since their coming to power in 41 A.H. (661 A.D.) to their downfall in 132 A.H. (749 A.D.)? These ninety years or so are formative years of the *Sunnah* too, and therefore, important. And is there a grain of truth in the claim that the internal policies of the Umayyads were more concerned about eradicating the memories of ^cAli and exterminating his followers than promoting the *Sunnah*? To a scholar of ^c*ilm al-Hadith* a Companion (*Sahabah*) was the most important link in the chain of *Isnad*. We have already noted in this article how a tradition is at once demoted from the status of *al-Sahih* to that of *al Mursal* if a *tabi*^c (who by definition, is supposed to have met one or more Companions) does not name the Companion he took the tradition from. Yet the most famous of the *fuqaha* (jurists) of the first century of the Muslim era, are compelled to convert their would-be *al-Sihah* into the less valued currency of *al-marasil*! Abu ^cAbdullah al-Hakim names them: "Most of the *marasil* traditions from amongst the traditionists of al-Madinah come from Sa^cid ibn al-Musaiyyib (died 93 A.H.−711 A.D.); from amongst the traditionists of Mecca, most of them come from ^cAta ibn Abu Rabah (died 115 A.H.−733 A.D.); from amongst the traditionists of Egypt, most of the *marasil* come from Sa^cid ibn Abu Hilal from amongst the traditionists of Syria, most *marasil* come from Makhul al-Shami (died in 116 A.H.−734 A.D.); from amongst the Kufi traditionists, most of the *marasil* come from Ibrahim al-Nakha^ci (died 96 A.H.-714 A.D.); from amongst the traditionists of Basrah, most of the *marasil* come from al Hasan al-Basri" (died 110 A.H.−728 A.D).

Why should these illustrious people of their time fail to reveal their Companion (*sahabah*), the source of their contribution to *Sunnah*? The answer given by the last mentioned, al Hasan al-Basri, may be representative of the rest of the *fuqaha*. Al-Zahabi records from Yunus ibn ^cAbid: "I said to al-Hasan, O Abu Sa^cid, you say: The Prophet said (such and such thing) but you have never met him?" al-Hasan replied: "O Son of my brother, you have asked me about something no one has asked me before. And if you were not as dear to me as you are, I would have not told you either. (My "*irsal*" is due to) the time I am living in and of which you know. But whenever you hear me say: "the Prophet said . . .", you must know it is through ^cAli ibn Abu Talib. I do not mention his name because I can not."

The time al-Hasan al-Basri has just mentioned began when the first Caliph of the Umayyads, Mu^cawiyah ibn Abu Sufyan, announced his caliphate in Shawwal 41 A.H. (660 A.D.) at Bayt al-Muqaddas. From then on it seems that the main concern of the government was ^cAli! Here is how Mu^cawiyah briefs his newly appointed governor of al-Kufa, Maghirah ibn Shu^cba: "I wanted to give you directions about many things but I leave it to your own good judgement (to do) that which will cause my pleasure, strengthen my rule, and "correct" my subjects. But I should not refrain from advising you never to cease from cursing ^cAli and speaking ill of him

Forgiveness for him; finding faults with the followers of ᶜAli (and thus) ex-(on the pulpits); invoking God's Mercy upon ᶜUthman and seeking God's pelling them (and while the faults are not found) refraining to hear from them (the traditions?). . . ."

As the Muslims have never quite been able to grasp the significance of "the Cross' and the philosophy of "Trinity" which in the end, still leaves a Christian to worship One God, the Western World too, may perhaps, misunderstood the enthusiasm and the zeal of the followers of ᶜAli. The above passage from al-Tabari may help to explain. The first Caliph of the Umayyads does not ask the governor to refute one particular act or acts of ᶜAli. He is concerned with the symbol "ᶜAli". To him, as to the followers of ᶜAli, "ᶜAli" was a name and a person but more so, a philosophy, an attitude, a particular way to approach God and a personal way to understand Islam.

The *Sunnah* which came into being after ᶜAli ibn Abu Talib (died 21st Ramadan 40 A.H.) was a strange one. Previously the traditionists were annoyed if a tradition was not blessed by the name of a Companion. The cities, the societies, the armies used to boastfully announce the presence of a Companion. Now the Companions stood to lose the very honor if they refused to denounce ᶜAli. Al-Masᶜudi tells us of a visit Saᶜd ibn Abu Waqqas made to the first Caliph of the Umayyad, Muᶜawiyah ibn Abu Sufyan: "He (Muᶜawiyah) made him sit next to him on the throne and began to attack and curse ᶜAli. Saᶜd shuddered and addressed him thus: (First) you honor me by sitting me next to you on the throne, next you start cursing ᶜAli? I swear by God that if I was given even one of his many distinctions it would have made me happier than if I were given all that the sun shines on.

Nothing happened to Saᶜd. It was Mecca at the time of holy pilgrimage and there were quite a sizeable crowd about. Also Saᶜd was one of the eminent Ten. But Hujr ibn ᶜAdi, comparatively young but learned and indeed the pride of al-Kufah, was another Companion who was made to pay with his life.

Together with his thirteen followers, their hands and feet secured with iron they were sent to Damascus. Their execution took place outside the city and the following indictment was read out: "The commander of the faithful has commissioned your execution, O head of the error, base of *kufr* and terrorisation and lover of *Abu Turab* (ᶜAli). Unless you denounce your *kufr* and curse your hero." But Hujr and his followers refused and were executed. Note that in the new *Sunnah* loving ᶜAli was *kufr*!

ᶜAmr ibn al-Himiq, another Companion, whose forehead was marked by the repetition of prostration and whose lectures were attended by the seekers of traditions was beheaded because he would not stop quoting traditions about and from ᶜAli. The Caliph made a gift to his imprisoned wife; of her husband's severed head! While she wiped the blood from it, there was no one to console her apart from solitude!

These events were followed by Karbala in 61 A.H., the sack of the city of the Prophet (*Madinah al-Nabi*) in 62 A.H., and the destruction of Kaᶜbah in 63 A.H. The point to remember concerning these well known episodes is that the outrages were perpetrated by a government which to the outside world, posed as the guardian of the Faith and the protector of the *Sunnah*.

Now consider the following tradition from ᶜAli ibn Khashram: "We were with Sufyan ibn ᶜUyaynah (died 198 A.H. – 813 A.D.) when Sufyan said: Al-Zuhri said . . ." Someone interrupted him saying: "Have you heard al Zuhri say this?" Sufyan ignored the question and repeated: "Al-Zuhri said . . ." But he was checked again with the same question. Then Sufyan said: "I have not heard it from al-Zuhri nor from someone who heard it from al-Zuhri. I was told by ᶜAbd al-Razzaq who heard it from *Muᶜmar* who was told it by al-Zuhri".

A scholar of ᶜ*ilm al-hadith* will not say that Sufyan, the famous Meccan jurist, was guilty of untruthfulness in the first instance. He is likely to point out that Sufyan was attributing to al-Zuhri that which in fact was said by him. The practice he will find Sufyan indulging in what is called *al-Tadlis*. The term therefore meant: "the omission on the part of the *rawi* of his immediate source or sources." The practice was so frowned upon that one of the jurists preferred the punishments of hell over the pleausres of *tadlis*!

Yet it was wide-spread. Because although *Ittisal al-asnad* (the continuity of links of *rawis*) was a faultless method to check a tradition and all its links, it also proved to be an effective weapon for the authorities to get to the source of the traditions which did not conform to the official *Sunnah*. Now turning to the table of the preferred *routes* by al-Hakim (see part one of this article) one notices in particular, that although al-Hakim acknowledges the best possible route to the traditions from *Ahl al-bayt*, is Jaᶜfar al-Sadiq, but then he merely says: "if the *rawi* is dependable, and does not name them! I suspect for the fear of exposing them to persecution."

Amongst the lessons history has taught mankind is the fact that causes are nursed by persecutions. The torments inflicted by Ziyad, the son of his father, and then later, by al-Hajaj ibn Yusuf al-Thaqafi, only served to rally the intellectuals of ᶜ*ilm al-hadith* round the forbidden name and cause of ᶜAli. For his name became the symbol of the only *albeit* silent opposition. The first century of the Muslim era which provided all the raw material for Imam Malik and others to base their work on, nevertheless, has not left us a work of its own. And it is from the second century onward that one finds *muhaddithin* turning to writing.

However, the jurists and the traditionists of the first century, in addition to transmitting the traditions to the second century, did leave the record of the struggle and the sufferings which started from the time the period of the Orthodox Caliphate terminated. In my opinion, the battle of Dair al-Jama-jim was no less in importance than that of al-Badr. For the contingent of *al-Qurra'* consisted of the persons who were *shuyukh* (the spiritual and professional leaders) to the entire community of the writers in ᶜ*ilm al hadith*. Amongst those who had left the mosques and the pulpits to take up arms were: Saᶜid ibn Jubayr, Hasan al-Basri, Ibrahim al-Nakhaᶜi, ᶜAbd al-Rahman ibn Abu Layla, Abu al-Bakhtari, Kumayl ibn Ziyad, al-Nakha'i, Muhammad ibn Saᶜd ibn Abu Waqqas and even, al-Shaᶜbi. To begin with these intellectuals succeeded in raising such a force that the "ironhanded" governor had to call Damascus for help repeating the word "Help" three times. But cunning and worldly shrewdness are not the strongest subjects of the true intellectuals. They chose to fight under ᶜAbd al-Rahman ibn al-Ashᶜath who cared less for the cause of *al qurra'* and the jurists and more for his personal gains.

Whatever the cause of the defeat may have been, the *Shuyukh* of ᶜ*ilm al-hadith* succeeded in printing the point on the pages of history. The first being that the Qur'an they knew, and the *Sunnah* they practiced and preached was so different that it was lawful for them to raise sword against supposedly a Muslim government. Secondly there was their adherence to ᶜAli. I translate the short speech of ᶜAbd al-Rahman ibn Abu Layla addressing the army before the battle began: "O group of *al-qurra'*, to run away from the battlefield is ignonimous and it is more so with you. I have heard ᶜAli, may God elevate further his rank amongst the pious and reward him with the best of the rewards He has set aside for the truthfuls and the martyrs, say; (when we met the Syrians): "O believers, whosoever sees an outrage being committed and a forbidden practice people are asked to adapt, and renounces those evils from his heart, earns exhoneration for himself and is a Muslim. The one who renounces those crimes with his tongue elevates himself over the first one and is rewarded. But the one who renounces the outrages with his sword in order that the Word of God may reign supreme and the word of the oppressors reduced to the lowest level, that is the person who treads the path of Guidance and whose heart is illumniated with the light of *al-yaqin*. . . ."

One finds the influence of ᶜAli pervading throughout the period the *Sunnah* took the final shape in. Abu ᶜAbd al-Rahman al-Nasa'i was asked, when he visited Damascus, about the distinctions (*fadail*) of Muᶜawiyah. And the reply quoted to be given by him proved to be the cause of his death. He said: "Is Muᶜawiyah not happy that his head too is counted with others (of Companions) and there is the talk about distinctions?

This was the author of one of the most correct books (*al-Sihah*) of the Sunnites!

And talking about the Imams of the majority, their contribution to the cause has not been less. ^cAli was renounced openly on the pulpits when Malik ibn Anas was born. But when Muhammad ibn ^cAbdullah, a grandson of ^cAli took up arms against the Umayyad government, Imam Malik declared Muhammad's support as lawful. In fact he encouraged people to join the rebellion. As a result he was punished. The writer of the earliest book (or perhaps one of the earliest books) in Islam could prove his allegiance to ^cAli by the marks left by the whip on his back!

To east of the empire, in al-Kafah, Imam Abu Hanifah was supporting the same cause of ^cAli at the same time. Of his Muhammad Abu Zuhrah writes: "Most of what traditions tell us about him is (the fact) that his heart forever remained with the sons of ^cAli whether they revolted against the government during the Umayyad period or ^cAbbasid. In his view the Umayyads had no right either to worldly authority or religious power."

His end came in the prison of al-Masur. And the historians tell us that it was due to his refusal to accept the post of the Chief Justice (*Qadi al-Quddat*) offered by the second Caliph of the ^cAbbasids. But that post was offered after he had been watched by government's security forces for a number of years. During that time he could not restrain himself from bitterly criticising the government for the wrongful imprisonment of ^cAbdullah ibn al-Hasan al-Muthana who was a grandson to ^cAli. Previously during the time of the Umayyads, when Zayd ibn ^cAli (*Zayn al ^cAbidin*) revolted against al-Hisham ibn ^cAbd al-Malik and Imam Abu Hanifah heard the news, he said: "His revolt resembles that of his grandfather, the Messenger of God, at al-Badr!" "Why did you not join him?" he was asked. "If I had not known that people will forsake him as they forsook his father, I would have fought with him. For the son of ^cAli is indeed the leader of righteousness". But, however, Imam Abu Hanifah is reported to have sent 10,000 Dinars to Zayd to assist him in the struggle.

It stands to the eternal credit of Hisham that, whatever else he may have done to enrage the Meccans and the Madinans, he spared Imam Abu Hanifah despite the latter's open allegiance to Zayd. Perhaps even in those medieval times it was recognised that, provided that it did not affect the lives and the property of the sovereign and the subjects, the *opposition* must be allowed. But Mansur, the second Caliph of the ^cAbbasids, who had no qualms in killing the founder, of his own empire, Abu Muslim Khurasani, was not going to be magnanimous to Abu Hanifah. The Caliph's opportunity came when Abu Hanifah advised one of his generals not to fight against Nafs al-Zakkiyah (the Pure Soul), another grandson of ^cAli. Imam Abu Hanifah was imprisoned and was taken out to be whipped 110 times daily. To me there is a significance in the numbers of whips decreed to be administered to the Imam. In Arabic each letter stands for a figure, and those who know the system will be able to read the name behind the number. No-one knows better than the professional men, how a vocation becomes part of one's life. Indeed the life itself. To those who believed that the Qur'an was the Word of God, and the Sermons, the Sayings and the Actions of His messenger so important as to be the basis of the constitution of an immense empire, the hallmark of a genuine material became the name of ʿAli. They were not ʿAli's worshipers but they regarded him as the first guardian and the protector of both the Qur'an and the *Sunnah.* In upholding ʿAli's cause they were not so much defending the name and the memories of a person but their profession.

Chapter Five

The Nahj al-Balaghah *and the Teachings of the Imams*

The third source of authority for the Shiᶜis after the Qur'an and the prophetic traditions is the exemplary sayings and conduct of their Imams. Among the latter genre of writings incorporating doctrinal teachings and ethical injunctions, ᶜAli's Nahj al-Balaghah *occupies the central position. In the following passage, Syed Husein M. Jafri provides a short exposition of some essential moral aspects of this source. The passages are taken from* Alserat, *pages 264–273 and* ESPMEHA, *pages 58–67, respectively.*

Syed Hussein M. Jafri

There is hardly any need to discuss in any deatil ᶜAli's authoritative position in early Islam. . . . Suffice it to say that he was not only the closest member of the Prophet's family but from his childhood also he was brought up by the Prophet, the recipient of Divine revelation, and thus ᶜAli and Islam grew together and he became an embodiment of the teachings of the Qur'an and the *Sunnah* of the Prophet. He has unanimously been recognized as the best qualified person to speak for Islam, its principles and ideals, its theories and practices, its thoughts and concepts and to interpret its fundamental beliefs and institutions. Besides, he has universally been credited with having a philosophical disposition and acclaimed as an unequalled man of letters in early Islam. His numerous speeches, orations, sermons, letters and maxims frequently recorded by Muslim historians and biographers from the earliest times, and compiled together by the Sharif al-Radi (d.405/1014) in his famous collection entitled *Nahj al-Balaghah*, bear testimony to the fact that he had no peer in literary accomplishment among the early Muslims.

We are presenting here, in English translation, the first sermon of the *Nahj al-Balaghah* which has been considered as the best interpretation and exposition of the fundamental beliefs and concepts of Islam. In the first part of the sermon ᶜAli deals with the question of the transcendence and immanence of God and the limitations of human intellect to comprehend Him. It explains the Qur'anic concept of the Unity of God and the essentials of faith which lead a man to the religious consciousness. ᶜAli then proceeds to depict God's power of creativity, creation of the heavens and the earth and the universe as a whole, the angels and their functions, and then the creation of man symbolized by Adam. Since mankind needs guidance, ᶜAli comes to the topic of God's selection and appointment of the prophets culminating in the choice of Muhammad as the last of the prophets, and the revelations of the Qur'an as the last of the revealed Books; and lastly, ᶜAli emphasises the importance of the *Shariᶜah* as the God-given code of human conduct and behaviour. In the last part of the sermon, as arranged by the Sharif al-Radi, ᶜAli speaks of the importance of the *Hajj* as one of the basic institutions of Islam... .

The external evidence may be taken from the fact that various parts of this Sermon are recorded by some of the earliest Muslim writes who flourished long before Sharif al-Radi. The way Sharif al-Radi records the

Sermon shows that he collected it in bits and pieces from different sources and put them together as one continuous speech. A careful reading of the whole Sermon, however, makes it almost certain that it is not one continuous speech but various parts of it have been delivered at different times and occasions which the compiler, because of the similarity of the theme, combined together as the opening Sermon of his collection. Had someone else written it to attribute it to ᶜAli it would not have lacked the coherence and logical sequence which it did not have. For example, the last part of the Sermon dealing with the institution of the *Hajj* with such an elaborate discussion apparently does not have any direct bearing on the main theme of the Sermon. Such an emphatic description of the *Hajj* at the end of the Sermon strongly suggests that at least the main part of it was delivered by ᶜAli during his Caliphate on the occasion of the *Hajj*. It seems logical that before speaking about the spiritual values of the *Hajj*, ᶜAli first discussed more fundamental questions pertaining to the faith and man's relation to his Creator.

The great importance of the Sermon, however, lies in the fact that it is one of the earliest interpretations of the fundamental beliefs of Islam given by a person who had the closest relationship with the recipient of Divine revelation, the Prophet of Islam.

*   *   *

"From one of his (ᶜAli's) Sermons in which he mentions the beginning of the creation of the sky and the earth as well as the creation of Adam." (Sharif al-Radi).

> Praise be to God whose praise cannot be attained by the (best of) orators, whose blessings cannot be counted by the enumerators and whose due cannot be paid by the strivers. He whom the utmost (human) ambitions cannot perceive and the deepest wisdom cannot reach; He for whose description there is no definable limit or available epithet, or countable time or stretchable duration. He created the creation (Universe) by His might, set loose the breezes by His mercy and pegged down the swaying earth by the rocky mountains.
>
> The first essential (i.e. beginning) of belief is His knowledge, the perfection of His knowledge is His verification, the perfection of verification is His unity, the perfection of His unity is to consider Him free (from human qualities) and the perfection of considering Him free (from anthropomorphic qualities) is the negation of (human) attributes for Him, as every attribute attests that it is other than the attributee and

every attributee testifies that it is other than the attribute. So he who ascribes attributes to God, the Glorious, associates something with Him, and he who associates something with Him duplicates Him, and he who duplicates him splits Him up, and he who splits Him up, is ignorant of Him, points towards Him, and he who points towards Him defines Him, and he who defines Him counts Him; and he who asks: "In what?" includes Him, and he asks: "On what?" detracts from Him. He is a Being, not by creation or accident, existent not by being ever nonexistent; with everything yet not by association, and other than everything but not by separation. He acts but not in the sense of movements or implements. He was seeing when there was none of His creatures to be seen by Him, aloof when there was no companion to whom He might have become attached or at whose absence He might have felt lonely.

* * *

He created all the creatures by His creative power, without any deep thinking which He might have employed, or any (previous) experience that He might have gained (utilized), or any movement that He might have made, or any mental exertion that might have perplexed Him. He placed all things in their proper places at the due time and made different things conform to one another. He endowed them with their respective natures and bestowed upon them their external forms, having been aware of them before their beginning, comprehending their limits and ends, knowing their essence and their inclination.

* * *

When creating the universe, He began the opening up of the atmospere, the splitting up of its sides and of the upper layers of the air and made the water (fluid) flow into it, the swelling water seething and surging, the abundant one layer upon layer. He placed it on the back of the violent wind and the strong gale which uproots everything. Then He forbade the wind to reject that water, empowered it to hold it tightly, and adjoined the former to the surface of the latter, so that the air beneath the water was open and the water above it flowing. Then He created a wind, the blowing of which did not bring any clouds and made it stay constantly in its place. He strengthened its blowing and made its source distant; He then commanded it to agitate the abundant water and raise high the sea-waves, and so it churned it up as one churns the milk in a leather bag, and moved it violently like its own violent motion in the atmosphere, turning back its first part on the last part and its quiescent part towards its surging one, till it rose up in high waves and its swelling billows threw up foam and froth. God then lifted up this froth in the opening air and the gaping atmosphere. Then from this watery froth He made the seven skies, the lowermost of them being a restrained wave and the topmost a safe ceiling and a lofty turret, without any pillars supporting them or any pegs keeping them together.

Then He decorated the skies with the ornaments of the stars and the dazzling heavenly bodies, and moved among them a light-shedding lamp and an illuminating moon, placed in a revolving sphere a moving roof and an oscillating tablet.

* * *

Then he opened out the space between the topmost skies and filled it up with different kinds of angels, some of whom lie prostrate and never rise up to genuflect, others genuflecting and never straightening up, others standing in rows and never leaving their places, and still others glorifying Him and never getting weary; the drowsiness of eyes never overtakes them, nor do the slackening of wits, the weakness of bodies or the heedlessness of forgetting. Some of them are the trustees of His revelation and like a tongue unto His apostles, coming and going with His decrees and commands. Some others are the guardians of His slaves (human beings) and the wardens of His Paradise. Some of them are such that their feet rest firmly on the lowermost layers of the earth, while their necks rise high above the topmost sky and their other limbs come out of its sides, their shoulders touching the Throne's legs, their eyes lowered before it, their wings folded beneath it, the Screen of majesty being placed between them and those other than they, and so also the curtain of might. They imagine not their Lord in any shape, and do not attribute to Him the qualities of the created beings; they do not limit Him with places and do not point at Him with similitudes.

* * *

Then God collected from the rugged and soft soils of the earth and from its sweet and salt ones, a handful of dust and poured water on it till it was cleansed, and He kneaded it up with moisture till it became hard and sticky. He then shaped from it a figure with curves and joints and limbs and parts. He solidified it till it stuck together and hardened it till it became resonating, for a fixed period and known duration of time. Then He breathed into the figure His own spirit and it assumed the form of a man with an intellect which he could employ, a thought which he could use, and limbs and parts (of the body) which he could utilize and operate in his service, and a knowledge by which he could differentiate between right and wrong, between tastes and smells, and between colours and kinds. His nature was imbued with varying colours, kindred similitudes, antagonistic contrasts and different admixtures of heat and cold, moisture and dryness. God then demanded back from the angels the thing He had entrusted to them and the fulfilment of His bequest to them, by ordering them to prostrate themselves before Adam and humble themselves to pay homage to him, and so He said: "Lie prostrate before Adam." They all prostrated themselves — all except *Iblis* who was swayed by self-conceit and overpowered by infamy, being proud of his own creation from fire and regarding with contempt a creature made from kneaded dust. Thereupon God granted him a respite in order to justify His displeasure, to complete his damnation and to fulfil the promise made to him, saying: "You shall be one of those respited for a known period of time." Then He settled Adam in an abode where he made his livelihood plentiful, made his stay secure and warned him of *Iblis* and his enmity. Then his enemy deceived him being jealous of the abode where he sojourned and his companionship of the virtuous ones, and so Adam bartered away his certainty for doubt and the firmness of his resolve for its weakness, and exchanged his happiness for fear and his self-satisfaction for regret. God then condescended to accept his repentance and taught him the word of His mercy. He promised to return him to the place he longed for and made him descend into the abode of affliction and procreation of children.

* * *

Imam ᶜAli

Health is increased by striving to obey God.

Reliance on God is the ultimate certainty.

Covetousness corrupts certainty.

The foundation of religion is certainty (of God).

Unbelief causes the flow of blessings to cease.

Faith is a tree whose root is certainty, whose branches are restraint (*al-taqwa*), whose blossoms are reserve (*al-haya*), and whose fruit is liberality (*al-sakha*).

Faith is the pinnacle of religion.

Patience is the fruit of faith.

Sincerity is the pinnacle of faith.

Patience is the vanguard of victory.

Deliverance lies in faith.

Avoid sins against God and you will be delivered.

The Remembrance of God (*zikr*) is the light of the reason, the life of souls, and the polisher of breasts.

Gnosis (*al-maᶜrifah*) is the light of the heart.

The aim of gnosis (*maᶜrifah*) and wisdom (*hikmah*) is preserving religion and tradition.

The ignorant see only superficially and by their opinions; the wise see by the eyes of their hearts and with insight.

Every secret is known to God.

I am astonished at how one who doesn't know himself claims to know his Lord.

The fruit of knowledge (*ᶜilm*) is to know God.

Knowledge is the light of wisdom and a fountain of beneficence.

Knowledge is the adornment of the wealthy and the wealth of the poor.

Three things bear witness to the knowledge of the wise; the messenger, the message, and the gift.

Knowledge is an inexhaustible treasure.

Knowledge is the supreme height of nobility.

Noble action is announced by the excellence of its intentions.

Firmly resolving upon the good extinguishes the fire of evil.

When firmness is combined with discretion, success follows.

Knowledge is the foundation of right actions.

The worst knowledge is that which is not acted upon.

To act without knowledge is error.

The ignorant worshipper is like an ass turning a mill: he goes round and round, but goes nowhere.

Ignorance is a mine of evil.

Ignorance is the greatest tragedy.

Blameworthy character is the fruit of ignorance.

The root of ignorance is overstepping limits.

Doubt is the fruit of ignorance.

The fruit of the tree of knowledge is harvested by fitting action, not by words.

Nobility, in God's sight, is in excellence of deeds, not excellence of words.

The best speech is that confirmed by fitting actions. The noblest speech is the truth.

Verily you are in greater need of doing well than of speaking well.

Learning is the greatest nobility; nothing takes precedence over it.

Associate with the learned; your knowledge will increase, your manners will improve, and your soul willl be purified.

Intimacy with the wise is the life of the spirit (*ruh*).

Hearts are cultivated by intimacy with the intelligent.

The learned man is alive among the dead; the ignorant man is dead among the living.

Association with the stupid is agony for the spirit.

The beauty of a learned man is what he does with his learning.

The learned rule the people by the power of their wisdom.

A fault of the learned is their fondness of assuming control.

The learned who do evil are a plague upon the people. Generosity carried to extremes is squandering.

The danger of cleverness is craftiness.

A wise man's error is worse than a felony.

Right attitude ensures against errors.

A wise man is diligent in deeds and sparing in expectations.

To pardon is the sign of intelligence.

Forgiveness is the highest virtue.

Forbearance is the evidence of much learning.

Chapter Six

Doctrinal Divisions Within Shiᶜism

As a thriving religious tradition, deeply rooted in the Qur'anic revelation and Muhammadan experience, Shiᶜism has been witness to and survived a number of fundamental divisions within its general doctrinal context. A historical and theological interaction between specific sociopolitical circumstances and the inner dynamics of Shiᶜi dogmas has given rise to major divisions within Shiᶜism. In the following passage ᶜAllamah Tabataba'i provides a historical-analytical exposition of these divisions. The passage is taken form SI, pages 75–82.

ᶜAllamah Tabatabaᵢ

Each religion possesses a certain number of primary principles which form its essential basis and other principles of secondary importance. When the followers of a religion differ as to the nature of the primary principles and their secondary aspects but preserve a common basis, the result is called division (*inshiᶜab*) within that religion. Such divisions exist in all traditions and religions, and more particularly in the four "revealed" religions of Judaism, Christianity, Zoroastrianism, and Islam.

Shiᶜism did not undergo any divisions during the imamate of the first three Imams: ᶜAli, Hasan, and Husayn. But after the martyrdom of Husayn, the majority of the Shiᶜis accepted the imamate of ᶜAli ibn Husayn al-Sajjad, while a minority known as the Kisaniyyah believed that the third son of ᶜAli, Muhammad ibn Hanafiyah, was the fourth Imam as well as the promised Mahdi, and that he had gone into occultation in the Radwa mountains and one day would reappear. After the death of Imam al-Sajjad the majority of the Shiᶜis accepted as Imam his son, Muhammad al-Baqir, while a minority followed Zayd al-Shahid, another son of the Imam al-Sajjad, and became known as Zaydis. Following Imam Muhammad al-Baqir, the Shiᶜis accepted his son Jaᶜfar al-Sadiq as Imam and after the death of Imam Jaᶜfar the majority followed his son Imam Musa al-Kazim as the seventh Imam. However, one group followed the older son of the sixth Imam, Ismaᶜil, who had died while his father was still alive, and when this latter group separated from the majority of Shiᶜis it became known as Ismaᶜilis. Others accepted as Imam either ᶜAbdallah al-Aftah or Muhammad, both sons of the sixth Imam. Finally, another party stopped with the sixth Imam himself and considered him as the last Imam. In the same way, after the martyrdom of Imam Musa al-Kazim the majority followed his son, Ali al-Rida, as the eighth Imam. However, some stopped with the seventh Imam and became known as the Waqifiyyah.

From the eighth Imam to the twelfth, whom the majority of the Shiᶜis believed to be the promised Mahdi, no division of any importance took place within Shiᶜism. Even if certain events occurred in the form of division, they lasted but a few days and dissolved by themselves. For exmaple, Jaᶜfar, the son of the tenth Imam, claimed to be Imam after the death of his brother, the eleventh Imam. A group of people followed him but scattered in a few days and Jaᶜfar himself did not follow his claim any further. Furthermore, there are differences between Shiᶜis in theological and juridical matters which must not be considered as divisions in religious schools. Also the Babi and Baha'i sects, which like the Batinis (The Qaramitah) differ in both the principles (*usul*) and branches (*furu*) of Islam from the Muslims, should not in any sense be considered as branches of Shiᶜism.

The sects which separated from the majority of Shiᶜis all dissolved within a short period, except two: the Zaydi and the Ismaᶜili which continue to exist until now. To this day communities of these branches are active in various parts of the world such as the Yemen, India, and Syria. Therefore, we shall limit our discussion to these two branches along with the majority of Shiᶜis who are Twelvers.

Zaydism and Its Branches

The Zaydis are the followers of Zayd al-Shahid, the son of Imam al-Sajjad. Zayd rebelled in 121/737 against the Umayyad caliph Hisham ᶜAbd al-Malik and a group paid allegiance to him. A battle ensued in Kufah between Zayd and the army of the caliph in which Zayd was killed.

The followers of Zayd regard him as the fifth Imam of the Household of the Prophet. After him his son, Yahya ibn Zayd, who rebelled against the caliph Walid ibn Yazid and was also killed, took his place. After Yahya, Muhammad ibn ᶜAbdullah and Ibrahim ibn ᶜAbdullah, who revolted against the ᶜAbbasid caliph Mansur al-Dawaniqi and were also killed, were chosen as Imams.

Henceforth for some time there was disorder in Zaydi ranks until Nasir al-Utrush, a descendant of the brother of Zayd, arose in Khurasan. Being pursued by the governmental authorities in that region, he fled to Mazandaran (Tabaristan) whose people had not as yet accepted Islam. After thirteen years of missionary activity in this region he brought a large number of people into the Zaydi branch of Islam. Then in the year 301/913 with their aid he conquered the region of Mazandaran, becoming himself Imam. For some time his descendants continued to rule as Imams in that area.

According to Zaydi belief any descendant of Fatimah (the daughter of the Prophet) who begins an uprising in the name of defending the truth may become Imam if he is learned in the religious sciences, ethically pure, courageous and generous. Yet for some time after Utrush and his descendants there was no Imam who could bring about an insurrection with the sword until recently when, about sixty years ago, Imam Yahya revolted in the Yemen, which had been a part of the Ottoman Empire, made it independent, and began to rule there as Imam. His descendants continued to rule in that region as Imams until very recently.

At the beginning the Zaydis, like Zayd himself, considered the first two
caliphs, Abu Bakr and ^cUmar, as their Imams. But after a while some of
them began to delete the name of the first two caliphs from the list of Imams and placed ^cAli as the first Imam.

From what is known of Zaydi beliefs it can be said that in the principles
of Islam (*usul*) they follow a path close to that of the Mu^ctazilites, while in
the branches or derivative institutions of the law (*furu^c*) they apply the jurisprudence of Abu Hanifah, the founder of one of the four Sunni schools of
law. They also differ among themselves concerning certain problems.

Isma^cilism and Its Branches

Imam Ja^cfar al-Sadiq had a son named Isma^cil who was the oldest of his
children. Isma^cil died during the lifetime of his father who summoned
witnesses to his death, including the governor of Medinah. Concerning this
question, some believed that Isma^cil did not die but went into occultation,
that he would appear again and would be the promised Mahdi. They further
believed that the summoning of witnesses on the part of the Imam for
Isma^cil's death was a way of hiding the truth in fear of al-Mansur, the ^cAb-
basid caliph. Another group believed that the true Imam was Isma^cil whose
death meant the imamate was transferred to his son Muhammad. A third
group also held that although he died during the lifetime of his father he
was the Imam and that the imamate passed after him to Muhammad ibn
Isma^cil and his descendants. The first two groups soon became extinct,
while the third branch continued to exist to this day and has undergone a
certain amount of division.

The Isma^cilis have a philosophy in many ways similar to that of the
Sabaeans (star worshippers) combined with elements of Hindu gnosis. In
the sciences and decrees of Islam they believe that each exterior reality
(*zahir*) has an inner aspect (*batin*) and each element of revelation (*tanzil*) a
hermeneutic and esoteric exegesis (*ta'wil*).

The Isma^cilis believe that the earth can never exist without a Proof (*hujjah*) of God. The Proof is of two kinds: "speaker" (*natiq*) and "silent one"
(*samit*). The speaker is a prophet and the silent one is an Imam or Guardian
(*wali*) who is the inheritor, or executor of the testament (*wasi*) of a prophet. In any case the Proof of God is the perfect theophany of the Divinity.

The principle of the Proof of God revolves constantly around the number
seven. A prophet (*nabi*), who is sent by God, has the function of prophecy
(*nubuwwat*), of bringing a Divine Law or *Shari^cah*. A prophet, who is the
perfect manifestation of God, has the esoteric power of initiating men into

the Divine Mysteries (*walayah*). After him there are seven executors of hi testament (*wasi*) who possess the power of executing his testamen (*wasayah*) and the power of esoteric initiation into the Divine Mysterie (*walayah*). The seventh in the succession possesses those two powers an also the additional power of prophecy (*nubuwwat*). The cycle of seven ex ecutors (*wasis*) is then repeated with the seventh a prophet.

The Isma'ilis say that Adam was sent as a prophet with the power o prophecy and of esoteric guidance and he had seven executors of whom th seventh was Noah, who had the three functions of *nubuwwah, wasayah* an *walayah*. Abraham was the seventh executor (*wasi*) of Noah, Moses th seventh executor of Abraham, Jesus the seventh executor of Moses Muhammad the seventh executor of Jesus, and Muhammad ibn Isma'il th seventh executor of Muhammad.

They consider the *wasi's* of the Prophet to be: 'Ali, Husayn ibn 'Ali (the do not consider Imam Hasan among the Imams), 'Ali ibn Husayn al Sajjad, Muhammad al-Baqir, Ja'far al-Sadiq, Isma'il ibn Ja'far, an Muhammad ibn Isma'il. After this series there are seven descendants o Muhammad ibn Isma'il whose names are hidden and secret. After then there are the first seven rulers of the Fatimid caliphate of Egypt the first o whom, 'Ubaydallah al-Mahdi, was the founder of the Fatimid dynasty. Th Isma'ilis also believe that in addition to the Proof of God there are alway present on earth twelve "chiefs" (*naqib*) who are the companions and elit followers of the Proof. Some of the branches of the Batinis, however, lik the Druzes, believe six of the "chiefs" to be from the Imams and six from others.

The Batinis

In the year 278/891, a few years before the appearance of 'Ubaydallah al Mahdi in North Africa, there appeared in Kufah an unknown person from Khuzistan (in southern Persia) who never revealed his name and identity He would fast during the day and worship at night and made a living from his own labor. In addition he invited people to join the Isma'ili cause an was able to assemble a large number of people about him. From among them he chose twelve "chiefs" (*naqib*) and then he set out for Damascus Having left Kufah he was never heard of again.

This unknown man was replaced by Ahmad, known as the Qaramit who began to propagate Batini teachings in Iraq. As the historians hav recorded, he instituted two daily prayers in place of the five in Islam, re moved the necessity of ablution after sexual intercourse, and made th drinking of wine permissible. Contemporary with these events, other Batin eaders rose to invite people to join their cause and assembled a group of followers. The Batinis had no respect for the lives and possessions of those who were outside their group. For this reason they began uprising in the cities of Iraq, Bahrain, the Yemen, and Syria, spilling the blood of people and looting their wealth. Many times they stopped the caravans of those who were making the pilgrimage to Mecca, killing tens of thousands of pilgrims and plundering their provisions and camels.

Abu Tahir al-Qarmati, one of the Qaramite leaders who in 311/923 had conquered Basrah and did not neglect to kill and plunder, set out with a large number of Batinis for Mecca in 317/929. After overcoming the brief resistance of government troops he entered the city and massacred the population as well as the newly arrived pilgrims. Even within the Masjid al-Haram (the mosque containing the Kaʿbah) and within the Holy Kaʿbah itself, there flowed streams of blood. He divided the covering of the Kaʿbah between his disciples. He tore away the door of the Kaʿbah and took the black stone from its place back to the Yemen. For twenty-two years the black stone was in Qaramite hands. As a result of these actions the majority of Muslims turned completely away from the Batinis and considered them outside the pale of Islam. Even ʿUbaydallah al-Mahdi, the Fatimid ruler, who had risen in those days in North Africa and considered himself the promised Mahdi, abhorred them.

According to the view of historians the distinguishing characteristic of the Batini school is that it interprets the external aspects of Islam in an esoteric manner and considers the externals of the *Shariʿah* to be only for simple-minded people of little intelligence who are deprived of spiritual perfection. Yet occasionally the *Batini* Imams did order certain regulations and laws to be practiced and followed.

The Nizaris, Mustaʿlis, Druzes and Muqannaʿah

The Nizaris

ʿUbaydallah al-Mahdi, who rose in North Africa in 292/904 and as an Ismaʿili declared his imamate and established Fatimid rule, is the founder of the dynasty whose descendants made Cairo the center of their caliphate. For seven generations this sultanate and Ismaʿili imamate continued without any divisions. At the death of the seventh Imam, al-Mustansir biʾllah Muʿidd ibn ʿAli, his sons, Nizar and al-Mustaʿli, began to dispute over the caliphate and imamate. After long disputes and bloody battles al-Mustaʿli was victorious. He captured his brother Nizar and placed him in prison, where he died.

Following this dispute those who accepted the Fatimids divided into two groups: the Nizaris and the Musta^clis. The Nizaris are the followers of Hasan al-Sabbah who was one of the close associates of al-Mustansir. After Nizar's death, because of his support of Nizar, Hasan al-Sabbah was expelled from Egypt by al-Musta^cli. He came to Persia and after a short while appeared in the Fort of Alamut near Qazwin. He conquered Alamut and several surrounding forts. There he established his rule and also began to invite people to the Isma^cili cause.

After the death of Hasan in 518/1124 Buzurg Umid Rudbari and after him his son, Kiya Muhammad, continued to rule following the methods and ways of Hasan al-Sabbah. After Kiya Muhammad, his son Hasan ^cAla Zikrihu'l-Salam, the fourth ruler of Alamut, changed the ways of Hasan al Sabbah, who had been Nizari and became Batini. Henceforth the Isma^cil forts continued as Batini. Four other rulers, Muhammad ibn ^cAla Zikruhu'l-Salam, Jalal al-Din Hasan, ^cAla' al-Din, and Rukn al-Din Khur shah, became Sultan and Imam one after another until Hulagu, the Mongol conqueror, invaded Persia. He captured the Isma^cili forts and put all the Isma^cilis to death, leveling their forts to the ground.

Centuries later, in 1255/1839, the Aqa Khan of Mahallat in Persia, who belonged to the Nizaris, rebelled against Muhammad Shah Qajar in Kerman, but he was defeated and fled to Bombay. There he propagated his Batini-Nizari cause which continues to this day. The Nizaris are today called the Aqa Khanids.

The Musta^clis

The Musta^clis were the followers of al-Musta^cli. Their imamate continued during Fatimid rule in Egypt until it was brought to an end in the year 567/1171. Shortly thereafter, the Bohra sect, following the same school, appeared in India and survives to this day.

The Druzes

The Druzes, who live in the Druze mountains in Syria (and also in Lebanon), were originally followers of the Fatimid caliphs. But as a result of the missionary activity of Nashtakin, the Druzes joined the Batini sect. The Druzes stop with the sixth Fatimid caliph al-Hakim bi'llah, whom others believe to have been killed, and claim that he is in occultation. He has ascended to heaven and will appear once again to the world.

The Muqanna^cah

The Muqanna^cah were at first disciples of ^cAta' al-Marwi known as Muqanna^c, who according to historical sources was a follower of Abu Muslim of Khurasan. After the death of Abu Muslim, Muqanna^c claimed that Abu

Muslim's soul had become incarnated in him. Soon he claimed to be a prophet and later a divinty. Finally, in the year 162/777 he was surrounded in the fort of Kabash in Transoxiana. When he became certain that he would be captured and killed, he threw himself into a fire along with some of his disciples and burned to death. His followers soon adopted Ismaʿilism and the ways of the Batinis.

Part II

The Shi^ci Position
vs. Other Divisions
Within Islam

Chapter Seven

Shi*c*ism and Sunnism

*Throughout the Islamic history, Sunnism and Shi*c*ism have constituted the central doctrinal tension within Islam. Out of the initial conflict over the questions of succession to Muhammad and the role and function of the successor, the Sunni-Shi*c*i conflict grew in theological and sociopolitical dimensions. The conflict has expressed itself repeatedly and in various ways in Islamic culture to the present time. In the following passage, Hamid Enayat takes a fresh look at this centuries-old conflict and examines its contemporary ramifications. The excerpt is taken from* MIPT, *pages 18–51.*

Hamid Enayat

...The distinguishing features of Shi'ism in relation to Sunnism should be sought not only in its fundamental principles, but perhaps more importantly in its ethos, in the tone of historically developed attitudes which have informed and infused the Shi'i stance on the controversial issues of Islamic history, society and dogma. The actual disagreements between the Sunnis and Shi'is in certain details of theology and legal practices have not been as important as this ethos, or in the words of the modern Shi'i scholar S. Husain M. Jafri, 'as the "spirit" working behind these rather minor divergences'. In trying to understand this ethos, one has to deal with 'Historical Shi'ism', namely,a Shi'ism which has taken shape in the actual, living experience of specific groups of Muslims, through attitudes which stemmed sometimes clearly from Shi'i tenets, and sometimes from individual interpretations and a slowly emerging consensus, without necessarily being recognised as fundamental principles in the Shi'i sources.

Considered in this light, perhaps the most outstanding feature of Shi'ism is an attitude of mind which refuses to admit that majority opinion is necessarily true or right, and — which is its converse — a rationalised defence of the moral excellence of an embattled minority. One can find numerous examples of this attitude in classical Shi'i sources. An anecdote, for instance, in the *Amali* of Shaykh Tusi (d. 461/1068), unquestionably the prime founder of Shi'i jurisprudence, typifies it vividly: Kumayl ibn Ziyad al-Nakha'i, a close disciple of the first Imam, 'Ali, relates:

> I was with the Prince of the Faithful at the Kufah Mosque. When we finished the last evening prayer, he ['Ali] took me by my hand, until we left the Mosque, until we left Kufah, and reached the suburb of the town. And all that time he had not uttered a word to me. Then he said: "O Kumayl, the hearts of men are like vessels, the best of them is the most retentive of them. So keep with yourself what you hear from me. The people are of three kinds: the divine scholar, those who seek knowledge and tread the path of salvation, and the rabble [*hamaj ra'a*] who follow every crowing creature, never partaking of the light of knowledge, never relying on a solid base."

This anecdote is significant in several respects: first, its adage is attributed to 'Ali, namely the only Imam among the twelve who became ruler of all Muslims. Secondly, the incident reported takes place in the Kufan period of

^cAli's career when after years of overt or covert opposition to 'usurping' Caliphs, he achieved political power: the reader is thus warned to take ^cAli's cenusre of popular fickleness not as the fulmination of an impractical, anti-social visionary but as the considered judgement of an experienced states-man. Thirdly, the extreme caution and discretion exercised by ^cAli in mak-ing his remark makes the bigotry, ignorance and unreliability of the 'rabble' to appear all the more reprehensible.

In his treatise *al-Idah*, to mention another example from a less important but earlier source, the third century jurisconsult and theologian Fadl ibn Shazan Nayshaburi (d. 290/902) is at pains to discredit the Sunnis' constant boasting of majority support as evidence of their righteousness, by arguing that the Qur'an, in an overwhelming number of verses, takes a sinister view of the majority, and only rarely accepts it as a factor of legitimacy; it deprecates the majority for following its whims and conjectures (VI, 116), lacking knowledge and understanding (VII, 187; XLIX, 4; V, 103), being poly-theists at heart (XII, 106), ungrateful (VII, 17; XII, 38) and transgressors to one another (XXXVIII, 24). That is why, in the history of the conflict of ideas 'many a small party has triumphed over a large party' (II, 249).

The reverse of the same attitude — the inherent virtue of belonging to a militant minority — is illustrated by Sayyid al-Murtada (d. 436/1043), the teacher of Shaykh Tusi. In his *Kitab al-Intisar*, enumerating in minute detail the legal and ritual points of difference between Shi^cism and other Muslim sects, he defiantly insists on the 'isolationist' character of Shi^cism (*ma'nfarad bihi'l-imamiyyah*) by arguing that the paucity of the following of an idea does not affect its validity, just as the immense popularity of another cannot be proof of its truth. But more relevant to the spirit of present-day Shi^cism is the expresson of this defiance in the revolt of the third Imam, Husayn ibn ^cAli, and his seventy-two companions, in 61/680. The memory of Husayn's martyrdom serves as an everlasting exhortation to the Shi^cis of all times to brave their numerical inferiority in the face of firm-ly established majorities.

In sustaining both aspects of their cautious attitudes towards majority amidst the global Muslim community, the Shi^cis have had to contend with powerful shibboleths. This has been partly due to the collective slant of Islamic political doctrines, greatly accentuated in the case of Sunnism because of its belief in the sanctity of the consensus *(ijma^c)* of the communi-ty. 'My community will never agree in error': the Prophet is thus claimed by the Sunnis to have conferred on his community the very infallibility that the Shi^cis ascribe to their Imams. The Shi^cis have tried to prove the Sunnis un-fitness to qualify as the community envisaged in the Prophet's prediction by pointing to their connivance in the misdeeds of their rulers during the greater part of Islamic history. An outcome of the Shi^cis refusal to be intimidated, let alone bound, by false 'public opinion' is the restricted permissibility of consensus among them as a source of jurisprudential rules. Whereas the Sunnis have defined consensus as 'the agreement among the "people who loose and bind"' (namely, the holders of power and position, according to Imam Fakhr al-Din al-Razi), and even as the agreement of the community in general (according to Ghazzali), the Shiᶜis hold consensus to be valid only when it includes the opinion of 'the infallible and the impeccable' (*maᶜsum*), namely the Imam. This doctrine has not caused the Shiᶜis to abandon consensus as an element of their legal system, since they always justify it by invoking the convenient maxim that 'the earth is never empty of the *maᶜsum*', which means that whenever a consensus is formed, one has to presume that the community of concurring scholars must have included a *maᶜsum* in their midst. But the doctrine has been a perfect safeguard against majority impositions.

The Shiᶜi view on majority seems to be primarily a result of its legitimist theory of succession to the Prophet, confining rightful government in the first instance to members of his House. Any political theory so exclusive in its outlook tends to breed exponents who jealously guard its purity from diffuse notions of authority. But as time went on, Shiᶜi authors resorted to diverse philosophical, theological and mystical vehicles to elaborate their principal beliefs. By their very nature, these vehicles too were elitist, capable of being developed and appreciated by only tiny literate groups. Significantly, of all these components in the Iranian Shiᶜi culture, literature which is alone suitable for popular appreciation has fared the worst, since it has been allocated mainly to recounting the lives of the Imams, often in stilted and morose style, and aimed merely at eliciting maximum grief over their sufferings.

Further explanations of the same attitude comes from the imperative of survival in hostile environments. Any minority constantly harassed and persecuted inevitably turns inward and, distancing itself increasingly from the majority, gradually develops its own mental habits and attitudes. In this capacity, the Shiᶜi attitude towards majority was supplemented by two other idiosyncratic practices: the esoteric style of teaching religious truths, which is mainly cherished by the Ismaᶜili school, and *taqiyyah*, which can temporarily be translated as expedient dissimulation... .

The Shiᶜis agree with the Sunnis that Muslim history since the era of the four Rightly-Guided Caliphs (11–40/632–61) has been for the most part a tale of woe. But whereas for the Sunnis the course of history since then has been a movement *away* from the ideal state, for the Shiᶜis it is a movement *towards* it:

'The incidence of fortune', say the Brethren of Purity, 'among certain peoples and nations, the increase in the power of some rulers, the outbreak of rebellions, the renewal of governorship in the kingdom, and other similar events [are aimed at] the betterment of the conditions of the world, and its elevation towards progress and wholeness. But often the factors of destruction prevail, such as wars, seditions and ravages, resulting in the ruin of the cities, the loss of the fortunes of a good people, and the demise of their prosperity, but *ultimately they all conduce to the good.*

True, the Sunnis too, in their fighting moments, like the militants of all times, produce rhetoric replete with expressions of faith in the final triumph of their cause—whether it is the fight against the infidels, or struggle for national independence, or confrontation with Israel. But there is nothing in their creed or theology which would make this triumph an inevitable occurrence in the divine scheme of things. Hence their general reluctance to indulge in philosophising about history. The few hitorians who have overcome this reluctance among them have usually come up with cyclical theories, expounding the notion that history consists of alternating patterns of the rise and fall of nations, or even of tedious repetitions of past events. Thus Ibn Khaldun explains the gradual decline and collapse of powerful dynasties and polities as an inexorable, and almost mechanical, transition from the virtuous ways of the desert life to the corrupting prosperity of urban settlement. And Maqrizi (d. 841/1437) sees the internecine conflicts between the Umayyads and Hashimites, and indeed the whole history of the Muslim Caliphate after the death of Muhammad, as a complete replica of the history of the Israelites.

By contrast, what lends an historicist thrust to the Shiᶜis confidence in the ultimate victory over the 'forces of injustice' is their millenarian anticipation of the Return of the hidden Imam. The Qur'anic verses usually invoked by Shiᶜi commentators as evidence of the doctrine of the Return, although making no apparent mention of a future Mahdi, promise the soversignty of the earth to the righteous and the oppreessed:

1. 'God hath promised to those of you who believe and do the things that are right, that He will cause them to succeed others in the land as He gave succession to those who were before them, and that He will establish for them that religion which they delight in, and that after their fear He will give them security in exchange. They shall worship Me: nought shall they join me' (XXIV,55).
2. 'And we were minded to show favour to those who were brought low in the land, and to make them spiritual chiefs [*Imams*], and to make them *Pharaoh's** heirs' (XXVIII,5).
3. 'My servants, the righteous shall inherit the earth' (XXI,105).

---

*Italics indicate addition by the translator (Rodwell).

4. 'The earth is God's: to such of His servants as He pleaseth doth He give it as a heritage' (VII,128).

Sunni commentators interpret the promise contained in the first verse as addressed to Prophet Muhammad's followers in his own time, that in the second to the Israelites, and that in the third and fourth to the entire community of the faithful. Shi͏ᶜi commentators, however maintain all of them to be referring to the Mahdi's followers at the end of time; they particularly substantiate their reading on the basis of a saying attributed to Muhammad to the effect that: 'Even if there remains but one single day of the world, God will lengthen that day until He has designated a righteous man from my House to fill it with justice and equity, just as it was filled with injustice and oppression.' This link between the Return and the ultimate, global sovereignty of the righteous and the oppressed makes Shi͏ᶜi historicism a *potential* tool of radical activism. But throughout the greater part of Shi͏ᶜi history, it never went beyond the potential state, remaining in practice merely a sanctifying tenet for the submissive acceptance of the *status quo.* This is apparent from the semantic structure of the term for the millenarian anticipation of the Return; *intizar,* which denotes an essentially submissive expectation of things to come. Hence a tendency grew among the Shi͏ᶜis to consider just government in the strict sense as an ideal which is impossible to achieve before the age of the Return. This eventually made the ideal state in Shi͏ᶜism to appear as a regime beyond the reach of ordinary human beings, and pushed it into the realm of meta-history:

'It is well established by the Tradition,' says Qadi Sa͏ᶜid Qumi (d. 1103/1691) a theosophist of the Safavid period,' that the Apostle of God, having been offered the choice between the status of servant and that of kingship, chose to be a Prophet Servant (*ᶜabd nabi*) rather than a Prophet King (*malik nabi*). Thus, there cannot be an exoteric kingship (*saltanah zahirah*) to succeed him, much less the kind of sovereignty exercised by the tyrants (*imamah al-jababirah*). Because, when such sovereignty did not belong to the Prophet himself, how could it belong to his successor? So if the Prophet is to have a successor, it is imperative that this succession should be of a religious nature (*khilafah diniyyah*), guaranteeing to the faithful the best conditions of viaticum and the Return, and that this spiritual kingship (*saltanah ruhaniyyah*) should fall on him who is of unshakeable devotion, he of whom it can be said that he is the very soul of the Prophet, just as the Prophet has declared it in the case of ᶜAli, Hasan and Husayn.'... .

* * *

It was the combination of the broad features — particularisms, esoterism, historicism, idealism, a pessimistic conception of human nature, a paradoxical apathy in politics, and emotionalism — that constituted the basic mood of historical Shiᶜism in contradistinction to Sunnism. There is certainly rational link between these features, so that not only do they all form a coherent whole, but each constituent of the whole — perhaps with the exception of historicism — can be considered as the logical result of the preceding, and the carrier of the following one. This does not mean that there was no tension between them. Tension was indeed inevitable not least because, as we said at the beginning of this chapter, while some of these features have flowed directly from Shiᶜi fundamental principles, others were the product of individual interpretation or collective understanding, sometimes at variance with those tenets. Thus particularism often collided with effusive popular rituals, and idealism stood ill at ease with a civic apathy which was in a way its distinct, but unwanted progeny. Most important of all, rationalism as an attribute of élitism, enshrined in the principle of *ijtihad* was outraged by all other features when these were carried to immoderate limits. Shiᶜi modernism has been aimed as much at resolving such tensions as at adapting Shiᶜism to altered social and political conditions.

We also noted at the beginning of our discussion that none of these features has been explicitly acknowledged by the Shiᶜis among their fundamental principles. This has been a source of both the strength and weakness of these features: strength, because they have always permeated Shiᶜi political attitudes merely as intangible and implicit agents, and have not, therefore, been able to be pinpointed easily whether by Sunni polemists or indigenous critics; weakness, because when Shiᶜi modernists launched their assault on orthodox strongholds, they could not be readily accused of contravening any specific canon of the faith... .

*   *   *

Of a completely different kind are the Sunni — Shiᶜi polemics. These are concerned, not with the imponderables of the 'spirits' of the two sects, but with the concrete details of Islamic history, theology, rituals and law. Most of the pivotal issues in the polemics have remained more or less unchanged throughout the ages. Thus the main themes of the al-Hilli-ibn Taymiyyah exchanges in the eighth/fourteenth century have been reproduced during the last hundred years or so in the Sunni censures of Shiᶜism by Rashid Rida, Ahmad Amin and ᶜAbdullah al-Qasimi, and the Shiᶜi responses by ᶜAbd al-Husayn Amini, Muhammad Husayn Kashif al-Ghita', Abu'l-Hasan al-Khunayzi and Sharaf al-Din al-Musawi. But the intellectual level of the arguments, the reasonings of the disputants, and the foci of emphasis have varied considerably from one period to another. The degree of tension has also varied as a function of the sectarian affiliations of the polemists. The most violent Sunni opposition to Shiᶜism has come from the Hanbalis, who nevertheless consider the moderate Twelver Shiᶜis as less blameworthy than the Ismaᶜilis, or the Batinis in general. For their part the Shiᶜis, while reciprocating this opposition, have been similarly careful not to antagonise other Sunni sects and have even sometimes paid compliments to the fair-mindedness of the Shafiᶜis and Hanafis, for instance in praising the third Shiᶜi Imam, Husayn. In recent times, the modernists in both camps have contributed their share to all these variations, either by introducing fresh issues into the controversy, or by efforts towards a reconciliation of the two sects.

In its original form the Sunni-Shiᶜi dispute is not concerned with the fundamentals of religion. Unlike, for instance, the disagreements among the Christians, it does not relate to the nature of God, or the function of his Emissary, or the manner of achieving human salvation. Rather, it involves issues which, as will be shown, are decidedly marginal to these matters, and in any case have no bearing on the basic duties of a Muslim (praying, fasting, pilgrimage, alms-tax, and the holy war). But over time, it has degenerated from a quarrel about the Prophet's successorship into a ritual, theological and legal rift which can, at least obliquely, affect certain basic beliefs and attitudes.

The polemics are clearly of two kinds: those dealing with historical personalities, especially some of the crucial figures in early Islam, and those dealing with concepts and doctrines. The predominance of each of these two sets of themes depends on which side has initiated the debate: the Shiᶜis are usually concerned with personalities, the Sunnis with concepts and doctrines, without, of course, this precluding a good deal of overlap. The reason for this customary 'division of labour' lies in the original cause of the controversy, which revolved around the few individuals aspiring for the succession to the Prophet. Since in the contest immediately after the Prophet's death, ᶜAli was defeated by his opponents, the initial reaction of his followers, the Shiᶜis, was confined to attacks on the particular misdeeds of the first three Caliphs as a converse vindication of his rightful succession. One could plausibly surmise that the later doctrinal altercations resulted from these early personal attacks. Before explaining this, we must briefly consider the Shiᶜi criticisms of the first three Caliphs.

The most serious objection to Abu Bakr is his complicity in convening the Saqifah assembly which appointed him as the first Caliph. That single act was enough in the Shiᶜi eyes to throw grave doubts on his integrity as a just and faithful follower of Muhammad. But then other wrongful deeds followed: he deprived Fatimah of her rightful inheritance from Muhammad

—the famous 'Fadak affair', relating to an oasis in Arabia near Khaybar, inhabited by the Jews who had submitted to Muhammad after his punitive assault on Khaybar. Abu Bakr refused to deliver Fadak to Fatimah, referring her to the words of the Prophet, 'No one shall be my heir; what I leave behind belongs to the poor.' If these acts harmed the rights of the Prophet's family, his other offences damaged the community at large: for instance, his pardoning of his general, Khalid ibn Walid, after the latter had murdered a Muslim notable, Malik ibn Nuwayrah, under the pretext that Khalid's services were indispensable for the young Islamic state; or his discontinuation of the practice of registering the Prophet's sayings, a measure which was later hardened by ᶜUmar, ostensibly to reinforce the authority of the Qur'an as the unique source of religious precepts.

ᶜUmar is taken to task primarily for his conduct in the 'Thursday Calamity': on the day of his death, the Prophet, who was gravely ill, bid his companions to fetch him paper and inkpot to write his will, so that they 'may not err after his death', a clear reference, according to the Shiᶜis, to his intention to designate ᶜAli as his successor. But ᶜUmar prevented those present from complying with the Prophet's request, arguing that 'his illness had reached a critical stage, and he has become delirious'. Another instance of his insubordination was that he twice refrained, together with Abu Bakr, from carrying out the Prophet's order to execute Hurqus ibn Zuhayr, whom the Prophet had found to be a renegade despite his pious appearances, and who later became a Khariji leader. But again like Abu Bakr, ᶜUmar is also censured for more fundamental reasons concerned with his legal and ritual innovations. His banning of temporary marriage (*mutᶜah*) is held to be in conflict with the Qur'an; so is his ruling that husbands could divorce their wives by 'triple repudiation', which was intended to discourage divorce, but which the Shiᶜis reject as a misinterpretation of the Qur'anic verse on the subject. His prohibition of *tamattuᶜ* (the act of performing the 'lesser pilgrimage' to Mecca until its completion, and then performing the pilgrimage proper or *Hajj* as a separate ceremony) and of the inclusion of the formula 'hasten to the best act' in the call to the prayer (because of his fear that this might divert people from the duty of waging the holy war against the infidels in a sensitive period) is said to have infringed Prophetic practices. Finally, his appointment of a council of six to designate his successor is denounced both on grounds of its composition (which was weighted in favour of ᶜUthman) and of its aggravating effect on factionalism among the Muslims.

The task of Shiᶜi polemists is relatively easier in the case of ᶜUthman since even Sunni opinion is divided about his Caliphal competence. In Shiᶜi estimation, his gravest weakness was nepotism, shown in the appointment of his close relatives as provincial governors. The reverse of this was his opɔressive attitude toward the partisans of ʿAli, it was in his time that ʿAbdullah bn Masʿud, an outstanding Companion of the Prophet, was killed ınder torture, and Abu Zarr al-Ghifari, the first 'socialist' in Muslim ıistory, was sent into exile at Muʿawiyah's insistence. There was thus widepread discontent against him, and his assassination took place by virtue of he consensus of the community, although ʿAli was not party to it. The hiʿis also question ʿUthman's record as a companion of the Prophet: they ɔarticularly point to his absence from the Prophet's campaigns at Badr and Jhud, and from the fateful ceremony known as *Bayʿat 'al-ridwan* at which he companions reaffirmed their allegiance to him. But like his predecessors, he s also accused of disregarding Qur'anic injunctions, for instance, by abroɡating the dispensation allowing travellers to shorten their prayer.

These criticisms would probably have passed as legitimate historical apɔraisals had it not been for two subsequent developments. The first was that hey took on an increasingly scurrilous tone, and were eventually instituionalised into the practices of *sabb* (vilification) and *rafd* (repudiation of he legitimacy) of the first three Caliphs. But the second development was nore important: the intrusion of Iranian nationalism into the controversy, ɔarticularly in the case of ʿUmar, whose Caliphate coincided with the Arab ɔonquest of Iran, and the destruction of Sassanian–Zoroastrianism culture. Γhis was enough to assure him a high place in Iranian folk demonology. hiʿi sources as early as the fourth/tenth century attack ʿUmar's discriminaion against the Iranian Muslims, and his prohibition of Arab–Iranian internarriage, which were considered to be all the more loathsome in view of a aying attributed to the eighth Imam, ʿAli ibn Musa al-Rida, confirming hat ever since Muhammad's death the Iranians had been accorded a special tatus among Muslims. Seven centuries later, the great codifier of Safavid– hiʿi jurisprudence, Muhammad Baqir Majlisi (d. 1111/1700) added furher ethnic spice to the debate by claiming that 'in the matter of faith, the ranians are superior to the Arabs.' He quoted the sixth Imam, Jaʿfar alɡadiq, as having said in justification of this superiority that: 'If the Qur'an ıad been revealed to the Iranians, the Arabs would not have believed in it. ɔo it was revealed to the Arabs, and the Iranians came to believe in it.' ɡometimes, ʿUmar's pro-Arab policies were contrasted with ʿAli's equitable reatment of the Arabs and Iranians. Meanwhile, popular, Iranian naionalistic hatred of ʿUmar manifested itself in numerous burlesque plays, arnivals and festivities celebrating the anniversary of his assassination ʿumar kushan) on the twenty-sixth day of the Muslim month of *Dhu '-hijjah*, or as part of the expiation for Husayn's martyrdom on the tenth ay of Muharram. They started to fall into desuetude only from the begining of the present century, out of respect for the Sunni Ottomans, but their races in some folk practices and colloquial expressions die hard.

There are similar objections levelled against the Prophet's favourite wife
ᶜA'ishah (whose hatred of ᶜAli knew no bounds), and many other Compa
nions, such as Talhah, Zubayr and Muᶜawiyah, although in terms of thei
implications for the Sunni–Shiᶜi breach, these are not as important as th
repudiation of the first three Caliphs. But the real issue behind sucl
polemics goes far beyond mere Shiᶜi carping at the members of the Sunn
'Establishment'. It concerns the choice between the *nass*, or divine ordi
nance, and arbitrary, personal discretion. The common denominator in al
the criticisms of the first three Caliphs and their followers is the accusatio
that by exercising their individual judgement, they all violated, ignored o
tampered with clear scriptural guidelines or Prophetic practices. This ac
cusation is all the more noteworthy because it involves the only case i
which the notion of 'exercising one's judgement' (*ijtihad*) is deprecated b
the Shiᶜis, who are otherwise its staunch exponents within the bounds of th
Qur'an and the Prophetic Tradition, as a device for the dynamic applicatio
of Islamic law to chaning circumstances. So if the Shiᶜis sometimes de
nounce the Companions, it is not because the latter exercised their in
dividual judgement, but because they exercised it in violation of the Qur'a
and the Tradition.

To the Shiᶜi, the most glaring example of this defiance is, of course, th
decision of the Saqifah assembly, which, in spite of the Prophet's previou
designation of ᶜAli at the Ghadir (pool or ditch) of Khumm as his successor
elected Abu Bakr as the Caliph; all othe examples are merely mentioned, o
the margin of the dispute about the Ghadir, as additional proof of th
disposition of the offending Companions to violate the norms. The implici
reasoning is that if after the Prophet's death, those Companions went aheac
with the election of a successor other than ᶜAli, this was a misdemeanour o
their behalf which fitted the general pattern of their behaviour. This raise
another issue which is a corollary to the dispute about the Prophetic succes
sion: were the Prophet's Companions endowed with any particular qualit
or virtue which placed them over and against the rest of the community, o
were they ordinary, fallible mortals? In countering the Shiᶜi criticisms of th
Companions, Sunni writers have often tended to assert that they all wer
men of unimpeachable character, a claim which is not easy to substantiat
when one remembers that their number has been put at around twelve thou
sand. Moreover, the Shiᶜis seize upon it as proof of the inconsistency of th
Sunnis, saying that the Sunnis on the one hand refute the dogma of infalli
bility (*ᶜismah*) of the Imams on the grounds that it confers on them super
human status, but on the other themselves ascribe a similar quality to th
Companions.

The polemics are thus gradually transposed from the domain of person
ages to that of ideas. But to consider the ideological differences further w

ave to shift our standpoint and look at the Sunni polemics which, as was oted earlier, are richer in conceptual disputation. The prime source for hese is undoubtedly *Minhaj al-sunnat al-nabawiyyah fi naqd kalam al-hiᶜat 'al-qadariyyah* ('The Way of the Prophetic Tradition in the Critique f the Theology of the Qadari Shiᶜism) by Ibn Taymiyyah (d. 728/1328). Iis arguments against Shiᶜism have remained influential to this day, and ave been forecfully revived in the works of modern Sunni fundamentalists. Iis treatise is in reply to *Minhaj al-sunnah fi maᶜrifat al-imamah* ('the Vay of the Tradition in Understanding the Imamate') by Hasan ibn Yusuf on Mutahhar al-Hilli, known as the ᶜAllamah (d. 726/1325), whose works ave an unprecedented scope to the practice of *ijtihad*, and made a major ontribution to the development of the Shiᶜi jurisprudential theory (*usul*). although mainly concentrating on al-Hilli's exposition of Shiᶜism, Ibn 'aymiyyah at times directs his attacks against the Ghullat and the Seveners (smaᶜilis), and occasionally lampoons the popular manifestations of hiᶜism—a device which is used in argument by many contemporary Sunni olemists as well, ignoring the important doctrinal and practical differences etween various Shiᶜi sects. But Ibn Taymiyyah is at pains to point out that vhile the Twelver Shiᶜis are only misguided Muslims, the Seveners are eretics and hypocrites. His main criticisms of Shiᶜism in general can be ummarised as follows:

There is nothing in the Qur'an and the Tradition to support the Shiᶜi laim that the Imamate is one of the 'pillars' of religion. How can it be otherwise when the Imam's disappearance has in practice reduced him to a seless being, unable to serve any of the worldly and other-worldly interests f the Muslims? The hidden Imam has now been absent for more than four undred years. The anticipation of his return has produced nothing but alse hopes, sedition and corrupt practices among certain groups of Muslims. Obeying God and the Prophet is enough to entitle every Muslim o Paradise (Qur'an, 4:13, 69). By requiring obedience to a hidden Imam vhom no one can see, hear or communicate with, Shiᶜism imposes a duty on Muslims above their capacity—an impossibility in view of God's justness. he doctrine of the Imamate thus aims at creating a regime which is impos-ible to achieve... .

* * *

Adoration of ᶜAli and 'Members of the House' has been a shared charac-eristic of many Sufi orders. What gives it a particular significance in the ase of the Kubrawiyyah is its merging with a strong plea for Sunni–Shiᶜi eace. Pro-ᶜAlid tendencies, however, became more marked in the doc-rines of Najm al-Din's followers, ᶜAli Hamadani, Ishaq Khatlani and most mportant of all, Muhammad Nurbakhsh, under whom the order veered towards Shi^cism. By virtue of his supposed descent from the seventh Imam of the Twelver Shi^cis, Musa al-Kazim, Nurbakhsh received the title of al Mahdi, and was proclaimed Caliph by some of his followers. These preten sions alarmed the ruling monarch, the Taymurid Shah-rukh, who ordered Nurbakhsh to be imprisoned on several occasions. In his formal teachings, Nurbakhsh also tried to strike a balance between Sunnism and Shi^cism. For instance, on the theory of the Imamate, he differentiated between what he called the 'conditions of the Imam', and his 'attributes'. The conditions are the same *a posteriori* prerequisites mentioned by the Sunni jurists with reference to the ^cAbbasid Caliphs (masculinity, majority, wisdom, Quraysh descent, etc.). But the 'attributes' or bases (*arkan*) are evidently those of the Shi^ci Imams (descent from Fatimah, knowledge, piety and generosity) Similarly, his view about the mystic unity of men with God purports to make it less offensive to orthodox taste by interpreting it in metaphorical terms, through the analogy of 'iron in the fire': so long as the iron is in the fire, it can truthfully say, 'I am the fire'. Once it is withdrawn from the fire it would be lying if it made the same claim. In the same manner, the proph ets and Friends of God (*awliya*) can assume God's attributes while they are in a state of ecstasy, but this does not mean that they become identical with God. But in spite of the conciliatory tone of many such doctrines, it seems that with the death of Nurbakhsh in 869/1464, the Kubrawi dream of Muslim unity also ended, perhaps because in his person, the movement had become too closely associated with the messianic connotations of Shi^cism Besides, the rise of the Safavid state, which made Shi^cism the official creed of Iran in 1502, intensified sectarian recrimination. The systematisation of Shi^ci jurisprudence, theology and philosophy — a gradual, but relentless process which lasted till the very end of the Safavid period — elevated the Shi^cis sense of self-confidence and identity to a level unprecedented since Buyid times. Against the background of ideological rigidity, and Iran's wars with the Ottoman state, any suggestion of a Sunni–Shi^ci dialogue, still more of a conciliation, could be no more than wishful thinking. Relations be tween the two communities deteriorated so much that the Sunnis now, con trary to Ibn Taymiyyah's differentiated judgement on the varieties of Shi^cism quoted earlier, considered the Shi^cis as outright infidels. This is clearly shown by an exchange of letters between the Shi^ci ^culama' of Khurasan and the Sunni ^culama' of Transoxiana following the Uzbak inva sion of Mashhad at the beginning of Shah ^cAbba's reign. In reply to the Shi^cis protest at the encirclement of Mashhad, and the destruction and pillaging of its surrounding fields by the Uzbak ^cAbdullah Khan, and his son ^cAbdul-Mu'min Khan, the Sunni ^culama' declared that by their persist ent vilification of the first three Caliphs the Shi^cis had forfeited their status as Muslims; it was therefore quite legitimate for the Sunni rulers to wage war against them, and destroy or confiscate their belongings. Little wonder, then, that the next significant step towards Sunni–Shiʿi understanding was taken almost three centuries after the death of Nur-bakhsh, in the interregnum between the Sunni Afghans' overthrow of the Safavid regime, and the emergence of the Qajar dynasty at the end of the eighteenth century. This time, the initiative was taken by a Shiʿi monarch, Nadir Shah, the founder of the short-lived Afsharid state in Iran. Exhaustion from more than a decade of anarchy and bloodshed caused by the Sunni–Shiʿi strife which accompanied the Afghan invasion of Iran and the destruction of the Safavid state, was good enough reason for this initiative. But as Hamid Algar has shown, there were possibly political motives behind it too: Nadir's ambitions to rule over an empire extending beyond Iran's frontiers, his need to maintain the loyalty of his troops who were mostly Sunnis, while offsetting the effects of the continued, 'religiously motivated loyalty' of many Iranians to the Safavids as legitimate rulers of Iran, and the advisability of achieving a *modus vivendi* with the Ottomans. But however lofty his political ambitions may have been, his scheme for Sunni–Shiʿi reconciliation, unlike that conceived by the Kubrawiyyah, was modest enough. It took the form of a twofold campaign, internal and external.

Internally, Nadir strove to put an end to those Shiʿi practices which perhaps more than any other aspect of Shiʿism were provocative to the Sunnis: *sabb*, public vilification of the first three Caliphs, and *rafd*, repudiation of the legitimacy of their Caliphate. These he formally prohibited, condemning them as 'vain and vulgar words' which cast discord and enmity among Muslims. Next, he tried to turn Shiʿism into a mere school of law, shorn of its esoteric Imamology. He therefore proposed that 'the separate identity and name of the Shiʿi *mazhab* be abandoned while 'part of its substance — that relating to *furuʿat* (branches of the law) be retained and renamed after Imam Jaʿfar al-Sadiq' the sixth Imam, the principal codifier of Shiʿi jurisprudence. In practice, this meant that Jaʿfar al-Sadiq be treated on a par with the founders of the four Sunni legal schools, so that there could be no doctrinal obstacle in Shiʿism being eventually incorporated into Sunni Islam.

Externally, Nadir demanded that the Ottoman Government, as the representative of Sunni Islam, recognise Shiʿism in its new garb, as the Jaʿfari *mazhab*, and then give substance to this recognition by several practical steps: the erection at Kaʿbah of a fifth *maqam* (ritual place) for the Shiʿis as the outward sign of the acceptance of their school on a par with the four Sunni schools; the appointment of an *Amir al-hajj* (pilgrimage leader) to accompany Iranian pilgrims travelling to Mecca by way of Damascus; the release of all prisoners taken during wars with Iran; and the exchange of ambassadors.

There was immediate opposition to Nadir's redefinition of Shiᶜism from those Iranian ᶜ*ulama'* who justifiably considered that it destroyed the very essence of Shiᶜism by reducing it to a mere corpus of legal niceties. This opposition was ruthlessly suppressed by measures characteristic of the Nadiri style of government – execution of the chief Mulla, Mirza ᶜAbd al-Husayn, and the confiscation of the endowments attached to the mosques and religious schools in Isfahan. But the whole project of a rapprochement with Sunnism foundered on the reaction of the Ottoman Government, which under the pressure of Sunni ᶜ*ulama'* rejected its principal points; the only positive element in its response was approval of Nadir's prohibition of *sabb* and *rafd*! The episode ended with Nadir's assassination in 1747.

From that year until the second half of the nineteenth century, when Islamic modernism appeared on the scene, no other attempt was made at reconciliation – at least none that was comparable, either in its political dimensions, or in its intellectual ingenuity, with those made by the Kubrawiyyah or Nadir. The climate was made even more inimical, if anything, for such efforts by the rise of Wahhabism in Arabia towards the end of the eighteenth century. Superimposing on Hanbali rigorism a puritan militancy seeking to root out all 'innovations' in Islam, Wahhabism represented the greatest fundamentalist challenge to Shiᶜism since the beginning of Islam. Although confined to a minority feared and denounced by most Sunnis, its excesses, particularly the ravaging of the Shiᶜi shrines, aroused lasting passions among the Shiᶜis, rendering them even more diligent in jealously guarding their separate identity... .

* * *

On the face of it, the failure of the attempts described so far at Sunni-Shiᶜi reconciliation was caused by the stubborn refusal of one side or the other, for political or confessional reasons, to compromise on what it held to be an eternal principle. But whenever not simply actuated by mundane political calculations, this refusal was itself the effect of a much more profound and damaging disability – the sclerosis of religious thinking. So long as the exponents of both sects treated their received prejudices as revealed truths, there could be no real prospect of a reconciliation. This sclerosis was reflected primarily in the rarity of serious dialogue between the controversialists. More significantly, it was reflected in the absence of that imperceptible outcome of any dialogue which is the interpretation of ideas and the slow transformation of a hitherto immutable system of thought through exposure to another system.

That is why, with modernistic trends gaining ground among religious circles in the Muslim world from the middle of the nineteenth century onwards, the barriers between Sunnis and Shiʿis gradually became less insuperable, allowing a good many cross-sectarian currents. The new situation held great promise, if not for concord, then at least for the diminution of age-old animosities. There were several reasons for this. First, in the altered moulds of political loyalties, the idea of the nation-state was replacing religious devotion as the ruling civic virtue of the modern age. This in itself had a dampening effect on sectarian divergences. Secondly, Islamic unity being one of the cardinal articles of their faith, the leaders of the first generation of Islamic modernists, notably Jamal al-Din Asadabadi (Afghani) (d. 1897) and Muhammad ʿAbduh (d. 1905), made strong pleas for Sunni-Shiʿi unity. Of the two, Asadabadi was the more consistent, mainly because his own background was steeped in both Sunni and Shiʿi traditions and because of his 'staleness' he could afford to preach supraconfessional tolerance. ʿAbduh, having been brought up in solidly Sunni environment, could not conceal his dislike of heterodox movements, especially those instigated by the Iranians in early Islam. This tendency became more pronounced in his disciple, Muhammad Rashid Rida, who, although committed to the modernists' ideal of Islamic unity, parted company with many of them by making anti-Shiʿism a major trait of his school, the *Salafiyyah*, after failing in his efforts to induce a Sunni–Shiʿi conciliation.

Third, unity was necessitated by other principles of modernism as well. Rationalism, which governed the better part of the modernist reformulation of the Islamic spiritual heritage, called for release from narrow parochial values in the interests of the universally applicable findings of reason: just as the Qur'anic unitarian teachings liberated the Arabs from tribalism, Islamic modernism was expected to dissolve all sectarian bonds. The fight against Western domination too required the unity of all Muslims, irrespective of their subsidiary beliefs. It was therefore expedient to tolerate and even support heterodox trends in so far as they contributed to the anti-imperialist struggle. Thus Asadabadi called on the Indian Muslims to demonstrate in favour of the Mahdi of Sudan, even if his standing as a real Mahdi was dubious, because this united them in their fight against the British. But in the same breath, Asadabadi refuted the Qadiyani reformist movement in India, because of its alliance with the British.

Later, in the twentieth century, politics exercised further pacifying influence on the relations between the two communities through another development. This was the creation of multi-confessional states, particularly Lebanon and Iraq, whose political structure depended on the Sunni-Shiʿi symbiosis. Preserving a minimum of mutual tolerance now became not so much a requirement of Islamic solidarity as a practical necessity. Equally restraining considerations stemmed from the diplomatic exigencies

of maintaining normal and friendly relations between states with predomi
nantly opposing confessional majorities. Thus the Saudi Arabs who in the
eighteenth century considered the Shi^{c}is as miscreants, and desecrated their
shrines in Iraq, now not only treat the Shi^{c}i Iranians at least officially, a
equal Muslims, but are also tolerant of their own Shi^{c}i subjects.

Islamic modernism, as construed by ^{c}Abduh's disciples, rapidly became
identified with Sunni Islam—and this in spite of their intention to make it a
movement transcending all sectarian divergences. Its counterpart among the
Shi^{c}is started under different circumstances, and took a different form. But
here also the modernists were agreed on the necessity of united action
against the West. This was vividly illustrated by the attitude of the Shi^{c}i
^{c}ulama' of Iraq, who, during the First World War, exhorted their followers
to wage war against the British under the Ottoman flag, while in principle
they considered the Ottoman rulers to be no more than 'usurpers'
(*mughtasibun*). They also led the national uprising in Iraq in 1920 against
the British mandate, thereby forging closer links between the two sects.

But the most ironical display of Shi^{c}i solidarity with the Sunnis took place
over the issue of the Caliphate—namely the very issue that had originally set
the two communities apart. When in 1922 . . . Mustafa Kemal's drive to establish a modern state threatened the instituton of the Caliphate in his country, the
Sunni Muslims outside Turkey, particularly in India, were greatly alarmed. But
their concern was conveyed to the Turkish Government by two Indian Shi^{c}is
—Sayyid Amir ^{c}Ali, and the leader of the 'extremist' Isma^{c}ili sect, the Aqa
Khan. After the abolition of the Caliphate in 1924, the Shi^{c}is kept up their
campaign of solidarity: they took an active part in the Jerusalem Congress
of 1931, held to discuss matters of common concern to all Muslims—including the fate of the Caliphate. In addition to the Yemeni delegate (the
only ruling prince attending the Congress), the Shi^{c}i ^{c}ulama' of Iraq sent an
accredited representative; two Iranian Shi^{c}is attended, and the Mufti of the
Shi^{c}is of Syria sent a message of sympathy. If one excepts the abortive Sun-
ni-Shi^{c}i consultations under Nadir, Gibb's remark in *Whither Islam?* is an
apt description of the significance of this event. 'Never before in Islamic
history,' he says, 'have the Sunni and Shi^{c}is met together to deliberate on
common problems, and while on the one hand the fact may be taken to illustrate the weakening of religious inhibition in political life, it no less truly
indicates a growing realisation of the common interest of all Moslems in the
modern world.'.. .

The revival of *ijtihad* and the new school of historical revisionism among
the Sunnis have affected the Sunni-Shi^{c}i dialogue by encouraging individual initiative for effecting some measure of reconciliaton. In February

1959, the official review of the University-Mosque of al-Azhar in Cairo published a *fatwa* (opinion or resposum) by its Rector, Shaykh Mahmud Shaltut, authorising instruction of Shiʿi jurisprudence. This was tantamount to the recognition of Shiʿism as on an equal footing with the four orthodox legal schools in Shiʿism. When Shaltut gave his *fatwa*, Shiʿi studies had been absent from the curriculum of that university for over nine hundred years. Although al-Azhar was created in 361/972 by an Ismaʿili Shiʿi, the Fatimid Caliph al-Muʿizz, two centuries later the Sunni Ayyubids turned it into a center of orthodox scholarship. Thus rather than constituting a simple case of curriculum reform, Shaltut's *fatwa* indicated a major psychological breakthrough.

Under the title 'Islam, the religion of unity', the *fatwa* is prefaced by two arguments in its justification, one historical, the other pragmatic. The historical argument is a reminder of the spirit of mutual respect and tolerance which permeated the relationship between the legal schools in early Islam. At that time, says Shaltut, *ijtihad* was a source of plurality of ideas, but not discord, because the different schools were united by their belief in the paramount authority of the Qur'an and the Tradition. The motto of the founders of all schools was: "When a *hadith* is proved authentic, it is my opinion; 'and do not care at all for my word'.... . This enabled all groups to co-operate with one another—the Sunnis among themselves, on the one hand, and the Sunnis with the Shiʿis, on the other—for the development of Islamic jurisprudence as a whole. It is obvious that in this argument, Shaltut is using the term *ijtihad* in the sense of the exercise of collective judgement (*al-ijtihad al-ʿammah*), because he goes on to say that legal plurality degenerated into antagonism once the individual form of *ijtihad* (*al-ijtihad al-khassah*) was introduced. Subordinated as it was to personal whims and wishes, *ijtihad* then became a factor of dissension, to be later exploited and intensified by the imperialist enemies who fostered enmity among the Muslims, setting every group against another.

Shaltut's second argument is simply a denunciation of prejudice or bigotry, and its harmful practical impact on the search for the best possible solutions to the present social problems of Muslims. He says that the legal schools of all persuasions should now be ready to accept from one another any idea which conforms to Islamic principles, and can best ensure the welfare of family and society. By way of example he mentions his own *fatwas* in favour of the Shiʿi rejection of the validity of 'suspended divorce' and divorce by triple repudiation in one sitting.

Shaltut advanced similar arguments in a more explicit *fatwa*, confirming the 'validity of worship according to the Imami Shiʿi doctrine'. (The word *sect* was deleted from the official document on the grounds that in ᶜIslam proper there are no sects, but only schools or doctrines'.) Combined with other conciliatory gestures such as the publication of ᶜAmili's *Wasa'il al-shiᶜah*, one of the most authoritative sources of traditional Shiᶜi, and Tabarsi's *Majmaᶜ al-bayan*, a Shiᶜi commentary on the Qur'an, both with al-Azhar's blessings, and a series of friendly communications between Shaltut and two Shiᶜi leaders in Iraq, Muhammad Khalisi and the afore-mentioned Muhammad Husayn Kashif al-Ghita', these *fatwas* established a distinct trend towards greater Sunni–Shiᶜi understanding. The credit for this should be largely put down to Shaltut's generally temperate vision of Islam. But also instrumental in bringing about this trend were the activities of the *Dar al-Taqrib al-Mazahib* (the Organisation for the Bringing Together of Schools) based in Cairo. Created in 1947 at the initiative of an Iranian Shiᶜi, Muhammad Taqli Qumi, *Dar al-Taqrib* soon became a forum in which, to quote Shaltut himself, 'the Hanafi, the Maliki, the Shafiᶜi and the Hanbali sit next to the Imami and Zaydi round one table 'discussing' literary accomplishments, Sufism and jurisprudence, in an atmosphere pervaded by a spirit of fraternity, a sense of affection, love and comradeship.

Paradoxically, another development which was to bring Shiᶜism close to the mainstream of Sunni Islam in the years to come took place in a world far removed from the euphoric atmosphere of these pious, speculative exercises – in the conflict between Jamal ᶜAbd al-Nasir's Arab nationalism, and Iran's pro-Western stance. In July 1960, Egypt broke off diplomatic relationship with Iran in retaliation for Iran's *de facto* recognition of Israel. In August, at a meeting of Al-Azhar, 150 ᶜ*ulama'* issued a proclamation calling on Muslims throughout the world to adopt an attitude of *jihad* against the Shah of Iran for his pro-Israeli policy. Three years later, the Shah launched his 'White Revolution', purporting to carry out reforms requiring the expropriation of large landowners, and female emancipation. This provoked a popular religious opposition, led by the hitherto relatively unknown Ayatullah Ruhullah Khumayni, who condemned what he regarded to be the illegality and falsity of these reforms as well as the Shah's connections with Israel and the United States.

The community of interests between this opposition in Iran, and the Nasirite Arab nationalist campaign against the Shah called into being a 'united front' between Iranian Shiᶜism and Arab Sunnism. Almost overnight, the militant Shiᶜi hierarchy of Iran was accorded in the Arab–Sunni circles a respectability rarely known in living memory. It is beyond the scope of this study to pursue the vicissitudes of this 'front' that lasted until recent times. Suffice it to say that with the triumph of Khumayni's Islamic Revolution in 1978–79, Sunni-Shiᶜi co-operation was placed under severe strain when sectarian passions were aroused both outside and inside Iran, and some Sunnis displayed fears of a Shiʿi revivalist threat to Islamic orthodoxy. This makes one doubtful about the ability of such limited Sunni–Shiʿi concord as has been surveyed in this chapter to survive a massive confrontation between Iranian and Arab nationalisms, of which the Iran–Iraq war of 1980–81 is but one catastrophic example. But the whole episode throws a revealing light on the extent to which religion can become a handmaid of politics, rendering any sectarian peace vulnerable to the unpredictability of international relations.

If the Sunni–Shiʿi concord has thus been proved to be dependent on political fortunes, Sunni–Shiʿi unity comes up against some more verifiable, but also more daunting obstacles. In the first place, so long as sectarianism is closely intertwined with nationalist idiosyncracies (Shiʿism with Iranian culture, Sunnism with Arab nationalism, Pakistan's Islamic identity, Kurdish separatism, etc.) any hope of unity is unrealistic. But the problem goes deeper than politics.... [T]he difference between Shiʿism and Sunnism is something more substantive and more far-reaching than pedantic squabblings over ritual, legal, and even theological matters: it impinges on the way in which the Qur'anic injunctions are applied to the nature of Man, the method of interpreting and conveying the divine message, the meaning of justice, and the philosophy of history. Thus as Algar points out, 'Sunnism and Shiʿism are two parallel orthodox perspectives of the Islamic revelation that cannot converge, in their exoteric aspects, for reasons inherent in the nature of each. No project of political motivation could alter this fact, although a conciliation of the two perspectives is possible, both at the level of action and, more importantly, at the level of the esoteric.'...

Chapter Eight

Shi^cism, Zaydism, Isma^cilism, and Shaykhism

The vitality of the Shi^cite doctrinal position of the Imamate, *according to which ^cAli and his male descendents assumed supreme authority after Prophet Muhammad, was always conducive to outburst of sectarian movements within Islam. In the following four passages, ^cAllamah Tabataba'i, Muhammad ibn ^cAbd al-Karim al-Shahrastani, Marshall Hodgson, and Mangol Bayat discuss these doctrinal-poilitical branches of Shi^cism. The passages are taken from SI, pages 82–83; MSD, pages 132–34; VI, Vol. 1, pages 378–84; and MDSTQI, pages 42.49.*

Allamah Tabataba'i

The majority of the Shi'is, from whom these groups have branched out, re Twelve-Imam Shi'is, also called the Imamites. As has already been men- ioned, the Shi'is came into being because of criticism and protest concern- ng two basic problems of Islam, without having any objections to the eligious ways which through the instructions of the Prophet had become revalent among their contemporary Muslims. These two problems con- erned Islamic government and authority in the religious sciences, both of which the Shi'i considered to be the particular right of the Household of the 'rophet.

The Shi'i asserted that the Islamic caliphate, of which esoteric guidance nd spiritual leadership are inseparable elements, belongs to 'Ali and his escendants. They also believed that according to the specification of the 'rophet the Imams of the Household of the Prophet are twelve in number. hi'ism held, moreover, that the external teachings of the Qur'an, which are he injunctions and regulations of the Shari'ah and include the principles of complete spiritual life, are valid and applicable for everyone at all times, nd are not to be abrogated until the Day of Judgment. These injunctions nd regulations must be learned through the guidance of the Household of he Prophet.

From a consideration of these points it becomes clear that the difference etween Twelve-Imam Shi'ism and Zaydism is that the Zaydis usually do ot consider the imamate to belong solely to the Household of the Prophet nd do not limit the number of Imams to twelve. Also they do not follow he jurisprudence of the Household of the Prophet as do the Twelve-Imam hi'is.

The difference between Twelve-Imam Shi'ism and Isma'ilism lies in that or the latter the imamate revolves around the number seven and prophecy oes not terminate with the Holy Prophet Muhammad. Also for them, hange and transformation in the injunctions of the Shari'ah are admissi- le, as is even rejection of the duty of following the Shari'ah, especially mong the Batinis. In contrast, the Twelve-Imam Shi'is consider the Proph- t to be the "seal of prophecy" and believe him to have twelve successors and

executors of his will. They hold the external aspect of the *Shariᶜah* to b
valid and impossible to abrogate. They affirm that the Qur'an has both a
exoteric and an esoteric aspect... .

* * *

Muhammad ibn ᶜAbd al-Karim al-Shahrastan

[Zaydin]: These are the followers of Zayd ibn ᶜAli ibn al-Husayn ib
ᶜAli ibn Abu Talib. They hold that the imamate belongs to the offspring c
Fatimah, and cannot legitimately be held by others. However, they recog
nize as Imam any Fatimid who is learned, pious, brave and generous, an
who declares his Imamate: allegiance, they maintain, must be given to suc
a one whether he is a descendant of Hasan or a descendant of Husayn. Actin
on this belief some of the Zaydiyyah recognize the Imamate of the Imam
Muhammad and Ibrahim, the sons of ᶜAbdullah ibn Hasan, who ha
revolted during the reign of Mansur, and were on that account put to deatl
They also admit the possibility of two imams in different regions; provide
they are both endowed with the above qualities, each has a right to allegianc∈
    While under the influence of these ideas Zayd ibn ᶜAli determined t
learn the sciences of theology and law in order to become adorned wit
knowledge. In theological matters he became a pupil of Wasil ibn ᶜAta', tl
"Weaver' and 'Stammerer', leader and chief of the Muᶜtazilites, even thoug
in Wasil's opinion, his grandfather, ᶜAli ibn Abu Talib, was not necessar
ly right in his battles with the People of the Camel, and in those against th
Syrians. According to Wasil one of the parties was wrong, but he did n∈
specify which. From Wasil, therefore, Zayd learned Muᶜtazilism, and all h
followers became Muᶜtazilites.
    One of Zayd's views was that it was possible for a man of lesser e≻
cellence, *al-mafdul*, to be imam, even though there was to be found a ma
of greater excellence, *al-afdal*. He said:

> ᶜAli ibn Abu Talib was the most excellent of the Companions, but the
> caliphate was entrusted to Abu Bakr partly for reasons of expediency,
> and partly from religious considerations. There was, for example, the

need to extinguish the fire of civil war and set at rest the hearts of the people, whose experience of the wars which took place at the time of the Prophet was still recent; and the sword of ʿAli, Commander of the Faithful, was still moist with the blood of the Qurayshite and other polytheists. Moreover, there was a lingering rancour in the hearts of men and a desire for vengeance. Men's hearts, therefore, were not fully disposed towards ʿAli, and they were not ready to give him wholehearted submission. Accordingly it was expedient that the man exercising the imamate should be one known to them to be gentle, kind, of mature age, an early adherent of Islam and close to the Prophet.

Do you not recall that during his last illness, when Abu Bakr proposed to confer the caliphate upon ʿUmar ibn al-Khattab, Commander of the Faithful, the people cried out in protest, saying to him, 'You have placed over us one who is severe and harsh.' Thus they did not approve of the choice of ʿUmar, Commander of the Faithful, because of his sternness and severity, his strict enforcement of religious laws and his harsh treatment of the enemy. Abu Bakr, however, reassured them by saying, 'If God were to call me to account I would answer that I appointed the best man among them and the best for them!" Accordingly it is permissible for a man of lesser excellence to be an Imam, even though there may be found a man of greater excellence, one to whom may be referred matters of law and whose decisions may be followed.

When the Shiʿis of Kufah heard that Zayd had expressed these views, and learnt that he did not dissociate himself from the two senior Companions, they rejected him for the rest of his life. It was for this reason that they were called Rafida (Rejectors).

Differences arose between Zayd ibn ʿAli and his brother Muhammad ibn ʿAli al-Baqir; not, however, on this issue, but rather on the question of Zayd being a disciple of Wasil ibn ʿAta, and of learning from a man who believed it possible that his grandfather was in error in fighting those who broke their allegiance; or those who deviated, or those who actively rebelled against him. They differed also in regard to Zayd's views on *qadar* which were contrary to those held by the descendants of the Prophet. A further point of disagreement was Zayd's opinion that an imam must rise up in revolt in order to be an imam. Finally, Baqir one day said to him, 'It would follow from your views that your father was not an Imam, for he did not at any time rise in revolt, nor did he show any sign of doing so.'

When Zayd ibn ʿAli was slain and his body crucified, Yahya ibn Zayd assumed the *Imamate*. Yahya went to Khurasan where many rallied in support of him. A prophecy from Jaʿfar ibn Muhammad al-Sadiq was communicated to him that he would be put to death just as his father had been, and crucified as he was. This came about as was foretold. The imamate then passed to the Imams, Muhammad and Ibrahim, who rose up in Medinah. Ibrahim afterwards went to Basrah where he gained support. Both of these men, however, were also killed. Sadiq had already foretold to them all that would happen to them, at the same time telling them that his predecessors had foretold it all to him. Sadiq also foretold that the Umayyads while conscious at the same time of the rancour of the descendants of the Prophet against them, would lift their heads so high above the people that if the mountains tried to rival them in height, they would raise their heads above them too. He also went on to say that it was not permissible for one of the descendants of the Prophet to rise up and proclaim himself until God permitted the collapse of their empire—pointing to Abu 'l-ᶜAbbas and Abu Jaᶜfar, the sons of Muhammad ibn ᶜAli ibn ᶜAbdullah ibn ᶜAbbas. Then, pointing to Mansur, he said, descendants have had their enjoyment of it.'

Zayd ibn ᶜAli was put to death in Kunasa in the city of Kufah by Hisham ibn ᶜAbd al-Malik; Yahya ibn Zayd in Juzjan of Khurasan by the governor; Muhammad the Imam in Medinah by ᶜIsa ibn Haman, and Ibrahim the Imam in Basrah—both of these latter by the order of Mansur. After that the Zaydiyyah remained disorganized till the appearance of their leader Nasir al-Utrush in Khurasan. Nasir was sought after so that he might be put to death, but he abandoned his campaign and went into hiding. Later he went into the districts of Daylam and al-Jabal which had not yet embraced Islam. He accordingly summoned the people to Islam, as taught by the school of Zayd ibn ᶜAli. This they embraced and followed. The Zaydiyyah remained strong in that region and were ruled over by a succession of their imams.

In certain matters of doctrine this group of the Zaydiyyah differs from their cousins, known as the Musawiyyah. In time most of the Zaydiyyah abandoned the belief in the Imamate of the one of lesser excellence. They also criticized the companions of the Prophet as did the Imamiyyah... .

Marshall Hodgson

Ismaᶜili Piety: Esotericism and Hierarchy

Quite a different turn was taken by others of the followers of Jaᶜfar al-Sadiq. Recognizing the line of his son Ismaᶜil as the true imams, they created a dynamic social and intellectual movement which fostered numerous rebellions and finally seized power in Egypt in the tenth century, on the decline of ^cAbbasid power. Esoteric Shi^cism played a more far-reaching role among the Isma^cilis (adherents of Ja^cfar's son Isma^cil) than among most Twelvers.

Indeed, they may be regarded as the most successful section of a movement which we may call the *Batiniyyah*, those who gave primacy to an 'inner meaning', a *batin*, in all religious words and formulations. (Some sections of the Batiniyyah owned the Twelver imams, however.) Growing out of the Ghullat theorists, such groups seem all to have been Shi^ci in tendency. Their piety was built on a sense of the esoteric hiddenness of truth and holiness. These were concealed from the masses, who were held capable only of the husks of faith, not its inner kernel. It was to ^cAli alone, the family confident of Muhammad, that the inward, secret meaning of the Qur'an had abeen confided; and only those spiritually alert enough to recognize ^cAli's position were vouchsafed such truths, for which they alone were ready.

There is something in the Batini mood that resembles that of the Manicheans; in fact, it is probable that some of the same sort of men who at the beginning of the ^cAbbasid regime secretly adopted Manicheanism, a century later were adopting Batinism and especially Isma^cilism (with equal secrecy). Both Manicheanism and Isma^cilism proposed to give their initiates a wisdom and a cosmic dignity which the coarse minds of ordinary mortals could scarcely aspirt to; outsiders were scarcely granted full human status. Like Manicheanism, Isma^cilism cultivated its own comprehensive body of science; this was based on that of the followers of Hellenic philosophy, but was modified in terms of an esoteric vision of the cosmos as a symbolic whole.

Isma^cilism contrasted with Manicheanism, however (and herein showed its Muslim character), is being oriented strongly to the practical development of the world's social order, to the movements of human history. Significantly, most Isma^cilis, like the other Piety-minded groups, recognized the binding force of the *Shari^cah* — regarded as the prime overt work of Muhammad. Its high position was symbolized in the primacy of Muhammad himself to the Isma^cilis' symbolic historical hierarchy — whereas some other Batinis went so far as to exalt ^cAli and his secret knowledge above Muhammad. Yet the Isma^cilis' *Shar^cism* was not merely reinforced by, but to a degree transcended by, their ^cAlid loyalism, interpreted as the basis for esoteric truth.

The purpose of the believer was to fulfill himself through the fulfillment of God's self-realization in the world — that is, of God's fulfillment here of His own rational cosmic possibilities. The world was no mere indiscriminate testing ground into which souls were placed to see how well they would do their duty; still less was it a work of blind evil; it presented, in all its details, a complex and beautiful divine plan. The Isma^cilis — in a tradition which went back at least to the Pythagoreans—loved to present their sense of an invisible underlying cosmic order in terms of numerical parallelisms: the seven openings in the human head answered to the seven visible planets, for instance, and to the seven days in each quarter of a lunar cycle, and to the seven intervals of a musical octave. This interest in numbers, though it sometimes took the subtler form of an interest in proportions, had in common with modern physical science only a very general trait, the expectation that rational, non-sensory uniformities were to be discovered, in whose light the most diverse phenomena would prove to have a common nature and a common meaning. The overriding interest was in finding a physical and moral unity in the cosmos and in its history, which would invest all details of an individual's life with cosmic meaning. The natural test of a religious system, then, was the degree to which it reflected the cosmic harmonies, even in its details, and allowed its adepts to reflect them through participating in it.

The cosmos itself was conceived in the traditional Irano-Semitic lore in which the Greek philosophical tradition played a large role, as hierarchically structured; the Creator was at the peak, working through the diverse circular motions of the heavenly spheres to evoke all the complex movements of our sublunar earthly sphere. Corresponding to this natural hierarchy of Creator and angelic heavens and ordinary mundane life was, for Isma'ilis, a religious hierarchy. The Prophet was at its head, of course; and the hierarchy was formed by delegation of authority from him. His single representative in each generation was the Imam of the time, designated by *nass* in the family of 'Ali; in him was invested the sacred 'ilm which knew the divine plan and could be unfolded to those who were worthy. But delegation did not end with the Imam. Indeed during most of High 'Abbasid times, in contrast to the group that was to become the Twelvers, the Isma'ilis had no accessible imam. Their Imam was 'hidden' since Isma'il's death—his son Muhammad had travelled off, it seemed, not even the initiates knew where. Instead of a single spokesman, the Isma'ilis acknowledged twelve chiefs, each with his own territory, to represent him; and the faithful under their command were further ranked in various increasingly numerous levels of hierarchy from the *da'is*, summoners or missionaries, down to the simple converts. Those of higher ranks taught those of lower ranks as much as they were ready to learn of the Imam's secret 'ilm.

This hierarchical organization was protected by an extreme use of an old principle. First those of the Kharijis who did not actually go out in military bands, and then many of the Shi'is who also had to accommodate themselves to authority which they could not in conscience accept, had developed the notion of *taqiyyah*, pious dissimulation of one's true opinions. It was not only to protect oneself but also to protect the community of which one was a member that a Shiᶜi was urged to practice *taqiyyah* dissimulation over against Sunni majorities or Sunni governments: at the least, not to press on their attention that Shiᶜi belief that the established Islam and the established government were illegitimate and should, in principle, be overthrown in the name of the imam. *Taqiyyah* came readily to include not making public among enemies those of the group's doctrines that would be most subject to misunderstanding. Among the Ismaᶜilis, now, took on a more extensive implication: it became the protecting of the sacred lore from profane ears — even from the less fully initiated on the adherents; eventually, it was still maintained even under an Ismaᶜili government. *Taqiyyah* dissimulation became the internal discipline which supported the hierarchy: the lore was protected at every level from those not yet ready for it.

Ismaᶜili Cyclicism

But the Ismaᶜili hierarchical discipline was designed not only to guarantee the soundness of the secret lore; it was appropriate also to conspiratorial political purposes. For the Ismaᶜilis expected, far more actively than the Twelvers with their quiescent Imams, a new dispensation for the world as a whole. A dramatic element was restored to the Muslim sense of history among the Ismaᶜilis, not however, in the sense of a nature cycle but on a strictly moral level.

A cyclical sense of history is very natural once the historical process (under conditions of literacy and urban life) is moving fast and steadily enough for the individual to be aware of it as a long-term process of change. If an infinity of space and time are assumed, but a finite range of formal possibilities, then a certain reflection, applied to the 'old man's sense of time' (the feeling that 'the younger generation is going to the dogs', extrapolated to include the implication that ever since some idealized starting point each generation has gotten, on the whole, worse), leads directly to an expectation of cycles in which renewal is followed by a steady decline. A somewhat different cyclicism can result from the same supposition of infinity applied to the 'young man's sense of time' (that the older generation are 'old fogies'), as we see in the presuppositions of many modern clichés, which assume patterns of progress that would recur not only in the other societies but even in future species if ours should destroy itself, or on other planets until some final cooling down. The fidelity of the religious traditions of Irano-Semitic heritage to the sense of the once-for-all linearity, which is strong even in Ismaᶜilism, bears witness to the high prestige among them of the moral insight that particular actions are absolutely decisive and not to be reversed or written off as mere incidents in a recurrent pattern.

The Isma^cili cyclicism, like its esotericism, represented a revival of view
points which had generally accompanied in the Irano-Semitic traditions -
perhaps as inevitable logical complement — the doctrine of a single irreversi
ble historical sequence, with beginning and end, which tended to dominate
those traditions. Elaborately as the world reflected, in some Isma^cili think
ing at least, a divine pattern, it was not free of corruption. As in all th
systems of Irano-Semitic monotheism, there had been a point of initial erro
and sin. The Isma^cilis (in the manner of the Gnostics) interpreted th
rebellion of Iblis (Satan), laconically sketched in the Qur'an, as a cosmi
turning point, necessitating an elaborate procedure of restoration, whicl
constituted human history. (In some Isma^cili philosophy, this initial aberra
tion was identified with the false sense of independence from overridin
cosmic rationality, which the vital will can be tempted to indulge in.) Th
greatest of the prophets (Adam, Noah, Abraham, Moses, Jesus, and
Muhammad made up the usual list) each had an 'executor' who taught th
secret meaning of the prophets' outward revelation and initiated a sequenc
of Imams who in turn remained unrecognized except by the élite. These mis
sions were to culminate in that of the Mahdi to come, who would form
seventh in the line and bring in the purifying Resurrection. (Sometimes thi
was distinguished from the individual resurrection of each of the faithful
which was made an essentially spiritual matter based on transformation o
the personality through the truth, while the great historical resurrection wa
to include the political establishment of truth and justice in the world.)

The sort of cyclicism worked out by the Isma^cilis can be traced in much o
the later esoteric Islam. However, the cyclicism of early Isma^cili thinkin
can be exaggerated. For the most part, the periodicity of the seven grea
public figures (*natiqs*), and of the seven Imams for each, was emotionall
and logically subordinate to the linearity of moral progression from the in
itial cosmic aberration to the restoration of cosmic harmony. Thei
readiness to adopt a politicial role demonstrates the history-mindedness o
the Isma^cilis, who were as convinced as any other Muslims of the specia
mission of Islam. Later, as the Isma^cili doctrine became more highl
developed, its philosophers interpreted it by way of neo-Platonism and thu
imposed on it an atemporal quality little in keeping with its historical role
Moreover, as it became involved in public political events without the ex
pected final consummation, the historical theory became steadily mor
refined and complex, incorporating explanations for all the contingencies
which in fact had arisen, in this process, also, its cyclicism was sometime
carried to the point of overshadowing its sense of linearity. (This happened

at least in the much later Nizari Ismaᶜili thinking.) But the Ismaᶜili core was chiliastic.

Counting from Hasan (for ᶜAli was not a mere Imam but the Prophet's executor), the seventh Imam was Muhammad ibn Ismaᶜil; as seventh, many expected him to be the Mahdi, he was to take power as soon as the effective organization of his followers was sufficient. The hierarchical authority and the esoteric secrecy thus served the individual not only in his personal spiritual development but at the same time through his participation in an ongoing historical cause; this social programme was as essential to the divine self-realization as was the personal development of the élite. (In the tenth century, in fact, an Imam did appear publicly — but only as a descendant of Muhammad ibn Ismaᶜil — and launched a campaign which first rallied the Ismaᶜili movement to the Imam and then hoped to win the whole of the Dar al-Islam.)

During High ᶜAbbasid times, Ismaᶜilism came to be the chief vehicle of the more esoteric of the chiliastic hopes that had gathered around Shiᶜism, though there continued other esoterically oriented Batini groups (notably that which separated from the Twelvers only at the end of the tenth century to become the Nusayris, of whom a body still survives in a peasant area in northern Syria). Ismaᶜilism offered much to many. To the speculatively inclined, it offered a remarkably well worked-out picture of the cosmos; in particular, the rich mythical symbolism which had found a place in the earlier parts of the Qur'an, but which the moralistic temper of many of the ᶜulama' scholars tended to reduce to rationalized prosaic irrelevance, was allowed its own vitality. To the intellectual, the shelter of its esotericism provided a worthy place within an Islamic framework for many interests which in the ordinary courtly order could well be dabbled in by Muslims, but scarcely *as* Muslims: philosphy and even natural science. It was under Batini, and probably Ismaᶜili, patronage that the most popular of the earlier compendia of Hellenic-type lore and science, the *Epistles of the Pure Brethren* (Ikhwan al-Safa) was composed . . . , and the chemical work of Jabir ibn Hayyan — foundation of the major corpus of early Islamicate chemical studies — likewise breathes this spirit. Finally, to the concerned man in the busy cities, trying to get a fairer share of prosperity, it offered hope of social justice and a sense of active participation in the struggle for this under the blessing of God. Wherever Shiᶜism was found, and sometimes elsewhere too, Ismaᶜilism was potentially influential in favourable circumstances. Nevertheless, the Ismaᶜilis, like the Manicheans, seem nowhere to have established their allegiance as commanding the daily faith of a whole population or even of a normal cross-section of it. Isma^{c}ilism remained the faith of an élite.

Mangol Bayat

The entire Shaykhi system of thought rests on the basic Muslim theosophical conception of the universe as consisting of a structured hierarchy of worlds and interworlds of reality which correspond to the different levels of being—matter, soul, and intellect. In the twelfth century, Suhrawardi, influenced by ancient Iranian thought which he interpreted in the light of neo-Platonic philosophy, had developed a scheme which put the world, the earthly realm of matter perceived through the senses, at the bottom of the scale. The interworld, or intermediary realm of the angels and of human souls—a world of "substances of light" perceived through the imaginative faculty—he placed in the middle. And at the highest level was the world of Pure Beings of Light, with no material or physical body and are perceived through the intellect.

A century later, Ibn ^{c}Arabi added a fourth realm, the sphere of the deity, and had elaborated on the concept of the intermediary world, the realm where the human soul imagines images which are as real as, if not more so than, the reality which is perceived through the senses. He depicted this interworld as an exact, ideal reflection of the physical world, a world of symbols or archetypal images of all earthly individuals and things, a transmaterial world that is "inaccessible to rational abstractions and to empirical materializations."

Suhrawardi reportedly experienced visionary dreams where Aristotle and Hermes, each in turn, enlightened him with their knowledge and helped him ascend to the intermediary world of light which, once reached, pushed the physical world back into darkness. Ibn ^{c}Arabi similarly asserted that human dreams, meditations and visions take place in this intermediate world of "real reality," and that it is possible to accomplish such "visionary voyages" from the earthly world. Both Suhrawardi and Ibn ^{c}Arabi, and most subsequent theosophers, firmly believed that human consciousness awakens to this reality, which is the reality of the eternal celestial soul, through the individual's active imagination, the organ of visionary perceptions. Thus, neo-Platonic metaphysics, which developed on the basis of the Sufi theories of Suhrawardi and Ibn ᶜArabi, made it possible for seekers of "true knowledge," who wished to escape from the contingency of existence, to reach a higher form of existence nearer the Absolute. Such a view of the ascent to the Absolute or "return to God," whereby all alienation, all uncertainty is gradually removed, offered a hopeful conception of the individual's spiritual and intellectual abilities to transcend human nature and to conquer what are essentially physical limitations and liabilities. Moreover, this conception of an intermediary, transmaterial world helped the theosophers solve a number of problematic issues of religious dogma.

Orthodox theologians, for example, traditionally emphasized a belief in the physical resurrection of the body on the day of judgment and in the physical afterlife, thus accepting a literal understanding of Qur'anic pronouncements on the subject. Majlisi, in his authoritative and comprehensive exposition of Imami Shiᶜi dogma, discussed at great lenth the issue of resurrection in a literal, physical sense. Such an interpretation always produced a dilemma for the philosophers who wished to comprehend the metaphysical issues rationally. They ended up by refuting the doctrine of the physical resurrection, and asserting their own belief in the spiritual survival of the soul. Ibn ᶜArabi, however, had the resurrection take place in this transmaterial world. In his view, it was a resurrection that was both physical (in the sense that it was the exact reflection of the earthly body) and spiritual, because the heavenly body is immaterial.

[Mulla] Sadra further insisted that the world of images and its contents are real: a real body, a real paradise, a real hell with its fire, none of which are material. Faithful to his theory of substantive change, he explained how the human form goes through a continuous process of renewal. The body upon death sheds its impure matter, and acquires a refined spiritual body in the intermediary world, thus undergoing a minor resurrection. There it prepares itself for the final metamorphosis, or greater resurrection, to reach the realm of the intellect. Sadra, therefore, categorically denied the physical resurrection of the body in its earthly form. His doctrine of substantive change, which is conceived to be unidirectional and irreversible, would not allow it. Similarly, Sadra emphatically refuted the theologians' conception of a physical afterlife. The Qur'an, he wrote, "repeatedly tells us that the afterlife is a new creation, a new level of existence. This clearly means that we cannot look for a reappearance of earthly elementary bodies there."

[Shaykh Ahmad] Ahsa'i, who was influenced by Sadra more than he wished to admit, accepted this conception of a hierarchical order of beings and realities, and used it to adapt many controversial theosophical ideas to the theological doctrine. He claimed that the transmaterial world, which he called *hurqalya*, can be perceived by the adept, the initiated. The degree of perception of things in *hurqalya* is directly proportionate to the degree of esoteric knowledge an individual possesses.

In order to accommodate his theosophical views to orthodox theology, Shaykh Ahmad drew a complicated and rather confusing scheme, whereby the human form is conceived as made of different layers of celestial and material substances, each corresponding to a different stage of its being. The scheme enabled him to accept, with minor differences, Sadra's argument that the progressive ascent of the human form—from the mineral, vegetable, and human stages to the final spiritual level of the pure intellect—is irreversible, and that there could be no physical resurrection.

Closely linked to the issue of resurrection is the question of *mi'raj*, the Prophet's nocturnal ascent to Heaven. Orthodox theologians, true to their literalist interpretaton of religion, postulate a belief in the physical *mi'raj*. Ahsa'i rejected this, and understood *mi'raj* to mean a spiritual experience symbolizing an ascent to the highest level of cognizance of the divine.

In accordance with the concept of the original spiritual substance of the human form, the Shaykh also asserted that the Prophet and the Imams, upon death, left behind their earthly garb, which they had temporarily worn during their terrestrial sojourn to make themselves visible to humans. Thereafter, they reassumed their original refined, immaterial substance to enter the heavens. Their physical bodies decomposed, and the material components reverted to their respective elements.

This unorthodox interpretation rejected the official view that the bodies of the Prophet and the Imams were, by divine grace, exempted from physical decomposition. Furthermore, Ahsa'i's conviction that the Hidden Imam does not live, though invisibly, in this world, but rather in the transmaterial world, *hurqalya*, and that his manifestation will not occur in this world but, again, in *hurqalya*, was contrary to the most fundamental Imami Shi'i doctrine. Orthodox theologians insisted, and still insist, that the Imam is alive and ever present on earth, though concealed from human sight. Majlisi had argued that it was biologically possible for the Imam to live so long. He even maintained that the Imam had been seen occasionally, had performed miracles, and had taken part, unrecognized, in annual pilgrimage rituals in Mecca. Similarly, Majlisi confirmed the orthodox view of the Imam's return to this world at the end of time as marking the physical resurrection of humans in this world... .

*   *   *

Of crucial importance to Ahsa'i's entire theophilosophical system is his conception of the nature, place and function of the Imams in the universe. Shaykhism, to use Corbin's definition, is essentially *"Imamismespeculatif."* It shares with the theophilosophical and theological schools the fundamental Shiᶜi idea of the Prophecy and the Imamate as being two separate stages of the Qur'anic revelation, one exoteric (*zahir*), the other esoteric (*batin*). Although the two stages were united in the person of the Prophet, the latter's mission was to reveal the exoteric meaning of the divine truth, thus leaving to the Imams the important task of gradually lifting the veil off the esoteric. Whereas the first stage ends with Muhammad, the second has its beginning with ᶜAli. To quote Ibn Babuyah, the tenth-century theologian: "The Imams are in authority. It is to them that Allah has ordained obedience, they are the witnesses for the people and they are the gates of Allah, the road to Him and the guides thereto, and the repositories of His knowledge and the interpreters of His revelations, and the pillars of His unity. They are immune from sins, and errors, they are those from whom Allah had removed all impurity and made them absolutely pure; they are possessed of the [power of] miracles and of [irrefutable arguments]; they are for the protection of people of this earth just as the stars are for the inhabitants of the heavens." He argued that the continued existence of the Imam, whether visible or concealed, is necessary because his nonexistence would deprive the earth of a witness from God. Hasan ibn Musa al-Nawbakhti, another mid-tenth-century Imami scholar, similarly insisted that the "earth cannot be void of a Proof. If the Imamate disappeared even for a moment, the earth and its inhabitants would perish." Ibn al-Mutahhar al-Hilli, writing in the thirteenth century, further reinforced this view of the Imamate as a universal authority in the things of religion and of the world. However, at this point Shaykhism departs from orthodox Shiᶜi. For, although the theologians implicitly grant the Imams a status almost equal to the Prophet's, and see them as endowed with a special divine grace, they do not recognize them as either independent or as divine beings. Ahsa'i, on the other hand, inspired by Sadra and his school of theosophy, drew a different conception of the Imams.

In Sadra's philosophical system, the being, after descending from the heavens into the abyss, returns to God. In its progressive ascent, it passes through three different stages of structured reality: the realm of matter, the realm of the soul, and finally, if it qualifies, back to the realm of pure intellect in the form of the Perfect Man who combines in himself all three realms. Whereas the human form in this world is material, in the other two worlds it is immaterial. The Perfect Beings are intermediate beings between the Necessary Being, God, and the contingent or earthly, world. (Fadlur] Rahman quite rightly notes an ambiguity in Sadra's description of them as pure existence and absolute beings, and as part of God, since there must also be within them something of the worldly. He explains that it was necessary for Sadra, in order to maintain continuity in the chain of hierarchical beings, to put them at the highest point, next to God, who transcends all, *ad infinitum*. "Their position," Rahman writes, "seems to be the same as that of the Attributes of God who are also said by Sadra to be intermediate between the absolute being of God's Essence and the world of contingency." These intellects constitute a manifestation of God, and "God contemplates Himself through this manifestation. Intellects are, therefore, forms or images of God, from this point of view." And they, in turn, contemplate God through their contemplation of themselves, as the effects of God. Thus, the Imam, the Perfect Man or the pure intellect, is truly the intermediary through whom, and only through whom, humans can reach and know God.

Ahsa'i took over their hierarchical system, adding to it, like Ibn ʿArabi before him, a fourth stage. This was the realm of the deity, whence the Fourteen Very Pure — that is, the Prophet, Fatimah and the twelve Imams — come and where they return. Aware of the theologians' uncompromising belief that there can be no separate immaterial substance besides God, and wishing to avoid criticism for attributing immateriality to other beings, Ahsa'i made use of Sadra's (which was originally Suhrawardi's) notion of a scale of graded beings. He explained how beings, which are made of both spiritual matter (light) and elemental matter ("solidified light"), materially differ in degree. The Primordial Intellect (that is, each of the Fourteen Very Pure) is more immaterial than, say, a mineral, but less so than God. However, Ahsa'i argument was too close to Sadra's to be accepted by the orthodox theologians. His notion of spiritual matter could, and did, sound like a euphemism for immateriality. Furthermore, the Shaykh explicitly stated that the Imams possess a spiritually divine reality, and that their temporary human condition in this world is only accidental. In other words, the Imams are pre-existential divine beings. This view is consistent with his firm conviction that the "biological status" of all beings is pre-existentially determined, and that the animal condition of human beings, just like the Imam's human condition, is accidental since their essence belongs to the intermediate world of the soul.

Ahsa'i further provoked shocked outcries from the orthodox ʿulama' with unorthodox statements regarding the universal function of the Imams. They are "the cause of Creation," the cause of the existence of everything that is not God. They are "the place" of God's will, they fulfill God's wish. "If it were not for the Imams, God would not have created anything." Such assertions, which abound in the Shaykh's works, echo Nasir al-Din Tusi's views on the Imamate. In his Ismaʿili phase, Tusi had defined the Imam as the "Deified Perfect Man," "the Manifestation of the Primal Divine Volition on earth," "the cause and origin of the existence of all beings and creations," and "the cause [while other beings are] the effects".

Ahsa'i was consequently accused of actually professing faith in ᶜAli, the first Imam, as the creator of the universe. To clarify his position and clear his name from such blasphemous charges, Ahsa'i argued that the Fourteen Very Pure, which are the Names and Attributes of the Divine, together constitute the eternal Muhammadan truth and through them, as God's agents, God's will manifests itself on earth. Hence, everything that exists, be it the intellect or the smallest particle of dust, exists as a result of this will and its agents. The entire world is the product of a voluntary act of the Imam, who derives his power and strength from God. Kazim Rashti futher emphasized this point: "Perhaps everything that exists in this world, be it visible or invisible, is linked to the thought of the Imam. Should the Imam turn his attention away from it, the entire world would disappear. His thought is thus the cause of existence." By themselves, Ahsa'i cautiously explained, the Imams have no independent power. Just as a hot iron bar derives its heat from the fire but, once hot, generates heat continuously even if taken out of the fire, the Imams act freely because God has endowed them with such an attribute. In fact, "The Imams Very Pure possess all the Divine Attributes, and through them all acts of the Divine Being are manifested." As Nicolas points out, Ahsa'i's argument meant to show that the act of creation cannot be attributed to the essence of God directly, but to the essence through the intermediary agency of the Imams. The Imams are, therefore, in the Shaykh's view, not the architect's of creation, but its contractors... .

Chapter Nine

Shiᶜism and Sufism

Through their long history, Shiᶜism, as a major division within the Islamic tradition, and Sufism, as the mystical and esoteric dimension of Islam, have been interrelated. The nature and vicissitudes of this complex interaction has been the subject of intensive scholarly investigation. In the following passage Seyyed Hossein Nasr discusses and analyzes the most important aspects of the relationship between Shiᶜism and Sufism. The passage is taken from SE, *pages 104–120.*

Seyyed Hossein Nasr

One of the most difficult questions touching the manifestation of Sufism in Islamic history is its relation with Shiᶜism. In discussing this intricate and somewhat complex relationship, in principle and essence or in the light of its metahistorical reality as well as in time and history, we need hardly concern ourselves with the too-often repeated criticism made by certain orientalists who would doubt the Islamic and Qur'anic character of both Shiᶜism and Sufism. Basing themselves on an *a priori* assumption that Islam is not a revelation and that even if it ranks as a religion, it is only an elementary 'religion of the sword' intended for a simple desert people, these would-be critics brush aside as un-Islamic all that speaks of gnosis (ᶜ*irfan*) and esotericism, pointing to the lack of historical texts in the early period as proof of their thesis — as if the non-existent in itself could disprove the existence of something which may have been there without leaving a written trace for us to dissect and analyse today. The reality of Shiᶜism and Sufism as integral aspects of the Islamic revelation is too dazzlingly clear to be ignored or explained away on the basis of a tendentious historical argument. The fruit is there to prove that the tree has its roots in a soil that nourishes it; and the spiritual fruit can only be borne by a tree whose roots are sunk in a revealed truth. To deny this most evident of truths would be as if one were to doubt the Christian sanctity of St. Francis of Assisi because the historical records of the first years of the Apostolic succession are not documented to fit academic standards. What the presence of St. Francis proves is in reality the opposite fact, namely, that the Apostolic succession must be real even if no historical records are at hand. The same holds true *mutatis mutandis* for Shiᶜism and Sufism. In this essay we will in any case begin by taking for granted the Islamic character of Shiᶜism and Sufism . . . . [U]pon this basis we can delve into their relationship. In fact Shiᶜism and Sufism are both, in different ways and on different levels, intrinsic aspects of Islamic orthodoxy, this term being taken not merely in its theological sense but more especially in its universal sense as tradition and universal truth contained with a revealed form.

The relationship between Shiᶜism and Sufism is complicated by the fact that in discussing these two spiritual and religious realities we are not dealing with the same level or dimension of Islam in both cases. As already mentioned, Islam has both an exoteric (*zahir*) and an esoteric (*batin*) dimension, which along with all their inner divisions represent the 'vertical' structure of the revelation. But it is also divided into Sunnism and Shiᶜism, which one might say represent its 'horizontal' structure. Were this the only aspect of the above relationship it would be relatively simple to explain. But as a matter of fact the esoteric dimension of Islam, which in the Sunni climate is almost totally connected with Sufism, in one way or another colours the whole structure of Shiᶜism in both its esoteric and even its exoteric aspect. One can say that Islamic esotericism or gnosis crystallized into the form of Sufism in the Sunni world while it poured into the whole structure of Shiᶜism especially during its early period. From the Sunni point of view Sufism presents similarities to Shiᶜism and has even assimilated aspects thereof. No less an authority than Ibn Khaldun writes: 'The Sufis thus became saturated with Shiᶜi theories. (Shiᶜi) theories entered so deeply into their religious ideas that they based their own practice of using a cloak (*khirqah*) on the fact that ᶜAli clothed al-Hasan al-Basri in such a cloak and caused him to agree solemnly that he would adhere to the mystic path. (The tradition thus inaugurated by ᶜAli) was continued according to the Sufis, through al-Junayd, one of the Sufi *shaykhs*. From the Shiᶜi point of view Shiᶜism is the origin of what later came to be known as Sufism. But here by Shiᶜism is meant the esoteric instructions of the Prophet, the *asrar* which many Shiᶜi authors have identified with the Shiᶜi 'concealment', *taqiyyah*.

Each of these two points of view presents an aspect of the same reality but seen within two worlds that are contained in the bosom of the total orthodoxy of Islam. That reality is Islamic esotericism or gnosis. If we take Sufism and Shiᶜism in their historical manifestation in later periods, then neither Shiᶜism nor Sunnism, nor Sufism within the Sunni world, derive from one another. They all derive their authority from the Prophet and the source of the Islamic revelation. But if we mean by Shiᶜism Islamic esotericism as such, then it is of course inseparable from Sufism. For example, the Shiᶜi Imams play a fundamental role in Sufism, but as representative of Islamic esotericism, not as specifically Shiᶜi Imams according to the later organization of the Shiᶜi faith. In fact there is a tendency among both later Muslim historians and modern scholars to read back into the first two centuries the clear distinctions that were established only later. It is true that one can discern Shiᶜi elements even during the life-time of th Prophet and that Shiᶜism and Sunnism have their roots in the very origin of the Islamic revelation, placed there providentially to accommodate different psychological and ethnic types. But the hard-and-fast divisions of later centuries are not discernible in the earlier period. There were Sunni elements with definite Shiᶜi tendencies, and there were Shiᶜi contacts with Sunni elements both intellectually and socially. In certain cases in fact it is difficult to judge as to whether a particular author was Shiᶜi or Sunni especially before the fourth/tenth century, although even in this period Shiᶜi and Sunni religious and spiritual life each possessed its own particular perfume and color.

In this less crystallized and more fluid environment, those elements of Islamic esotericism which from the Shiᶜi point of view are considered as particularly Shiᶜi, appear as representing Islamic esotericism as such in the Sunni world. No better instance of this can be found than the person of ᶜAli ibn Abu Talib. Shiᶜism may be called the 'Islam of ᶜAli', who in Shiᶜism is both the 'spiritual' and 'temporal' authority after the Prophet. In Sunnism also nearly all Sufi orders reach back to him and he is the spiritual authority *par excellence* after the Prophet. The famous *hadith* 'I am the city of knowledge and ᶜAli is its gate', which is a direct reference to the role of ᶜAli in Islamic esotericism, is accepted by Shiᶜi and Sunni alike, but the 'spiritual vicegerency' (*khilafah ruhaniyyah*) of ᶜAli appears to Sufism within the Sunni world not as something specifically Shiᶜi but as being directly connected with Islamic esotericism in itself.

Yet the case of ᶜAli, the reverence in which he is held by Shiᶜi and Sufis alike, shows how intimately Shiᶜism and Sufism are connected together. Sufism does not possess a *Shariᶜah*; it is only a spiritual way (*Tariqah*) attached to a particular *Shariᶜite* rite such as the Maliki or Shafiᶜi. Shiᶜism possesses both a *Shariᶜah* and a *Tariqah*. In its purely spiritual or *Tariqah* aspect it is in many instances identical with Sufism as it exists in the Sunni world, and certain Sufi orders such as the Niᶜmatullahi have existed in both the Shiᶜi and Sunni worlds. But in addition Shiᶜism possesses even in its *Shariᶜite* and theological aspects certain esoteric elements which make it akin to Sufism. In fact one could say that Shiᶜism, even in its outward aspect, is oriented toward the spiritual stations (*maqamat-i ᶜirfani*) of the Prophet and the Imams, which are also the goal of the spiritual life in Sufism.

A few examples in the vast and intricate relationship between Shiᶜism and Sufism may make more clear some of the points discussed so far. In Islam in general, and Sufism in particular, a saint is called a *wali* (abbreviation of *waliallah* or friend of God) and sanctity is called *wilayah*. As already mentioned in Shiᶜism the whole function of the Imam is associated with the power and function of what in Persian is called *walayat*, which comes from the same root as *wilayah* as is closely connected with it. Some have even identified the two. In any case according to Shiᶜism, in addition to the power of prophecy in the sense of bringing a divine law (*nubuwwah* and *risalah*), the Prophet of Islam, like other great prophets before him, had the power of spiritual guidance and initiation (*walayah*) which he transmitted to Fatimah and ᶜAli through them to all the Imams. Since the Imam is always alive, this function and power is also always present in this world and able to guide men to the spiritual life. The 'cycle of initiation' (*da'rat al-walayah*) which follows the 'cycle of prophecy' (*da'irat al-nubuwwah*) is therefore one that continues to this day and guarantees the ever-living presence of an esoteric way in Islam.

The same meaning pertains to *wilayah* in the sense that it too concerns the ever-living spiritual presence in Islam which enables men to practice the spiritual life and to reach a state of sanctity. That is why many Sufis since the time of Hakim al-Tirmizi have devoted so much attention to this cardinal aspect of Sufism. There is to be sure a difference between Shi°ism and Sufism on how and through whom this power and function operates as well as who is considered as its 'seal'. But the similarity between the Shi°i and the Sufis concerning this doctrine is most startling and results directly from the fact that both are connected in the manner mentioned above with Islamic esotericism as such, which is none other than *wilayah* or *walayah* as used in the technical sense in both Shi°i and Sufi sources.

Among the practices of the Sufis there is one that is closely associated in its symbolic meaning with *wilayah* and in its origin with the Shi°i *walayah*. It is the practice of wearing a cloak and handing it from the master to the disciple as a symbol of the transmission of a spiritual teaching and the particular grace associated with the act of initiation. Each state of being is like a cloak or veil that 'covers' the state above, for symbolically the 'above' is associated with the 'inward'. The Sufi cloak symbolizes the transmission of spiritual power which enables the disciple or *murid* to penetrate beyond his everyday state of consciousness. By virtue of being presented with this cloak or veil in its symbolic sense he is able to cast aside the inner veil that separates him from the Divine.

The practice of wearing and transmitting the cloak and the meaning of this act are closedly associated with Shi°ism, as affirmed by Ibn Khaldun in the quotation cited above. According to the famous *Hadith-i kisa'* (the tradition of the garment) the Prophet called his daughter Fatimah along with °Ali, Hasan and Husayn and placed a cloak upon them in such a manner that it covered them. The cloak symbolizes the transmission of the universal *walayah* of the Prophet in the form of the partial *walayah* (*walayat-i fatimiyyah*) to Fatimah and through her to the Imams who were her descendents. There is a direct reference to the esoteric symbolism of the cloak in a well-known Shi°i *hadith* which because of its significance and beauty is quoted fully here:

> 'It has been accounted of the Prophet — upon him and his family be peace — that he said: "When I was taken on the nocturnal ascension to heaven and I entered paradise, I saw in the middle of it a palace made of red rubies. Gabriel opened the door for me and I entered it. I saw in it a house made of white pearls. I entered the house and saw in the middle of it a box made of light and locked with a lock made of light. I said, 'Oh

Gabriel, what is this box and what is in it?' Gabriel said, 'Oh Friend of God (*Habiballah*), in it is the secret of God (*sirrallah*) which God does not reveal to anyone except to him whom He loves.' I said, 'Open its door for me'. He said, 'I am a slave who follows the divine command. Ask thy Lord until He grants permission to open it.' I therefore asked for the permission of God. A voice came from the Divine Throne saying, 'Oh Gabriel open its door', and he opened it. In it I saw spiritual poverty (*faqr*) and a cloak (*muraqqaᶜ*). I said, What is this *faqr* and *muraqqacᶜ*?' The voice from heaven said, 'Oh Muhammad, there are two things which I have chosen for thee and the people (*ummah*) from the moment I created the two of you. These two things I do not give to anyone save those whom I love, and I have created nothing dearer than these.'" Then the Holy Prophet said, "God—Exalted be His Name—selected *faqr* and the *muraqqaᶜ* for me and these two are the dearest things to Him." The Prophet directed his attention toward God and when he returned from the nocturnal ascent (*miᶜraj*) he made ᶜAli wear the cloak with the permission of God and by His command. ᶜAli wore it and sewed patches on it until he said, "I have sewn so many patches on this cloak that I am embarrassed before the sewer." ᶜAli made his son Hasan to wear it after him and then Husayn and then the descendants of Husayn one after another until the Mahdi. The cloak rests with him now.'

Ibn Abi Jumhur as well as the later Shiᶜi commentators upon this *hadith* add that the cloak worn and transmitted by the Sufis is not the same cloak cited in the *hadith*. Rather, what the Sufis seek to do is to emulate the conditions for wearing the cloak as the Prophet wore it and through this act to become aware to the extent of their capability of the divine mysteries (*asrar*) which the cloak symbolizes.

The whole question of *walayah* and the cloak that symbolises it makes clear the most important common element between Sufism and Shiᶜism, which is the presence of a hidden form of knowledge and instruction. The use of the method of *ta'wil* or spiritual hermeneutics in the understanding of the Holy Qur'an as well as of the 'cosmic text', and belief in grades of meaning within the revelation—both of which are common to Sufism and Shiᶜism—result from the presence of this esoteric form of knowledge. The presence of *walayat* guarantees for Shiᶜism and Sufism alike a gnostic and esoteric character, of which the doctrine and the characteristic manner of instruction present in both are natural expressions.

Closely associated with *walayah* is the concept of the Imam in Shiᶜism, for the Imam is he who possesses the power and function of *walayat*. The role of the Imam is central to Shiᶜism, but we cannot deal here with all its ramifications. But from the spiritual point of view it is important to point to his function as the spiritual guide, a function that closely resembles that of the Sufi master. The Shiᶜi seeks to encounter his Imam, who is none other than the inner spiritual guide—so that some Shiᶜi Sufis speak of the Imam of each person's beings (*imam wujudiha*). If one leaves aside the Shariᶜite and also cosmic functions of the Imam, his initiatory function and role as spiritual guide is similar to that of the Sufi master. In fact just as in Sufism each master is in contact with the pole (*Qutb*) of his age, in Shiᶜism all spiritual functions in every age are inwardly connected with the Imam. The idea of the Imam as the pole of the Universe and the concept of the *Qutb* in Sufism are nearly identical, as asserted so clearly by Sayyid Haydar Amuli when he says, 'The *Qutb* and the Imam are two expressions possessing the same meaning and referring to the same person.' The doctrine of the universal or perfect man (*al-insan al-kamil*) as expounded by Ibn ᶜArabi is very similar to the Shiᶜi doctrine of the *Qutb* and the Imam, as is the doctrine of the Mahdi developed by later Sufi masters. All these doctrines refer essentially and ultimately to the same esoteric reality, the *haqiqat al-muhammadiyyah*, as present in both Shiᶜism and Sufism. And in this case as far as the formulation of this doctrine is concerned there may have been direct Shiᶜi influences upon later Sufi foundations.

Another doctrine that is shared in somewhat different forms by Shiᶜi and Sufis is that of the 'Muhammadan light' (*al-nur al-muhammadi*) and the initiatic chain (*silsilah*). Shiᶜism believes that there is a 'Primordial Light' passed from one prophet to another and after the Prophet of Islam to the Imams. This light protects the prophets and Imams from sin, making them inerrant (*maᶜsum*), and bestows upon them the knowledge of divine mysteries. In order to gain this knowledge man must become attached to this light through the Imam who, following the Prophet, acts as man's intermediary with God in the quest for divine knowledge. In the same way, in Sufism, in order to gain access to the methods which alone make spiritual realisation possible, man must become attached to an initiatory chain or *silsilah* which goes back to the Prophet and through which a *barakah* flows from the source of revelation to the being of the initiate. The chain is thus based on a continuity of spiritual presence that much resembles the 'Muhammadan light' of Shiᶜism. In fact later Sufis themselves also speak of the 'Muhammadan light'. In the early period, especially in teachings of Imam Jaᶜfar al-Sadiq, the Shiᶜi doctrine of the 'Muhammadan light' and the Sufi doctrine of the spiritual chain meet, and as in other cases have their source in the same esoteric teachings of Islam.

Finally, in this comparison between Shiᶜi and Sufi doctrines one should mention the spiritual and gnostic stations (*maqamat-i ᶜirfani*). If we turn to a study of the life of the Prophet and the Imams as, for example, found in the compilation of Majlisi in the *Bihar al-anwar*, we will discover that these accounts are based more than anything else upon the inner spiritual states of the personages concerned. The goal of the religious life in Shiᶜism is, in fact, to emulate the life of the Prophet and the Imams and to reach their inward states. Although for the majority of Shiᶜi this remains only a latent possibility, the élite (*khawass*) have always been fully aware of it. The spiritual stations of the Prophet and the Imams leading to union with God can be considered as the final goal toward which Shiᶜi piety strives and upon which the whole spiritual structure of Shiᶜism is based.

Now in Sufism also, the goal, which is to reach God, cannot be achieved except through the states and stations (*hal* and *maqam*) which occupy such a prominent position in the classical treatises of Sufism. The Sufi life is also one that is based on the achievement of these states, although the Sufi does not seek these states in themselves but seeks God in His Exalted Essence. Of course in Sufism nearly all the members of any order are conscious of the states and stations whereas in Shiᶜism concerns a whole community, possessing its own exoteric and esoteric division and having its own élite as well as its common believers (*ᶜawamm*). But in the special significance given to the spiritual stations in the Shiᶜi account of the lives of the Prophet and the Imams, there is a striking similarity with what one finds in Sufism. Here again both refer to the same reality, Islamic esotericism, with the practical and realised aspect of which the spiritual stations are concerned... .

Today in the Shiᶜi world and particularly Shiᶜi Persia one can distinguish between three groups of gnostics and mystics: those who belong to regular Sufi orders such as the Niᶜmatullahi or the Zahabi and who follow a way very similar to those of Sufis in the Sunni world; those who also have had a definite spiritual master and have received regular initiation but whose master and those before him do not constitute an organized and 'institutionalized' Sufi order with an openly declared *silsilah* and established centre or *khaniqah*; and finally those who have definitely received a gnostic and mystical inspiration and have authentic visions (*mushahadah*) and experience spiritual states (*ahwal*), but who do not possess a human master. Of this latter group some are Uwaysis, others belong to the line of *Khadir* or *Khidr* in Persian, and most reach spiritual contact with the Imam who is also the inner spiritual guide. The overflow of esotericism in Shiᶜism into even the more outward aspects of the religious has made this third type of possibility more common here than one would find in Sunni Islam. Some of the great theosophers and gnostics in fact, who have definitely reached the state of spiritual vision as attested by their works, belong to this latter category and also perhaps to the second category because in that case likewise it is difficult to discern the spiritual lineage outwardly.

Shiᶜism and Sufism, then, possess a common parentage in that they are both linked with the esoteric dimension of the Islamic revelation and in their earliest history drew inspiration from the same sources. In later periods they have had many mutual interactions and influenced each other in innumerable ways. But these historical manifestations have been no more than applications to different moments of time of an essential and principal relationship which belongs to the eternal and integral reality of Islam itself and which in the form of the gnosis that characterizes Islamic esotericism has manifested itself in both segments of the Islamic community, the Sunni and Shiᶜi alike.

Part III

Shi*c*i Doctrines and Beliefs

Chapter Ten

The Shiʿi View of God

As Supreme Authority, Allah is at the center of the Islamic revelation. He is the Truth (Haqq), the Reality (Haqiqah), and the Necessary Being (Wajib al-Wujub). He is omnipotent (al-Qadir), Omniscient (al-ʿAlim), and Omnipresent (al-Qayyum). In the following two passages, first ʿAllamah Tabatabaʾi provides a succinct formulation of the Shiʿi understanding of its Supreme Authority, and then William Chittick translates a number of traditional statements by Prophet Muhammad and Shiʿi Imams on the Unity of God. The excerpts are taken from SI, *pages 123–33, and* SA, *pages 23–31, 42–43, and 44–48, respectively.*

ʿAllamah Tabatabaʾi

Consciousness and perception, which are intertwined with man's very being, make evident by their very nature the existence of God as well as the world. For, contrary to those who express doubt about their own existence and everything else and consider the world as illusion and fantasy, we know that a human being at the moment of his coming into existence, when he is already conscious and possesses perception, discovers himself and the world. That is to say, he has no doubt that "he exists and things other than he exist." As long as man is man this comprehension and knowledge exist in him and cannot be doubted, nor do they undergo any change.

The perception of this reality and existence which man affirms through his intelligence, in opposition to the views of the sophist and skeptic, is immutable and can never be proven false. That is to say, the claim of the sophist and the skeptic which negates reality can never be true, because of man's very existence. There is within the immense world of existence a permanent and abiding reality which pervades it and which reveals itself to the intelligence.

Yet each of the phenomena of this world which possesses the reality that we discover as conscious and perceiving human beings loses its reality sooner or later and becomes nonexistent. From this fact itself it is evident that the visible world and its parts are not the essence of reality (which can never be obliterated or destroyed). Rather, they rely upon a permanent Reality through which they gain reality and by means of which they enter into existence. As long as they are connected and attached to it they possess existence and as soon as they are cut off from it they become nonexistent. We call this Immutable Reality, which is imperishable (that is, the Necessary Being), God.

*   *   *

The path chosen in the previous section to prove the existence of God is a very simple and evident one which man treads with his God-given nature and intelligence without any complication. Yet, for the majority of people, because of their continuous preoccupation with material things and their being drowned in the pleasures of the senses, it has become very difficult to return to their God-given, simple, primordial, and untainted nature. That is why Islam, which describes itself as universal, and which believes all people to be equal in religion, has made it possible for such people to find another way to prove the existence of God. It seeks to speak to them and to make God known to them by means of the very path through which they have turned away from their simple, primordial nature.

The Holy Qur'an instructs the multitude of men in the knowledge of God through different ways. Most of all, it draws their attention to the creation of the world and the order which reigns over it. It invites men to contemplate the "horizons" and "their own souls," for man in his few days of earthly life, no matter what path he chooses or what state he loses himself in, will never step outside the world of creation and the order which reigns over it. His intelligence and power of comprehension cannot overlook the marvelous scenes of heaven and earth which he observes.

This vast world of existence which stretches before our eyes is, as we know, in its parts and as a whole continuously in the process of change and transformation. At each moment it manifests itself in a new and unprecedented form. It becomes actualized under the influences of laws which know no exception. From the farthest galaxies to the smallest particles which form the parts of the world, each part of creation possesses an inward order and runs its course in a most amazing manner under laws which do not admit any exceptions. The world extends its domain of activity from the lowest to the most perfect state and reaches its own goal of perfection.

Above these particular orders stand more universal orders and finally the total cosmic order which brings together the countless parts of the universe and relates the more particular orders with each other, and which in its continuous course accepts no exceptions and permits no breaches.

The order of creation is such that if, for example, it places a man upon the earth, it constitutes him in such a way that he can live in harmony with his environment. It arranges the environment in such a way that it raises him like a loving nurse. The sun, the moon, the stars, water and earth, the night and the day, the seasons of the year, the clouds, wind and rain, the treasures beneath the earth and on its surface, in other words all the forces of nature, use their energy and resources in providing well-being and peace of mind for him. Such a relation and harmony can be discovered among all phenomena and also between man and his neighbors near and far, as well as within man's own habitat.

Such a continuity and harmony can also be observed within the internal structure of every phenomenon in the world. If creation has given man bread, it has also given him feet to seek it, hands to grasp it, a mouth to eat it, and teeth to chew it. It has related man through a series of means, which are connected with each other like the links of a chain, to the final goal envisaged for this creature, which is subsistence and perfection.

Many men of science have no doubt that the countless relations among things which they have discovered as a result of several thousand years of effort are but humble samples and a foretaste of the secrets of creation and their myriad ramifications. Each new discovery declares to man the existence of an endless number of unknown elements. Could anyone say that this vast world of existence, all of the parts of which either separately or in unity and interconnection bear witness to an infinite knowledge and power, need not have a creator and could have come into being without reason and cause? Or could it be said of these particular and universal domains of order and equilibrium, and finally of this total cosmic order which through innumerable interrelations has made the world a single unit running its course according to laws which know no exceptions, that all this has occurred without plan and only through accident and chance? Or could anyone say that each of the phenomena and domains in the cosmos has chosen for itself, before coming into being, an order and law which it puts into effect after coming into being? Or could anyone claim that this world, which is a single unit and which possesses complete unity, harmony and the interconnection of parts, could be the result of multiple and different commands issuing from different sources?

Obviously, an intelligent man, who relates every event and phenomenon to a cause, and who sometimes spends long periods in investigation and efforts to gain knowledge of a cause that is unknown to him, will never accept the possibility of a world existing without a Being as its cause. Such a person, who by observing a few bricks placed upon one another in an orderly manner considers them to be the effect of an agent possessing knowledge and power and who denies the possibility of chance and accident in the putting of the bricks together and therefore concludes that a plan and purpose must have existed beforehand, will not regard the cosmic order as being the result of an accident or the play of chance.

A deeper awareness of the order reigning in the world is enough to show that the world, along with the order reigning over it, is the creation of an omnipotent Creator who has brought it into being through His limitless knowledge and power and who directs it toward an end. All the partial causes which bring about individual events in the world ultimately end in Him. They are in every way under His dominance and are guided by His widsom. Everything that exists is in need of Him, while He has need of nothing and does not depend on any causes or conditions.

God, the Exalted, says, "Lo! in the heavens and the earth are portents for believers. And in your creation, and all the beasts that He scattereth in the earth, are portents for a folk whose faith is sure. And the difference of night and day and the provision that Allah sendeth down from the sky and thereby quickeneth the earth after her death, and the ordering of the winds, are portents for a people who have sense. These are the protents of Allah which we recite unto thee (Muhammad) with truth. Then in what fact, after Allah and His portents, will they believe?" (Qur'an, XLV, 3-6).

Every reality in this world which we can possibly imagine is a limited reality, that it, one whose actualization depends upon certain necessary causes and conditions. If these do not exist that reality cannot exist in the world. Every reality has a boundary beyond which it cannot extend its existence. Only God is such that He has no limit or boundary, for His reality is absolute and He exists in His Infinity no matter how we try to conceive of Him. His Being does not depend upon and is not in need of any causes or conditions. It is clear that in the case of something limitless we cannot conceive of multiplicity, for any supposedly second reality will be other than the first, as a result of which each would be limited and bound and would set a boundary to the reality of the other. For example, if we consider a limitless volume we cannot conceive another limitless volume alongside it. And if we do suppose another, it will be the same as the first. Therefore, God is one and has no partner.

[A] . . . Bedouin approached cAli in the middle of the fighting during the Battle of the Camel and asked if he asserted that God was one. In answer cAli said, "To say that God is one has four meanings: Two of those meanings are false and two correct. As for the two incorrect meanings, one is that one should say 'God is one' and be thinking of number and counting. This meaning is false because that which has no second cannot enter into the category of number. Do you not see that those who said that God is the third of a trinity [i.e., the Christians] fell into infidelity? Another meaning is to say that so and so is one of this people, namely a species of this genus or a member of this species. This meaning also is not correct when applied to God, for it implies likening something to God and God is above all likeness.

"As for the two meanings which are correct when applied to God, one is that it should be said that God is one in the sense that there is no likeness unto Him among things. God possesses such uniqueness. And one is to say that God is one in the sense that there is no multiplicity or division conceivable in Him, neither outwardly nor in the mind nor in the imagination. God possesses such a unity." (*Bihar al-anwar*, vol. II, p. 65)

cAli has also said, "To know God is to know His Oneness." (*Bihar al-anwar*, vol. II, p. 186). This means that to prove that the Being of God is unlimited and infinite suffices to prove His Oneness, for to conceive a second for the Infinite is impossible. There is therefore no need of any other proofs, although there exist many others.

*   *   *

If we analyze the nature of a human being, we see that he has an essence which is his individual humanity and also qualities through which his essence is known, such as the quality of being born in such a land, or being the son of such a person, or being learned and capable, or tall and handsome; or he possesses the contrary of these qualities. Some of these qualities, like the first and second, can never be separated from the essence, and others, like being learned or capable, have the possibility of separation and alternation. Yet all are different from the essence and at the same time different from each other.

This point, namely the difference between the essence and qualities and between the qualities themselves, is the best proof that an essence that has qualities, and a quality that makes known in essence, are both limited and finite. For if the essence were limitless and infinite it would encompass the qualities as well, and also the qualities would include each other, and as a result all would become one. For example, the essence of man would be the same as capability and also capability the same as knowledge; height and beauty would be the same; and all of these would possess the same meaning.

From this example it is clear that the Divine Essence cannot be conceived to have qualities in the sense that human beings have qualities. A quality can come about only through setting limits and the Divine Essence transcends all limitations (even the limitation of this transcendence which in reality is a quality).

* * *

In the world of creation we are aware of many perfections which appear in the form of qualities. These are positive qualities which, wherever they appear, make the object of which they are the quality more perfect and increase its ontological value, as can be seen clearly in the comparison between the live being such as man and a lifeless one such as a stone. Doubtless God has created and bestowed these perfections upon creatures; if He had not possessed them in their fullness Himself He could not have bestowed them upon otherse and perfected others through them. Therefore, if we follow the judgment of sound reasoning we must conclude that God, the Creator, has knowledge, power, and every other real perfection. Furthermore, as has already been mentioned, the marks of His knowledge and power and, as a result, the marks of life are seen in the order of the cosmos.

But because the Divine Essence is limitless and infinite these perfections which are shown to be His Qualities are in reality the same as His Essence and one with each other. The difference observed between the Essence and the Qualities and at the same time between the Qualities themselves is only on the plane of concepts. Essentially there is but one Reality involved which is one and indivisible.

In order to avoid the inadmissible error of limiting the Essence through attributing qualities to it or denying the principle of perfection in it, Islam has commanded its followers to preserve a just balance between affirmation and negation. It has ordered them to believe that God has knowledge but not like the knowledge of others. He has power but not like the power of others. He hears but not with ears. He sees but not with eyes like those of men, and so on.

* * *

Qualities in general are of two types: qualities of perfection, and qualities of imperfection. Qualities of perfection, as mentioned above, are of a positive nature and give higher ontological value and greater ontological effect to the object that they qualify. This is clear from the comparison between a live, knowing and capable being and a dead being which lacks knowledge and capability. Qualities of imperfection are the reverse of such qualities. When we analyze these imperfect qualities we see that they are negative and show a lack of perfection, such as ignorance, impatience, ugliness, illness, and the like. Therefore, it can be said that the negation of the quality of imperfection is the quality of perfection. For example, the negation of ignorance is knowledge and the negation of impotence is power and capability.

For this reason the Holy Qur'an has related each positive quality directly to God and negated every quality of imperfection from Him, attributing the negation of such imperfections to Him, as He says: "He is the knower, the Omnipotent," or He says, "He is the Alive" or "Neither slumber nor sleep overtaketh Him," or "Know that ye cannot frustrate Allah."

The point that must never be forgotten is that God, the Most Exalted, is Absolute Reality without any limit or boundary. Therefore, a positive quality attributed to Him will not possess any limitation. He is not material and corporeal or limited to space and time. While possessing all positive qualities He is beyond every quality and state which belongs to creatures. Every quality which in reality belongs to Him is purified from the notion of limitedness, as He says, "Nought is as His likeness." (Qur'an, XLII, 11)

* * *

In addition, qualities are also divided into qualities of essence and qualities of action. A quality sometimes depends only on the qualified itself, such as life, knowledge and power, which depend on the person of a living, knowing and capable human being. We can conceive of man in himself possessing those qualities without taking into consideration any other factor.

At other times a quality does not depend only on the qualified in itself, but, in order to qualify, it also requires the existence of something external as in the case of writing, conversation, desire, and the like. A person can be a writer if he possesses ink, pen, and paper, and he can converse when there is someone with whom to speak. In the same way he can desire when there is an object of desire. The sole existence of man is not sufficient to bring these qualities into existence.

From this analysis it becomes clear that the Divine Qualities which are the same as God's Essence, as already pointed out, are only of the first kind. As for the second kind, whose actualization depends upon an external factor, they cannot be considered as Qualities of the Essence and the same as the Essence, for all that is other than God is created by Him and so, being situated in the created order, comes after Him.

Qualities that pertain to God after the act of creation such as creator, omnipotent, giver of life, giver of death, sustainer, etc., are not the same as His Essence but are additional to it; they are Qualities of Action. By Quality of Action is meant that after the actualization of an act the meaning of a quality is understood from that act, not from the Essence (that performs the act), such as "Creator", which is conceived after the act of creation has taken place. From the creation is understood the quality of God as Creator. That quality depends upon creation, not upon the sacred Essence of God, the Most Exalted, Himself, so that the Essence does not change from one state to another with the appearance of that quality. Shi^cism considers the two qualities of will (*iradah*) and speech (*kalam*) in their literal meaning as Qualities of Action (will meaning wanting something and speech meaning conveying a meaning through an expression). Most of the Sunni theologians consider them as implying knowledge and thereby take them to be Qualities of Essence.

* * *

The law of causality reigns throughout the world of existence without any breach or exception. According to this law each phenomenon in this world depends for its coming into being upon causes and conditions which make its actualization possible. If all of these causes, which are called the complete cause (the sufficient and necessary cause), are actualized, the coming into being of that phenomenon, or the assumed effect, becomes determined and necessary. And assuming the lack of all or some of these causes, the actualization of the phenomenon is impossible. Investigation and analysis of this thesis will clarify this point for us.

(1) If we compare a phenomenon (or effect) with the whole, complete (or sufficient) cause, and also with the parts of the complete cause, its relation

to the complete cause is based on necessity and on a completely determined relationship. At the same time its relation to each of the parts of the complete cause (which are called incomplete or partial causes) is one of possibility and lack of complete determinism. These causes provide the effect only with the possibility of existence, not with its necessity.

The world of existence, in its totality, therefore, is governed throughout by necessity because each of its parts has a necessary connection with its complete cause by the very fact of coming into being. Its structure is composed of a series of necessary and certain events. Yet, the character of possibility is preserved in its parts if we consider each part separately and in itself in the phenomena which are related and connected to partial causes which are other than their complete cause.

The Holy Qur'an in its teachings has called this reign of necessity Divine Destiny (*qada'*), for this necessity issues from that Source that gives existence to the world and is therefore a command (*hukm*) and "Divine Decree" that is certain and is impossible to breach or disobey. It is based on justice and accepts no exception or discrimination. God Almighty says, "verily His is all creation and commandment" (Qur'an, VII, 54), and "When He decreeth [*qada*] a thing. He saith unto it only: Be! and it is" (Qur'an, II, 117), and also "(When) Allah doometh there is none that can postpone His doom [*hukm*]" (Qur'an, XIII, 41).

(2) Each part of the cause provides the appropriate measure and "model" for the effect, and the coming into being of the effect is in accordance with the totality of the measures determined for it by the complete cause. For example, the causes that make respiration possible for man do not cause respiration in the absolute and unconditioned sense; rather they send a determined time and with a determined shape. Likewise, the causes of men's vision (including man himself) do not bring into being vision which, through the means and organs provided, is limited and measured for men in every respect. This truth is to be found without exception in all the phenomena of the world and all the events that occur in it.

The Holy Qur'an has called this aspect of the truth "Providence" (*qadar*) and has related it to God Almighty who is the origin of creation, as has been said, "And there is not a thing but with Us are the stores thereof. And we send it not down save in appointed measure [*qadar*]" (Qur'an, XV, 21).

In the same way that according to Divine Destiny the existence of each phenomenon and event which occurs in the cosmic order is necessary and cannot be avoided, so also according to Providence each phenomenon and event that occurs will never trespass or disobey in the least degree the measure which God has provided for it... .

William Chittick (Tr.)

Prophet Muhammad

Abu ᶜAbdullah (the sixth Imam) has related from his fathers that the Prophet of God — God bless him and his household — said in one of his sermons, "Praise belongs to God, who in His firstness (*awwaliyyah*) was solitary and in His beginninglessness (*azaliyyah*) was tremendously exalted through divinity and supremely great through His magnificence and power. He originated that which He produced and brought into being that which He created without a model (*mithal*) preceding anything that He created. Our Lord, the eternal (*al-qadim*), unstitched (the heavens and the earth) through the subtlety (*lutf*) of His lordship and the knowledge within His omniscience, created all that He created through the laws of His power (*qudrah*), and split (the sky) through the light of dawn. So none changes His creation, none alters His handiwork, 'none repels His law' (XIII, 45), non rejects His command. There is no place of rest away from His call (*daᶜwah*), no cessation to His dominion and no interruption of His term. He is the truly existent (*al-qaymum*) from the first and the truly enduring (*al-daymum*) forever. He is veiled from His creatures by His light in the high horizon, in the towering might, and in the lofty dominion. He is above all things and below all things. So He manifested Himself (*tajalla*) to His creation without being seen, and He transcends being gazed upon. He wanted to be distinguished by the profession of Unity (*tawhid*) when he withdrew behind the veil of His light, rose high in His exaltation and consecrated Himself from His creation.

"He sent to them messengers so they might be His conclusive argument against His creatures and so His messengers to them might be witnesses against them. He sent among them prophets bearing good tidings and warning, 'that whosoever perished might perish by a clear sign, and by a clear sign he might live who lived' (VIII, 42) and that the servants might understand of their Lord that of which they had been ignorant, recognize Him in His Lordship after they had denied (it) and profess His Unity in His divinity after they had stubbornly resisted."

*   *   *

Ibn ᶜAbbas related that a Jew, called Naᶜthal, stood up before the Prophet of God — upon whom be blessings and peace — and said, "O Muhammad, verily I will ask thee about certain things which have been repeating themselves in my breast for some time. If thou answerest them for me I will embrace Islam at thy hand."

The Prophet said, "Ask, O Abu ᶜUmmarah!"

Then he said, "O Muhammad, describe for me thy Lord."

He answered, "Surely the Creator cannot be described except by that with which He has described Himself—and how should one describe that Creator whom the senses cannot perceive, imaginations cannot attain, thoughts (*khatarat*) cannot delimit and sight cannot encompass? Greater is He than what the depicters describe! He is distant in His nearness and near in His distance. He fashions (*kayyaf*) 'howness' (*kayfiyyah*), so it is not said of Him, 'How?' (*kayf*); He determines (*ayyan*) the 'where' (*ayn*), so it is not said of Him, 'Where?' (*ayn*). He sunders 'howness (*kayfufiyyah*) and 'whereness' (*aynuniyyah*), so He is "One. . . . the Everlasting Refuge" (CXII, 1-2), as He has described Himself. But depicters do not attain to His description. 'He has not begotten, and has not been begotten, and equal to Him is not any one' (CXII, 3-4).

Naᶜthal said, "Thou hast spoken the truth. O Muhammad, tell me about thy saying, 'Surely He is One, there is none like (*shabih*) Him.' Is not God one and man one? And thus His oneness (*wahdaniyyah*) resembles the oneness of man."

He answered, "God is one, but single in meaning (*ahadi al-maᶜna*), while man is one but dual in meaning (*thanawai al-maᶜna*); corporeal substance (*jism*) and accidents (*ᶜarad*), body (*badan*) and spirit (*ruh*). Similarity (*tashbih*) pertains only to the meanings."

Naᶜthal said, "Thou hast spoken the truth, O Muhammad."

ᶜAli, the First Imam

It was related by ᶜAli ibn Musa al-Rida (the eighth Imam) from the earlier Imams in succession that al-Husayn ibn ᶜAli (the third Imam) spoke as follows: The Commander of the Faithful—upon whom be peace—addressed the people of the mosque at Kufah and said:

"Praise belongs to God, who did not originate from anything, nor did He bring what exists into being from anything. His beginninglessness is attested to by the temporality (*huduth*) of things, His power by the impotence with which He has branded them, and His everlastingness (*dawam*) by the annihiliation (*fana'*) which He has forced upon them. No place is empty of Him that He might be perceived through localization (*ayniyyah*), no object (*shabah*) is like Him that He might be described by quality (*kayfiyyah*), nor is He absent from anything that He might be known through situation (*haythiyyah*)... .

"The first step in religion is knowledge (*ma'rifah*) of Him. The perfection of knowledge of Him is to confirm Him (*tasdiq*). The perfection of confirming Him is to profess His unity (*tawhid*). The perfection of profession His Unity is sincerity (*ikhlas*) towards Him. And the perfection of sincerity towards Him is to negate attributes (*nafy al-sifat*) from Him, because of the testimony of every attribute that it is not that which possesses the attribute (*al-mawsuf*) and the testimony of everything that possesses attributes that it is not the attribute.

"So whoso describes God—glory be to Him—has given Him a comrade (i.e. the description). Whoso gives Him a comrade has declared Him to be two (*tathniyah*). Whoso declares Him to be two has divided Him. Whoso divides Him is ignorant of Him. (Whoso is ignorant of Him points to Him). Whoso points to Him has delimited Him. Whoso delimits Him has numbered Him. Whoso says, 'In what is He?', has enclosed Him. Whoso says, 'On what is He?' has excluded Him (from certain things).

'He is a being (*ka'in*) not as the result of temporal origin (*hadath*), an existent (*mawjud*) not (having come) from nonexistence (*'adam*). He is with everything, not through association (*muqaranah*); and He is other than everything, not through separation (*muzayalah*). He is active (*fa'il*), not in the sense of possessing movement and instruments. He was seeing when there was none of His creatures to be observed by Him. He was 'alone' (*mutawahhid*) when there was none with whom to be intimate and at whose loss to feel lonely.

"He originated creation and gave to it its beginning without employing deliberation, profiting from experience, occasioning movement (*harakah*, i.e. in Himself), or being disrupted by the cares of the soul (*hamamah nafs*). He delays things to their times, mends their discrepancies, implants (in them) their natural dispositions, and makes these (dispositions) adhere to their objects. He has knowledge of them before their beginning, encompasses their limits (*hudud*) and their end (*intiha'*) and knows their relationships (*qara'in*) and aspects (*ahna'*).".. .

* * *

Ja'far al-Sadiq, the Sixth Imam

Abu Basir has related that he said to Abu 'Abdallah—upon whom be peace—"Tell me about God, the Mighty and Majestic. Will believers see Him on the Day of Resurrection?"

He answered, "Yes, and they have already seen Him before the Day of Resurrection."

Abu Basir asked, "When?"

The Imam answered, "When He said to them, 'Am I not your Lord? They said: 'Yes, verily' (VII, 172). Then he was quiet for a time. Then he said, "Truly the believers see him in this world before the Day of Resurrection. Doest thou not see Him now?"

Abu Basir then said to him, "That I might be made thy sacrifice! Shall I relate this (to others) from thee?"

He answered, "No, for if thou relatest it, a denier ignorant of the meaning of what thou sayest will deny it. Then he will suppose that it is a comparison and unbelief (*kufr*). But seeing with the heart (*al-ru'yah bi-l-qalb*) is not like seeing with the eyes (*al-ru'yay bi-l-ᶜayn*). High be God exalted above what the comparers (*mushabbihun*) and heretics (*mulhidun*) describe!"

* * *

It has been related that Abu ᶜAbdallah said, "The name of God is other than God, and everything that can be called by the name of a 'thing' (*shay'*) is created, except God. Therefore all that tongues express or is worked by hands is created. God is the goal of him who sets Him as his goal, but the determined goal (*al-mughayya*, i.e., in the mind of man) is other than the (real) goal. The goal possesses attributes (*mawsuf*), and all that possesses attributes has been fashioned (*masnuᶜ*). But the Fashioner (*saniᶜ*) of things does not possess the attributes of any stated limit (*hadd musamma*). He has not come into being that His Being (*kaynunah*) should be known through fashioning (*sunᶜ*) (carried out) by other than He. He does not terminate at a limit unless it be other than He. Whoso understands this principle (*hukm*) will never fall into error. It is the unadulterated profession of Unity (*al-tawhid al-khalis*), so believe in it, confirm it, and understand it well, with God's permission—the Mighty and Majestic.

"Whoso maintains that he knows God by means of a veil (*hijab*) or a form (*surah*) or a likeness (*mithal*) is an associator (*mushrik*), for the veil, the likeness and the form are other than He. He is utterly and only One. So how should he who maintains that he knows Him by means of other than Him be professing Unity? Surely He alone knows God who knows Him by means of God (*billah*). Therefore, whoso knows Him not only by means of Him knows Him not. On the contrary, he only knows other than Him. There is nothing between the Creator and the created. God is the Creator of things, but not from something. He is *named* by His names, so He is other than His names, and His names are other than He. The described (*al-mawsuf*) is other than the describer (*al-wasif*).

"Then whoso maintains that he has faith in that which he does not know has gone astray from knowledge (*ma'rifah*). A created thing (*makhluq*) perceives nothing unless by means of God: the knowledge of God is perceived only by means of God. But God is empty of His creatures and His creatures are empty of Him. When He desires a thing, it is as He desires, by His command (*amr*) and without speech (*nutq*). His servants have no refuge from that which He decrees (*ma qada*), and they have no argument against that which is His pleasure. They have no power to act or to deal with that which is brought about in their bodies, created (by God), except by means of their Lord. So whoso maintains that he is able to perform an act which God, the Mighty and Majestic, does not desire, has maintained that his will (*iradah*) prevails over the Will of God. 'Blessed be God' the Lord of all beings!" (VII, 54).... .

'Ali al-Rida, the Eighth Imam

It has been related that when al-Ma'mun desired to install al-Rida (as his successor), he collected together Banu Hashim and said to them, "Verily I desire to install al-Rida in this affair after me.

Banu Hashim envied al-Rida and said, "Thou appointest an ignorant man who possesses not the insight to direct the caliphate. Therefore send for him. He will come to us and thou wilt see how his ignorance decides thee against him." So he sent for him and he came. Banu Hashim said to him, "O Abu al-Hasan! Ascend the pulpit and display for us a sign whereby we may worship God."

So he ascended the pulpit and sat for a long time, his head bowed in silence. Then he trembled a great trembling and stood up straight, praised and lauded God, and asked His blessing for His prophet and his household. Then he said, "The first element in the worship of God is knowledge of Him, the root (*asl*) of knowledge of Him is to profess His Unity (*tawhid*), and the correct way (*nizam*) to profess the Unity of God is to negate attributes from Him. For the powers of reason testify that every attribute and everything possessing an attribute (*mawsuf*) is created. Everything possessing an attribute testifies that it has a Creator which is neither attribute nor possesses an attribute. Every attribute and everything possessing an attribute testify to connection (*iqtiran*), between the attribute and that to which it is attributed. Connection testifies to temporality (*hadath*). And temporality testifies that it accepts not the Beginningless, which accepts not the temporal.

"So it is not *God* whose Essence is known through comparison. It is not *His* Unity that is professed by someone who attempts to fathom Him. It is not *His* reality (*haqiqah*) that is attained by someone who strikes a similitude for Him. It is not *He* who is confirmed (*tasdiq*) by him who professes an end for Him. It is not *He* to whom repairs he who points to Him. It is not *He* who is meant by him who compares Him (to something). It is not to *Him* that he who divides Him into parts humbles himself. And it is not *He* who is desired by him who conceives of Him in his imagination.

"Everything that can be known in itself (*bi-nafsihi*) is fashioned (*masnuᶜ*). All that stands apart from Him is an effect (*maᶜlul*). God is inferred from what He fashions (*sunᶜ*), the knowledge of Him is made fast by the powers of reason, and the argument (*hujjah*) for Him is established by (man's) primordial nature (*al-fitrah*).

"God's creating of the creatures is a veil between Him and them. His separation (*mubayanah*) from them is that He is disengaged from their localization (*ayniyyah*). That He is their origin (*ibtida'*) is proof for them that He has no origin, for none that has an origin can originate others. That He has created them possessing means (of accomplishing things) is proof that He has no means (*adah*), for means are witness to the poverty of those who use them.

"So His names are an expression (*taᶜbir*), His acts (*afᶜal*) are (a way) to make (Him) understood (*tafhim*), and His Essence is Reality (*haqiqah*). His innermost center (*kunh*) separates (*tafriq*) Him from creation, and His otherness (*ghuyur*) limits (*tahdid*) what is other than He. Therefore ignorant of God is he who asks for Him to be described! Transgressing against Him is he who seeks to encompass Him! Mistaken is he who imagines to have fathomed Him!

"Whoso says 'how?' has compared Him (to something). Whoso says 'why?' has professed for Him a cause (*taᶜlil*). Whoso says 'when?' has determined Him in time (*tawqit*). Whoso says 'in what?' has enclosed Him (*tadmin*). Whoso says 'to what?' has professed for Him a limit (*tanhiyah*). Whoso says 'until what?' has given Him an end (*taghiyah*). Whoso gives Him an end has associated an end with Him. Whoso associates an end with Him has divided Him. Whoso divides Him has described Him. Whoso describes Him has deviated from the straight path (*ilhad*) concerning Him.

"God does not change with the changes undergone by creation, just as he does not become limited by delimiting (*tahdid*) that which is limited (*al-mahdud*). He is One (*ahad*), not according to the explanation offered by number (*ta'wil ᶜadad*); Outward, not according to the explanation of being immediate (to the senses); Manifest, not through the appearance of a vision (of Him); Inward (*batin*), not through separation (*muzayalah*); Apart (*muba'in*), not through distance; Near, not through approach; Subtle, not through corporealization; Existent, not after nonexistence; Active, not through coercion; Determining, not through the activity of thought (*jawl fikrah*); Directing (*mudabbir*), not through movement; Desiring, not through resolution; Willing (*shaʾ*), not through directing attention (*himmah*); Grasping (*mudrik*), not through touch (*majassah*); Hearing, not through means; and Seeing, not through organs.

"Times accompany Him not, places enclose Him not, slumber seizes Him not, attributes delimit Him not, and instruments (*adawat*) are of no use to Him. His being (*kawn*) precedes times (*al-awqat*), His existence (*wujud*) non-existence and His beginninglessness (*azal*) beginning (*al-ibtidaʾ*).

"By His giving senses to the sense organs it is known that He has no sense organs. By His giving substance to substance it is known that He has no substance. By His causing opposition among things it is known that He has no opposite. By His causing affiliation among affairs it is known that He has no affiliate. He opposes darkness to light, obscurity to clarity, moisture to solidity, and heat to cold. He joins together those things which are hostile to one another and separates those which are near. They prove (the existence of) their Separator by their separation and their Joiner by their junction. That is (the meaning of) His words — He is the Mighty and Majestic — 'And of everything created We two kinds; haply you will remember' (LI, 49).

"So through them He separated 'before' and 'after' that it might be known that He has no before and after. They testify with their temperament that He who gave them temperaments has no temperament. They prove by their disparity (*tafawut*) that He who made them disparate has no disparity. They announce through their subjection to time that He who subjected them to time is not subject to it Himself.

"He veiled some of them from others so that it might be known that there is no veil between Him and them other than them. His is the meaning of lordship (*al-rububiyyah*) when there was none over whom He was Lord, the reality of godhood (*al-ilahiyyah*) when there was nothing for whom He was God, the meaning of Knower when there was nothing to be known, the meaning of Creator (*khaliq*) when there was nothing created (*makhluq*) and the import of hearing when there was nothing to be heard. It is not because He created that He deserves the meaning (of the term) 'Creator' and not because He brought the creatures into being that the meaning of 'making' is derived.

"How (should it not be so)? For *mudh* ('ever since') conceals Him not, *qad* ('already') brings Him not near, *laʿalla* ('perhaps') veils Him not, *mata* ('when?') limits Him not in time, *hin* ('at the time of') contains Him not, and *maʿ* ('with') brings Him not into association. Instruments (*adawat*) limit only themselves and means (*alah*) allude only unto their own like. Their activities are found only in things. *Mudh* withholds things from being eternal (*qidmah*), *qad* shields them from beginninglessness, and *law la* ('if only') wards off perfection (*al-takmilah*). Things become separate and prove (the existence of) their Separator. They become distinguished and prove their Distinguisher (*muba'in*). Through them their Maker manifests Himself to the powers of reason. Through (these power) He becomes veiled to sight, to them imaginations appeal for a decision, in them is substantiated (only) other than Him, from them is suspended the proof and through them He makes known to them the acknowledgement (*al-iqrar*).

"Confirmation (*tasdiq*) of God is made fast by the powers of reason, and faith (*iman*) in Him reaches perfection through acknowledgment. There is no religiosity (*diyanah*) except after knowledge (*ma'rifah*), no knowledge except through sincerity (*ikhlas*) and no sincerity along with comparison. There is no negation (*nafy*) of comparison if there is affirmation (*ithbat*) of attributes.

"So nothing in creation is found in its Creator. All that is possible in it is impossible in its Maker. Movement (*harakah*) and stillness (*sukun*) do not affect Him. How should that which He effects (in others) have effect upon Him, or that which He has originated recur for Him? Then His Essence would be disparate, His inmost center divided, His signification (*ma'na*) prevented from eternity. How would the Creator have a meaning different from the created?

"If something from behind limited Him, then something in front would limit Him. If perfection (*tamam*) were seeking Him, imperfection would be upon Him. How should that which does not transcend (*imtina'*) temporality be worthy of (the Name) 'Beginningless'? How should that which does not transcend being produced (*insha'*) the producer of things (of the world?) There then would have arisen in Him a sign of having been made (*al-masnu'*) and He would become a proof (*dalil*) after having been the proven (*madlul 'alayh*).

"There is no argument in absurd opinions (such as the above), no answer when it (absurdity) is asked about, no glorification of Him in its meaning. Nor is there any ill in distinguishing Him from creation, unless it be that the Eternal accepts not to be made two, nor the Beginningless to have a beginning.

"There is no god but God, the All-high, the Tremendous. They have cried lies who ascribe equals to God! They have gone astray into far error and suffered a manifest loss! And God bless Muhammad and his household, the pure.".. .

Chapter Eleven

The Shi'i View of Revelation and Prophecy

Revelation and prophecy are complementary channels, doctrinally speaking, through which the Divine Will is transmitted to humanity. According to Islam, the cycles of revelations come to a closure with Prophet Muhammad. This closure is both final and primal. Thus the Qur'an is the last revelation and the revelation; Muhammad is the last Prophet and the Prophet; and umma is the last divinely ordained community as well as its universal expression. In the following two passages, first, ʿAllamah Tabataba'i analyzes the central significance of revelation for the human community, and then ʿAllamah al-Hilli, in a passage translated by I. K. A. Howard and S. M. Waris Hasan, discusses the position of the messenger or the transmitter of Divine Will. The passages are taken from SI, pages 142–49 and 151–56, and Alserat, pages 3–11, respectively.

ᶜAllamah Tabataba'i

If we delve into the matter carefully, we will discover that man seeks continuously those laws which can bring him happiness in the world; that people as individuals and in groups recognize, in accordance with their God-given nature, the necessity for laws which provide felicity for them without discrimination or exception, laws which establish a general norm of perfection among mankind. Obviously, up to now, during the different periods of human history, there have not come into being any such laws which were devised by human reason. If the laws of existence had placed the burden of creating such human laws upon the shoulders of human reason, then during the long period of history such laws would have been established. In that case, each individual who possesses the power of reasoning would comprehend this human law in detail in the same way that everyone realizes the necessity for such laws in society.

In other words, if it had been in the very nature of things that it be the duty of human reason to create a perfect common law which must provide happiness for human society, and that man should be guided to that perfect law through the process of creation and the generation of the world itself, then such laws would have been apprehended by each human being through his reason in the same way that man knows what is of benefit or detriment to him throughout the determined course of daily life. There is, however, as yet no sign of the presence of such laws. Laws which have come about by themselves, or have been devised by a single ruler, or individuals, or nations, and have become prevalent in different societies are considered by some as certain, and by others as doubtful. Some are aware of these laws and others are ignorant of them. Never has it come to pass that they are endowed by God with reason, should have a common awareness of the details of the laws which can bring about happiness in the world of man.

* * *

Thus, in the light of the discussion above, it becomes clear that the laws which can guarantee the happiness of human society cannot be perceived by reason. Since according to the thesis of general guidance running throughout creation the existence of an awareness of these laws in the human species is necessary, there must be another power of apprehension within the human species which enables man to understand the real duties of life and which places this knowledge within the reach of everyone. This consciousness and power of perception, which is other than reason and sense, is called the prophetic consciousness, or the consciousness of revelation. Of course the presence of such a power in mankind does not mean that it should necessarily appear in all individuals, in the same way that although the power of the enjoyment of marriage and being prepared for this enjoyment is possible only for those who have reached the age of puberty. In the same way that the consciousness of revelation is a mysterious and unknown form of consciousness for those who do not possess it, the apprehension of the joy of sexual union is a mysterious and unknown feeling for those who have not reached the age of puberty.

God, the Exalted, makes reference in His Word to the revelation of His Divine Law (*Shari'ah*) and the inability of human reason to comprehend this matter in the verses: "Lo! We inspire thee as We inspired Noah and the prophets after him, as We inspired Abraham and Ishmael and Isaac and Jacob and the tribes, and Jesus and Job and Jonah and Aaron and Solomon, and we imparted unto David the Psalms; and messengers We have mentioned unto thee before and messengers We have not mentioned unto thee; and Allah spoke directly unto Moses; Messengers of good cheer and of warning, in order that mankind might have no argument against Allah after the messengers" (Qur'an, IV, 163–165).

* * *

The appearance of prophets affirms the conception of revelation outlined above. The prophets of God were men who propagated the call of revelation and prophecy and brought definitive proofs for their call. They propagatged among people the elements of the religion of God (which is the same divine law that guarantees happiness) and made it available to all men.

Since in all periods of history the number of people endowed with the power of prophecy and revelation has been limited to a few individuals, God — the Most Exalted — has completed and perfected the guidance of the rest of mankind by placing the mission of the propagation of religion upon the shoulders of His prophets. That is why a prophet of God must possess the quality of inerrancy (*'ismah*). In receiving the revelation from God, in guarding it and in making possible its reaching the people, he must be free from error. He must not commit sin (*ma'siyah*). The reception of revelation, its preservation and its propagation are three principles of ontological guidance; and error in existence itself is meaningless. Furthermore, sin and opposition to the claims of the religious call and its propagation are impossible in a prophet for they would be a call against the original religious mission; they would destroy the confidence of the people, their reliance upon the truth and the validity of the call. As a result they would destroy the purpose of the religious call itself.

God, the Exalted, refers in His word to the inerrancy of the prophets, saying, "And We chose them and guided them unto a straight path" (Qur'an, VI, 88). And also, "(He is) the Knower of the Unseen, and He revealeth unto none His secret, save unto every messenger whom He hath chosen, and then He maketh a guard to go before him and a guard behind him, that He may know that they have indeed conveyed the messages of their Lord" (Qur'an, LXXII, 26-28).

* * *

What the prophets of God received through revelation and as a message from God and conveyed to mankind was religion (*din*), that is, a way of life and human duties which guarantee the real happiness of a man.

Revealed religion in general consists of two parts: doctrine and practice or method. The doctrinal part of revealed religion consists of a series of fundamental principles and views concerning the real nature of things upon which man must establish the foundations of his life. It is comprised of the three universal principles of unity (*tawhid*), prophecy (*nubuwwah*), and eschatology (*macad*). If there is any confusion or disorder in one of these principles the religion will not be able to gain any following.

The practical part of revealed religion consists of a series of moral and practical injunctions covering the duties man has before God and human society. That is why the secondary duties which have been ordered for man in different Divine laws are of two kinds: morals (*akhlaq*), and actions (*acmal*). The morals and actions related to the Divine are of two kinds, such as: first, the quality of faith, sincerity, surrender to God, contentment and humility; and second, the daily prayers, fasting, and sacrifice (called acts of worship and symbolizing the humility and servitude of man before the Divine Throne). The morals and actions related to human society are also of two kinds, such as: first, the quality of love for other men, wishing well for others, justice and generosity; and second, the duty to carry out social intercourse, trade and exchange, etc. (called transactions).

Another point that must be considered is that since the human species is directed toward the gradual attainment of perfection, and human society through the passage of time becomes more complete, the appearance of a parallel development must also be seen in revealed laws. The Holy Qur'an affirms this gradual development, which reason has also discovered. It can be concluded from its verses that each Divine Law (*Sharicah*) is in reality more complete than the *Sharicah* before; for instance, in this verse where He says, "And unto thee have We revealed the Scripture with the truth, confirming whatever Scripture was before it, and a watcher over it." (Qur'an V, 48) Of course, as scientific knowledge also confirms and the Qur'an states, the life of human society in this world is not eternal and the development of man is not endless. As a result, the general principles governing the duties of man from the point of view of doctrine and practice must of necessity stop at a particular stage. Therefore, prophecy and the *Sharicah* will also one day come to an end when in the perfection of doctrine and expansion of practical regulations they have reached the final stage of their development. That is why the Holy Qur'an, in order to make clear that Islam (the religion of Muhammad) is the last and most complete of the revealed religions, introduces itself as a sacred book that cannot be abrogated (*naskh*), calls the Prophet the "Seal of the Prophets" (*khatam al-anbiya'*), and sees the Islamic religion as embracing all religious duties. As He says, "For lo! it is an unassailable Scripture. Falsehood cannot come at it from before it or behind it" (Qur'an, XLI, 41-42). And also, "Muhammad is not the father of any man among you but he is the messenger of Allah and the Seal of the prophets" (Qur'an, XXXIII, 40). And, "We reveal the scripture unto thee as an exposition of all things" (Qur'an, XVI, 89).

*   *   *

Many modern scholars who have investigated the problem of revelation and prophecy have tried to explain revelation, prophecy and questions connected with them by using the principles of social psychology. They say that the prophets of God were men of a pure nature and strong will who had great love for humanity. In order to enable mankind to advance spiritually and materially and in order to reform decadent societies, they devised laws and regulations and invited mankind to accept them. Since people in those days would not accept the logic of human reason, in order to make them obey their teachings the prophets, according to such modern scholars, claimed that they and their thoughts came from the transcendent world. Each prophet called his own pure soul the Holy Spirit; the teachings which he claimed came from the transcendent world were called "revelation and prophecy"; the duties which resulted from the teachings were called "revealed *Sharicah*"; and the written record of these teachings and duties were called a "revealed book."

Anyone who views with depth and impartiality the revealed books and especially the Holy Qur'an, and also the lives of the prophets, will have no doubt that this view is not correct. The prophets of God were not political men. Rather they were "men of God," full of truthfulness and purity. What they perceived they proclaimed without addition or diminution. And what they uttered they acted upon. What they claimed to possess was a mysterious consciousness which the invisible world had bestowed upon them. In this way they came to know from God Himself what the welfare of men was in this world and the next, and propagated this knowledge among mankind.

It is quite clear that in order to confirm and ascertain the call of prophecy there is need of proof and demonstration. The sole fact that the *Shariᶜah* brought by a prophet conforms to reason is not sufficient in determining the truthfulness of the prophetic call. A man who claims to be a prophet, in addition to the claim of the truth of his *Shariᶜah*, claims a connection through revelation and prophecy with the transcendent world, and therefore claims that he has been given by God the mission to propagate the faith. This claim in itself is in need of proof. That is why (as the Holy Qur'an informs us) the common people with their simple mentality always sought miracles from the prophets of God in order that the truthfulness of their call might be confirmed.

The meaning of this simple and correct logic is that the revelation which the prophet claims is his cannot be found among others who are human beings like him. It is of necessity an invisible power which God miraculously bestows upon His prophets, through which they hear His word and are given the mission to convey this word to mankind. If this be true, then the prophet should ask God for another miracle so that people would believe the truth of his prophetic call.

It is thus clear that the request for miracles from prophets is according to correct logic and it is incumbent upon the prophet of God to provide a miracle at the beginning of his call, or according to the demand of the people, in order to provie his prophecy. The Holy Qur'an has affirmed this logic, relating miracles about many prophets at the beginning of their mission or after their followers requested them.

Of course many modern investigators and scientists have denied miracles, but their opinions are not based upon any satisfactory reasons. There is no reason to believe that the causes which until now have been discovered for events through investigation and experiment are permanent and unchanging, or that no event ever occurs for reasons other than those which usually bring it about. The miracles related about the prophets of God are not impossible or against reason (as is, for example, the claim that the number three is even). Rather they are a "break in what is habitual" (*kharq-i ᶜadat*), an occurrence which, incidentally, has often been observed in a lower degree among people following ascetic practices.

* * *

It is known through tradition that in the past many prophets appeared, and the Holy Qur'an affirms their multitude. It has mentioned some of them by name or by their characteristics, but has not given their exact number. Through definitive traditions also it has not been possible to determine their number except in the well-known saying which Abu Zarr Ghifari has recited from the Holy Prophet, according to which their number has been set at 124,000.

* * *

From what can be deduced from the Qur'an, it can be concluded that all the prophets of God did not bring a *Shari͑ah*. Rather, five of them — Noah, Abraham, Moses, Jesus, and the Prophet Muhammad — are "possessors of determination" (*ulu'l-͑azm*), those who have brought a *Shari͑ah*. Other prophets follow the *Shari͑ah* of those who "possess determination." God has said in the Qur'an, "He hath ordained for you that religion which He commended unto Noah, and that which We inspire in thee (Muhammad), and that which We commended unto Abraham and Moses and Jesus" (Qur'an, XLII, 13). He has also said, "And when We exacted a covenant from the Prophets, and from thee (O Muhammad) and from Noah and Abraham and Moses and Jesus son of Mary, We took from them a solemn covenant." (Qur'an, XXXIII, 7).

* * *

The last prophet of God is Hadrat-i Muhammad — upon whom be blessings and peace — who possesses a book and a *Shari͑ah* and in whom Muslims have placed their faith. The Prophet was born fifty-three years before the beginning of the hegira calendar in Mecca in the Hijaz amidst the family of Banu Hashim of the Tribe of Quraysh, who were considered the most honored of the Arab families.

* * *

. . . According to Divine instruction, the Prophet began to propagate his mission openly. With the beginning of open propagation the people of Mecca reacted most severely and inflicted the most painful afflictions and tortures upon the Prophet and the people who had become newly converted to Islam. The severe treatment dealt out by the Quraysh reached such a degree that a group of Muslims left their homes and belongings and migrated to Abyssinia. The Prophet and his uncle, Abu Talib, along with their relatives from the Banu Hashim, took refuge for three years in the "mountain pass of Abu Talib," a fort in one of the valleys of Mecca. No one had any dealings or transactions with them and they did not dare to leave their place of refuge.

The idol-worshipers of Mecca, although at the beginning they considered inflicting all kinds of pressures and tortures such as striking and beating, insult, ridicule and defamation on the Prophet, occasionally would also show kindness and courtesy toward him in order to have him turn away from his mission. They would promise him great sums of money or leadership and the rule of the tribe. But for the Prophet their promises and their threats only resulted in the intensification of his will and determination to carry out his mission. Once, when they came to the Prophet promising him wealth and power, the Prophet told them, using metaphorical language, that if they were to put the sun in the palm of his right hand and the moon in the palm of his left hand he would not turn away from obeying the unique God or refrain from performing his mission.

About the tenth year of his prophecy, when the Prophet left the "mountain pass of Abu Talib," his uncle Abu Talib, who was also his sole protector, died, as did also his devoted wife. Henceforth there was no protection for his life nor any place of refuge. Finally the idol-worshipers of Mecca devised a secret plan to kill him. At night they surrounded his house from all sides with the aim of forcing themselves in at the end of the night and cutting him to pieces while he was in bed. But God, the Exalted, informed him of the plan and commanded him to leave for Yathrib. The Prophet placed ᶜAli in place of himself in his bed and at night left the house under Divine protection, passing amidst his enemies, and taking refuge in a cave near Mecca. After three days when his enemies, having looked everywhere, gave up hope of capturing him and returned to Mecca, he left the cave and set out for Yathrib.

The people of Yathrib, whose leaders had already accepted the message of the Prophet and sworn allegiance to him, accepted him with open arms and placed their lives and property at his disposal. In Yathrib for the first time the Prophet formed a small Islamic community and signed treaties with the Jewish tribes in and around the city as well as with the powerful Arab tribes of the region. He undertook the task of propagating the Islamic message and Yathrib became famous as "Madinat al-rasul" (the city of the Prophet). Islam began to grow and expand from day to day. The Muslims, who in Mecca were caught in the mesh of the injustice and inequity of the Quraysh, gradually left their homes and property and migrated to Medinah, revolving around the Prophet like moths around a candle. This group became known as the "immigrants" (*muhajirun*) in the same way that those who aided the Prophets in Yathrib gained the name of "helpers" (*ansar*).

Islam was advancing rapidly but at the same time the idol-worshipers of Quraysh, as well as the Jewish tribes of the Hijaz, were unrestrained in their harassment of the Muslims. With the help of the "hypocrites" (*munafiqun*) of Mecca, who were amidst the community of Muslims and who were not known for their holding any particular positions, they created new misfortunes for the Muslims every day until finally the matter led to war. Many battles took place between the Muslims and the Arab polytheists and Jews, in most of which the Muslims were victorious. There were altogether over eighty major and minor battles. In all the major conflicts such as the battles of Badr, Uhud, Khandaq, Khaybar, Hunayn, etc., the Prophet was personally present on the battle scene. Also in all the major battles and many minor ones, victory was gained especially through the efforts of ᶜAli. He was the only person who never turned away from any of these battles. In all the wars that occurred during the ten years after the migration from Mecca to Medinah less than two hundred Muslims and less than a thousand infidels were killed.

As a result of the activity of the Prophet and the selfless effort of the muhajirun and ansar during this ten-year period, Islam spread through the Arabian peninsula. There were also letters written to kings of other countries such as Persia, Byzantinum and Abyssinia inviting them to accept Islam. During this time the Prophet lived in poverty and was proud of it. He never spent a moment of his time in vain. Rather, his time was divided into three parts: one spent for God, in worshiping and remembering Him; a part for himself and his household and domestic needs; and a part for the people. During this part of his time he was engaged in spreading and teaching Islam and its sciences, administrating to the needs of Islamic society and removing whatever evils existed, providing for the needs of the Muslims, strengthening domestic and foreign bonds, and similar matters.

After ten years of stay in Medinah the Prophet fell ill and died after a few days illness. According to existing traditions the last words on his lips were advice concerning slaves and women.

* * *

It was demanded of the Prophet, as it had been of other prophets, that he produce a miracle. The Prophet himself also confirmed the power of prophets to produce miracles as has been asserted clearly by the Qur'an. Many miracles by the Prophet have been recounted, the transmission of some of which is certain and can be accepted with confidence. But the enduring miracle of the Prophet, which is still alive, is the sacred book of Islam, the Holy Qur'an. The Holy Qur'an is a sacred text consisting of six thousand and several hundred verses (*ayah*) divided into one hundred and fourteen large and small chapters (*surah*). The verses of the Holy Qur'an were revealed gradually during the twenty-three year period of prophecy and mission of the Prophet. From less than one verse to a whole and complete chapter were revealed under different circumstances, both at day and night, on journeys or at home, in war or peace, during days of hardship or moments of rest.

The Holy Qur'an in many of its verses introduces itself in unambiguous language as a miracle. It invited the Arabs of that day to rivalry and competition in composing writings of comparable truth and beauty. The Arabs, according to the testimony of history, had reached the highest stages of eloquence and elegance of language, and in the sweetness of language and flow of speech they ranked foremost among all people. The Holy Qur'an claims that if it be thought of as human speech, created by the Prophet himself or learned through instruction from someone else, then the Arabs should be able to produce its like or ten chapters like it, or a single one of its verses, making use of whatever means were at their disposal to achieve this end. The celebrated Arab men of eloquence claimed in answer to this request that the Qur'an was magic and it was thus impossible for them to produce its like.

Not only does the Qur'an challenge and invite people to compete with its eloquence and elegant language, but also it occasionally invites rivalry from the point of view of its meaning and thus challenges all the mental powers of men and *jinn*, for the Qur'an is a book containing the total program for human life. If we investigate the matter carefully we will discover that God has made this vast and extensive program which embraces every aspect of the countless beliefs, ethical forms and actions of mankind and takes into account all of their details and particularities, to be the "Truth" (*haqq*) and to be called the religion of the truth (*din-i haqq*). Islam is a religion whose injunctions are based on the truth and the real welfare of mankind, not the desires and inclinations of the majority of men or the whims of a single, powerful ruler.

At the foundation of this vast program is placed the most cherished word of God which is belief in His Unity. All the principles of the sciences are deduced from the principle of Unity (*tawhid*). After that, the most praiseworthy human ethical and moral virtues are deduced from the principles of the religious sciences and included in the program. Then, the countless principles and details of human action and individual and social conditions of man are investigated, and the duties pertaining to them which originate from the worship of the One are elaborated and organized. In Islam the relation and continuity between the principles (*usul*) and their applications (*furuᶜ*) are such that each particular application to whatever subject it may be, if it is brought back to its source, returns to the principle of Unity or *tawhid*, and Unity if applied and analyzed becomes the basis for the particular injunction and rule in question.

Of course, the final elaboration of such an extensive religion with such unity and interconnection, or even the preparation of an elementary index for it, is beyond the normal powers of the best authorities on law in the world. But here we speak of a man who in a short span of time was placed amidst a thousand difficulties concerning his life and property, caught in bloody battles and faced with internal and external obstacles and furthermore placed alone before the whole world. Moreover, the Prophet had never received instruction nor learned how to read and write. He had spent two-thirds of his life before becoming a prophet among a people who possessed no learning and had had no taste of civilization. He passed his life in a land without water or vegetation and with burning air, among a people who lived in the lowest social conditions and were dominated by neighboring political powers.

Besides the above, the Holy Qur'an challenges men in another way. This book was revealed gradually, during a period of twenty-three years, under totally different conditions in periods of difficulty or comfort, war or peace, power or weakness, and the like. If it had not come from God but had been composed and expounded by man, many contradictions and contrasts would be observed in it. Its ending would of necessity be more perfect than its beginning, as is necessary in the gradual perfection of the human individual. Instead, the first Meccan verses are of the same quality as the Medinan verses and there is no difference between the beginning and end of the Qur'an. The Qur'an is a book whose parts resemble each other and whose awe-inspiring power of expression is of the same style and quality throughout.

^c*Allamah al-Hilli*

The evidence for the goodness of the prophetic mission is that it has encompassed benefits and has been free from corrupting influences. Therefore, it was absolutely good. The author has mentioned some of the benefits of the prophetic mission.

Among these is the fact that reason is supported by the prophetic transmission of laws which reason can also deduce for itself, like the unity of the Creator and other such things. Then there is the fact that through the prophetic mission information of the law is provided in matters which reason cannot deduce, like the stipulations of the divine law and other such problems of the principles of religion.

These benefits include the removal of the fear (of uncertainty) which comes to the *mukallaf* with regard to his own actions; for he knows from rational evidence that he is owned by another (i.e. God) and that using another's possession without his permission is evil. Without the prophetic mission, he would not know of the goodness of actions and thus, he would be afraid of acting and not acting. Since reason allows the master (i.e. God) to demand the servant to perform certain actions, the only way in which they can be performed is through (the information brought) by the prophetic mission.

Another of these matters is the fact that some actions are good and some are evil. These include what reason can know to be good independently and what it cannot know to be good independently. The same applies to evil actions. As a result of the prophetic mission knowledge is acquired of the good and evil actions of which reason had no knowledge indepently.

Also included in these matters is the fact that some things are useful to us, like many kinds of food and medicine, while others are harmful to us, like many kinds of poison and drugs. Reason does not acquire full knowledge of all of these . This great benefit comes through the prophetic mission.

Then, there is the fact that mankind was not created like any of the other animals. He is an urban creature by nature, who depends on many factors without which the organisation of his livelihood would be incomplete. He would be unable to achieve most of this without partnership and cooperation. The tendency to dominate others is also present in human nature, as a result of which conflict, which is contrary to the rationale of social life, arises. Therefore it is necessary that a unifying factor prevail over society. Such a unifying factor is the *sunnah* of the Prophet and the divine law. A *sunnah* must have some one to introduce it, who will establish it and lay down its regulations. Such a person would have to be different from others of his species because of the absence of the (required) superiority in them. That distinguishing (feature) could not be anything which is given him by his fellow men because of the possibility of resentment arising in some through him being singled out by othres. Therefore he (a prophet) must be distinguished by God through a miracle, by which men will be led to believe the claim which he makes, and through which he can cause men to be afraid of disobeying him and promise them (rewards) for following him. As a result of this the organisation of life may be fulfilled and the preservation of the human species maintained to the highest possible degree.

There is also the fact that individual humans differ in attaining the elements of perfection, in acquiring knowledge and in gaining virtues. Some do not need any other person to help them in this because of their own strength of spirit, complete awareness, and strong disposition to be in contact with higher matters. Others are entirely unable to do those things, while there are others who reach an intermediate state. The degrees of perfection within this scale vary in accordance with their nearness to one of the two extreme groups and their distance from the other. The benefit which a prophet brings is that he supplements the deficient individuals of the species according to their varying dispositions' need for more or less.

Furthermore, there is the fact that the human species needs tools and beneficial things for its continuation, like clothes and houses and other such things. These are things which require knowledge of their techniques in order for them to be acquired. Human faculties (left to themselves) are incapable of that. Thus, the benefit which the Prophet brings is to teach these hidden crafts which are beneficial.

In addition, it is known that degrees of morality vary. In this, there is need for one who is perfect to give instruction in morality, and beneficial policies to the extent that human affairs, in terms of both country and home, may be properly organised.

Finally, Prophets make known the rewards for obedience and the punishments for disobedience. Thus grace comes to the *mukallaf* through their mission.

Because of these benefits, the mission of prophets is necessary.

* * *

The Brahmins argued for the non-existence of the prophetic mission by maintaining the view that the Messenger would either bring what conformed to reason or what opposed it. If he brought what conformed to reason, there was no need for him nor advantage in having him. If he brought what opposed reason, it would be necessary to reject his statement. This specious argument is invalid according to what was said earlier with regard to the first benefit of the prophetic mission. That was that we say: "Why is it not possible for prophets to bring what conforms to reason? For the advantage in that would be a confirmation of the deduction of reason." Or we say: "Why is it not possible for prophets to bring that which reason does not require and to which (reason) does not guide, even though it does not oppose reason in the sense that they do not bring anything which reason would be required to contradict?" Many of the stipulations of the divine law and acts of worship, to whose detailed exposition reason does not give any guidance, are like this.

Concerning the Necessity of the Prophetic Mission

> It (the prophetic mission) is necessary because it encompasses the grace (required) for the responsibilities which are enjoined on man according to reason.

Here the people differ. The Mu^ctazila maintain that the Prophetic mission is necessary while the Ash^carites maintain that it is not necessary. The Mu^ctazila argue that the responsibilities which are enjoined on man through revelation (*takalif sam^ciyya*) are the grace which enables man to perform the responsibilities which are enjoined on man through reason (*takalif ^caqliyyah*). Grace is necessary (for men to perform these rational responsibilities), therefore, the responsibility enjoined on man through revelation (*taklif sam^ci*) is necessary. However, it is only possible to know about it through the Prophet. Therefore the existence of the Prophet is necessary because that, by which the necessary can only be fulfilled, is (itself) necessary. They argue for the responsibility enjoined on man through revelation (*taklif sam^ci*) being a grace for (the performance of) that responsibility enjoined on man according to reason (*^caqli*), by maintaining the view that when man is diligent in carrying out duties enjoined by revelation and in avoiding things forbidden by the divine law, he would be close to one who was carrying out the duties enjoined by reason and avoiding those things forbidden by reason. These latter are necessarily known by every rational being. We have explained earlier that grace is necessary.

Concerning the Necessity of Infallibility

> Infallibility is necessary for the Prophet in order that he may gain men's confidence and thus attain his purpose, and because of the necessity for

men to follow him and the necessity of the contrary of that (i.e. not following a sinner) and the necessity of repudiating the acts of a sinner.

The people differ on this point. A group of the Mu^ctazila concede the possibility of minor sins to prophets either through forgetfulness, as some of them think, or on the basis of interpretation, as a group of them believe, or because they (minor sins) occur in men surrounded by an abundance of rewards (i.e. thus diminishing the effect of these minor sins). The Ash^carites and the *Hashwiyyah* hold the view that minor sins and major sins, other than unbelief and lying, are possible for prophets. The *Imamiyyah* maintain that they must have infallibility from all sins, whether minor or major. The evidence for this comes in a number of arguments:

1. The purpose of the mission of prophets can only be attained through the infallibility of the prophets. It is necessary that the purpose be attained. That explains that if those to whom a prophet had been sent allowed the possibility of prophets lying and being sinful, they could also allow the possibility of such a thing in what prophets ordered and forbade and in their actions which they enjoined them to follow. Then the prophets could not call them to obey their orders, and that would be a contradition of the purpose of the prophetic mission.

2. It is necessary to follow the Prophet. Therefore if he perpetrated an act of disobedience to God, it would either be necessary to follow him or not. The second (i.e. not following him) is invalid because it is a denial of the main purpose of the prophetic mission. The first (i.e. following him) is invalid because performing a disobedient action is not allowed. He (al-Tusi) indicates the above argument by his statement ". . . because of the necessity for men to follow him and the necessity of the contrary of that". For through regarding him to be a prophet, it is necessary to follow him; while if the action was regarded as being sinful, it would not be allowed to follow him.

3. A sinful act must be repudiated because of the universal application of the obligation to forbid all sin (*al-nahy ^can al-munkar*). That would require hurting him while it is forbidden to do that. All such views on the Prophet sinning are logically absurd.

(It is necessary for the Prophet to have) the perfection of reason, intelligence, perspicacity and sound judgement. He must not have any form of forgetfulness or anything which would cause people to shun him, such as a base father, an unchaste mother, coarse manners, physical defects and the like, nor any bad habit such as eating on the road and similar things.

It is necessary that the Prophet should have these qualities which he has mentioned. His statement ". . . the perfection of reason" is connected to (his earlier requirement of) infallibility. It is clear that he must have the ultimate in intelligence, perspicacity and sound judgement in so far as he could not be weak in judgement, and hesitant and bewildered in affairs because that would be the greatest inducement for people to shun him. It is clear that forgetfulness is not possible for him lest he should forget about some matter he was enjoined to communicate. He should be free from a base father (i.e. born of a good father) and an unchaste mother (i.e. born of a chaste mother) because those are things which would cause people to shun him. He should be free from coarseness and harshness of manner lest he should make people avoid him. He should be free from sicknesses like physical deformities, constant wind and leprosy, as also from many things ordinarily permitted, which should not be in him since they are matters which diminish his greatness, such as eating on the road and other things like that. For all such things would be reasons for people avoiding him and as such would negate the prupose of his prophetic mission.

Concerning the Means of Knowing the Truthfulness of the Prophet

> The means of knowing his truthfulness is through the appearance of miracles performed by him. A miracle is the bringing into existence of something which is abnormal or the removal of something which normally would exist in a way which breaks throug normality and which conforms to the claim (of prophethood which is made).

After he has mentioned the qualities of the Prophet, it is necessary for him to mention the explanation of how he is known. This is by one thing, through the appearance of miracles performed by him. We mean by miracles "the bringing into existence of something which is abnormal or the removal of something which normally exists, in a way which breaks through normality and which conforms to the claim (of prophethood which is made)". Bringing into existence and removal are both equal in the performance of miracles. Thus there is no difference in the stick being turned into a snake and preventing the powerful from removing the weakest things. We have made the condition breaking through normality because performing a normal action, or not performing an action which is abnormal, does not give evidence of the truthfulness (of a prophet). We have said "in a way which conforms with the claim", because whoever claims prophethood and bases his miracles (in support of the claim) on the healing of a blind man who, then, becomes deaf without the blindness being cured, will not be a true prophet. In miracles there must be the (following) conditions:

1. The community to whom he was sent must be unable to do the like or what is equivalent to it.
2. It must be done through God, the Most High, or at His command.
3. It must be done during the time of *taklif* because normality will be broken on the appearance of the signs of the Day of Judgement.
4. It must occur after the claim of the claimant to prophethood or come within the terms of that. We mean by "come within the terms of that" that he puts forward the claim of prophethood during his life while no-one else makes a (valid) claim of prophethood. Then he makes known that miracle after he has made known other miracles following his claim. Thus the appearance of the second type of miracle would be like that which followed his claim because its association with his claim is known and because he has made it known for the sake of that claim, just as the miracle which followed the claim.
5. It must be (something) which breaks the course of normality.

Concerning Miracles of Proofs of Great Holiness (karamat)

> The story of Mary, and of others, indicates the possibility of miracles being performed by the righteous.

The people differ here. A group of Mu^ctazila hold the view of the impossibility of miracles being performed by the righteous as acts of great holiness or of them appearing, on the contrary, from liars as a proof of their lying. However, Abu'l-Husayn from that group, and another group of the Mu^ctazila as well as the Ash^carites maintain that that is possible. The latter view is the more correct. The author proves this with the story of Mary. That indicates that miracles could be performed by her and others, as does the story of Asif and (also) the well-substantiated (*mutawatur*) stories reported of ^cAli and the other Imams. Those who deny miracles apart from the miracles of prophets interpret the story of Mary on the basis of it being an extension (of the miracles) of Jesus, and the story of Asif on the basis of it being a mircale of Solomon with Bilqis, as if Solomon was saying: "My followers can do this while yours cannot." Because of this, she submitted after becoming aware of his miracles. (They interpret) the story of ^cAli as the completion of the miracles of the Prophet.

> It is not necessary for (such miracles) to be excluded (from the status) of being miracles, nor for them to cause the Prophet to be abandoned, nor for them to require the absence of the Prophet's distinction from others, nor for them to invalidate his evidence for his prophethood, nor does it require them to become comnmon (to every class or person).

These are the arguments which those of the Muctazila, who deny that the righteous may perform miracles, use:

1. They say that if it was possible for miracles to appear from those who are not prophets as a mark of their being honoured, it would be possible for miracles to be performed even though no-one else knew of them, because the purpose (of these miracles) is the happiness of those involved in them. If that was possible, then miracles in such large numbers would come to be excluded from the status of being miracles.

   The answer is to deny the consequences of the argument (i.e. no-one knowing about them) because the fact that such miracles are excluded from the status of being miracles is an unacceptable argument. We only concede the possibility of the performance of miracles when it is free of such unacceptable aspects. Thus the performance of miracles is possible so long as they are not in such large numbers as to come to be excluded from the status of being miracles.

2. They say that if the performance of miracles was possible by those who are not prophets, it would be necessary to abandon prophets since the reason for the necessity of obeying them is the performance of miracles by them. For, if those, to whom obedience was not required, participated in that, the prophets' position would be diminished. In support of this, they maintain that if the leader honored (whatever the nature of that honor might be) everyone then the type of that honor would certainly be degraded were it to be extended to someone who did not deserve that honor.

   The answer is to deny the idea of a miracle being reduced in merit it if has been performed by another prophet. Thus if it had been only performed by one prophet his status would have been exalted. But similarly, if it had been performed by a group of prophets, no reduction in its merit is required. In the same way, there is no reduction in the merit (of prophets) through the miracle being performed by the righteous.

3. Abu Hashim argues that the miracle is evidence (of prophethood) through distinguising him and specifying him. The *Qadi al-qudat* explains that by arguing that the miracle points to the distinction of the Prophet from others. For individuals of the community share humanity and its inherent characteristics with him, and if it was not for miracles, he would not be distinguished from them. Thus if others share this ability to perform miracles with him, no distinction between them occurs.

The answer is that the distinction of a prophet from others occurs through miracles and through their association with his claim to prophethood. This latter is something which he is characterised by, apart from others. The fact that others can share the performance of miracles with him, does not mean that they share in everything with him.

4. (They say that) If the performance of miracle is allowed to people other than a prophet, then its (miracles) validity for being the exclusive evidence to the prophethood is nullified. And since it is not so, the whole premise is void. (To explain it further they say) If miracles were performed by all and sundry it would deprive the claimant of the prophethood of the exclusivity of the evidence. As we know that a general (evidence) cannot be applied to the specific (claim).

The answer is to deny the requirement (of miracles alone proving prophethood) because what is particular to the Prophet is the miracle in association with the claim (to prophethood). If a miracle is performed by a person, either he claims prophethood or he does not. If he claims it, we know that he is speaking the truth, since reason cannot accept the performance of a miracle by a liar. If a man did not claim prophethood, there would be no consideration of prophethood for him. Thus the result is that the miracle does not initially point to prophethood, rather it points to the truth of a claim (to prophethood when such a claim is made). Thus if the claim embraces prophethood, the miracle points to the truthfulness of the claimant with regard to his claim, and that necessitates the reality of prophethood.

5. They maintain that if the performance of a miracle is possible for someone who is not a prophet, it could be performed by every truthful person. Thus a miracle could be performed by one who gives information about being full and being hungry and other such things.

The answer is that the performance of miracles does not have to be common (to every class of person), i.e. the appearance of miracles from every truthful person is not required. For we only require the appearance of a miracle from one who claims prophethood, or from the righteous as a mark of their being honoured and exalted. That does not occur for every person who gives true information.

The Prophet's miracles before his prophethood gave (the picture) of setting the way (to his prophethood).

The people differ on this. Those who deny the appearance of miracles (as acts of honouring a person), deny the performance of miracles as a way of setting the way (to prophethood), except for a group of them. The rest concede it. The author points to its possibility through the occurrence of miracles from the Apostle before (his) prophethood, such as is reported of the bursting of the courtyard of Khusraw, the causing of the water of the sea of Sawih to sink, the extinguishing of Persian fire, the story of the companions of the Elephant, and the clouds which shaded him from the sun, and the stones which greeted him, and others like that which are confirmed of him before prophethood.

> The stories of Musaylimah, Pharoah and Abraham, (all) provide for the possibility of the performance of miracles which contradict the claims (of liars).

The people differ on this point. Those who deny miracles as acts of honoring persons deny the performance of miracles by liars as a contradiction of what they claim, through showing their lie. The author demonstrates the possibility through the occurrence of such incidents as the one reported of Musaylimah, the liar, when he claimed prophethood. He was told that the Apostle prayed for a one-eyed man and God restored the eye which had gone. Then Musaylimah prayed for a one-eyed man, but the one-eyed man lost his sound eye. Similarly it is reported that when God made the fire over Abraham cold and secure (so that it did not burn him), Nimru said at that: "The fire has only become like this out of fear of me." Then, in that circumstance, a fire descended suddenly upon him and burnt his beard. Thus it could not be said that the absence of a miracle after the claim (of false prophets) was sufficient to demonstrate their lying. For the appearance of a miracle in contradiction to their wicked claims exists as an act which breaks through normality without bringing any advantage to them. Thus it is fruitless for them because we maintain that sometimes the general interest is served through the appearance of a miracle in contradiction to wicked claims as a demonstration of their lying about the circumstances. In this way doubt is removed of the possibility of it being said that there will be a delay of the (supporting) miracle (appearing) after their (false) claim because of some (false) public interest, and that it would appear at another time, so that complete certainty of their lying would not occur.

Concerning the Necessity of the Prophetic Mission at All Time

> The evidence of the necessity of the prophetic mission provides for its generalisation (to all times).

The people differ here. A group of the Mu^ctazila say that the prophetic mission is not necessary at all times, but rather in one circumstance apart from another and that is when there is public benefit in the prophetic mission. The ^culama' of the Imamiyyah maintains that the prophetic mission is necessary at every time insofar as there can never be a time without the revealed law (shar^c) of a prophet. The Ash^carites maintain that the prophetic mission is not necessary at every time because they deny the rationally good and the rationally evil, and the study of this has taken place earlier. The author demonstrates the necessity of the prophetic mission at all times, by stating the fact that the evidence for the necessity of the prophetic mission provides for its generalisation, namely the evidence of the prophetic mission provides for the generalisation of the prophetic misson at all times, because in the prophetic mission is that which drives away wrong and urges obedience. Therefore it is (a means of) grace. Since, in it, there is a warning for those who are unaware, the removal of differences, the defence against turmoil and confusion and all matters of necessary public interest which could only be fulfilled through the prophetic mission, the prophetic mission must be necesary at all times.

It is not necessary (for a prophet to have) a revealed law (shari^cah).

The two shaykhs differ on this point. Abu ^cAli concedes the possibility of a prophetic mission for the purpose of confirming what has been suggested by reason, and does not require that he should have a revealed law. On the other hand, Abu Hashim and his companions maintain that a prophet cannot be sent without a revealed law because reason is sufficient for knowledge of the things necessary according to reason. Therefore the prophetic mission (without a revealed law) would be pointless.

The answer is that it is possible for there to be a prophetic mission which has embraced a kind of public benefit, by the fact that knowledge of his prophethood and his call to men to what has been suggested by reason is in their interest. Therefore the prophetic mission does not necessarily bring a revealed law. Men must observe a prophet's miracle and then public benefit will occur to them which would not have occurred without the prophetic mission. Abu ^cAli has argued on the basis of the view that it is possible for the mission of a prophet to follow the mission of a prophet with one revealed law and similarly it is possible for the mission of a prophet to require what has been suggested by reason.

Concerning the Prophethood
of the Prophet Muhammad

The appearance of the miracle of the Qur'an and other miracles in association with the claim of our Prophet Muhammad prove his proph-

ethood. The challenge to copy it in association with the impossibility of
doing so despite the many motives to try to do so prove the inimitability
of the Qur'an. Well-substantiated reports of other miracles, in addition
to it, also support (his claim to prophethood).

When he has finished with the study of prophethood in general, he begins
to confirm the prophethood of our Prophet Muhammad. The evidence for
it is the fact that miracles have appeared from him and he has claimed
prophethood. Therefore he is true. As for the miracles that have been performed by him, there are two aspects:

1. The Qur'an is a miracle and it is appeared through him. As for the
   inimitability of the Qur'an, he challenged the eloquence of the Arabs
   according to God's verse: "Produce a *surah* like it"; "Then produce
   ten *surahs* forged like it"; "Say: if man and *jinn* agreed to produce
   the like of the Qur'an, they could not produce its like, even if some
   of them were helping others". The challenge (to produce the like)
   coupled with the impossibility of producing its like, together with
   the abundant motives for (people) to do so as a demonstration of
   their merit, a refutation of his claim and a security from being killed, demonstrate their deficiency and their inability to compete with
   it. As for it occurring through him, that the Qur'an revealed exclusively to him is well-authenticated.
2. Numerous miracles are reported of him. Examples are the spring of
   water which came from between his fingers so that many were satisfied by littled water after his return from the raid of Tabuk, the
   causing of the water to sink at the well of Hudaybiyyah when his
   companions all sought for water and the well was dry. He gave his
   arrow to al-Bara' ibn ᶜAzib and ordered him to go down and stick it
   into the well. He stuck it in and immediately the water was so abundant that there was fear that al-Bara' would be drowned. On
   another occasion the Prophet spat in a well when the people com-
   plained to him of the disappearance of the water, and then cold
   water burst forth from it. Then the people of Yamama learnt about
   that and asked Musaylimah to do that when there was only a little
   water in their well. He spat in it and the water disappeared completely. When God's verse descended "Warn your clan who are
   kinsmen", he said to ᶜAli: "Go and take a ewe and bring me a jug
   full of milk. Then summon to me the sons of your father, the Banu
   Hashim." He did that and summoned them. There were forty men.
   They ate until they were full, yet the only sign that any of it had
   been eaten was the traces on their fingers. They drank from the jug
   until they were sated and still the milk remained in its earlier state

(i.e. it looked as it it hadn't been drunk). Then when he wanted to summon them to Islam, Abu Lahad said: "Muhammad is likely to bewitch you". Therefore they got up before he called them to (believe) God, the Most High. Then he said to ᶜAli: "Do the same as you did". So he did the same on the second day., Then when he wanted to call them to (believe) God, Abu Laham repeated his words. Again he said to ᶜAli: "Do the same as you did". He did it again on the third day. After this he made a pledge to ᶜAli of the caliphate after his death land in succession of him... .

* * *

"What do you have?" Jabir answered: "I have a young female goat in the fire and a *saᶜ* of barley, which we have baked." He said: "Make my companions sit ten by ten (i.e. in rows of ten)." He did so and all of them ate.

Little stones in the hands of the Prophet raised God. A wolf gave testimony to his mission, for when Ruhban ibn Aws was pasturing his sheep a wolf came and seized a ewe and made off towards him. The wolf said to him: "Is there surprise in my taking a sheep when this Muhammad summons people to the truth and is not answered?" Then Ruhban went to the Prophet and accepted Islam. After, he was called "the one who talked to the wolves".

He (the Prophet) spat in the eye of ᶜAli, when it suffered from opthalmia. It never suffered from the disease after that.

The Prophet prayed that God might keep the heat and cold from ᶜAli, as a result ᶜAli's dress in summer and winter were the same. For the Prophet the moon was split and he called to a tree and it answered him, coming through the ground without anything pulling or pushing it and then returned to its place. He used to preach at the trunk of a palm tree, and then a *minbar* (pulpit) was made for him and he moved to it. The palm trunk lamented for him as a she-camel laments for her offspring. Therefore (he went) and embraced it and it became silent. He told us of what was as yet unknown concerning many people and places, such as when he told of the killing of Husayn, and the place at which the killing would take place. Then he was killed in that place. He told of the killing of Thabit ibn Qays ibn Shammas and he was killed. He informed his Companions of the conquest of Egypt and told them to treat the Copts well, for they had the right of a protected minority (*zimma*) and a right through relationship to him. He told them of the claims of Musaylimah to prophethood in Yamama and the claims of al-ᶜAbsi to prophethood in Sanᶜa, and that they both would be killed. Fayruz al-Daylami killed al-ᶜAbsi around the time of the death of the

Prophet and Khalid ibn al-Walid killed Musaylimah. He told ᶜAli about the report of Zu 'l-Thaddiyyah and (what) would happen.

He invoked God against ᶜUtba ibn Abu Laham when he recited: "By the star". ᶜUtba said "You have disbelieved in the Lord and the star". Thereupon (the Prophet) called on God to set a dog upon him. ᶜUtba went to Syria and a lion came out and violent fear gripped him. His colleagues said to him: "What are you shaking at?" He answered: "Muhammad has invoked God against me. By God, the heavens have never shaded a speaker more truthful than Muhammad." Then the people surrounded him with themselves and their equipment. But the lion came and bit off their heads one by one until it came to him, and it took a mouthful of him, and he was terrified of it.

The Prophet gave information of the death of the Najashi (of Ethiopia) and the killing of Zayid ibn Harithah at Muᶜta. He told of his death in Medinah (as if was watching the battle) and how Jaᶜfar took the standard. Then he told of Jaᶜfar's being killed. He stopped for a moment and said that ᶜAbdullah ibn Rawaha had taken the flag. After that he reported the killing of ᶜAbdullah ibn Rawaha. He went to the house of Jaᶜfar and took out the latter's children. Tears filled his eyes as he announced the news of Jaᶜfar's death to his family. The matter was later shown to have happened as he had told it.

He (the Prophet) said to ᶜAmmar: "A group which will usurp (authority) will kill you," and the followers of Muᶜawiyah killed him. Because of the fact that this report was widespread Muᶜawiyah was not able to deny it, but he deceived the common people and said that ᶜAmmar was killed by those who brought him. However Ibn ᶜAbbas refuted this, maintaining that by the same argument it could be said that the unbelievers had not killed Hamzah and only the Apostle had killed him since it was he who had brought him against them until they killed him.

The Prophet said to ᶜAli: "After me you will fight against those who break their allegiance, those who act unjustly and those who stray from the true path of religion." The ones who broke their allegiance were Talha and al-Zubayr because they pledged allegiance to him (ᶜAli) and then they broke that allegiance. The ones who acted unjustly were Muᶜawiyah and his followers because they were oppressive usurpers. Those who strayed from the true path of religion were those who left the community; they were the Kharijites.

These are some of the miracles which have been reported. We have shortened their number because there are so many, and these will attain our purpose. We have reported other miracles in our book *Nihayat al-maram*.

> It is said that the Qur'an is inimitable because of its eloquence; and it is said to be so because of both its eloquence and its style together; and it is said to be so because of the fact that it turns (men) away (from copying it). All of these are likely.

The people differ on this point. The two Jubba^cis maintain that the reason for the inimitability of the Qur'an is its eloquence. The *Ahl al-haqq* declare that it is its eloquence and style together. While al-Nazzam and al-Murtada maintain that it is the element in it which turns men away (from copying it), in the sense that God turned them away from, and prevented them from, competing with it. The first (i.e. the two Jubba^cis and their supporters) argue that the Arabs regarded its eloquence as magnificent. It was for this reason that al-Nabighah wanted to embrace Islam when he heard the Qur'an and recognized its eloquence. Abu Jahl attempted to stop him and said to him: "Forbidden to you is (everything) except the best." Because of that God gave information about them in His statement: "He thinks, and he plots; yet he was killed. How can he plot and then be killed, how can he plot and then look . . ." etc. to the end of the verse. It is argued against the view of the element which averts men from copying the Qur'an that if the element of averting men from copying it was a reason for its inimitability, it would be necesary for it to be extremely indistinct because indistinctness is the most profound form of inimitability, and thus this reason is necessarily invalid. However al-Sayyid Murtada argues that the Arabs were able to produce the individual words and structures (of the Qur'an) but they were unable to produce its like as a result of their being turned away from doing what they had the power to do. All these different views are possible.

Abrogation is a factor which involves different elements of public benefit.

This is an indication of the reply to the Jews when they maintain the continuation of the revealed laws of Moses. For they said that abrogation was invalid because if that which was abrogated was an advantage, forbidding it would be evil. Thus since abrogation is invalid, the doctrine of the continuation of the revealed law of Moses is required. The outline of the answer is that we maintain that the laws are dependent upon public benefit. However, public benefits change with changing times and they differ through the differences of those on whom responsibility is placed (*mukallafin*). Therefore it is possible that there may be a law appointed for the benefit of one people at one time, while for another people to be ordered to carry it out at another time would be a corrupting (influence). Thus it is forbidden.

It happened that some things permitted to those before Noah, were forbidden to him. Thus circumcision was made obligatory when (previously that law) had been withheld, and marriage of two sisters (to one man) was forbidden and other things (like that).

This is corroboration of the invalidity of the Jewish doctrine when they deny abrogation. He has explained first the possibility of its occurrence. Here he explains its occurrence in their own revealed law. That (also) occurs in other contexts. It comes in the Torah that God said to Adam and Eve: "I have permitted to you everything which crawls on the face of the earth." Thus snakes were permitted to him (Adam). While it also comes in the Torah that (God) said to Noah: "Take with you of the permitted animals such and such, and the forbidden animals, such and such." Thus he forbade to Noah some of the animals he had permitted to Adam. Another example from the Torah is that he had allowed Noah to defer his own circumcision until he grew up, while he forbade other prophets to do so. He allowed Abraham to delay circumcision (longer) than seven days. Anotehr example from the Torah is that while he allowed Adam to marry two sisters, he forbade it to Moses.

> The Jews' report from Moses about the eternal nature of the revealed law is a lie. Even if it was conceded, it would not indicate (such a meaning absolutely).

A group of Jews concede the possibility, in terms of reason, of the occurrence of abrogation but yet deny the abrogation of the revealed law of Moses. They adhere to the (fact) that it is related that Moses said: "Keep the Sabbath for ever". Eternity points to continuation and continuation of the condition of the Sabbath denies the doctrine of the prophethood of Muhammad. The answer (includes several) points:

1. This tradition is forged and it has been attributed to Ibn al-Rawandi.
2. Even if we conceded the report of it, its authentication by the Jews has come to an end because the fortunes of victory uprooted them and annihilated them so that there does not remain any of them whose report can be relied upon.
3. The expression "eternity" does not indicate absolute continuation. For it comes in the Torah without the meaning of continuation. For example, with regard to the slave, he served for six years and then his freedom was offered to him in the seventh. However, the slave refused, and his ears were pierced (as a slave) and therefore he served "for ever", and in another passage "he served for fifty years". They were enjoined with regard to the cow which they were entrusted to slaughter, that that should be *sunnah* for them "for ever". Then their worship of it came to an end. In the Torah it says: "Sacrifice two lambs, a lamb at morning and a lamb in the evening between sunset and nightfall as an 'eternal' sacrifice required of you." Their worship in this manner has ceased. Since "eternity" in these passages does not refer to continuation, the evidence for it is absolutely absent. The most which can be said in this connection is

that it points to a superficial meaning. But the superficial meanings of expressions should be abandoned when the contrary evidence exists.

Revelation (*sam^c*) points to the universality of the prophethood of the Prophet.

A group of the Christians hold the view that Muhammad was sent to the Arabs in particular. However, revelation gives the lie to this doctrine of heirs. For God said: "So that I may warn you and whoever is (able to be) reached;" and He said: "We have not sent you except to all the people". The *Surah* of the Jinn points to his being sent to them. The Prophet said: "I have been sent to the black and to the red." It could be argued: How could his mission to those who do not understand his speech be possible? For God said: "We have not sent an apostle except with the language of his people." However, we maintain that there is no impossibility in that because a translator could translate his speech to anyone who did not understand his language. It does not say in the verse that God did not send an apostle except to a people who could understand his language. It is only reported that He did not send him except with the language of his people. The *Qadi al-quddat* allows two possibilities with regard to Gog and Magog:

1. That they were not people originally capable of responsibility (*mukallafin*) and that they were corrupters of the earth, like the beasts who were corrupters of the earth.
2. That they were people capable of responsibility (*mukallafin*) and that the Prophet's summons reached them to come near to the places where they might hear the speech of him who was beyond the barrier (*sadd*).

Some people concede that there were in some places those whom the Prophet's summons did not reach, and they could not be subject to the responsibility of following his revealed law. In my view, if the meaning of that was that responsibility (*taklif*) was completely absent from them whether the call reached them after that or it didn't, then it (the meaning) is absolutely invalid because of what we have explained of the universality of the Prophet's prophethood. If the meaning was that they were not responsible as long as they did not know, and when the call reached them they became responsible, it is correct.

The Prophet is greater in merit than the angels, as are the other prophets, because of the existence in the Prophet of that which conflicts with rational power and his compelling it to submit to reason.

The people differ on this. The majority of the Muslims hold the view that prophets are greater in merit than angels, while others and a group of the ancients hold the view that angels are greater in merit. The ancients argue on the basis of reasons, some of what the author has mentioned, and they are not aware of the inadequacy of their argument. The fact is that in prophets there is the appetitive faculty, the anger faculty, and the rest of the bodily faculties like imagination and fancy and things like these. The majority of the laws of these faculties are contrary to the law of rational power and oppose it so that the majority of people have recourse to the faculties of appetite, anger and fancy, and they abandon rational power. However prophets conquer their nature and act in accordance with their rational powers and avoid the appetitive faculties and the other bodily faculties. Therefore their acts of worship and their actions are more difficult than the acts of worship of the angels insofar as the angels do not have these bodily faculties. Since prophets' acts of worship are more difficult, they are greater in merit, according to the Prophet's saying: "The actions which are greater in merit are those which are the hardest." There are other arguments from the two points of view which we have mentioned in our book *Nihayat al-maram*.

Chapter Twelve

The Imams and the Imamate

According to the Shiᶜis, the continuity of the Muhammadan mission was ordained to be preserved through the Imamate. *Once established by Muhammad, the* ummah *had to be led by Imams, who had inherited the divinely ordained guidance from God's last messenger. Muhammad's* risalah *(messengership) was to be perpetuated in the Imam's* walayah *(guardianship). In the following passage ᶜAllamah Tabataba'i provides the most authoritative definition of* Imamate *in its doctrinal context, and Charles Adams's translation of Henry Corbin relates the concept of Imam in Shiᶜi spirituality. The excerpts are from SI, 174–189 and Adams's previously unpublished translation of En Islam Iranien.*

ᶜAllamah Tabataba'i

Man through his god-given nature realizes without any doubt that n⟨
organized society, such as a country or city or village or tribe or even ⟨
household consisting of a few human beings, can continue to subsis⟨
without a leader and ruler who puts the wheel of the socity in motion an⟨
whose will governs each individual's will and induces the members of tha
society to perform their social duty. Without such a ruler the parts of thi⟨
society become dispersed in a short time and disorder and confusion reign
Therefore, he who is the ruler and governor of a society, whether it be grea⟨
or small, if he is interested in his own position and the continued existenc⟨
of his society, will appoint a successor for himself if he is to be absent fron
his function temporarily or permanently. He will never abandon the domair
of his rule and be oblivious to its existence or annihilation. The head of ⟨
household who bids farewell to his house and household for a journey of ⟨
few days or months will appoint one of the members of the household o⟨
someone else as his successor and will leave the affairs of the house in hi⟨
hands. The head of an institution, or the principal of a school, or the owne⟨
of a shop, if he is to be absent even for a few hours will select someone t⟨
represent him.

In the same way Islam is a religion which according to the text of the Holy
Book and the *Sunnah* is established upon the basis of the primordial natur⟨
of things. It is a religion concerned with social life, as has been seen by ever⟨
observer near and far. The special attention God and the Prophet hav⟨
given to the social nature of this religion can never be denied or neglected. I⟨
is an incomparable feature of Islam. The Holy Prophet was never obliviou⟨
to the problem of the formation of social groupings wherever the influenc⟨
of Islam penetrated. Whenever a city or village fell into Muslim hands h⟨
would, in the shortest time possible, appoint a governor or ruler in whos⟨
hands he would leave the affairs of the Muslims. In very important militar⟨
expeditions ordered for the Holy War (*jihad*), he would appoint more than
one leader and commander, in order of succession. In the war of Mu'tah h⟨
even appointed four leaders, so that if the first were to be killed the second
would be recognized as the head and his command accepted and if the second were to be killed, then the third, and so on.

The Prophet also displayed great interest in the problem of succession
and never failed to appoint a successor when necessary. Whenever he left
Medinah he would appoint a governor in his own place. Even when h⟨
migrated from Mecca to Medinah and there was as yet no idea as to wha⟨

would occur, in order to have his personal affairs managed in Mecca for those few days and to give back to people what had been entrusted to him, he appointed ᶜAli—may peace be upon him—as his successor. In the same way, after his death ᶜAli was his successor in matters concerning his debts and personal affairs. The Shiᶜis claim that for this very reason it is not conceivable that the Prophet should have died without appointing someone as his successor, without having selected a guide and leader to direct the affairs of Muslims and to turn the wheels of Islamic society.

Man's primordial nature does not doubt the importance and value of the fact that the creation of a society depends on a set of common regulations and customs which are accepted in practice by the majority of the groups in that society, and that the existence and continuation of that society depend upon a just government which agrees to carry out these regulations completely. Anyone who possesses intelligence does not neglect or forget this fact. At the same time one can doubt neither the breadth and detailed nature of the Islamic *Shariᶜah*, nor the importance and value the Prophet considered it to possess, so that he made many sacrifices for its application and preservation. Nor can one debate about the mental genius, perfection of intelligence, perspicacity of vision or power of deliberation of the Prophet (beside the fact that this is affirmed through revelation and prophecy).

According to established traditions in both Sunni and Shiᶜi collections of *hadith* (in the chapter on temptations and seditions and others) transmitted from the Prophet, the Prophet foretold seditions and tribulations which would entangle Islamic society after his death, and the forms of corruption which would penetrate the body of Islam, and later worldly rulers who would sacrifice this pure religion for their own impure, unscrupulous ends. How is it possible that the Prophet should not neglect to speak of the details of events and trials of years or even thousands of years after him, and yet would neglect the condition that had to be brought into being most urgently after his death? Or that he should be negligent and consider as unimportant a duty that is on the one hand simple and evident and on the other significant to such a degree? How could he concern himself with the most natural and common acts such as eating, drinking and sleeping and give hundreds of commands concerning them, yet remain completely silent about this important problem and not appoint someone in his own place?

Even if we accepted the hypothesis (which Shiᶜism does not accept) that the appointment of the ruler of Islamic society is given by the *Shariᶜah* to the people themselves, still it would be necessary for the Prophet to give an explanation concerning this matter. He would have had to give the necessary instructions to the community so that they would be aware of the problem upon which the existence and growth of Islamic society and the life of religious symbols and observances depended and relied. Yet there is no trace of such a prophetic explanation or religious instruction. If there had been such a thing, those who succeeded the Prophet and held the reins of power in their hands would not have opposed it. Actually, the first caliph transferred the caliphate to the second caliph by bequest. The second caliph chose the third caliph through a six-man council of which he was himself a member and whose order of procedure he had himself determined and ordered. Muᶜawiyyah forced Imam Hasan to make peace and in this way carried away the caliphate. After this event the caliphate was converted into an hereditary monarchy. Gradually many religious observances identified with the early years of Islamic rule (such as holy war, commanding what is lawful and prohibiting what is forbidden, the establishment of boundaries for human action) were weakened, or even disappeared from the political life of the community, nullifying in this domain the efforts of the Prophet of Islam.

Shiᶜism has studied and investigated the primordial nature of man and the continuous tradition of wisdom and has survived among men. It has penetrated into the principal purpose of Islam, which is to revivify man's primordial nature, and has investigated such things as the methods used by the Prophet in guiding the community; the troubles which entangle Islam and the Muslims and which led to division and separation; and the short life of the Muslim governments of the early centuries, which were characterized by negligence and lack of strict religious principles. As a result of these studies Shiᶜism has reached the conclusion that there are sufficient texts left by the Prophet to indicate the procedure for determining the Imam and successor of the Prophet. This conclusion is supported by Qur'anic verses and hadiths which Shiᶜism considers as sound, such as the verse on *walayat*, and the *hadiths* of Ghadir, Safinah, Thaqalayn, Haqq, Manzilah, Daᶜwat-ᶜashirah-i aqrabin and others. But of course these *hadiths*, most of which are also accepted by Sunnism, have not been understood in the same way by Shiᶜism and Sunnism. Otherwise the whole question of succession would not have arisen. Whereas these hadiths appear to Shiᶜis as a clear indication of the Prophet's intention in the question of succession, they have been interpreted by Sunnis in quite another way so as to leave this question open and unanswered.

To prove the caliphate of ᶜAli ibn Abu Talib, Shiᶜis have had recourse to Qur'anic verses, including the following: "Your friend [*wali*] can be only Allah; and His messenger and those who believe, who establish worship and pay the poor-due, and bow down (in prayer) [or, and this reading is accepted by ᶜAllamah Tabataba'i: [". . . pay the poor-due while bowing down in prayer)"]" (Qur'an, V, 55). Shiᶜi and Sunni commentators alike agree that this verse was revealed concering ᶜAli ibn Abu Talib, and many Shiᶜi and Sunni traditions exist supporting this view. Abu Zarr Ghifari has said: "One day we prayed the noontime prayers with the Prophet. A person in need asked people to help but no one gave him anything. The person raised his hands to the sky saying, 'Oh God! Be witness that in the mosque of the Prophet no one gave me anything.' ᶜAli ibn Abu Talib was in the position of genuflection in the prayers. He pointed with his finger to the person, who took his ring and left. The Prophet, who was observing the scene raised his head toward heaven and said: 'Oh God! My brother Moses said to Thee, "Expand my breast and make easy my tasks and make my tongue eloquent so that they will comprehend my words, and make my brother, Harun, my help and vizier" [cf. Qur'an, XXVIII, 35]. Oh God! I am also Thy prophet; expand my breast and make easy my tasks and make ᶜAli my vizier and helper.' " Abu Zarr says, "The words of the Prophet had not as yet finished when the verse [cited above] was revealed."

Another verse which the Shiᶜis consider as proof of the caliphate of ᶜAli is this: "This day are those who disbelieve in despair of (ever harming) your religion; so fear them not, fear Me! This day have I perfected your religion for you and completed My favour unto you, and have chosen for you as religion AL-ISLAM" (Qur'an, V, 3). The obvious meaning of this verse is that before that particular day the infidels had hopes that a day would come when Islam would die out, but God through the actualization of a particular event made them lose forever the hope that Islam would be destroyed. This very event was the cause of the strength and perfection of Islam and of necessity could not be a minor occasion such as the promulgation of one of the injunctions of religion. Rather, it was a matter of such importance that the continuation of Islam depended upon it.

This verse seems to be related to another verse which comes toward the end of the same chapter: "O Messenger! Make known that which hath been revealed unto thee from thy Lord, for if thou do it not, thou will not have conveyed His message. Allah will protect thee from mankind." (Qur'an, V, 67). This verse indicates that God commanded a mission of great concern and importance to the Prophet which if not accomplished would endanger the basis of Islam and prophecy. But the matter was so important that the Prophet feared opposition and interference and in awaiting suitable circumstances delayed it, until there came a definite and urgent order from God to execute this command without delay and not to fear anyone. This matter also was not just a particular religious injunction in the ordinary sense, for to preach one or several religious injunctions is not so vital that if a single one of them were not preached it would cause the destruction of Islam. Nor did the Prophet of Islam fear anyone in preaching the injunctions and laws of religion.

These indications and witnesses add weight to the Shiᶜi traditions which assert that these verses were revealed at Ghadir Khumm and concern the spiritual investiture (*walayat*) of cAli ibn Abu Talib. Moreover, many Shici and Sunni commentators have confirmed this point.

Abu Sacid Khudari says: "The Prophet in Ghadir Khumm invited people toward cAli and took his arm and lifted it so high that the white spot in the armit of the Prophet of God could be seen. Then this verse was revealed: "This day have I perfected your religion for you and completed My favor unto you, and have chosen for you as religion AL-ISLAM.' Then the Prophet said, 'God is great (*Allahu akbar*) that religion has become perfected and that God's bounty has been completed. His satisfaction attained and the walayat of cAli achieved,' Then he added, 'For whomever I am the authority and guide cAli is also his guide and authority. Oh God! Be friendly with the friends of cAli and the enemy of his enemies. Whoever helps him, help him, and whoever leaves him, leave him.'"

In summary we can say that the enemies of Islam who did everything possible to destroy it, when they lost all hope of achieving this end, were left with only one hope. They thought that since the protector of Islam was the Prophet, after his death Islam would be left without a guide and leader and would thus definitely perish. But in Ghadir Khumm their wishes were brought to nought and the Prophet presented cAli as the guide and leader of Islam to the people. After cAli this heavy and necessary duty of guide and leader was left upon the shoulders of his family.

Some of the hadiths pertaining to Ghadir Khumm, the investiture of cAli, and the significance of the Household of the Prophet are cited here:

Hadith-i ghadir: The Prophet is Islam upon returning from the farewell pilgrimage stopped in Ghadir Khumm, assembled the Muslims and, after delivering a sermon, chose cAli as the leader and guide of Muslims.

Bara' says: "I was in the company of the Prophet during the farewell pilgrimage. When we reached Ghadir Khumm he ordered that place to be cleaned. Then he took cAli's hand and placed him on his right side. Then he said, 'Am I the authority whom you obey?' They answered, 'We obey your directions.' Then he said, 'For whomever I am his master (*mawla*) and the authority whom he obeys, cAli will be his master. Oh God! Be friendly with the friends of cAli and enemy of the enemies of cAli.' Then cUmar ibn al-Khattab said to cAli, 'May this position be pleasing to you, for now you are my master and the master of all the believers.''

Hadith-i safinah: Ibn cAbbas says, "The Prophet said, 'My household is like the ship of Noah; whoever embarks upon it will be saved and whoever turns away from it will be drowned.'"

Hadith-i thaqalayn: Zayd ibn Arqam has recounted that the Prophet said, "It seems that God has called me unto Himself and I must obey His call. But I leave two great and precious things among you: the Book of God and My Household. Be careful as to how you behave toward them. These two will never be separated from each other until they encounter me at Kawthar (in paradise)." *Hadith-i thaqalayn* is one of the most strongly established hadiths, and has been transmitted through many chains of transmission and in different versions. Shi^cis and Sunnis agree concerning its authenticity. Several important points can be deduced from this haidth and its like: (1) In the same way that the Holy Qur'an will remain until the Day of Judgment, the progeny of the Holy Prophet will also remain. No period of time will be without the existence of the figure which Shi^cism calls the Imam, the real leader and guide of men. (2) Through these two great trusts (*amanat*), the Prophet has provided for all the religious and intellectual needs of the Muslims. He has introduced his Household to Muslims as authorities in knowledge and has pronounced their words and deeds to be worthy and authoritative. (3) One must not separate the Holy Qur'an from the Household of the Prophet. No Muslim has a right to reject the "sciences" of the members of the Household of the Prophet and remove himself from under their direction and guidance. (4) If people obey the members of the Household and follow their words they will never be led astray. God will always be with them. (5) The answers to the intellectual and religious needs of men are to be found in the hands of the members of the Household of the Prophet. Whoever follows them will not fall into error and will reach true felicity; that is, the members of the Household are free from error and sin and are inerrant. From this it can be concluded that by "Members of the Household" and "progeny" is not meant all the descendants and relatives of the Prophet. Rather, specific individuals are meant who are perfect in the religious sciences and are protected against error and sin so that they are qualified to guide and lead lmen. For Shi^cism these individuals consist of ^cAli ibn Abu Talib and his eleven descendants who were chosen to the imamate one after another. This interpretation is also confirmed by the Shi^ci traditions. For example, Ibn ^cAbbas has said, "I said to the Prophet, 'Who are your descendants whose love is obligatory [upon Muslims]?' He said, ^cAli, Fatimah, Hasan and Husayn.'" Jabir has transmitted that the Prophet has said, "God placed the children of all prophets in their 'backbone' but placed my children in the backbone of ^cAli.'"

* * *

Much of the argument of Shi^cism concerning the succession to the Prophet rests on the belief that during the last days of his illness the Prophet in the presence of some of his companions asked for some paper and ink so that something could be written which, if obeyed by the Muslims, would prevent them from going astray. Some of those present considered the Prophet to be too ill to be able to dictate anything and said, "The Book of God is sufficient for us." There was so much clamor raised over this matter that the Holy Prophet told those present to leave, for in the presence of a prophet there should not be so any noise or clamor.

Considering what has been said above about hadiths concerning succession and the events that followed upon the death of the Prophet, especially the fact that ᶜAli was not consulted in the question of selecting the Prophet's successor, Shiᶜis conclude that the Holy Prophet had wanted to dictate his definitive views about the person who was to succeed him but was not able to do so.

The purpose of the utterances of some of those present seems to have been to cause confusion and prevent this final decision from being clearly announced. Their interruption of the Holy Prophet's discourse does not seem to be what it appears outwardly, that is concern with the possibility that the Prophet might utter incongruous words due to the intensity of his illness. For, first of all, throughout his illness the Holy Prophet was not heard to have uttered any meaningless or incongruous words and no such thing has been transmitted concerning him. Moreover, according to the principles of Islam the Prophet is protected by God from uttering delirious or senseless words and is inerrant.

Secondly, if the words mentioned by some of those present on that occasion before the Prophet were meant to be of a serious nature there would have been no place for the next phrase, "The Book of God is sufficient for us," In order to prove that the Prophet might utter incongruous words under unusual circumstances the reason of his serious illness would have been used rather than the claim that with the Qur'an there was no need of the Prophet's words. For it could not be hidden from any Muslim that the very text of the Book of God considers the obedience to the Holy Prophet to be obligatory and his words to be in a sense like the Word of God. According to the text of the Holy Qur'an, Muslims must obey the injunctions of both God and the Prophet.

Thirdly, an incident involving illness occurred during the last days of the life of the first caliph, who in his last will and testament chose the second caliph as his successor. Whene ᶜUthman was writing the will according to the order of the caliph, the caliph fainted. Yet the second caliph did not repeat the words that had been uttered in the case of the Prophet according to the *hadith* of "Pen and Paper." This fact has been confirmed in a *hadith* related by Ibn ᶜAbbas. And it has been accounted of the second caliph that he said, ᶜAli deserved the caliphate but the Quraysh would not have been able to bear his caliphate, for had he become caliph he would have forced the people to accept the pure truth and follow the right path. Under his caliphate they would not have been able to transgress the boundaries of justice and thus would have sought to engage in war with him."

Obviously according to religious principles one must force him who has deviated from the truth to follow the truth; one must not abandon the truth for the sake of one who has abandoned it. When the first caliph was informed that some of the Muslim tribes had refused to pay religious tax, he ordered war and said, "If they do not give me the titles which they gave the Prophet, I shall fight against them." Evidently by this saying he meant most of all that truth and justice must be revived at all costs. Surely the problem of the legitimate caliphate was more important and significant than titles, and Shi‘ism believes that the same principle applied by the first caliph to this matter should have been applied by the whole early community to the problem of succession to the Holy Prophet.

*   *   *

In the discussion of prophecy it was mentioned that, according to the immutable and necessary law of general guidance, each created species is guided through the path of genesis and generation toward the perfection and felicity of its own kind. The human species is not an exception to this general law. Man must be guided through the very "instinct" of seeking reality and through thought concerning his life in society in such a way that his well-being in this world and the next is guaranteed. In other words, to attain human happiness and perfection, man must accept a series of doctrines and practical duties and base his life upon them.

It has, moreover, already been said that the way to understand that total program for life called religion is not through reason but through revelation and prophecy, which manifests itself in certain pure beings among mankind who are called prophets. It is the prophets who receive from God, through revelation, the knowledge of men's duties and obligations as human beings and who make these known to men, so that by fulfilling them men may attain felicity.

It is evident that in the same way that this reasoning proves the necessity for knowledge to guide men to the attainment of happiness and perfection, it also proves the necessity for the existence of individuals who preserve intact the total body of that knowledge and who instruct the people when necessary. Just as the Divine Compassion necessitates the existence of persons who come to know the duties of mankind through revelation, so also it makes it necessary that these human duties and actions of celestial origin remain forever preserved in the world and as the need arises be presented and explained to mankind. In other words, there must always be individuals who preserve God's religion and expound it when necessary.

The person who bears the duty of guarding and preserving the Divine message after it is revealed and is chosen by God for this function is called the Imam, in the same way that the person who bears the prophetic spirit and has the function of receiving Divine injunctions and laws from God is called the Prophet. It is possible for the imamate and prophecy (*nubuwwat*) either to be joined in one person or to be separate.

The proof given previously to demonstrate the inerrancy of prophets, also demonstrates the inerrancy of the Imams, for God must preserve His true religion intact and in such a state that it can be propagated among mankind at all times. And this is not possible without inerrancy, without Divine protection against error.

* * *

The previous argument about the reception of Divine injunctions and laws by the prophets only proves the basis of prophecy, namely the receiving of Divine injunctions. The argument does not prove the persistence and continuity of prophecy, even though the very fact that these prophetic injunctions have been preserved naturally raises the idea of persistence and continuity. That is why it is not necessary for a prophet (*nabi*) always to be present among mankind, but the existence of the Imam, who is the guardian of Divine religion, is on the contrary a continuous necessity for human society. Human society can never be without the figure whom Shiᶜism calls the Imam whether or not he is recognized and known. God, the Most Exalted, has said in His Book: "So if these disbelieve in it, We have already entrusted it to a people [i.e., the Imams] who do not disbelieve in it" (Qur'an, VI, 90).

As mentioned above, the functions of prophecy and imamate may be joined in one person who is then appointed to the functions of both prophet and Imam, or to both the reception of the Divine law and its preservation and explanation. And sometimes they can be separated, such as in periods during which there is no prophet living but when there is a true Imam living among men. It is obvious that the number of God's prophets is limited and the prophets have not been present in every period and age.

It is also of significance to note that in God's Book some of the prophets have been introduced as Imams such as the Prophet Abraham, about whom is said, "And (remember) when his Lord tried Abraham with (His) commands, and he fulfilled them, He said: Lo! I have appointed thee a leader [imam] for mankind. (Abraham) said: And of my offspring (will there be leaders)? He said: My covenant includeth not wrongdoers" (Qur'an, II, 124). And God has also said, "And We made them chiefs [imams] who guide by Our command . . ." (Qur'an, XXI, 73).

* * *

In the same way that the Imam is the guide and leader of men in their external actions so does he possess the function of inward and esoteric leadership and guidance. He is the guide of the caravan of humanity which is moving inwardly and esoterically toward God. In order to elucidate this truth it is necessary to turn to the following two introductory comments. First of all, without any doubt, according to Islam as well as other Divine religions the sole means of attaining real and eternal happiness or misery, felicity or wretchedness, is by means of good or evil actions which man comes to recognize through the instruction of Divine religion as well as through his own primordial and God-given nature and intelligence. Second, through the means of revelation and prophecy God has praised or condemned man's actions according to the language of human beings and the society in which they live. He has promised those who do good and obey and accept the teachings of revelation a happy eternal life in which are fulfilled all desires that accord with human perfection. And to the evildoers and the iniquitous He has given warning of a bitter perpetual life in which is experienced every form of misery and disappointment.

Without any doubt God, who stands in every way above all that we can imagine, does not, as we do, possess "thought" moulded by a particular social structure. The relations of master and servant, ruler and ruled, command and prohibition, reward and punishment, do not exist outside our social life. The Divine Order is the system of creation itself, in which the existence and appearance of everything is related solely to its creation by God according to *real* relations and to that alone. Furthermore, as has been mentioned in the Holy Qur'an and prophetic hadith, religion contains truths and verities above the common comprehension of man, which God has revealed to us in a language we can comprehend on the level of our understanding.

It can thus be concluded that there is a real relationship between good and evil actions and the kind of life that is prepared for man in eternity, a relation that determines the happiness or misery of the future life according to the Divine Will. Or in simpler words it can be said that each good or evil action brings into being a real effect within the soul of man which determines the character of his future life. Whether he understands it or not, man is like a child who is being trained. From the instructions of the teacher, the child hears nothing but do's and don'ts but does not understand the meaning of the actions he performs. Yet, when he grows up, as a result of virtuous mental and spiritual habits attained inwardly during the period of training, he is able to have a happy social life. If, however, he refuses to submit to the instructions of the teacher he will undergo nothing but misery and unhappiness. Or he is like a sick person who, when in the care of a physician, takes medicine, food and special exercises as directed by the physician and who has no other duty than to obey the instructions of his doctor. The result of this submission to his orders is the creation of harmony in his constitution which is the source of health as well as every form of physical enjoyment and pleasure. To summarize, we can say that within his outward life man possesses an inner life, a spiritual life, which is related to his deeds and actions and develops in relation to them, and that his happiness or misery in the hereafter is completely dependent upon this inner life.

The Holy Qur'an also confirms this explanation. In many verses it affirms the existence of another life and another spirit for the virtuous and the faithful, a life higher than this life and a spirit more illuminated than the spirit of man as we know it here and now. It asserts that man's acts have inner effects upon his soul that remain always with him. In prophetic sayings there are also many references to this point. For example, in the *Hadith-i mi'raj* (*hadith* of the nocturnal ascension) God addresses the Prophet in these words: "He who wishes to act according to My satisfaction must possess three qualities: he must exhibit a thankfulness that is not mixed with ignorance, a remembrance upon which the dust of forgetfulness will not settle, and a love in which he does not prefer the love of creatures rather than My love. If he loves Me, I love him; I will open the eyes of his heart with the sight of My majesty and will not hide from him the qualities of My creatures. I will confide in him the darkness of the night and the light of the day until conversation and intercourse with creatures terminates. I will make him hear My word and the word of My angels. I will reveal to him the secret which I have veiled from My creatures. I will dress him with the robe of modesty until the creatures feel ashamed before him. He will walk upon the earth having been forgiven. I will make his heart possess consciousness and vision and I will not hide from him anything in Paradise or in the Fire. I will make known to him whatever people experience on the Day of Judgement in the way of terror and calamity."

Abu ͨAbdallah—may peace be upon him—has recounted that the Prophet of God—may peace and blessing be upon him—received Harithah ibn Malik ibn al-Nu ͨman and asked him, "How art thou, Oh Harithah?" He said, "Oh Prophet of God, I live as a true believer." The Prophet of God said to him, "Each thing possesses its own truth. What is the truth of thy word?" He said, "Oh Prophet of God! My soul has turned away from the world. My nights are spent in a state of awakedness and my days in a state of thirst. It seems as if I am gazing at the Throne of my Lord and the account has been settled, and as if I am gazing at the people of paradise who are visiting each other in heaven, and as if I hear the cry of the people of hell in the fire." Then the Prophet of God said, "This is a servant whose heart God has illuminated."

It must also be remembered that often one of us guides another in a good or evil matter without himself carrying out his own words. In the case of the prophets and Imams, however, whose guidance and leadership is through Divine Command, such a situation never occurs. They themselves practice the religion whose leadership they have undertaken. The spiritual life toward which they guide mankind is their own spiritual life, for God will not place the guidance of others in someone's hands unless He has guided him Himself. Special Divine guidance can never be violated or infringed upon. The following conclusions can be reached from this discussion:

1. In each religious community the prophets and Imams are the foremost in the perfection and realization of the spiritual and religious life they preach, for they must and do practice their own teachings and participate in the spiritual life they profess.
2. Since they are first among men and the leaders and guides of the community, they are the most virtuous and perfect of men.
3. The person upon whose shoulders lies the responsibility for the guidance of a community through Divine Command, in the same way that he is the guide of man's external life and acts, is also the guide for the spiritual life, and the inner dimension of human life and religious practice depends upon his guidance.

Henry Corbin

The Meaning of the Imam for Shi°i Spirituality

Shi°ism as the Religion of Spiritual Love that Initiates One into Knowledge of the Self

The term *walayah* has been used frequently, and we know that Shi°ism is the religion of the *walayah*. The richness of this term is evident already, along with the difficulty we have in finding an equally expressive single term in our languages, since it denotes a specifically Shi°i sentiment of manifold aspects. But the contexts in which it appears and the Persian term used most frequently to translate it (*dusti*), as well as the Arabic terms that sometimes are paired with it and sometimes are substituted for it (*hubb, mahabbat, mawaddat*), all enable us to grasp at once its basic meaning: The religion of the *walayah* is the religion of spiritual love.

Our authors frequently explain that *walayah* is *mahabbat* (dilection, love); the *wali* is the *muhibb* (the friend, the one who loves). This immediate significance, the profound resonance of the term, is lost if we yield to the routine and the approximate, and if we translate *wali* simply as saint. Doubtless, the words have certain aspects in common, but the connotations of *wali and walayah* go beyond what customarily and *canonically* is understood in our language by *saint* and *saintliness*. For this very reason, we are no longer surprised that the essence of Shi^cism so frequently has been misunderstood; it is important to recognize that *walayah* is its central concept, that which it presents in various aspects, framing the whole horizon of its view of the world; and it is important to understand its basic meaning.

The Shi^ci were fully aware through the teaching of their Imams that their Shi^cism was basically a devotion of love. This, plus the distinctive tonality that as a result marks their sense of man and of being human is what we would like briefly to summarize here. In fact, it is by virtue of the premises and implications that emerge from Islam professed as religion of love that the concept and the figure of the Imam appear to us in their ineluctable necessity. At the same time, the central problem of Shi^cism is posed, met, and solved, without the occasion even to speak of Sufism. Here, as we have said, is the key to a spiritual situation that even now scarcely has been analyzed. In the end, the meaning of the Imam for the most personally experienced kind of Shi^ci spirituality will be found, of course, in the *walayah* itself. The meaning of the Imam as the object of the *walayah* manifests itself as being the initiation of the adept to the knowledge of himself. Once initiated, he understands how and why the love of God is impossible without love of the Imam, for it is in the *walayah*, as the form of his love, that he discovers and verifies the meaning of the famous maxim: "He who knows himself knows his Lord." That being the case, the titles assumed by the Imams in the *hadith* are understandable directly in relation to this experienced spirituality, as leading to the encounter with the "Soul of the soul" (*Jan-i jan*) who is the Imam. Since elsewhere we have analyzed this fructification of imamology as a spiritual experience in Isma^cilism, we devote ourselves here to its Twelver Shi^ci aspect.

First of all let us note this. To speak of Islam as a religion of love bears little resemblance to the current representation of Islam in general, or at least of Sunni Islam, as a strictly legalistic religion, as observance of the *Shari^cah*. The paradox normally becomes apparent only when one speaks of Sufism. But it is Shi^ci Islam in itself, without any necessity to refer explicitly to Sufism, that presents itself as the religion of the *walayah*. Testimonies to this effect are found assembled in all Shi^ci literature. They are presented in a particularly systematic fashion in a monumental, already-cited work, the book of *Prolegomenas to the Shi^ri Hermeneutics of the Qur'an*," composed in Isfahan in the seventeenth century by Abu al-Hasan Sharif Isfahani, who was a student of the great theologian Muhammad Baqir Majlisi. The work presents a considerable number of glossed *hadith*, derived from the Prophet and the Imams, attesting that the *walayah* is the inner, esoteric meaning (*batin*) of the Qur'anic Revelation. The *walayah*, to be sure, is a "category" that makes hierohistory comprehensible, but beyond that, and for that very reason, it modalizes the conscience of every Shiᶜi believer. For the validity of every religious act, Shiᶜi doctrine postulates an intention of love, an interior attitude molded by this intention. Hence, the famous *hadith* cited several times already, in which one Imam after another has repeated that to join their cause demands an effort so heroic that it can be assumed only by an angel drawn nigh, a messenger-prophet, or a believer whose heart God has tested for faith — this *hadith* and all those related to it are intended, our author stresses, to exclude and deny that there can be complete surrender to the threefold *Shahadah* (attestation to the Unique One, to the prophetic revelation, and to the Imamic initiation) without the fervor of ardent desire (*shawq*), assent, and perfect love (*mahabbah kamilah*) in regard to the supreme purity (ᶜismah) of the Fourteen Immacultae Ones.

Moreover, the profession of this love, of this *walayah*, takes precedence over all the obligations of the *Shariᶜah*, not only in the sense that it alone authenticates the performance of these obligations but also becuase it can compensate for failure to meet them. This the Imams teach in numerous *hadith*, affirming that "the first thing about which a man is questioned after his death is his love for Us. If he has professed this love (*walayah*) and died professing it, then his prayer, his fasting, his alms, and his pilgrimage, are acceptable to God. If he has not professed this love, then none of his works will be capable of being accepted by God."

Since, in Shiᶜi ethics, actions originate in the inner-being (the *batin*), pious works and the performance of ritual duties must necessarily originate in a sentiment of love; otherwise they are empty formality. Abu al-Hasan Sharif wrote: "Our shaykh (i.e., Muhammad Baqir Majlisi) states explicitly in his *Bihar al-anwar*: 'All the Imamis agree that the spiritual validity of deeds and God's approval of them are conditioned by faith (*Iman*); this point is as integral a part of faith as is love for the Twelve Imams and their imamate." Nothing could be less legalistic than a religion thus conceived in its essence. The consequences are far reaching for the very vocation of Shiᶜi Islam in this world. It is important to grasp well in what sense and why the Imam is the object of this *walayah* (when we say simply "the Imam," the word refers both to each Imam and to the Fourteen Immaculate Ones, since in the unity of their essence each one is equivalent to all the others).

To clarify the discussion for which we have been preparing throughout the preceding pages, we may say that all the knowledge that man can have of God, not only the knowledge resulting from his own efforts but also all that the *Deus absconditus* might give of Himself as *Deus revelatus*, i.e., comprising all knowledge born of the inspired revelations to the prophets — all this knowledge, *eo ipso*, is *human* knowledge of God, whether it be acquired through man's effort or revealed to and for man. This human meaning of all human knowledge of God is recapitulated in the dictum, "He who knows himself knows his Lord".

Now, we could not pass from one element of this sentence to the other if the Imam were not the form of knowledge of the self, the form by virtue of which a relationship was established between the human subject and the *absconditum*. The truth of this dictum is then established as through an interiorization of imamology: The imam *is* the human meaning of all human knowledge of God. For to know and recognize the Imam (not only a certain one of the Twelve Imams but also each of the Twelve and the entire group of Twelve in their essence and their pre-eternal theophanic function) is to avoid the double trap to which *tawhid* is exposed and the simplistic monotheism to which common people and theologians alike succumb, the double trap of *taᶜtil* and *tashbih*.

We know already that the former (*taᶜtil*) consigns the Divine Reality to an absolute beyond in order to surmount the "human meaning" of the Divine Names and Attributes. Shiᶜism also posits this "beyond" of the Names and Attributes expressed in human language, but it holds that if we remain content purely and simply with this consignment to the beyond (*taᶜtil*), we plunge into the depths of agnosticism, because we thereby dissolve the personal human–divine bond that every believing consciousness postulates. On the other hand, if we make the divine Super-essence (*hyperousia*) the support of the Names and Attributes, we plunge into the depths of *tashbih* (anthropomorphism). Whoever says, "What good is the Imam? God without an intermediary is enough for me" plainly forgets that, in speaking of this God who is immediate for him, he can never speak save of the God who reveals Himself to him, of God as he knows Him, in and through the form in which God reveals Himself to him. Even if he speaks of God as of something impersonal or transpersonal, he does so only by virtue of the form shown to him or withheld from him. Without this *mazhar*, without this "theophanic form" in which God manifests Himself — in the widest sense of the term — it is impossible even to speak of God. This form is the "Face" of God, and several texts have already shown us the importance of this theme for Shiᶜism. We have been told that this "Face of God" is the Imam. Later we shall also see that he is what is *pre-posed*, what goes in "advance of the theory of the being of his devotee (*muqaddam ᶜala wujudihi*)."

If, then, we lose or destroy the meaning of the Imam — and with him the validity of the human meaning of the human knowledge of God or of the divine Revelation to man — we shall find ourselves trapped in the circle of *ta^ctil* and *tashbih*. Because this meaning is human, "too human," it is suspected and rejected, and we advance no further than agnositicism, pure and simple (*ta^ctil*); or else it is accepted but without a consciousness of what it really is, so that we fall into the trap of metaphysical idolatry (*tashbih*). Only the theophanic person of the Imam upholds the validity of this human meaning because it transcends the "too human." Thus, outside Shi^cism, certain Sufi masters, for example, have meditated to the point of vertigo in order to escape infernal dialectic in which *ta^ctil* and *tashbih* have imprisoned their *tawhid*, their "unification of the Unique." But the mystery of *tawhid* is the mystery of the divine solitude, of "God alone is unique."

This does not mean a solitary, mathematical unity, dominating or surpassing an infinity of other unities or individuations of being. It is the mystery of the every-instance-unique of all the Uniques, of the One multiplied to infinity through itself but that is always the unique One; the Face of God that remains unique for every unique being; that is what the Imam is and what is expressed in the diversity of the titles that the Imams assign themselves in their *hadith*. These titles are repeated in Shi^ci prayers that are spread throughout a complex liturgical calendar to such an extent that the commentary on each of these prayers alone might constitute a whole treatise or imamology. An example was cited above.

The universality of the *walayah* with the Imam as its object and the idea of the Imam as the human meaning of the divine Revelation to and for man, such that without the Imam no authentic *tawhid* is possible, is what lends coherence to what might be called *Shi^ci ecumenism*, in the sense that Shi^cism aims at combining in the unity of this *walayah* (in this religion of love, all the elements and all the figures of a permanent, prophetic religion as a religion for the whole of humanity) which is the spiritual posterity of Abraham. All the prophets and all their believers have professed this same *walayah*; together, they all form a single, immense *corpus mysticum* (the Isma^cilis for their part, speak of the "Temple of Light" of the Imamate), which cannot be denied except by a denial that is *ipso facto* a repudiation of the prophetic Revelations prior to Islam. An *hadith* of the second Imam, Hasan ibn ^cAli, declares: "Whoever denies the pre-eminence of the Prince of the Believers (^cAli, the first Imam) gives the lie to the Torah, the Gospel, the Psalms, the writings of Abraham, and all the other Books of God that have descended from Heaven. For of everything that is revealed in these Books, nothing is more important, after the attestation to the Unique (*tawhid*) and the attestation to the mission of the prophets, than the attestation to the *walayah* in respect to ^cAli and the Imams."

In any case, this affirmation is the corollary of the Prophet's declaration, which we already know, that the Imam was sent with each prophet secretly but that with him, the Seal of the Prophets, the Imam was sent openly. The *walayah*, the divine dilection whose object is the pleroma of the Fourteen Immaculate Ones, is the secret, the esoteric aspect of the divinely inspired Revelations to the prophets; the secret of the Treasure that is hidden but aspires to be known. The Imam is this Treasure becoming knowable and the object of love. Christian theologians are faced with this question: Since the Redemption is an accomplished historical fact that is a part of historical chronology alongside other historical facts, how can we conceive of salvation for men prior to this historical fact? As we have gradually come to see, such a question could not be posed in these same terms in the context of a prophetic religion that stretches uninterruptedly from Adam to the last Imam.

Before the Seal of the Prophets, prior prophets already had brought to men the same message, calling them to the same religion of love directed towards the divine Face that their prophetic inspirations had revealed to the prophets. Paradise and Hell lay in man's assent or rejection. In a long conversation with his disciple, Mufaddal, the sixth Imam explains that the Imam is the one who separates the people of Paradise from the people of Hell; he does not even have to judge them; it is their love or their hate for the Imam that *is* their Paradise or Hell respectively. It is in this sense that one may speak of Ridwan (the Angel of Paradise) and Malik (the Guardian of Hell) as emanating from the order of the Imam. It has been thus from the beginning of the mission of the prophets and thus it will be throughout the cycle of the *walayah*. "The Shiᶜi find their salvation in an act of love for their Imam" (this statement entails others that at times afford a degree of consonance with the idea of salvation in Pure Land Buddhism). Initiating his disciple to the mystery of this universal religion of love that encompasses all believers, Imam Jaᶜfar rightly concludes: "Oh Mufaddal, gather all this with care, for it is a Treasure of knowledge, secret and hidden. Show it only to those who are worthy of it."

In fact, this Treasure can be shown only to those whose gaze is raised to that level of the horizon that previously showed us the mystery of the primordial Muhammadan Reality, a mystery situated in the preexistence of pure spiritual beings, where everything takes place in the world of the Spirit, even before there were terrestial beings and biographies; for what all the prophets proclaimed was this eternal Imam as "site of the mission and message of the prophets". . . . That is what the Imam explains to his disciple. But at first Mufaddal does not understand. How could the earlier prophets profess this love for the Imam? How could their followers find their Paradise and their adversaries find their Hell therein? So Imam Jaᶜfar explains to him: "Dost thou not know that God Most-High sent His Messenger, a Spirit (the Logos-Prophet), to the prophets, themselves Spirits who were created 2000 years before the creation of creatures? Dost thou know that this Spirit called them to the triple Attestation?" Here again is verification that Shi^c^i theosophy could not conceive of hierohistory except on the plane of metahistory, where preexistence and postexistence are *copresent*. We know that the number that "encodes" the duration in "subtle time" of the anteriority of the world of spiritual beings may vary. Nevertheless, the disjunction of the before and after, the law of irreversibility, concerns only the order of succession in our historical time ("opaque time", *zaman kathif*), not the simultaneous order of events that endure permanently in the world of the Spirit. There is neither chronology nor anachronism in the Imam's explanation; there is a perfect synchronism that, however, is inconceivable anywhere but on the plane where imamology situates us.

Thus, we find this synchronism subjacent to the idea of the *corpus mysticum* formed of all those in existence who have professed or do profess the religion of the one eternal *walayah*. This *walayah* has its source in God Himself in that He reveals Himself in those who are the object of His love. At the same time, because they are the object of this love, they are granted a "right" that was invoked before "their time" in this world and that, accordingly, already has responded to the question posed by Mufaddal. In a *hadith* in which the Prophet alludes to the events of his "celestial assumption"—when he was "two bows'-length away," to which the *surah* of the Star refers (53:9)—he tells Imam ^c^Ali that he heard God say to him: "I wrote thy Name and his Name on my Throne before creating the creatures because of my love of you both. Whoever loves you and takes you as friends numbers among those drawn-nigh to Me. Whoever rejects your *walayah* and separates himself from you numbers among the impious transgressors against Me."

This tradition in its various implications, is among those tirelessly contemplated in Shi^c^ism as establishing the very source of the *walayah*, the divine dilection, the dilection for the Hidden Treasure, inclining toward the primordial Light that rises from it and that reveals it to creatures, the divine dilection that gives rise to and motivates the dilection (*walayah* and *mahabbah*) borne by their followers towards those who are its objects—the Fourteen Figures of primordial light—and that gives rise to the ethical law of Shi^c^ism (expressed in the two familiar Persian words, *tawalla wa-tabarra*, to choose as friends the Friends of God and their friends and to break with their enemies). Thus at the origin, through this predilection, God confers a kind of right to Himself upon those who are the pre-eternal objects of this predilection: Hence that formula of invocation, frequent in Shi^c^i prayers, which sounds forth like a supreme conjuration, as if by invoking this "right to Himself" conferred by God upon His Friends, the prayer formulated by their friends bore in itself the force of accomplishment. The Imams themselves proferred the formula *bi-haqqina*, which can be translated "by our right" or "in the name of our cause".

In certain contexts, as we have said, recourse to this "right" is itself a response to Mufaddal's question. Indeed, since this "right" originates in metahistory, it could be invoked by means of a synchronism, which, though it baffles our sense of history, serves as the key to hierohistory, because it was recourse to this "right," the invocation of this "cause," that provides the denouement to the drama experiences in this world by the prophets one after another. It is "in the name of this cause" that God "returned to Adam," who was exiled from paradise; and because this same "cause" also is the secret of the denouement of Qur'anic Christology—Christ victoriously preserved from death of God, who raised him up to Himself. (IV, 156)—this same cause, invoked by the prophets, makes even the idea of an impossible decide to disappear. In a *hadith* going back to the eighth Imam, the Imam ᶜAli Rida, and through him to the earlier Imams, it is said: "When Noah was in danger of being inundated, he invoked God by invoking our cause (or our right), and God saved him from inundation. When Abraham was cast into the fire, he invoked God by invoking our cause, and God caused the fire to become a harmless coolness. When Moses opened a path into the sea, he invoked God by invoking our cause, and God made the sea dry land. And when the Jews wanted to kill Jesus, he invoked God by invoking our cause; then God saved him from death and raised him up to Himself (Qur'an, IV, 156)."

Here now is another text, among a great many others, affirming the synchronism of this religion of the *walayah* common to all the prophets. This time, there is a conversation between the fifth Imam, Imam Muhammad Baqir, and his disciple Jabir al-Juᶜfi, which forms part of a whole set of conversations constituting, as it were, the Shiᶜi hermeneutic of the Old Testament of our Bible. "'I asked the Imam' his disciple relates, 'about the interpretation of dream visions given by Daniel. Is it authentic, or not?'— 'Of acourse it is authentic,' the Imam replied. 'Daniel truly had a divine revelation, for he was a prophet (*nabi*). Daniel was one of those to whom God taught the symbolic meaning of events (*ta'wil al-ahadith*). He was truthful and a sage. And the divine religion that he professed was the religion of our love (of love for us, the *Ahl al-Bayt*).'" The assertion makes sense, of course, only on the plane of the primordial Muhammadan Reality. Taken by surprise, Jabir asks the same question as Mufaddal is supposed to have put to Imam Jaᶜfar: "Of your love, of love for you, *Ahl al-Bayt*?' And the Imam replied: 'Yes, God be my witness! There was never a Prophet nor an angel who did not profess the religion of our love (*illa wa-kana yadinu bi-mahabbatina*)'"

This is all perfectly clear. At issue is a "religion of love," and it is not a Sufi master who speaks, but the fifth Shiᶜi Imam. In addition, this religion always has been professed by the followers of all the prophets, because the revelation of the divine Face to which this love is addressed was the secret of their message. Here, then, we reach the heart of the matter. Given the idea of the religion of the *walayah* as being that of the permanent prophetic religion of humanity because "the Imam was secretly sent with each prophet", given, accordingly, the meaning of the Imam and the Imamate for hierohistory, that is to say, for the history of spiritual events that occurred in the dimension of a time other than the time of profane history, we are in a position to understand the primordial meaning of the Imam for Shiᶜi spirituality. The universalistic aspect of Shiᶜism is linked to the universality of the devotion of love to the theophanic Figure who is the revealed Face of God. Now, man's recognition of this divine Face comes about through his knowledge of himself. It is on the rock of a faith in which love is an integral part that Shiᶜism is conscious of gathering together all the believers in the prophetic religion, by means of the message that summons them to the quest for the Soul of their soul. The progression that passes from the meaning of the Imam for hierohistory to his meaning for the most private spirituality can only result in putting into operation the principle of the Shiᶜi hermeneutic on which we have been so insistent.

Since its inner, esoteric meaning (the meaning with respect to the *walayah*) is constantly being attained in each new believer, the Holy Book remains alive for the whole duration of our Eon. Throughout the periods of the whole cycle of prophecy, it is the center of the "plane of historical permanence" represented by hierohistory, which means that during every period of the cycle the same protagonists and antagonists reappear, the same enthusiasms for the faith, and the same militantly negative refusals: the dramatic personae remain the same under other names and with different actors. This permanence is expressed in the idea of the *walayah*, which is eternal, whereas the prophetic mission is temporary; it is expressed also in the relationship that unites all the prophets and spiritual adepts to the "Seal of the Prophets" and to the "Seal of the Friends of God." It is the *walayah* as the esoteric aspect, the secret element of the message repeated by one prophet after another up to the "Seal of Prophets" that unites all the prophets and all their believers in one and the same *corpus mysticum* (the Temple of Light of the Imamate). What is it, then, to belong to this *corpus mysticum*? How does the *walayah* in respect to the Imam make the faithful adept, the "believer with tested heart," a member of this mystical body ultimately represented by the notion of *Ahl al-bayt* (members of the holy Family, of the "house" or the prophetic "temple")? How, according to the terms of the first Imam himself, is it the "believer with tested heart" who discovers this love in his heart?

We know already that without the Imamate, only a strictly negative theology (that of *tanzih*, designated by Christian tradition as "apophatic" theology) would be possible, in view of the *Deus absconditus*. If the *Deus absconditus* becomes an object of knowledge and an object of love, this happens thanks to the Face, the epiphanic Form (the *mazhar*), that makes of it a *Deus revelatus*. To say that the Imam is this revealed Face, this epiphanic Form, *eo ipso* is to do a great deal more than make an "objective" statement arising from a theoretical theosophy, for such a proposition directly engages the innermost life of the adept, that is to say, the meaning of the Imam for the spirituality experienced by Shiᶜism. In fact, assent to this proposition presupposes entering actively into a personal relationship, and the actualization of this relationship is achieved to the extent that the recognition of the Imam as epiphanic Form *eo ipso* is also initiation of the adept to knowledge of himself. When he has attained this, he is himself an epiphanic form of the Imam, just as the Imam is the epiphanic Form of the *Deus absconditus*. Thus, the fifth Imam was able to say, "We are the Treasurers and the Treasures of God in this world and the other world (cf. *infra* the full meaning of this proposition), and our Shiᶜi are treasurers and treasures for us, the Imams," since, in fact, the Imamate is the content (treasure) of the divine science and something of the knowledge of the Imam is realized in each Shiᶜi "with tested heart.".. .

We conclude the following: The Imam is *the* theophanic Forum (*mazhar*); in this Form, God is the object of knowledge and love; to attain this theophanic form *eo ipso* is to attain knowledge of God in the only form in which He is knowable and that, as such, constitutes the supreme degree to which the Lowly can attain, the highest degree of its being, its knowledge, and its love. Since theophany as such means the establishment of a rapport between the One who shows himself (*mutajalli*) and the one to whom He is shown (*mutajalla lahu*), the One who shows Himself does so of necessity in a form proportionate to and commensurate with the one to whom He shows Himself. Ibn ᶜArabi has insisted on this point. But here the rapport clearly is imamology itself, for imamology alone makes possible this rapport, without which *tawhid* would be undermined.

This relationship of homogeneity posited by theophany (*tajalli*), coupled with the fact that theophany is the highest summit that the Lowly, the being of the lower world, can attain, means that by reaching the "place" of this theophany (that mystical Sinai where God is revealed to him), the believer reaches the summit or the heart of his being, his self, his anima (*nafs*). But the form this theophany takes, that it, the Face of this God revealed to him at the summit of his soul, is the Imam. Therefore, to know one's self, one's soul, one's anima, and therewith all the universe of the soul, is to know one's Imam; it is this knowledge that constitutes for every man the knowledge of his Lord, his knowledge of God. The Imam is the form that the *Deus revelatus* assumes in the knowledge of self that is the knowledge of

God. The Imam is the form of his knowledge and of his love of God. The knowledge of the Imam reveals to his adept that it is, as such, the form of his love and consequently the secret of his being, for his being is his itself. Thus, the love of the Imam, the religion of the *walayah*, so conceived by our Shi'i authors as to embrace all the stages of an eternal prophetic religion, all the followers of all the prophets, is initiation to knowledge of the self, a self who is not an impersonal Absolute devoid of qualities but is the Soul and the Beloved of the soul (*jan-i jan*), the self in the second person that "goes in advance of me," the Imam (in the purely etymological meaning of the word).

Thus, Shi'i piety and spirituality culminate in the *walayah* devoted to the Imam as the theophanic Form in which the *absconditum* is revealed to man and in which the hidden God becomes the object of love (this Form being *mahbubiyat*). For this reason, all love of God is *walayah* of the Imam by virtue of the fact that love postulates a God who is the object of love. Non-Shi'i Sufism searched for such an outcome in anguish, in order to escape what Ruzbihan called the "madness of the inaccessible." But it is important to note that the imamology represents precisely the result of it. For this is the meaning of the Imam in the manifold titles conferred upon him in the Shi'i invocations, which only repeat the titles that the Imams give to themselves in their *hadiths*: the Imam as Guide and as Pole, as *A'raf*, as Witness of God, etc. Each of these illustrates the basic theme of a knowledge of self that is knowledge of the Imam and that *eo ipso* is knowledge of God, because there is no knowledge of God accessible to man other than the knowledge of his Imam.... .

The Imam as Guide and as Pole

This fundamental theme of prophetic philosophy has already been illuminated in the preceding pages. Here it will suffice to sum up the essentials. First of all, there is the situation about which one is questioned in such abrupt terms as the following: What happens when there is no longer, and never will be, another prophet; when, in addition, the *true meaning* of the prophetic Revelation does not lie in the apparent letter; when the true meaning is derived not from conclusions reached through deductions or inference but can be unveiled and transmitted only by "the one who knows"? This question is answered by the bi-unity of the Imam and the Qur'an, affirmed in numerous Shi'i *hadiths*: The Qur'an is the "silent Imam", the Imam is the "speaking Qur'an".

As the "speaking Qur'an," the Imam is the Guide, the permanent Guide, who provides initiation to the true meaning of the Qur'anic Revelation and who thereby preserves the Book in the state of the living Word. We have already referred to the *hadith* of the fifth Imam that evades the trap of historicism when it is confronted with the letter. For the same reason the sixth Imam, Ja^{c}far al-Sadiq, tests one of his disciples by asking him: "Oh Abu Muhammad, the Prophet was the Warner. ^{c}Ali was the Guide: But is there a Guide (*Hadi*) today?" The disciple answers: "Yes, I swear to thee by my life: In thy House there has always been a Guide, one succeeding the other, and now thy turn has come." "May God have mercy upon thee, Oh, Abu Muhammad," the Imam replies. "If a verse were revealed for a certain man and the man then died, the verse would die with him; the whole Book would by now be dead. No! The Qur'an is alive and will continue to exist for those who will live in the future as it existed for those who lived in the past." Here again, it is impossible to state more clearly that if the matter in question were to understand the Holy Book simply in relation to "its time," in relation to the historical or social circumstances in which the verses emerged, then the Qur'an would have long since been dead. In other words, without the *walayah* of the "Friends of God" who always exist in this world, there would be no future for the Book of God. In this world, the life of the Imam and the life of the Holy Book are bound together.

The presence of the Imam and his friends therefore must be perpetuated. Such was the theme of the dialogue between the first Imam and Kumayl ibn Ziyad cited above, where we encountered the motif of the mystical *pole*, without which the world of man could not endure. Echoing the statements of the first Imam, Mulla Sadra wrote: "The earth can never be devoid of an Imam, a Guide for every era. Otherwise the Qur'an would die, owing to the death of those who support it. But the Qur'an lives and will never die until the Day of Resurrection. The one who guides us towards the Qur'an lives in every moment of time, until the coming of the last Hour." These lines merely recapitulate the content of the *hadith* comprising Kulayni's chapter on the Imam as Guide and Guarantor of God (*hujjah*), he who "answers for" God before men. We should keep in mind some of those *hadith* that affirm the inviolable consciousness that the Imams have of themselves. From the fifth Imam Muhammad Baqir: "As God is my witness, since the gathering in of the soul of Adam (i.e. since the death of Adam), God has not allowed the existence of a terrestrial world without an Imam to guide men to God; he is the Guarantor of God to His servants. The terrestrial world has never been left without an Imam who is Guarantor and Guide for men." From the tenth Imam, ^{c}Ali Naqi: "In truth the terrestrial world is never devoid of a Guarantor and Guide, and, as God is my witness, I am at present he." From the sixth Imam, Ja^{c}far Sadiq, a disciple, Abu Hamzah, relates: "I asked Imam Ja^{c}far, 'Can the Earth remain without an Imam?' He replied, 'If the Earth has no Imam, it would sink.'" Again the fifth Imam: "If the Imam were removed from the Earth for a single hour, it vould roll like waves which would rock its inhabitants as the sea rocks the nhabitants of its waves." These statements, which cement a mysterious bond, a sacramental bond, so to speak, between the presence of the Imam and the continuance of the terrestrial world of men, are pregnant with certain consequences. First, there is every evidence that the necessity of the Imam is not just one social-political theme among others. We here confront a metaphysical theme that concerns the order and the suprasensible structure of the universe, namely, the theme of the Imam as mystical Pole, Pole of poles (*qutb al-aqtab*). This, Mulla Sadra explains in a very pithy passage. The necessity of the Imam expresses an inner law of being, which requires that every higher degree of being be the goal, the finality, of a lower degree; the lower exists through the higher degree; it cannot find its fulfillment and perfection save in the higher degree. The degree of lower being presupposes the existence of the higher degree but not inversely. More than a law of evolution, it is a law of the *ascension* of being toward the higher degree that is preexistent to it. The same holds true for humanity. It cannot find its fulfillment except at the degree that marks its supreme perfection. Such is the meaning of the Imamate, for, according to Mulla Sadra, "the degree of the Imamate signifies the Perfect Man (*al-insan al-kamil, Anthropos teleios*), who is the *king* of the terrestrial world. But precisely because it is the kingdom of the Perfect Man as the finality of being, this kingship neither results from nor depends on political considerations that would make the Imam a mere rival of the Umayyids and the ᶜAbbasids. It has to do with something other than what is treated by social history, for it is a kingship that by its very essence implies neither the necessity nor even the idea of temporal political success, still less the idea that majorities are always right, under the pretext that they "make" history. Instead it pertains to a history that "is made" without their knowledge; a spiritual kingship above the visible world that operates incognito, something like the role of the dynasty of the Grail.

Other implications also arise. This idea of the incognito, we have seen, had been implied to be essential to the Imamate as early as the Prophet's statements limiting the number of the Imams descended from him to twelve. In effect this limitation implies of necessity the return of the Imamate into occultation (*ghaybah*) at a given moment. Hence, *ipso facto*, the present relationship of the Shiᶜi believer with his Imam as the *pole* of his being is not a relationship with an institution of this world but a relationship with the suprasensible world. The permanent but invisible presence of the twelfth Imam after his fleeting appearance in this world, implies for him a mode of existence superior to the conditions that pertain in the biological world—a suprasensible presence and existence manifested only as visions or incognito encounters. But this invisible presence of the Imam polarizes Shiᶜi devotion; both its simple believers and its doctors live in familiarity with it. It is no more necessary for the Imam to be physically visible to the eyes of the flesh than it is for him to be known or recognized by the masses and the power of this world. The Imamate is the intrinsic qualification of his being, that of the Perfect Man. Neither man's ignorance nor his blindness can abolish that element in his being that makes the Imam the Imam.... .

The Imam as the Aᶜraf

This theme sends us back to the Qur'anic verses that allude to the mysterious rampart erected between Paradise and Hell — the Aᶜraf, which gives its name to the seventh *surah* (verses 44–45): "On the Aᶜraf stand men who recognize each by his appearance" (VII, 44). A disciple relates that the sixth Imam (himself repeating a remark of the first Imam) replied as follows to a question about the men of the Aᶜraf):

> "It is we (the Imams) who are on the Aᶜraf; we recognize our companions by their faces. And we are ourselves the Aᶜraf, for God can be the object of knowledge only to those who pass through our knowledge. And we are the Aᶜraf, for on the Day of Resurrection we are those whom God recognizes as being the Way (*sirat*). No one enters Paradise save those who recognize us and those whom we ourselves recognize. No one enters the Fire save those who deny us and whom we ourselves deny. If God Most High had wished, He would have made Himself known to men. But he made us his Thresholds, his way, his path, the Face toward which it is necessary to be oriented. Therefore, one who strays from our *walayah* (i.e. refuses us his devotion of love), or gives others preference over us, strays from the Way."

This relationship of the Imam and the Aᶜraf proceeds through three stages to their mutual identification. Mulla Sadra begins here by showing that in their purely exoteric exegeses all the literalist commentators more or less stray around the countryside while the exegeses of the non-Shiᶜi esotericists allow the essential element in the idea of the Aᶜraf to escape them. He himself works out this idea by scrutinizing, the intentions of the Imam, sentence by sentence, in order to give a genuinely Imami exegesis of the Aᶜraf. Once it is established that the proper noun Aᶜraf is derived from the root ᶜ-r-f, which denotes the idea of knowing, of being acquainted with, a three-stage process contained in the Imam's reply can be broken down as follows:

> 1. At the first stage, the Imam begins by stating: "It is we (the twelve Imams) who are on the Aᶜraf," which means "at the summit of

knowledge" (*ma^crifat*), its highest rampart, elevation being understood here as spiritual not spatial.

2. At the second stage, there has been noteworthy progress: The Imam no longer simply asserts that the Imams are at the summit of the *A^craf* but affirms that they *are* themselves the *A^craf*, meaning that their knowledge mediates all human knowledge of God. They are not, then, merely the *subjects* of knowledge, *those who know* and those whose knowledge is the summit of knowledge; they also are *that through which* there is knowledge (*ma^crifat*), that through which, and thanks to which, there is an *object* corresponding to this knowledge, for they are the very thing attained by the highest knowledge, the *object* of that knowledge. In this case, we may make use of either the person or his title to designate and name the thing itself, by which we mean here the knowledge that is the cause and the source. In the first phase of the reaply, the word *A^craf* is used to denote knowledge, or gnosis itself (*ma^crifat*). "We are at the summit of the *A^craf*," at the summit of this gnosis. In progressing to the second phase of the reply, the word denotes the cause of this gnosis, that through which it exists. "We are the *A^craf*," which means we are *that through which* there is knowledg of God on the part of man. We are the content of the human knowledge of God, for we are the theophany. In other words, there is no *ma^crifat Allah*, God is not knowable, and there is no human knowledge of God except for the man who knows us. We have already seen that the Imam *is* the theophanic form, that is tot say, the Imam is the "Face that God ineluctably assumed in all knowledge that man has of Him or in which God reveals Himself to him; without this "Face" there is only the *Absconditum*. The Imam, being the *A^craf*, therefore, is that supreme face, that through which a human knowledge of God exists.

The meaning of the Imam for Shi^ci spirituality again is seen here to be the same as we analyzed above. The Imams themselves teach the reciprocity of the two maxims, since the Imam can say, "He who knows *us*, knows his Lord," and, on the other hand, all our spiritual devotees repeat, "He who knows *himself* (his soul), knows his Lord." Thus, by knowing himself (his soul, his anima), he knows his Imam, and whoever knows his Imam knows his Lord. Accordingly, there is alternation or substitution between the notions of Imam and Self: to know one's Imam is to know oneself; to know oneself is to know one's Imam (the Soul of the soul) and to know one's Lord. What Shi^ci spirituality offers to its adepts in the person, in the "form of light" of its twelve Imams is access to that knowledge of the self, outside of which there is no knowledge of God, that is, access to consciousness of the personal relationship that makes God to be what he is—as He shows Himself—for the one who worships him. Hence, the importance of the visions of the Imams in dreams, visions that reveal to the believer favored with them - his innermost secret, the Imam as "Soul of his Soul", the secret of his own knowledge of God. Or, as we said above, "the human meaning of the knowledge of God." Here, at the same time, the Imam announces the divine meaning of this human knowledge.

3. Then, at the third stage, by a new progression, the Imam affirms: "We are the *A^craf*, for on the Day of Resurrection we are those whom God recognizes as being the way . . ." Here, by the *A^craf*, the Imam means "that which is the essential object of knowledge," not what is external and is known *per accidens*. What is this essential knowledge? Just as at the second stage of the reply the Imam *is* the knowledge that man has of God, that *through which* man knows God, here, too, at the third stage, He is the divine knowledge of man, that *through which* God knows man. The Imam says in effect: the one who knows us, God knows as a being of Paradise. At the second stage, the Imam asserts: The knowledge that the believer has of us is the knowledge that he has of God. At the third stage: The knowledge that God has of the believer is the knowledge that the believer has of us. By knowing us he has knowledge of himself as a being of paradise, and this knowledge is that which God has of him. Inversely, whoever rejects us has a perception of himself that *is* his ball. "No one enters the Fire save those who deny us and whom we ourselves deny," and such is the knowledge that God has of those who deny us. It is the denier himself who drives God from his paradise, and that is what hell is. Thus, at the boundary where knowledge of the Imam and knowledge of self are conjoined, the exoteric meaning of the *A^craf* as "rampant" takes on its fullest truth: The Imam actually is the *rampart* that separates heaven and hell.

The teaching or meditation of a philosopher brings to light limitless possiblities: The Imam *is* the knowledge that man has of God, and as such he *is* the knowledge that God has of man. These twin propositions mark the *situs* of the Imam at the level of the primordial theophany, at the dawn of all divine cognoscibility. Other texts . . . already have allowed us to witness the breaking of this dawn. There, too, it was a particular divine Will that shone through from the horizon of a universal primordial Will, and that dawn made possible the appearance of the form (*tajalli*) in which divinity became an object of love (its *mahbubiyyat*). The voluntarist aspect corresponds to a metaphysics of being that, according to a master of the Shaykhi schools such as Muhammad Karim Khan Kirmani, must refuse to include the ineffable divine Being, of whom nothing can be predicated, in an indivisible unity of being (*wahdat al-wujud*). In Mullla Sadra Shirazi, however, we have a thinker who accepts this indivisibility, and his metaphysics is expressed initially in terms of knowledge.

There is a global divine knowledge, essential and perfect, that is identical with the simple divine Essence and that involves no multiplicity, because this Essence (*zat*) is the source from which the existence of all things springs and because, by knowing Himself, God knows the totality of things in virtue of that knowledge identical with His essence. And, there is a divine knowledge of individual things consisting either in the fact that their Ideas are actualized in being "prior to" their existence *in concreto*. The whole presents a hierarchy of causes and of things caused. According to Mulla Sadra then, there is a strict symmetry and parallelism in the ascending and descending order of this hierarchy. Just as the Angels are active causes (*faᶜᶜal*), which give rise gradually to the potential existence of creatures, similarly the prophets and Imams, all the "Friends of God," are causes and intermediaries acting upon the potential angelicity of human beings, causing them to leave the states of animality in order to lead them to the actual angelic state that makes them beings of paradise (*ahl al-jinnat*). Just as in the cosmological order the knowledge that God has of beings of this world of becoming is knowledge mediated by the knowledge that He Himself has of their Angels (the *angeli intellectuals* and the *angeli caelestes* of the Avicennian hierarchies), so that it is said that the Angels are the Witnesses (*shuhada'*) before God of His creation; likewise, in the eschatological order, God's knowledge of the fidelity of his believers is mediated through the knowledge that he Himself has of the prophets and the *Awliya'*. For this reason, they will be the "Witnesses" for men before God on the Resurrection Day.

It is through the idea of these Witnesses that the saying of the Imam leads the philosopher spontaneously to discover the symmetry between the function of angelology for cosmogenesis and cosmology (the order of the *Mabda'*) and the role of imamology in the return of souls to their Origin (the order of *Maᶜad*), that is to say in their role in soteriology and eschatology. Imamology, like angelology, has its metaphysical foundation in the divine Knowledge; both culminate in the notion of *Witness*. In this notion a metaphysics and a spirituality of the Presence converge, a Presence toward which all the motifs of prophetic philosophy are oriented. The Imam *is* that point of convergence at which the Witness, the contemplator (*shahid*) — the Imam atop the *Aᶜraf* — is at the same time the contemplated one (*mashhud*), the Witness-of-contemplation — the *Aᶜraf* itself — because this Witness, by attesting to men the God whom he himself contemplates (by "answering for" Him), also is the same whom men contemplate when this God "shows Himself" to them. He is the eye with which God looks at and relates to men because it is with this same eye that man looks at and relates to God (this motif is fully developed in the mysticism of Ruzbihan). The Imams are at once the eyes through which God watches the world and the eyes through which men contemplate the divine Attributes, since the divine Essence is inaccessible to them. The Imam is indeed the contemplator-contemplated (*shahid-mashhud*, contemplated by God and men), guarding against *ta^ctil* and *tashbih*; and the knowledge that I have of the Imam is the knowledge that God has of me. Hence, the Imam is truly the "rampart," separating the inhabitants of paradise from those of hell.

Therefore, it is true to say, Mulla Sadra wrote, "that the knowledge which God has of the spiritual state of the two groups is mediated by the knowledge that He has of these Witnesses in their dual aspect (attesting to paradise for some and hell for others). Such is the deepened understanding (*tahqiq*) of the fact that the prophets and the Imams *are* the Witnesses of God for men, and of the meaning of the following Qur'anic verse: "How then shall it be, when We bring forward from every nation a Witness, and bring them to witness against those! (IV, 45)." The three progressive stages in the reply of the Imam then reveal their final truth: "We are the *A^craf*," that is to say, we are those who by essence are the object of divine knowledge (the *ma^crufun bi-'al-zat*), the objects of the divine contemplation (the *mashhudun li-'Allah*), his Witnesses-of-contemplation, without intermediary, since, being intermediaries for others, we are the exalted degrees of the Path (*sirat*) through which man must pass in order to reach the supreme human proximity to God.

The theme of the *A^craf* thus takes on the outline of the summit, of the "rampart" of "prophetic and imamic philosophy," which is the gift of supreme wisdom. In the words of Imam Ja^cfar, commenting to a disciple, upon Qur'anic verse II, 272: "He who has been given wisdom has received a great good" (the Proverbs of Solomon), "this wisdom (*hikmah*) consists of having spiritual consciousness, gnosis (*ma^crifah*) of the Imam." There is a whole set of motifs that lie behind the definition of this widsom, the foremost of which is the motif of the *Hujjah*, to which Sadra Shirazi frequently returns in his commentary on the texts of the Imams. There is a double *Hujjah*, a double Witness, Guide, Guarantor. In its first form, there is an external Guide, the prophet-herald to men; and after him came the Imams for those men who needed a visible guide. But Twelver Shi^cism under the direction of the "hidden Imam" is oriented in essence toward the second aspect of the *Hujjah*, the invisible, inner Guide, the inner Imam (*Hujjah batinah, Imam dakhili*): a gleaming light that originates from the Throne, that dawns in the Orient of the soul, on its supreme horizon, illuminates the

"sense faculty of the heart" through which the prophetic message is understood in its esoteric meaning, that is the *walayah* of the Imams; the inner,
secret prophecy (*nubuwwah batiniyyah*), relating to the hidden universe and
the inner things of the soul. The idea of the "Inner Guide," far from
eliminating the necessity of prophetology and Imamology, is their ultimate
realization; it is precisely to this that imamology provides initiation. The Inner Guide toward whom the interiorization of imamology leads is he who
preserves the mystic from any Luciferian intoxication. Before embarking on
the Path, the mystic can be characterized by this remark of the fifth Imam:
"Thou knowest even less about the roads of Heaven than about those of
Earth." The "quest of the Imam" to which the Shi'i adept therefore is invited, does not mean an encounter with a guide familiar with astronomical
space. Another world is intended here, a world "corresponding to the interior, invisible forms that cannot be perceived by our physical, but only by
our spiritual, senses."

When the Imam speaks of wisdom (whose degrees are defined as faith in
God, in his Angels, his revealed Books, his Messengers and the Resurrection), Sadra reminds us that parallel to the two aspects of the *Hujjat* or
Guide — exterior and interior — there are two wisdoms: — unveiled (*hikmah
makshufah*) and veiled (*hikmah masturah*). "Wisdom unveiled" consists of
the visible persons of the Sages, personifications of wisdom. Whoever sees
one of them (with the "eyes of the heart" that reveal his qualities to the
observer) *sees* the form and the person of wisdom. For men in general, this
wisdom is a divine gift, "which is a great good", i.e. the visible person of the
Imam, since he is wisdom in person (*nafs al-hikmah*). "Veiled wisdom" is
that in the heart of the Friends of God (the *awliya'*), the prophets, the
Imams, *hukama' ilahiyun*, Sages of God, "theosophists" in the fullest sense
of the word. And the teaching of the Imams about the *A'raf* enables us to
understand that if each of them is a Sage in one aspect, he is also wisdom in
another.

Here Mulla Sadra's meditation pulsates with a profound joy, when he
reaches the point where Shi'i spirituality and the metaphysics of being and
knowledge that he professes as an *ishraqi* philosopher converge in the unity
of the spiritual consciousness of the *ishraqi* Shi'i. The same thing takes
place, he says, when the Sage becomes one with wisdom, as occurs in the act
of intellection when the subject who intellectualizes (*'aqil*) becomes one
with intelligence (*'aql*). This assertion illustrates the characteristic feature
alrealdy noted, that of *ishraqi* Shi'i spirituality in which the philosopher's
effort cannot be separated from spiritual realization, and vice versa.

The theme of the double *Hujjah* is but an echo of the theme of the double
wisdom. In the Imam, there is both manifest and hidden (*makhfiyyah*)
wisdom. Manifest wisdom is the person of the invisible Imam. Hidden

wisdom is the interior, spiritual, intellective light (*nur batini ^{c}aqli*), a light that *is* the spiritual life of the Imam and that illuminates for the adept whom he guides the world of the Beyond and the celestial beings and figures that it contains. Such is the gift of wisdom. Just as in the act of intellection the subject who intellectualizes *is* himself the intelligence in action (the latter is not superimposed upon him, it *is* his being), so the person of the Sage (the Imam) *is* wisdom. To know by gnosis (*ma^{c}rifah*) the person of the Sage (the Imam) is to know the wisdom that is himself in person. But in the act of spiritual knowledge, the wisdom of the Imam, like the intelligence in the case of one who intellectualizes, becomes the wisdom of the adept, of him who takes the Imam as guide and who therby is made aware of the convertibility of the two maxims: "He who knows his Imam knows his Lord," and "He who knows himself knows his Lord," meaning the Imam. To have complete spiritual consciousness of his Imam, his interior, personal, invisible Guide, is himself to become someone in whom the wisdom ofthe Imam is actualized, someone in whom there dwells the "inner Witness," precisely the Imam himself as inner Imam (*Imam dakhili*), the "divine Face" who endures when everything else perishes. As we said above, the Imam is the theophanic form in the same way that the adept is the epiphanic form of the Imam. Imami spirituality is initiation to the interior Imam through the exterior Imam, to the knowledge of one self through the knowledge of the Imam.

Thus, we must consider the meaning of each of the Shi^{c}i Imams and of the whole pleroma of the Imams for Shi^{c}i spirituality. All the teaching regarding the *A^{c}raf* culminates in a metaphysics of the Witness (*shahid*) and the testimonial Presence (*shuhud*), such that the Imam becomes the active consciousness, so to speak, of his follower. And thanks to this, there is perpetuated in this world the *silsilat al-^{c}irfan*, the line of gnosis, unknown to most men, a secret line of the heroes of the hierohistory of the cycle of *walayah*, composed of all those individuals in this world who are "living" in the real sense of the word.

This "community of the living" stretches to the extent of being a prophetic "ecumenism," which has the same esoterism as its foundation. The idea of the universal *walayah* (above §1), having the Imam as its Seal, already has led us to use this term above: All the prophets of earlier periods, along with all their followers, all the believers of the same eternal prophetic religion compose together a *corpus mysticum* (the "Temple of light" of the Imamate in Isma^{c}ili terminology). "It has been the same in all eras, and it will be the same in the future. Indeed, all the Sages of God (*^{c}ulama' rabbaniyyun*, the *Theosophoi*) all the prophets, and all their Imams, are all of one religion (din wahid), one school (*mazhab wahid*). More precisely, they are like one spiritual person, total and unique (*shakhs wahid kulli ^{c}aqli*). Moreover, the believers who follow them, in whatever place and whatever time they may exist, are like a single Soul; the school of each Imam also is that of another Imam, and at the same time the school of the totality of the prophets and the *awliya'*.

Chapter Thirteen

Shi'i Hermeneutics

Shi'ism emphasizes the inner reality (batin) of all things, which complements and is the "source" of the outward (zahir). Not only the sacred text but also the world of nature possesses both a batin and a zahir. Hermeneutics (ta'wil), which is so central to Shi'ism, means going from the zahir to the batin and making use of the outward as a gate for reaching the inward. This process is applied especially to the Qur'an that, according to many Shi'i hadiths, possesses many inner levels of meaning. Ta'wil denotes, literally, going back to the origin or beginning for the inward is the origin of the outward. This process is central to all aspects of Shi'i thought, especially the science of Qur'anic commentary, where ta'wil or esoteric commentary is contrasted with tafsir that remains bound to only the outward form or literal meaning of the Sacred Text. In the following passage, Henry Corbin has explained the dynamics of Shi'i hermeneutics through the works of Sayyid Haydar Amuli. The excerpt is from the previously unpublished translation of Corbin's En Islam Iranien by Charles Adams.

Henry Corbin

The *Jamjiᶜ al-asrar wa manbaᶜ al-anwar* is literally: "The Compendium of Esoteric Doctrines and the Source of Light." The *asrar* are the secrets, hidden, internal, esoteric realities to be discovered by the cognitive act known as *kashf*, an internal revelation, a mystic intuition, a visionary perception. In their entirety, they constitute theosophy, while rational intellection (*ᶜaql*) is the organ of philosophy, and positive tradition (*naql*) is that which nourishes theology. It is the great treatise mentioned above and a few pages of which, extracted from the exordium and from the conclusion, one can read below. It was written at the beginning of the Iraqi period about the year 725/1351-52. We already have mentioned its main purpose; let us add that the work includes numerous autobiographical allusions. It consists of three books designated respectively as *asl* (source, principle); each book is then subdivided into four large chapters of *qaᶜidah* (basic doctrine). The structure of the whole is thus built around the number twelve.

Book I presents what constitutes the essence and the truth of the *tawhid*. It establishes the differentiation between theological *tawhid* (*uluhi*, exoteric monotheism) and ontological or esoteric *tawhid* (*tawhid wujudi*), the latter being the affirmation of the transcendental unity of being (*wahdat al-wujud*, not a so-called "existential monism"). The author indicates that theological *tawhid* conceals a *shirk* or occult dualism, an unconscious idolatry. Ontological *tawhid* is presented in a fashion conforming to the metaphysics of the Ibn ᶜArabi. Finally, it is linked to the hermeneutics of verse XXXIII, 72, from which it follows that the burden assumed by man, in an act of sublime madness, is the very secret of the Imams. Indeed, they have repeated it: Their cause is so difficult and so heavy, that it can be borne only by an angel, a prophet, or a believer with tested heart. The context serves to strengthen the affirmation that the Sufis, insofar as they employ the gnosis transmitted from the Imams, are the "Shiᶜi in the true sense"; those Shiᶜi who accept the teachings of the Holy Imams in its entirety, are "the believers with tested heart" and therefore the Sufis in the real sense.

Book II continues the previous account by bringing forward supporting evidence in the form of Qur'anic verses, sayings of the Prophet, sayings of the Holy Imams and remarks of the great masters (the *Mashayikh*).

Book III is of a perfect symmetry. Each of its four chapters deals with three notions fundamental for Shiᶜi theosophy, in an order that shows how the words forming each triad are homologues of one another: (1) the literal exoteric religion (*sharicah*), the mystic way (*tariqah*), the truth of gnosis, and spiritual realization (*haqiqah*). (2) The prophetic message (*risalah*), the prophetic vocation (*nubuwwah*), the *walayah* of the Imam (his qualification as *Wali Allah*, Friend of God and guide of spiritual initiation). (3) The revelation of divine communication through the Angel (*wahy*), inspiration (*ilham*), interior revelation (*kashf*), mystical intuition, (hierognosis). (4) Islam (the act of surrender to God); *iman* (faith-belief), according to the Shici requirements, implying the adherence of the heart to the triple attestation (of divine Unity, of the prophetic mission, and of the *walayah* of the Imams); *iqan* (the certitude that at the same time is *pistis* and gnosis). The chapter on prophecy and the *walayah* is composed on a grand scale. There, Haydar Amuli demonstrates, against Ibn cArabi, that it is impossible historically and structurally to accept that Jesus, son of Maryam, is the "Seal" of the absolute *walayah*, and to accept along with some of his disciples that Ibn cArabi was himself in person the Seal of the particular or Muhammadan *walayah*. The Seal of the absolute *walayah* can be only the first Imam; the Seal of the Muhammadan *walayah* can be only the one recognized by Twelver Shicism as the twelfth Imam, the Hidden Imam, the awaited Mahdi, son of the Imam Hasan cAskari. The discussion is taken up again some thirty years later, in even greater detail, in the prolegomena to the commentary on the *Fusus* of Ibn cArabi. Because the work of Haydar Amuli draws all its conclusions from the fact that the *walayah* is the esoteric aspect of prophecy, it is a great moment in the "prophetic philosophy" in Shici Islam.

*   *   *

The writing of the "Treatise on the Knowledge of Being" (*Risalah f macrifat al-wujud*) was completed at Najaf on the 15th of Jumada II of the year 768 H./17 February 1367. It is this date that serves to distinguish the two parts of the Iraqi period of the life of our Sayyid (periods *B* and *C*). The composition of the treatise was motivated by the request of a friend, whose name is not given by the author but with whom the author had a tie of deep affection. This treatise is a summary (a long one, in spite of what the author indicates) of a very vast work on metaphysics of which we have not yet found a manuscript. In fact, Sayyid Haydar declares that he had just finished a great treatise in which he had envisaged all the aspects of being and explained the opposition between the *Mutakallimun* (the scholastics) and the philosophers who profess the transcendental unity of being, as well as produced testimonies from the Word of God, the Word of the Prophets and the *awliya'*, when "one of my brothers," he writes, "who is dearer to me than the pupil of my eye asked me with insistence immediately to give a concise and

useful summary of it, a summary little in volume but great in teaching."
Like the work that it summarizes, the treatise includes an introduction
and three pillars (*rukn*) or chapters, dealing respectively with (1) the problem of being (*status quaestionis*), of being as understood in the sense of absolute being (*itlaq al-wujud*) and of being as an immediate given. It points
out the impossibility of deducing being, of replying rationally by a principle
of reason that is sufficient to the question of the *tarjih*: Why does being
prevail over nonbeing? Why being rather than nothingness? (2) The necessity of being and of its unity. (3) The epiphany of being (*zuhur al-wujud*) and
its multiplicity. The author states clearly from the beginning that he is
dealing with the metaphysics of being, encompassing a triple point of view:
that of the philosophers, by way of the intellect (*ᶜaql*); that of the theologians, by way of tradition (*naql*); that of mystical theosophists, by the way
of intuitive perception (*kashf*). This is entirely in conformity with the position characteristic of the author and with the method used in the great Sum-
ma, the *Jamiᶜ al-asrar*. Also, when giving the title of his book, Sayyid
Haydar declares that he dedicates it to those who possess the required state
of preparation, the perfect aptitude, the needed finesse and penetration; he
withholds it from all negators and disputers, from all those who are far
away from God, and from the Friends of God.

It is needless to underline the importance of such works for the Islamic
philosophy that historians so long had thought to have ended with Averroes
in Andalusia. Haydar Amuli does not deal with the metaphysics of being
either in the fashion of Avicenna or in that of Averroes. Nevertheless, it is
in fact the very same problem inherited from Greek philosophy with which
he deals. But he tackles it in a manner and with resources, that he himself
derives from his thorough knowledge of the work of Ibn ᶜArabi and his
continuous meditation on the Book of God and the tradition of the Imams
of Shiᶜism. It would be inconceivable to him, as well as to the whole group
of our Shiᶜi philosophers, to pretend to deal with the metaphysics of being
while professing the dualism common in the West, which separates philosophy and theology from one another. To persist in separating them is to
mutilate the problems (and the program) of one and the other, and to close
the access that allows them, one through the other, to issue onto the
superior level that is theosophic metaphysics. Thus, one reaches the absurd
extremity where some claim that our philosophers deal with philosophical
problems, while it would be simpler and more "objective" to admit that the
program of their philosophy goes beyond the limits of what "modern"
philosophy means by the name *philosophy*. Haydar Amuli and those like
him are in affinity with our neo-Platonic theosophists of the Renaissance. It
is as a neo-Platonist that Sayyid Haydar meditates upon the triad of the
bismillah: Allah refers to the absolute One, Unitude (*ahadiyyah*), while *al-*

Rahman (the Merciful) refers to the multiple One, the Nous, the Intelligence, the Imam or the metaphysical Adam, and *al-Rahim* (the Compassionate) refers to the Soul of the world, the metaphysical Eve. Shiᶜi philosophy, as Haydar Amuli intends to present it in its entirety, will be expanded still more by Mulla Sadra Shirazi, Qadi Saᶜid Qumi, and several others; it appears to us of an unequalled interest for the phenomenology of the religious consciousness.

* * *

The two works analyzed above have been published recently. What remains to be mentioned here are two basic works of considerable magnitude about which we have already given some information. The first work is the *Tafsir ᶜirfani*, the monumental spiritual and mystical commentary on the Qur'an, completed in 777/1375-76, and consisting of seven large volumes preserved in the autograph manuscript, the recent discovery of which at Najaf and at Qum has been reported above. This *Tafsir* carries a complex title loaded with symbols. This is how Haydar Amuli explains it, when in the introduction to his commentary on the *Fusus* of Ibn ᶜArabi, he comes to talk about it while discussing the books he had previously written.

> As to our own books, they form two categories: there are those that can be considered as effusions from above, and those that emanate from within us. As to the effusions from above, these are the *ta'wilat* (spiritual exegeses) of the Holy Qur'an, which include the most precious and the most venerable of the sciences and the divine doctrines of the Qur'an and which gather together the symbols and the figures particular to the Prophet, the subtle doctrines and Muhammadan realities that have their faithful expression in what God says about those who form the elite of his servants: 'I have prepared for my servants, the just ones, what the eye has never seen, the ear never heard, what has not yet reached the heart of any man.' Consequently this book was entitled: 'The Supreme Ocean and the Culminating Mountain, A Book Dealing with the Spiritual Hermeneutics of the Precious and Unshakable Book of God.' (*al-Muhit al-aᶜzam wa'l-tawd al-ashamm fi ta'wil Kitab Allah al-ᶜaziz al-muhkam*). It was divided into seven volumes in order thus to be able to put it under the auspices of seven great prophets, the seven poles, and the seven *abdal*, in such a fashion that the prolegomena and the *Fatihah* (first surah) form one volume together, while each sixth of the Qur'an in turn forms another volume. This *tafsir* is to us like what the *Fusus al-hikam* are to Shaykh Muhi al-Din ibn ᶜArabi, and like what the Qur'an is to the Prophet. The plan of our *tafsir* is the following: We start by establishing nineteen premises and circles, corresponding with the external world and the spiritual world, with the *Book of Horizons* and the *Book of Souls*, each of these universes being limited to nineteen.

Two remarks are due here. On the one hand, Sayyid Haydar alludes here to the fact that the *Fusus* can be considered as an "inspired book," since this book was transmitted in a dream to Ibn ꜥArabi by the Prophet, the Prophet himself having received it in the *malakut*. By assimilating the case of his own *Tafsir* to that of the *Fusus* of Ibn ꜥArabi, our Sayyid illustrates and confirms what he had just said a few lines above; that is, that this *Tafsir* is not a book that emanated from him, but a book that he was conscious of having been "effused upon him from above," by means of the inspiration that is kept open by Shiꜥi gnoseology even after the closure of the cycle of prophecy. On the other hand, the structure of the prolegomena to the *Tafsir*, as announced by Haydar Amuli, corresponds to the structure of the esoteric hierarchy: the seven prophets and the twelve Imams, a total of nineteen figures. When our Sayyid speaks of circles, this idea appears to be linked to the complex diagram he knew how to construct so artfully. We have already recalled earlier the significance of what we propose to call the "diagrammatic art," which illustrates the works of Haydar Amuli.

Elsewhere also, in the same introduction, Sayyid Haydar describes his magnum opus as

> divided into seven large volumes, corresponding to the *ta'wil* of the eminent shaykh, Najm al-Din Razi, known as Dayih. The latter, in fact has divided his work into seven large volumes and entitled it *Ocean of Spiritual Truths and Mystical Realities* (*Bahr al-haqa'iq wa'l-daqa'iq*). Our aim was to have a book comparable to it in every respect as well as one that would satisfy the *hadith* appealed to in both: the Qur'an has an exterior (or exoteric) and an interior (or esoteric) aspect; the latter in turn has an esoteric aspect, and so forth down to seven esoteric depths. This *tafsir* (of Najm Dayih) is famous in all climes and in all countries. The theosophic truth of its structure is recognized among the most eminent of the mystic philosophers and theosophists, and it is accepted by them as having neither its equal nor its like, especially with respect to the sciences of the Qur'an and for the fact that it was not obtained by an exterior acquisition or a prolonged dialectic research but rather by a secret dispensation that came from the Merciful by means of mystical perception (*kashf*).

Thus, Sayyid Haydar allows us at least to have a glimpse of his mystical *tafsir* and the secret of its content. While awaiting the time when we can study it carefully and provide for its publication, we know already in what perspective the author situates it. In referring to the work of Najm Dayih Razi, Haydar Amuli also is evoking the whole body of the mystical *tafsirs*. This literature is considerable; classification and systematic study of its are yet to be done, and this kind of work can be done only by researchers specialized in the philosophical and religious sciences. For what is of primary interest to the latter and what they consider important is the way in which the Qur'an has been read by the spiritual adepts and metaphysicians of Islam. They have no objection to the fact that their hermeneutics do not conform to the program and aims of our "positive criticism"; the objection would be perfectly inoperative. As we were saying above about the metaphysics of being, we Western interpreters should not impose a so-called modern program on our authors. Our task is to take up and give true value to the meaning of the questions that were or are "on the program" of our philosophers. The works in which this program unfolds are immense. We may mention here the *ta'wilat* of Ruzbihan Baqli Shirazi, ᶜAbd al-Razzaq, Kashani, Sayyid Ahmad ᶜAlawi, and Mulla Sadra Shirazi, even the great mystical *tafsir* of Sultan ᶜAli Shah in the nineteenth century. To this can be added the fact that Shiᶜi *tafsirs* (including those of the Ismaᶜilils), as a whole, belong to the mystical hermeneutics of the Qur'an in the broad sense of the word *mystical*, i.e., to the extent to which they heighten or deepen the letter of the Qur'an to show its hidden meaning, which concerns the person of the Imam and embraces all the levels of being on which imamological metaphysics situate the Imam... .

Theological Tawhid and Ontological Tawhid

The analysis of the *Jamiᶜ al-asrar*, as we have presented it, shows that of the three books forming the work; the first two are dedicated to the theosophy of the *tawhid*. However, there is no disequilibrium, for all the themes of theosophy, those of prophetology and imamology, as well as those of gnoseology, which are the degrees of knowledge corresponding respectively to the levels of the *shariᶜah*, the *tariqah*, and the *haqiqah*—all these themes, the author believes, are nothing but the implications or the applications of the doctrine of the *tawhid*. This doctrine both shows and motivates the gradation of theological or exoteric *tawhid* and ontological or esoterical *tawhid*. Haydar Amuli is bent on explaining it himself.

> In the outline I have just presented there is a secret intention address-
> ed to the elite of the spiritual adepts, a secret, I mean to say, that will
> not escape whoever is worthy of it, for to the superior man a hint is suf-
> ficient. If I have added the themes of the *shariᶜah*, of the *tariqah* and of
> the *haqiqah*, and in general the themes treated in Book III of the present
> work—if I have added them, I say—to the theme of the *tawhid* and its
> categories, although the present work essentially is devoted to the theme
> of the *tawhid* and its categories, although the present work essentially is
> devoted to the theme of the *tawhid*, this primarily is because there is not
> deeper mystery than the abscondity of the *tawhid* with its consequences
> and implications, and it is this, therefore that we have to show and that

we must orient ourselves towards. Moreover, those who have asked me to write the present work, have not asked me for anything else.

But secondly, we also had to deal with the theosophic secrets reserved here for Book III, and that is because the *tawhid* includes obscurities and subtleties, some corresponding to the level of men of literal religion *(shariʿah)*, and others to the level of those who follow the mystical Path *(tariqah)*, and others to the level of those who have reached gnostic truth *(haqiqah)*. The meaning of this gradation can be understood only by one who is at its level. I had to show the degrees and levels of the *tawhid*, in such a way that one would understand its true meaning and give up casting anathemas on others. Therefore, if we have had to deal with the *nubuwwah* (prophetic vocation), the *risalah* (mission of the messenger prophet), and the *walayah* (charisma of the Imam), it is becuase they are the points of origin and birth of the whole and because the *tawhid* proceeds from them alone, and is manifested through their holders (the prophet, the Messenger, the Imam) alone. It therefore was important to give a spiritual consciousness *(maʿrifah)* of these three things. The same is true for divine communication, inspiration, and interior revelation (third *qaʿidah* of Book III), and for the notions of *Islam*, *iman*, and *iqan* (fourth *qaʿidah*), for all these things are the consequences and implications of the former.

Actually, the totality of all these themes forms but a single theme, to such a degree that if only one of these problems were to be neglected, the problem as a whole would not appear as it should; the solution would remain hidden, would escape the consciousness, as anyone with knowledge of these things would realize. Therefore, the strongest of the reasons motivating our plan is the fact that presentation of the *tawhid* requires that we deal with those who profess it. This is why the whole of the present book will deal with the *tawhid*, and this will be the subject matter of Books I and II; it will then be the subject matter of Books I and II; it will then deal with those who profess it, and that will be the subject of Book III. And, in reality, there is no other way of proceeding.

The framework having been thus outlined, the exposé concerning the theosophy of the *tawhid*, the affirmation of the Unique, is carried out in all faithfulness to the teaching of Ibn ʿArabi. But it inevitably leads to prophetology and imamology, to the idea of the cycle of the *walayah*, i.e., to the cycle of spiritual initiation by the "Friends of God," succeeding to the cycle of legislative prophecy. This time, as we have already said, the fidelity of our Sayyid to the teaching of Ibn ʿArabi whom he admires, yields to a more imperious requirement, that of fidelity to the teachings of the Imams of Twelver Shiʿism. He will find himself, to his great regret, under the obligation of mounting a fundamental critique against Ibn ʿArabi, because Ibn ʿArabi, by substituting the person of Jesus for that of the Imam as

"Seal of the *walayah*," shakes the whole structure of prophetology and imamology.

The problems posed by the *tawhid* take us back to the admirable Qur'anic verse whose hermeneutic treatment by Haydar Amuli has already appeared earlier as an illustration of what we have called "the spiritual struggle of Shicism." In fact, in this verse our Sayyid was "reading" the eternal vocation of Shicism, i.e., of esoteric Islam. Each time this vocation is expressed, we notice the same profound tonality. It is expressed in the interpretation of the verse of the divine Deposit (XXXIII, 72); it is expressed, we have noted, in the answer of Adam to the anonymous questioner: "I ignored all things apart from God," as it is expressed in the last words of the last visible representative of the hidden Imam, cAli al-Samarri: "Henceforth the matter beiongs to God alone." A single ethos, created by an unshakable confidence and a radical pessimism. It is this very same ethos that vibrates throughout the pages in which Haydar Amuli exerts himself to explain the meaning of the profession of Islamic faith: *La ilaha illa allah* (*Non deus nisi Deus*).

Basically, it will be this. By assuming the trust of the divine secret, Adam did violence to himself, to "his soul," by blotting out his self in divine Ipseity, and by *ignoring*, from then on, that anything else existed but God. But was it in the power of the man to assume this trust that had been refused by all beings? In fact, Adam had preceded and usurped what could have been the privilege only of the last Imam. The realization of the integral *tawhid*, comprising the two forms, theological and ontological, cannot but accompany the integral manifestation of the *walayah*. Now this Manifestation cannot take place until the time of the *parousia* of the twelfth Imam, coming out of his occultation as Imam of the Resurrection. The sublime violence and the sublime ignorance of Adam are turned back upon man; they have degenerated into oppression and stupidity, for it was inevitable that man should consider *other* than God. This in fact, precisely the stake that rides upon the *tawhid*, the Attestation and the Unique.

In appearance, nothing is simpler than the statement of the profession of Islamic faith: *la ilah illa allah*. Through this it seems, one affirms that, on the one hand, there is a divinity that is unique, and on the other hand, the multitude of beings who are its creatures. In fact, there is nothing more difficult, for this simple explanation "in general usage" shows from the beginning that the naive understanding of the *tawhid* considers something *other* than God. Also, the *tawhid* has absorbed the efforts of all the generations of thinkers of Islam, as it has absorbed the meditations of the mystics. Ismacili theosophy, for instance, has liberated itself from it by a powerful dialectic, from which it becomes clear that exoteric monotheism, at the very moment when it believes that it has exalted and isolated the Unique, falls into the worst of metaphysical idolatries. This precisely is the peril and the illusion that Haydar Amuli denounces. The fact is that for the problem of the relationship between the *Ens increatum* and the *Ens creatum* to be envisaged as it should be, it cannot be envisaged except in an esoteric teaching. That the matter is not a simple one, even that the secret of the *tawhid* appears as the secret assumed by Adam at his great peril, is shown to us by a certain exclamation of one, who in spite of his young age, was among the most celebrated companions of the Prophet, ᶜAbdullah ibn ᶜAbbas. His repute and his importance are due to the fact that, thanks to the declarations ascribed to him, it is possible to trace certain mystical exegeses of Qur'anic verses back even to the entourage of the Prophet. Thus, in reference to Qur'anic verse LXV, 12 ("It is God who created the seven Heavens and of Earth their like"), Haydar Amuli reminds us that ᶜAbdullah ibn ᶜAbbas, one day during the pilgrimage month (the ninth of Zu'l-Hijjah, the day of ᶜ*arafah*) on the mountain of ᶜArafat (twelve miles from Mecca), cried out in a very loud voice, brandishing his stick: "O men! if I commented on this verse to you as I have heard it commented on by the Prophet himself, you would stone me." (Let us recall here the poem where the fourth Imam declares himself unable to divulge the secret of the gnosis.) In fact, to explain this verse to his intimates, ᶜAbdullah ibn ᶜAbbas used to refer to this other: "God is *the* One (CXII, 1)". And it is by this solitude or divine *unitude* that he explained in turn the famous verse of Light, beginning with these words: "God is the light of the Heavens and of the Earth . . ." (XXIV, 35). For, to those who have understood the *true meaning*, light is *being*, and darkness is non-being. The Light, which is God, therefore is the constitutive being of the Heavens and of the Earth; it, and it alone, exists in the *true sense*, when one speaks of the Heavens and the Earth.

This means that God is *alone* in being, along with His Names, His Attributes, His Actions, i.e., His theophanies. The totality of being therefore is He, through Him, comes from Him, and returns to Him. God is not *a being* next to or above other beings, his creatures; He is being, the absolute act of being (*wujud mutlaq*). The divine unitude does not have the meaning of an arithmetical *unity*, among, next to, or above other unities. For, if there were being *other* than He (i.e., creatural being), God would no longer be the *Unique*, i.e., the *only* one to be. This does not by any means destroy the plurality of *beings*, neither does it make them an illusion; the illusion would be to deceive oneself about the modality of their act of being. That which is *other* than being, is simply nothingness; the alternative to unitude or divine solitude, is nihilism. This is what it means for man to assume the secret of the *tawhid* while ignoring everything *other* than God. This is why theological *tawhid*, under the threat of disintegrating into its contrary, must culminate in the *tawhid of being* that our author, guided by his master Ibn ᶜArabi, designates as ontological tawhid. And he derives its teaching from all the mystical theosophists who have preceded him in Islam.

There then is a theological *tawhid* (*tawhid uluhi*): it is the exoteric *tawhid* (*tawhid zahir*), the one to which the prophets have invited the whole of humanity, by inviting them to affirm a unique divinty, unconditioned, *absolute*, i.e., *absolved* of any determination which links it to local or historical determinations. The formula for it is *La ilaha illa allah* (there is no God but God). And, there is ontological *tawhid* (*tawhid wujudi*): It is the esoteric *tawhid* (*tawhid batin*) the one to which the Initiated (the "Friends of God", the *awliya'*) summon by inviting men to consider being in its *absolute* act of being, i.e. absolved from the determinations that it actualizes, for there can be no being *other* than being. To understand the esoteric meaning of this verse: — "All that dwells upon the earth is perishing, yet still abides the Face of thy Lord, majestic, splendid" (LV, 26–27) – is to understand the solitary reality of the unique being. The formula for it is this: *Laysa fi al-wujud siwa allah* (there is no being but God). Let us avoid creating confusion with certain modern Western systems that are not at all appropriate here by not speaking of *monism*; we should rather speak of *theomonism*, or even *theomonadism*.

To illustrate this *unitude* of being in its epiphanies (*mazahir*) by a comparison, Haydar Amuli takes the example of ink and its manifestation by the letters of the script. If one refrains for a moment from considering the letters of the script and their particular forms to consider as such the reality of the ink that constitutes them, the existence of the letters itself appears as a certain way of considering the existence of the ink, but this consideration does not add a new real existence to the existence of the ink. As to the material reality of the act of being, there is nothing in the letters but the ink itself: The letters of the script are the ink taking the *shape*, the quiddity of this or that letter. It is not a matter of denying the existence of letters, in the plural, but of seeing *how* they exist. For, in a reciprocal fashion, what we preceive directly, is never being in its in-itselfness, but being manifested in its forms; we perceive the epiphanies of being. In the same fashion, ink appears only in the shape of letters (the shape of the inkwell, even the shape of a blot, does not alter the reasoning). The letters would be nothing without the ink, but the ink does not become *another* ink; similarly, being in its epiphanies only multiplies itself by itself (1×1). In each case it is the ink that, by being, *is* this or that letter. All is individual, yet all is One. This is the transcendental unicity of being (*wahdat al-wujud*). Thus, it goes for our thinkers with respect to the relationship of the Necessary Being with the forms of its Manifestations. If we lose sight of that, we *associate* being with the Unique. Then there is no more *tawhid*: Monotheism turns into idolatry.

Precisely the important word has just been uttered. The nightmare of the faithful *muslim* as of the theologian, is that which is designated by the word *shirk*. It is usually translated by *associate*: it is the act of associating other gods to God, *other* being to Being. The idea of *disintegration* can, perhaps, help us better to catch its meaning. For a double peril threatens the double *tawhid*—a disintegration of being, and a disintegration of the divine—the latter being the result of the former. In other words, without the esoterist *tawhid* of the Initiated, the exoteric *tawhid* of naive monotheism turns into its contrary. Haydar Amuli distingishes a double *shirk*: There is a patent, obvious *shirk* (*shirk jali*), and there is an occult, secretive *shirk* (*shirk khafi*). The first is that of the man who has never heard the call of the prophets, and who particularly adores such and such a determinate divinity. The second *shirk* is infinitely subtle. It secretly threatens the literalist believer as well as the doctor of the Law who refuses the *tawhid* of being professed by the mystics. Only he who turns towards being *absolved* of any determination that fetters it and understands that there *is only God in being*, only he escapes the secret, unconscious *shirk*, professes the Unity in its true meaning and is an *^carif*, a gnostic. But the threat is so subtle, it corrodes the secret depths of the monotheistic consciousness so thoroughly, that the Prophet has declared: "The *shirk* moves in my community, more invisible than a black ant moving on a black stone on a black night."

There, therefore, is no truth for a *tawhid* that does not simultaneously accomplish the integration of the divine and the integration of being. The *tawhid* in the true sense (*haqiqi*) and not in the metaphorical sense (*majazi*) is the theosophical *tawhid* that includes both forms of the *tawhid*, theological and ontological. This is the "Right Path" (*sirat mustaqim*). It is easy to describe it, but the difficulty of following it is comparable to the difficulty of Adam in assuming the divine trust. Haydar Amuli goes so far as to say: "Of a Hundred million souls, there may be only one that succeeds, for this Path is more hidden than the mystical Phoenix (the *^canqa' al-maghrib*), more difficult to find than red sulphur and the philosopher's stone."

However, if on the one hand, the manifestation of all of the Prophets (*nabis*) during the "cycle of prophecy" from Adam up to Muhammad, the Seal of the prophets, has had as its aim the invitation (*da^cwah*) of creatures to theological *tawhid*, on the other hand, the mission of all the *Initiated* (*awliya'*) (all those of the hierarchies described earlier here, the whole of which forms the *imamah* of the Imam) has as its aim, during the "cycle of the *walayah*", from the death of the Prophet to the *parousia* of the last Imam, to summon men to ontological *tawhid*, and to deliver them from the secret, unconscious *shirk* that forms its antithesis, however pious their motives may be.

When one tries to envisage the position of the theosophy of Twelver Shi^cism vis á vis the Law (the *shari^cah*), it is important to realize the following. If theological *tawhid* is that which considers the exoteric letter of positive religion and is applied in this world, it is so because the *sharicah* is limited to the present state of the world; and the legislative prophetic mission, which is the source of the *sharicah* and of theological *tawhid*, is itself already closed in this world. On the other hand, the *walayah*, which is the initiatory function of the Imam, is eternal; it applies to the present state of the world, as to the state that preceded it and the state that will follow it. To Shici theosophists, the *walayah* is anterior to prophecy and to the prophetic mission of which it is the source and the origin. And just as the Manifestation started with the *walayah*, it is in and by the *walayah* that its completion must occur. Or again, in the same way as the ordering of being (*tartib wujudi*) began with the ontological *tawhid*, likewise the latter will be its completion, for the End is the return to the Beginning. The cyclical way of thinking common to all our authors is affirmed here by the refusal of a rectilinear evolution: The cycle takes its origin in *metahistory* and leads back to it. It therefore would be invalid to oppose this cyclical conception and the "history and salvation." Soteriology itself presupposes a cyclical history and a cyclical time.

It therefore is to this integration of being that the resurrector Imam (*Qa'im*) finally will call; he will not reveal a new *sharicah*, but will unveil the hidden meaning of all earlier Revelations. It will be the reign of the pure spiritual meaning, of the eternal Religion (*din baqi, qayyim*), which, being founded on the theosophical *tawhid* that is the integration of being, will allow men to gather together in a unique community, as they did at the beginning of Adam's period. The call for theological *tawhid*, for exoteric monotheism, has been closed with the "Seal of the prophets." Now comes the call of the Initiated (*awliya'*) to esoteric *tawhid*, to this eternal Religion the last Imam of which will be the Seal (*Khatim al-awliya'*), he who for the twelve Shici is now the twelfth Imam, the hidden Imam.

Thus, there is an essential connection between the *walayah*, and esoteric *tawhid*. Not only is it this to which the "Friends of God," the *awliya'*, refer, but the advent of the "Seal" of the Muhammadan *walayah* must mark the final establishiment of integral *tawhid*, hitherto esoteric. It is of capital importance, therefore, not to err concerning the person of the final "Seal" of the *walayah*. As long as it is a matter of explaining ontological and esoteric *tawhid*, Haydar Amuli remains faithful to the theosophy of Ibn cArabi, though he also employs a lexicon of his own. But one understands that he has to part from Ibn cArabi as soon as it comes to the doctrine about which a Shici thinker cannot compromise. It is to the extent to which he is faithful to this doctrine that the schematization of the cycle of prophecy and the cycle of *walayah* either remains coherent or breaks up... .

It is here, as great as is his admiration for Ibn ^cArabi, that Haydar Amuli clearly departs from him, and he will be followed in this by all the Shi^ci ^curafa, as penetrated as they are by the doctrines of the great Andalusian theosophist. Ibn ^cArabi professes that the Seal of the universal *walayah* was Jesus (^cIsa ibn Maryam), while he himself claimed to be the Seal of the particular Muhammadan *walayah*. On this second point, however, it is possible to have a certain reservation as to whether this was actually the claim of Ibn ^cArabi himself. We ourselves believe, that his dream vision concerned the secret of his personal destiny, as he had to experience it for himself, in the same way as every mystic has his secret. But to transpose the meaning of the dream to the objective plane of hierohistory, as Dawud Qaysari his commentator has done, does not seem to correspond to what Ibn ^cArabi thought. This also is the point of view of several contemporary Iranian shaykhs, to whom the work of Ibn ^cArabi is familiar. Moreover, there is the testimony of Ibn ^cArabi himself, attesting in veiled terms to his mysterious encounter with the Imam of that time. Accordingly, he did not identify himself with the Imam.

Unfortunately, it remains true that the first thesis, clearly presented by Ibn ^cArabi, that makes Jesus the Seal of the universal *walayah*, is radically incompatible with the prophetology that in Islam is the contribution of Shi^cism. This prophetology implies that the Seal of the *walayah*, of this *walayah*, which is the esoteric aspect of the prophetic mission, can be only the Imam. But Ibn ^cArabi transfers this title to Jesus. He therefore makes a prophet, the last great prophet before Muhammad, the Seal of the *walayah*. Hence, the incoherence in the fundamental relation between prophetic mission and the *walayah* was introduced, a confusion that seems to have no other aim but to do away with Shi^ci imamology, to culminate in an imamology without an Imam. On the other hand, the position of the Shi^ci theosophist is unshakable: The Seal of the universal *walayah* can be only the first Imam, ^cAli ibn Abu Talib; the Seal of the particular Muhammadan *walayah* can be only the twelfth Imam, the awaited Imam, "presently hidden to the senses, but present in the heart of his followers," Muhammad al-Mahdi, son of the eleventh Imam, Hasan al-^cAskari. This is so, because it is the Muhammadan *Imamah*, the pleroma of the Twelve Imams, that in its entirety is the Seal of the *walayah*, to which is linked the manifestation of integral *tawhid*.

These few indications give us an inkling of the importance of the work of Haydar Amuli in the whole of Shi^ci though and spirituality. It will be easier to return to it, when progress has been made in publishing those of his works which we have been able to recover. Understood in its *^cirfani* essence, which makes it into the gnosis of Islam, whether according to Sa^cd al-Din

Hamuyih or Haydar Amuli, Mulla Sadra, or Shaykh Ahmad Ahsa'i, and whatever may be the opinions of one or the other regarding other problems, Shi^cism leads us to ask anew with Haydar Amuli, the question of Sufism in its essence and its significance, the question of knowing whether non-Shi^ci Sufism has not aimed essentially at the imamology without an Imam, and whether it has not transposed to the person of the Prophet the whole content of imamology, leaving aside all that did not agree with Sunni feeling.

This question inevitably is encountered whenever one goes in depth into the spirituality of Iranian Islam in the company of those who have experienced it or are experiencing it today. Every study of the theme of the Muhammadan *walayah* finds itself centered on the idea of a "pole," the *qutb*. This mystical "pole" of the world, which gives its "polar" dimension to each being who enters into relationship with it, is the Imam. Thus, if this idea of a "pole" comes to be separated from the Imam and to continue to exist independently from imamology, it *eo ipso* will lean toward the metaphysical usurpation denounced by Shi^ci gnostics. This is because their imamology aims beyond the empirical person of the Imam. We have already pointed out that the twelve Imams, or rather the twelve Imams with the Prophet and Fatimah the Radiant, the "Fourteen Immaculate Ones" are the primordial theophany; their spiritual entity of "persons of light" pre-existed the manifested worlds and, consequently, their own earthly manifestation and their epiphanic form in the sensual world. As such, they are invested with a cosmogonic function to which corresponds their eschatological function, in the return of things to their origin and the return of the soul to itself. The Fourteen Immaculate Ones "inhabit" the consciousness of the Shi^ci spiritual adept; they occupy it in the state of wakefulness, just as they populate its visions whether in dream or in an intermediary state... .

Chapter Fourteen

Taqiyyah

Taqiyyah *(prudent fear, or dissimulation) is a doctrine that developed out of the political persecution of the Shiᶜis throughout Islamic history, especially under the Umayyads (661-750 A.D.). Here ᶜAllamah Taba-taba'i and Hamid Enayat locate the theological and social significance of* taqiyyah, *within its Shiᶜi context. The passages are taken from* SI, *pages 223-25, and* MIPT, *pages 175-81, respectively.*

cAllamah Tabataba'i

One of the most misunderstood aspects of Shicism is the practice of dissimulation or *taqiyyah*. With the wider meaning of *taqiyyah*, "to avoid or shun any kind of danger," we are not concerned here. Rather, our aim is to discuss that kind of *taqiyyah* in which a man hides his religion or certain of his religious practices in situations that would cause definite or probable danger as a result of the actions of those who are oppsed to his religion or particular religious practices.

Among followers of the different schools of Islam, Shicis are well known for their practice of *taqiyyah*. In case of danger they dissimulate their religion and hide their particular religious and ritual practices from their opponents.

The sources upon which the Shicis base themselves in this question include the following verse of the Holy Qur'an: "Let not the believers take disbelievers for their friends in preference to believers. Whoso doeth that hath no connection with Allah unless (it be) that ye but guard yourselves against them [*tattaqu minhum*, from the same root as *taqiyyah*] taking (as it were) security [*tuqatan*, again from the same root as *taqiyyah*]. Allah biddeth you beware (only) of Himself. Unto Allah is the journeying" (III,28). As is clear from this sacred verse, God, the Most Exalted, forbids with the utmost emphasis *wilayah* (meaning in this case friendship and amity to the extent that it affects one's life) with unbelievers and orders man to be wary and have fear in such a situation.

In another place He says, "Whoso disbelieveth in Allah after his belief — save him who is forced thereto and whose heart is still content with Faith — but whoso findeth ease in disbelief. On them is wrath from Allah. Theirs will be an awful doom" (Qur'an, XVI, 106). As mentioned in both Sunni and Shici sources this verse was revealed concerning cAmmar ibn Yasir. After the migration (*hijrah*) of the Prophet the infidels of Mecca imprisoned some of the Muslims of that city and tortured them, forcing them to leave Islam and to return to their former religion of idolatry. Included in this group who were tortured were cAmmar and his father and mother. cAmmar's parents refused to turn away from Islam and died under torture. But cAmmar, in order to escape torture and death, outwardly left Islam and accepted idol worship, thereby escaping from danger. Having become free, he left Mecca secretly for Medinah. In Medinah he went before the Holy Prophet—upon whom be blessings and peace—and in a state of penitence and distress concerning what he had done asked the Prophet if by acting as he did he had fallen outside the sacred precinct of religion. The Prophet said that his duty was what he had accomplished. The above verse was then revealed.

The two verses cited above were revealed concerning particular cases but their meaning is such that they embrace all situations in which the outward expression of doctrinal belief and religious practice might bring about a dangerous situation. Besides these verses, there exist many traditions from the members of the Household of the Prophet ordering *taqiyyah* when there is fear of danger.

Some have criticized Shiᶜism by saying that to employ the practice of *taqiyyah* in religion is opposed to the virtues of courage and bravery. The least amount of thought about this accusation will bring to light its invalidity, for *taqiyyah* must be practiced in a situation where man faces a danger which he cannot resist and against which he cannot fight. Resistance to such a danger and failure to practice *taqiyyah* in such circumstances shows rashness and foolhardiness, not courage and bravery. The qualities of courage and bravery can be applied only when there is at least the possibility of success in man's efforts. But before a definite or probable danger against which there is no possibility of victory—such as drinking water in which there is probably poison or throwing oneself before a cannon that is being fired or lying down on the tracks before an onrushing train— any action of this kind is nothing but a form of madness contrary to logic and common sense. Therefore, we can summarize by saying that *taqiyyah* must be practiced only when there is a definite danger which cannot be avoided and against which there is no hope of a successful struggle and victory.

The exact extent of danger which would make permissible the practice of *taqiyyah* has been debated among different *mujtahids* of Shiᶜism. In our view, the practice of *taqiyyah* is permitted if there is definite danger facing one's own life or the life of one's family, or the possibility of the loss of the honor and virtue of one's wife or of other female members of the family, or the danger of the loss of one's material belongings to such an extent as to cause complete destitution and prevent a man from being able to continue to support himself and his family. In any case, prudence and the avoidance of definite or probable danger which cannot be averted is a general law of logic accepted by all people and applied by men in all the different phases of their lives.

Hamid Enayat

Etymologically, *taqiyyah* comes from the root *waqa, yaqi* in Arabic, which means to shield or to guard oneself, the same root from which the important word *taqwa* (piety, or fear of God) is derived. There is thus nothing in the term itself to justify its standard translation in English either as dissimulation or (expedient) concealment, although both acts may be necessary to guard oneself from physical or mental harm on account of holding a particular belief opposed to that held by the majority. The Shiᶜi case for the necessity of *taqiyyah* is based on a commonsense 'counsel of caution' on the part of a persecuted minority. Since for the greater part of their history the Shiᶜis have been a minority amidst the global Islamic community and have lived mostly under regimes hostile to their creed, the only wise course for them to follow has been to avoid exposing themselves to the risk of extinction resulting from an open and defiant propagation of their beliefs, although they have not shunned their mission, whenever the opportunity has presented itself, to give a jolt to the Muslim conscience by revolting against impious rulers. This precautionary attitude has not been confined to the Shiᶜis alone in Islamic history; other sects and movements have resorted to the same tactic whenever threatened by oppressors. But the practice has come to be almost exclusively associated with Shiᶜism, partly because of the enduring status of the Shiᶜis in history as a minority, or 'unorthodox' group, and partly because their opponents have found in it valuable ammunition for their propaganda. Hence the inclusion, in almost every classical work of Shiᶜi jurisprudence (*fiqh*), of a chapter which either justifies or outlines the rules of the *taqiyyah*. The justification primarily rests on three Qur'anic verses. The first is a general warning to the faithful not to associate themselves with infidels: 'Let not believers take infidels for their friends rather than believers; whoso shall do this has nothing from God — unless, indeed, ye fear a fear from them: But God would have you beware of Himself; for to God ye return' (III, 28). The second verse exempts from divine punishment those believers who retract their profession of faith under duress: 'Whoso, after he hath believed in God denieth him , if he were forced to it and if his heart remain steadfast in the faith *shall be guiltless*' (XVI, 106). Shiᶜi exegetes believe this verse to refer to ᶜAmmar, the son of Yasir, who was a prominent pro-ᶜAli companion of Prophet Muhammad. Being a frail old man, ᶜAmmar was tortured by the Quraysh infidels into expressing belief in polytheism, but Muhammad defended him on the grounds that he was a staunch believer 'from head to toe'. Finally, the third verse is part of the story of Moses: when Pharaoh, Haman and Korah (Qarun) ordered Moses' followers to be killed, 'a man of the family of Pharaoh who was a believer, but hid faith' questioned the wisdom of killing a man for the sake of his faith (XL, 28). In addition to these verses there are numerous sayings ascribed to the Imams, particularly the sixth, al-Sadiq, confirming the imperative necessity of *taqiyyah*, even to the point of identifying it with the essence of religion itself: 'He who has no *taqiyyah*, has no religion (*din*)'; 'The *taqiyyah* is [a mark] of my religion, and that of my forefathers.'

There is another argument in defence of the *taqiyyah* which is mysticophilosophical, and is predicated on the esoteric character of Shi^cis . . . If the *raison d'être* and the essential function of the Imams should be sought in their status as the repository of the truth of the religion, or the 'sacred trust' placed exclusively at their disposal, then their knowledge of that truth cannot be communicable through propagation (*iza^cah*), otherwise not only will their claim to a privileged position be forfeited, but the knowledge itself will be in danger of being misrepresented and vulgarised. This view of the *taqiyyah* is most elaborately stated by one of the convinced Western exponents of mystico-philosophical schools of Shi^cism, Henry Corbin, who asserts that the practice was instituted by the Imams themselves, not only for reasons of personal safety, 'but as an attitude called for by the absolute respect for high doctrines: nobody has strictly the right to listen to them except those who are capable of listening to, and comprehending, the truth. To act otherwise, is to abandon ignominimously the trust which has been confided in you, and to commit lightly a grave spiritual treachery.' On this basis, Corbin tries to explain a number of distinctive features of Shi^ci culture. One cannot, he says, '*ex abrupto*, notebook and questionnaire at hand, ask a Shi^ci about his faith. To do so would be the surest means of making him shut himself off to further questions, and inducing him to get rid of the questioner by giving inoffensive, [but] derisory answers'. This attitude, continues Corbin, may have to do with long periods of fierce persecution, but only in the most ephemeral sense, because the deeper reason is the refusal to allow religious knowledge to be debased through superficial dissemination. As an illustration of this point, he relates how he once heard 'a young *mulla* in his thirties, declaring that while Shi^cism addresses the whole people, it could not receive the consent of but a spiritual minority'. He explains the absence of 'the missionary spirit, and of proselytisations in Iranian Shi^cism in the same terms, and shows *taqiyyah* and Shi^ci esoterics to be mutually dependent. According to a statement by the great Shi^ci theologian Shaykh Sadduq (d. 381/991), which he quotes, 'abolition of *taqiyyah* is not allowed until the appearance of the Imam announcing the resurrection [*al-Imam al Qa'im*], by whom the religion will be made integrally manifest.' If, concludes Corbin, 'the teachings of the Imams concerned only the explanation of the *Shariʿah*, the Law and the ritual, as some have claimed and still do claim, the imperative of the *taqiyyah* would have been incomprehensible.'

Such sophisticated interpretations of the *taqiyyah* have now come as much under the devastating attacks of the modernists as the more down-to-earth, popular perceptions of the term. For although both the Qur'anic verses and the sayings attributed to the Imams, and the glosses by authoritative Shiʿi jurists and theologians, indicate that *taqiyyah* is an exceptional dispensation granted only in cases of emergency and compulsion (*idtirar*), in practice it has become the norm of public behaviour whenever there is a conflict between faith and expediency. Small wonder, then, that it has at times degenerated into an excuse for downright hypocrisy and cowardice. For the same reason, one of the first tasks facing the Shiʿi modernists has been to effect a thorough affirmation of its original meaning with a view to transforming it from a camouflage for political passivity into an instrument of activism. They have realised that unless they overcome this mental barrier among the ordinary Shiʿi to oppositional politics, they have little chance of translating their other militant doctrines into a veritable, sustained mass movement. Hence their efforts to demonstrate how far the current notion of *taqiyyah*, both in Sunni polemics and in popular Shiʿi usage, has deviated from its real meaning.

The first important point to emerge from the modernist treatment of the subject is that what is commonly assumed to be a simple, monolithic concept is, according to its proper definition, in fact a convenient rubric for a variety of acts, each having a clearly defined purpose. It is, therefore, wrong to think that all acts of *taqiyyah* are either sanctioned or repudiated with unvarying force in religion. Four categories are particularly mentioned: (1) the enforced (*ikrahiyyah*), (2) precautionary or apprehensive (*khawfiyyah*), (3) arcane (*kitmaniyyah*), and (4) symbiotic (*mudarati*). The enforced *taqiyyah* consists of acting in accordance with the instructions of an oppressor, and under necessity, in order to save one's life. Although being the simplest of all the four to define, it is also the most controversial kind, because it applies most readily to the political conditions of the Shiʿis in most places — now as much as in the past — and involves the difficulty of reaching consensus as to who an oppressor is. The precautionary or apprehensive *taqiyyah* consists of the performance of acts and rituals according to the *fatwas* (authoritative opinions) of the Sunni religious leaders, and in the Sunni countries. Alternatively, it consists of the 'complete precaution of a minority in its way of life, and dealings with the majority, for the sake of protecting oneself and one's co-religionists'. The arcane *taqiyyah* is to conceal one's faith or ideology, as well as the number and strength of one's faith or ideology, as well as the number and strengh of one's co-religionists, and to carry out clandestine activity for furthering the religious goals, in times of weakness and lack of preparation for conducting an open propaganda. It is this kind of *taqiyyah* which is the opposite of *iza^cah* (propaganda). Finally, the symbiotic type is simply a code of coexistence with the Sunni majority, and of participation in their social and ritual congregations for maintaining Islamic unity, and establishing a powerful state comprising all the Muslims.

The point of this classification is twofold: on the one hand, it attests the Shi^cis' realistic understanding of the practical problems which arise in reconciling the conflicting demands of a pure faith, and the physical survival of an unlawful minority; on the other, it purports to emphasise that concealing one's faith or ideology is simply a tactical device which should by no means interrupt the efforts towards its triumph, or conceived as a warrant for suspending essential religious duties. But the modernists seem to admit that even the fullest enumeration of the correct forms of the *taqiyyah*, and of their specific purposes, still leaves enough loop-holes for the feeble-minded and the comfort-seekers to use the whole practice as a convenient excuse for neglecting the obligation to speak and fight for the truth, thus acting as silent accomplices in rampant injustice. How can it be otherwise when safeguarding one's life is explicitly recognised as a legitimate aim in the observance of at least two of the four varieties of the practice? A substantial portion of the modernist arguments is allocated, therefore, to a semi-scholarly, semi-ideological debate on the limits of self-protection, on the demarcation line beyond which safeguarding oneself, or one's co-religionists, turns from a legitimate and judicious act of self-defence into a cowardly flight from the unmistakable summons of the religious conscience. The most frequent warning accompanying these arguments is that *taqiyyah* is definitely an illicit act whenever it entails 'a corruption in religion'. What 'corruption in religion' exactly means is never quite clear, but the modernists use one or two vital clues in the sayings attributed to the Imams, and in the works of distinguished jurists of the past, to elucidate its application. There is, for instance, the statement reportedly made either by the fifth Imam, al-Baqir, or the sixth, al-Sadiq, that they 'never practise *taqiyyah* [although not proscribing it for others] in three things: wine-drinking, wiping over the shoes [instead of bare feet in the ablution for prayer, *mash al-khuffayn*], and abandoning the *tamattu^c* pilgrimage'. Wine-drinking is banned by all Muslims, but the latter two acts are supposed to be Sunni innovations'. The Imam is thus saying that he will never perform these acts for the sake of pleasing the rulers or the majority although he does not prohibit them for others, because his own position as the leader of the Shi^ci community requires absolute avoidance of all offences even those which others may be allowed to commit to escape molestation on the part of the rulers or the majority. Moreover, the Prophet Muhammad and the Imam al-Sadiq are both quoted as having denounced anybody who glorifies the innovators (*zu bidᶜah*); and the Prophet is said to have cursed the *ᶜalims* who do not 'proclaim their knowledge' to awaken the public upon the appearance of an innovation. In another saying attributed to the Imam ᶜAli, the *ᶜalims* 'who do not proclaim their knowledge in time' have been described as the 'most stinking (*antan*) individuals on the Day of Judgement'. Leaving aside the traditions associated with the Imams, the behaviour of the militant Shiᶜis under the Umayyids and ᶜAbbasids is also recounted to demonstrate that *taqiyyah* was never used as a means of evading moral responsibility: those militants who were arrested by the authorities never revealed the names or hide-outs of their fellow-fighters even under the severest torture. This attitude is reflected even in the opinion of classical jurists such as Shaykh Tusi and Ibn Idris, who unequivocally rule out the permissibility of the *taqiyyah* whenever it results in the killing of people. Having thus established that genuine Shiᶜism never permits dissimulation if what is at stake is the very essence of religion, the modernists proceed to argue that all the statements ascribed to the Imams which stress the incumbency of the *taqiyyah*, and identify it as an integral part of the religion, should be understood as a mere pleading for clandestine activity, to create 'a secret organisation for protecting and propagating the doctrines of a Shiᶜi Imam'.

Discussion on *taqiyyah* sometimes involves a more delicate issue which concerns the principle of *al-amr bi'l-maᶜruf wa'l-nahy ᶜan al-munkar* (enjoining the good and forbidding the evil), since one possible result of any kind of concealment or dissimulation can be the suspension of this cardinal religious duty. A person who is allowed to hide his real belief or practice to protect himself in a hostile environment should, by the same token, be permitted to abstain from advising others what to do and what not to do. The two attitudes are indeed so interrelated that sometimes *taqiyyah* is thought to be the opposite of, not *izaᶜah*, but *al-amr bi'l maᶜruf*, etc. So if Shiᶜism is to retrieve its pristine character as a creed of militancy, then it must go on the offensive in all areas of social and political life, and this makes 'enjoining the good and forbidding the evil' the strongest sanction of its campaign for the total regeneration of the community. Classical authors paid a great deal of attention to the questions of whether 'enjoining the good and forbidding the evil' is an individual duty (*fard ᶜayn*, which should be performed by every Muslim, like prayer), or a collective duty (*fard kifayah*, which needs only to be performed by a group of Muslims, like *jihad*, the 'holy war'); and of whether it is necessitated by reason or the law (*sharᶜ*). They also pointed out the different forms in which the duty may be implemented: primarily by speech, and, if this does not produce the desired result, by hand—although the latter is believed to be the exclusive function of the Imams or their representatives. The modernists mostly refuse to be drawn into discussions of a purely theoretical nature, dismissing them as pedantic digressions. Instead, their debate is focused on the pre-conditions and the forms of the fulfilment of the duty. Most Shiᶜi authorities of the past agreed that a Muslim cannot perform the duty unless he meets three requirements: first, he should have the knowledge required to distinguish good from bad; second, he must be fairly certain that his advice will be effective; and third, he must be sure that no harm will come to his or her person as a consequence of performing the duty. The modernists consider the classical treatment of these preconditions to be unsatisfactory on two main grounds. First, they believe that even the absence of these pre-conditions does not negate the 'obligatoriness' of the act itself, unlike, for instance, the prerequisite of solvency in the case of paying pilgrimage to Mecca. The latter act ceases to be obligatory for a Muslim who does not have sufficient financial means. But 'enjoining the good and forbidding the evil' remains incumbent on every Muslim even in the absence of its pre-conditions, just as prayer is still obligatory for a person who is not physically clean. The only effect that the absence of these pre-conditions can and must have is to create a further obligation to achieve them. Thus a Muslim who does not have the knowledge of good and evil in Islam should do all in his or her power to obtain it, rather than using his ignorance as a pretext for indifference to problems of public morality. Second, the modernists refute the second and third conditions as absurdly obstructive, and an encouragement to quietism, arguing that if the great heroes of social and political struggle in Islamic history—men like ᶜAli, Husayn and Abu Zarr—wanted to observe such conditions, they could have never revolted against the inequities of their times. The whole debate acquires an all the more disputations tone against the background of the controversy that has raged in the past among classical Shiᶜi jurists on the subject: while men like Shaykh Muhammad Hasan Najafi, author of *Jawahir al-kalam*, the most widely-used textbook of *fiqh* in centres of religious teaching in Iran, emphasise the essentiality of the preconditions, there are jurists like Shahid Thani ('the Scond Martyr') and Muhaqqiq Karaki whose arguments favour the militants' case.

The Shiᶜi modernist views on *taqiyyah*, such as those outlined here, present one of the rare examples of genuine critical thinking in present-day Islam. While aiming at a radical reformation of a traditional concept and attitude, they seldom depart, as some quasi-religious modernist works do, from the accepted terms and categories of theology and jurisprudence. The arguments are often 'immanent', remaining always within Islamic idiom and thought, hardly invoking any notion drawn from any of the fashionable ideologies of our time, to substantiate or discredit a viewpoint. Misrepresentation of *taqiyyah* is denounced in the name of upholding religious sincerity, removing a major barrier in the way of unity with Sunni Muslims, and exhibiting its virtue as a method of clandestine struggle. And the duty of 'enjoining the good and forbidding the evil' is exalted not in order to foster an attitude of inquisitiveness, or to pry into the private life and manners of individuals, but to stress the value of personal example as the most effective way of persuading others to rectify their ways, and stand up to corruption and tyranny. Meanwhile, the fact that the two issues are examined in conjunction with each other signifies an awareness that no traditional or conventional practice, which is likely to have momentous ramifications in the political behaviour of Muslims, can be meaningfully studied without examining it with the entire system of religious behaviour.

Chapter Fifteen

Mutᶜah *or*
Temporary Marriage

Mutᶜah *(temporary marriage) is one of the particularities of the Shiᶜi
family law and, in modern times, has been the subject of considerable
controversy. In the following passage,* ᶜAllamah Tabataba'i and Seyyed
Hossein Nasr *provide a concise statement of the Shiᶜi position on this
issue. The passage is taken from* SI, *pages 227–30.*

*Allamah Tabataba'i and Seyyed Hossein Nasr

Another of the misunderstood practices of Shi^cism that has often been criticized, especially by some of the moderns, is temporary marriage or *mut^cah*.

It is a definitely established historical fact that at the beginning of Islam, namely between the commencement of the revelation and the migration of the Holy Prophet to Medinah, temporary marriage, called *mut^cah*, was practiced by Muslims along with permanent marriage. As an example one can cite the case of Zubayr al-Sahabi, who married Asma', the daughter of Abu Bakr, in a temporary marraige; from this union were born ^cAbdallah ibn Zubayr and ^cUrwah ibn Zubayr. These figures were all among the most famous companions of the Holy Prophet. Obviously if this union were to have been illegitimate and categorized as adultery, which is one of the most grievous sins in Islam and entails heavy punishments, it would never have been performed by people who were among the foremost of the companions.

Temporary marriage was also practiced from the time of the migration until the death of the Holy Prophet. And even after that event during the rule of the first caliph and part of the rule of the second, Muslims continued to practice it until it was banned by the second caliph, who threatened those who practiced it with stoning. According to all of the sources the second caliph made the following statement: "There are two *mut^cahs* which existed in the time of the Prophet of God and Abu Bakr which I have banned, and I will punish those who disobey my orders. These two *mut^cahs* are the *mut^cah* concerning the pilgrimage and the *mut^cah* concerning women."

Although at first some of the companions and their followers were opposed to this ban by the second caliph, since that time the Sunnis have considered *mut^cah* marriages to be unlawful. The Shi^cis, however, following the teachings of the Imams of the Household of the Prophet, continued to consider it legitimate as it was during the lifetime of the Prophet himself.

In the Qur'an, God says concerning the believers: "And who guard their modesty. Save from their wives or the (slaves) that their right hands possess, for them, they are not blameworthy, But whoso craveth beyond that, such are the transgressors" (Qur'an, XXII, 5-7). Also, "And those who preserve their chastity Save with their wives and those whom their right hands possess, for thus they are not blameworthy; But whoso seeketh more than that, those are they who are transgressors" (Qur'an, LXX, 29-31). These verses were revealed in Mecca and from the time of their revelation until the *Hijrah*, it is well known that *mut^{c}ah* marriage was practiced by Muslims. If *mut^{c}ah* marriage had not been a true marriage and women who had married according to it had not been legitimate wives, certainly according to these Qur'anic verses they would have been considered to be transgressors of the law and would have been forbidden to practice *mut^{c}ah*. It is thus clear that since temporary marriage was not forbidden by the Prophet it was a legitimate marriage and not a form of adultery.

The legitimacy of the *mut^{c}ah* marriage continued from the time of the *hijrah* until the death of the Holy Prophet as this verse, revealed after the *hijrah*, proves, "And those of whom ye seek content [*istamta^{c}tum*, from the same root as *mut^{c}ah*] (by marrying them), give unto them their portions as a duty" (Qur'an, IV, 24). Those opposed to Shi^{c}ism contend that this verse from the "Chapter on Women" was later abrogated, but the Shi^{c}i do not accept this view. In fact, the words of the second caliph cited above are the best proof that up to the time of his ban such marriages were still practiced. It is inconceiveable that if *mut^{c}ah* had been abrogated and forbidden it would have continued to be commonly practiced by Muslims during the lifetime of the Holy Prophet and after his death until the time of the second caliph; that if *mut^{c}ah* had been abrogated no action would have been taken to forbid it. We cannot accept the claim that the only thing that the second caliph did was to put into action an order of prohibition and abrogation of *mut^{c}ah* given by the Holy Prophet, for such a possibility is negated by the clear words of the second caliph, "There are two *mut^{c}ahs* which existed in the time of the Prophet of God and Abu Bakr which I have banned, and I will punish those who disobey my orders."

From the point of view of legislation and the preservation of public interest also we must consider the legitimacy of temporary marriage, like that of divorce, one of the noteworthy features of Islam. It is obvious that laws and regulations are executed with the aim of preserving the vital interests of the people in a society and providing for their needs. The legitimization of marriage among mankind from the beginning until today is an answer to the instinctive urge for sexual union. Permanent marriage has been continuously practiced among the different peoples of the world. Yet despite this fact, and all the campaigns and efforts at public persuasion that are carried out against it, there exist throughout the countries of the world, in large and small cities, both hidden and public places where illegitimate sexual union or fornication takes place. This in itself is the best proof that permanent marriage cannot fulfill the instinctive sexual desires of everyone and that a solution must be sought for the problem.

Islam is a universal religion and in its legislation takes all types of human beings into consideration. Considering the fact that permanent marriage does not satisfy the instinctive sexual urge of certain men and that adultery and fornication are according to Islam among the most deadly of poisons, destroying the order and purity of human life, Islam has legitimized temporary marriage under special conditions by virtue of which it becomes distinct from adultery and fornication and free of their evils and corruptions. These conditions include the necessity for the woman to be single, to become married temporarily to only one man at one time, and after divorce to keep a period during which she cannot be remarried (*ciddah*), half of the time that is required after the permanent marriage. The legitimizing of temporary marriage in Islam is done with the aim of allowing within the sacred law possibilities that minimize the evils resulting from the passions of men, which is not channeled lawfully manifest themselves in much more dangerous ways outside the structure of religious law..

Chapter Sixteen

Eschatology

*In the earlier chapters of the Qur'an revealed in Mecca pronouncements about the Day of Judgement (*Yawm al-qiyamah*) abound. This Day remains the focal point of human life according to the Islamic revelation. Human terrestrial experience begins with a descent from the world of the spirit and ends with a return to God. In the following passage ᶜAllamah Tabataba'i summarizes Shiᶜi eschatology in its metaphysical significance. The excerpt is taken from* SI, *pages 161–71.*

Allamah Tabataba'i

Those who are acquainted to a certain extent with the Islamic sciences know that within the teachings of the Holy Book and the traditions of the Prophet there are many references to spirit and corpus, or soul and body. Although it is relatively easy to conceive of the body and what is corporeal, or that which can be known through the senses, to conceive of spirit and soul is difficult and complicated.

People given to intellectual discussions, such as the theologians and philosophers, Shi'i and Sunni alike, have presented different views concerning the reality of the spirit (*ruh*). Yet, what is to some extent certain is that Islam considers spirit and body to be two realities opposed to each other. The body through death loses the characteristics of life and gradually disintegrates, but it is not so with the spirit. When the spirit is joined to the body, the body also derives life from it, and when the spirit separates from the body and cuts its bond to the body — the event that is called death — the body ceases to function while the spirit continues to live.

From what can be learned through deliberation upon the verses of the Holy Qur'an and the sayings of the Imams of the Household of the Prophet, the spirit of man is something immaterial which has some kind of relation and connection with the material body. God the Almighty in His Book says, "Verily We created man from a product of wet earth; Then he placed him as a drop (of seed) in a safe lodging; Then fashioned We the drop a clot, then fashioned We the clot a little lump, then fashioned We the little lump bones, Then clothed the bones with flesh, and then produced it as another creation" (Qur'an, XXIII, 12-14). From the order of these verses it is clear that at the beginning the gradual creation of matter is described and then, when reference is made to the appearance of the spirit, consciousness, and will, another kind of creation is mentioned which is different from the previous form of creation.

In another place it is said, in answer to skeptics who ask how it is possible for the body of man, which after death becomes disintegrated and whose elements become dispersed and lost, to have a new creation and become the original man, "Say: The angel of death, who hath charge concerning you, will gather you, and afterwards unto your Lord ye will be returned" (Qur'an, XXXII, 11). This means that your bodies disintegrate after death and are lost amidst the particles of the earth, but you yourselves, namely, your spirits, have been taken from your bodies by the angel of death and remain protected with Us.

Besides such verses the Holy Qur'an in a comprehensive explanation expresses the immateriality of the spirit in itself when it asserts, "They will ask thee concerning the Spirit. Say: The Spirit is by command of my Lord" (Qur'an, XVII, 85).

In another place in explaining His command (*amr*) He says, "But His command, when He intendeth a thing, is only that He saith unto it: Be! and it is. Therefore glory be to Him in Whose hand is the dominion over all things!" (Qur'an, XXXVI, 81–82). The meaning of these verses is that the command of God in the creation of things is not gradual nor is it bound to the conditions of time and space. Therefore, the spirit which has no reality other than the command of God is not material and in its being does not have material characteristics; that is, it does not have the characteristics of divisibility, change, and situation in time and space.

* * *

Intellectual investigation confirms the view of the Holy Qur'an about the spirit. Each of us is aware of a reality within himself which he interprets as "I" and this awareness exists continuously within man. Sometimes man even forgets his head, hands, feet and other members or the whole of the body. But as long as himself exists, the consciousness of "I" does not leave his awareness. Thus perception cannot be divided or analyzed. Although the body of man is continuously undergoing change and transformation and chooses different locations in space for itself and passes through different moments of time, the reality of "I" remains fixed. It does not undergo any change or transformation. It is clear that is the "I" were material it would accept the characteristics of matter which are divisibility, change, and situation in time and space.

The body accepts all the characteristics of matter and, because of the relocation of the spirit and the body, these characteristics are also considered to belong to the spirit. But if we pay the least attention, it becomes evident to man that this moment in time and the next, this point in space or another, this shape or another shape, this direction of motion or any other, are all characteristics of the body. The spirit is free from them; rather each of these determinations reaches the spirit through the body. This same reasoning can be applied in reverse to the power of consciousness and apprehension or knowledge which is one of the characteristics of the spirit. Obviously if knowledge were a material quality, according to the conditions of matter it would accept divisibility and analysis, and be determined by time and space.

Needless to say, this intellectual discussion could go on at length and there are many questions and answers related to it which cannot be considered in the present context. The brief discussion presented here is only an

indication of the Islamic belief concerning body and spirit. A complete
discussion will be found in works on Islamic philosophy.

* * *

Although a superficial view would regard death as the annihilation of
man and see human life as consisting of only the few days that stand between birth and death, Islam interprets death as the transfer of man from
one stage of life to another. According to Islam man possesses eternal life
which knows no end. Death, which is the separation of the spirit from the
body, introduces man to another stage of life in which felicity or disappointment depends upon good or evil deeds in the stage of life before death.
The Holy Prophet has said: "You have been created for subsistence, not annihilation. What happens is that you will be transferred from one house to
another."

* * *

From what can be deduced from the Holy Book and prophetic traditions
it can be concluded that between death and general resurrections man
possesses a limited and temporary life which is the intermediate stage (*barzakh*) and link between the life of this world and eternal life. After death
man is interrogated concerning the beliefs he has held and the good and evil
deeds he has performed in this life. After a summary account and judgement he is subjected to either a pleasant and felicitous life, or an unpleasant
and wretched one, depending on the results of the account and judgement.
With this newly acquired life he continues in expectation until the day of
general resurrection. The condition of man in the life of the intermediate
state (purgatory) is very similar to the condition of a person who has been
called before a judicial organization in order to have the acts he has committed investigated. He is questioned and investigated until his file is completed. Then he awaits trial.

The soul of man in the intermediate state possesses the same form as in
his life in this world. If he be a man of virtue, he lives in happiness and
bounty in the proximity of those who are pure and close to the Divine
Presence. If he be a man of evil, he lives in affliction and pain and in the
company of demonic forces and "leaders of those who have gone astray."

God, the Most Exalted, has said concerning the condition of a group of
those in the state of felicity, "Think not of those, who are slain in the way of
Allah, as dead. Nay, they are living. With their Lord they have provision.
Jubilant (are they) because of that which Allah hath bestowed upon them of
His bounty, rejoicing for the sake of those who have not joined them but

are left behind: that there shall be no fear come upon them neither shall they grieve. They rejoice because of favor from Allah and kindness, and that Allah wasteth not the wage of the believers" (Qur'an, III, 169–171). And in describing the condition of another group who in the life of this world do not make legitimate use of their wealth and possessions, He says, "Until, when death cometh unto one of them, he saith: My Lord! Send me back, that I may do right in that which I have left behind! But nay! It is but a word that he speaketh; and behind them is a barrier [*barzakh*] until the day when they are raised" (Qur'an, XXIII, 99–100).

* * *

Among sacred texts the Qur'an is the only one to have spoken in detail about the Day of Judgment. Although the *Torah* has not mentioned this Day and the Gospels have only alluded to it, the Qur'an has mentioned the Day of Judgment in hundreds of places, using different names. It has described the fate awaiting mankind on this Day sometimes briefly and on other occasions in detail. It has reminded mankind many times that faith in the Day of Recompense (Day of Judgment) is on the same scale of its importance as faith in God and is one of the three principles of Islam. It has mentioned that he who lacks this faith, that is, who denies resurrection, is outside the pale of Islam and has no destiny other than eternal perdition.

And this is the truth of the matter because if there were to be no reckoning in God's actions and now reward or punishment, the religious message, which consists of an assemblage of God's decrees and what He has commanded and forbidden, would not have the least effect. Thus the existence or nonexistence of prophecy and the religious mission would be the same. In fact, it nonexistence would be preferable to its existence, for to accept a religion and follow the regulations of a Divine Law is not possible without the acceptance of restrictions and loss of what appears as "freedom." If to submit to it were to have no effect, people would never accept it and would not give up their natural freedom of action for it. From this argument it becomes clear that the importance of mentioning and recalling the Day of Judgment is equivalent to that of the principle of the religious call itself.

From this conclusion it also becomes evident that faith in the Day of Recompense is the most effective factor which induces man to accept the necessity of virtue and abstention from unbecoming qualities and great sins, in the same way that to forget or lack faith in the Day of Judgment is the essential root of every evil act and sin. God the Almighty has said in His Book, "Lo! those who wander from the way of Allah have an awful doom, forasmuch as they forgot the Day of Reckoning" (Qur'an, XXXVII, 27). As can be seen in this sacred verse, the forgetting of the Day of Judgment is considered to be the root of every deviation. Meditation on the purpose of the creation of man and the Universe, or on the purpose and end of Divine Law, makes it evident that there will be a Day of Judgement.

When we meditate on creation, we see that there is no action (which of necessity is also a kind of motion) without an immutable end and purpose. Never is the action, considered independently and in itself, the end. Rather action is always the prelude to an end and exists by virtue of that end. Even in actions which superficially appear to be without purpose such as instinctive actions or the play of children and the like, if we study them carefully we will discover purposes in conformity with the kind of action in question. In instinctive actions, which are usually a form of motion, the end toward which the motion takes place is the purpose and aim of the action. And in the play of children there is an imaginary end, the attainment of which is the purpose of playing. The creation of man and the world is the action of God and God is above the possibility of performing a senseless and purposeless act such as creating, nourishing, taking away life and then again creating, nourishing and taking away life, that is, of making and destroying, without there being an immutable end and a permanent purpose which He pursues in these actions. There must of necessity be a permanent aim and purpose in the creation of the world and of man. Of course, its benefit does not accrue to God, who is above every need, but rather to the creatures themselves. Thus, it must be said that the world and man are directed toward a permanent reality and a more perfect state of being which knows no annihilation and corruption.

Also, when we study with care the conditions of men from the point of view of religious education and training, we see that as a result of Divine guidance and religious training people become divided into the two categories of the virtuous and the evil. Yet in this life there is no distinction made between them. Rather, on the contrary, success usually belongs to those who are evil and unjust. To do good is combined with difficulty and hardship and every kind of privation and endurance of oppression. Since this is so, Divine Justice requires the existence of another world in which each individual receives the just reward his actions deserve, and lives a life in conformity with his merits.

Thus it is seen that careful consideration of the purpose of creation of the Divine Laws leads to the conclusion that the Day of Judgment will come for every person. God, the Exalted, makes this clear in His Book, saying, "And We created not the heavens and the earth, and all that is between them, in play. We created them not save with truth; but most of them know not" (Qur'an, XLIV, 38–39). Also, "And We created not the heavens and the earth and all that is between them in vain. That is the opinion of those who disbelieve. And woe unto those who disbelieve and do good works as those who spread corruption in the earth; or shall We treat the pious as the wicked?" (Qur'an, XXXVIII, 28–29). In another place He says, "Or do those who commit ill-deeds suppose that We shall make them as those who believe and do good works, the same in life and death? Bad is their judgment! And Allah hath created the heaves and the earth with truth, and that every soul may be repaid what it hath earned. And they will not be wronged" (Qur'an, XLV, 21–22).`

* * *

In discussing the outward and inward meaning of the Qur'an we pointed out that the Islamic sciences are explained in the Qur'an through different means and that these are in general divided into the two dimensions of the exoteric and the esoteric. The exoteric explanation is the one that conforms to the level of the simple thought patterns and understanding of the majority, in contrast to the esoteric, which belongs to the elite alone and which can be comprehended only with the aid of the vision which comes through the practice of the spiritual life.

The explanation that emanates from the exoteric view presents God as the absolute ruler of the world of creation, all of which is His dominion. God has created many angels, whose number is legion, to carry out and execute the commands He issues for every aspect of creation. Each part of creation and its order is connected to a special group of angels who are the protectors of that domain. The human species is His creation and human beings are His servants who must obey His commands and prohibitions; and the prophets are the bearers of His messages, the conveyors of the laws and regulations which He has sent to mankind and has demanded that mankind obey . God has promised reward and recompense for faith and obedience, and punishment and painful retribution for infidelity and sin, and will not break His promise. Also since He is just, His justice demands that in another state of being the two groups of virtuous and evil men, who in this world do not have a mode of life in accordance with their good and evil nature, become separated, the virtuous to possess a good and happy life, and the evil a bad and wretched existence.

Thus God, according to His Justice and the promises He has made, will resurrect all men who live in this world after their death, without exception, and will investigate in detail their beliefs and works. He will judge them according to the truth and give everyone who has a right his due. He will carry out justice on behalf of all who have been oppressed. He will render to each person the reward for his own actions. One group will be assigned to eternal heaven and the other group to eternal hell.

This is the exoteric explanation of the Holy Qur'an. Of course it is true and correct. But its language is composed of terms and images born of man's social life and thought in order that its benefit might be more general and the radius of its action more widespread.

Those who have penetrated into the spiritual meaning of things and are to a certain extent familiar with the esoteric language of the Holy Qur'an, however, understand from these sayings meanings which lie above the level of simple and popular comprehension. The Holy Qur'an, amidst its simple and uncomplicated expositions, occasionally alludes to the esoteric aim and purpose of its message. Through many allusions the Holy Qur'an affirms that he world of creation with all its parts, of which man is one, is moving in its "existential becoming" which is always in the direction of perfection toward God. A day will come when this movement will come to an end and will lose completely its separate and independent existence before the Divine Majesty and Grandeur.

Man, who is a part of the world and whose special perfection is through consciousness and knowledge, is also moving with haste toward God. When he reaches the end of this becoming, he will observe plainly the Truth and Oneness of the Unique God. He will see that power, dominion and every other quality of perfection belong exclusively to the sacred Divine Essence; the reality of each thing *as it is* will be revealed to him. This is the first stage in the world of eternity. If, through his faith and good works in this world, man is able to have communication, relation, familiarity, and friendship with God and the beings in His proximity, then with a felicity and joy that can never be described in human language he will live near God and in the company of the pure beings of the world above. But if, because of desire and attachment to the life of this world and its transient and baseless pleausres, he is cut off from the world above and has no familiarity with or love for God and the pure beings of His Presence, then he becomes afflicted with painful torment and eternal adversity. It is true that a man's good and evil acts in this world are transient and disappear, but the forms of these good and evil acts become established in the soul of man and accompany him everywhere. They are the capital of his future life, be it sweet or bitter.

These affirmations can be drawn from the following verses: God says, "Lo! unto thy Lord is the (absolute) return" (Qur'an, XCVI, 8). And He says, "Do not all things reach Allah at last?" (Qur'an, XLII, 53); and "The (absolute) command on that day is Allah's" (Qur'an, LXXXII, 19). Also in the account of the address made to certain members of the human race on the Day of Judgment He says, "(And unto the evildoer it is said): Thou wast in heedlessness of this. Now We have removed from thee thy covering, and piercing is thy sight this day" (Qur'an, L, 22).

Concerning the hermeneutic interpretation (*ta'wil*) thereof? On the day when the fulfillment thereof cometh, those who were before forgetful thereof will say: The messengers of our Lord did bring the Truth! Have we any intercessors, that they may intercede for us? Or can we be returned (to life on earth), that we may act otherwise than we used to act? They have lost their souls, and that which they devised hath failed them" (Qur'an, VII, 53). He says, "On that day Allah will pay them their just due, and they will know that Allah, He is the Manifest Truth" (Qur'an, XXIV, 25). And, "Thou verily, O man, art working toward thy Lord a work which thou wilt meet (in His presence)" (Qur'an, LXXXIV, 6). Also, "Whoso looketh forward to the meeting with Allah (let him know that) Allah's reckoning is surely nigh . . ." (Qur'an, XXIX, 5). And, "And whoever hopeth for the meeting with his Lord, let him do righteous work, and make none sharer of the worship due unto his Lord" (Qur'an, XVIII, 111). And, "But ah! thou soul at peace! Return unto thy Lord, content in His good pleasure! Enter thou among My bondmen! Enter thou My Garden!" (Qur'an, LXXXIX, 27–30). Also He says, "But when the great disaster cometh, The Day when man will call to mind his (whole) endeavor, And hell will stand forth visible to him who seeth. Then, as for him who rebelled, And chose the life of the world, Lo! hell will be his home. But as for him who feared to stand before his Lord and restrained his sould from lust, Lo! the Garden will be his home" (Qur'an, LXXIX, 34–41).

Concerning the identity of the reward of actions God says, "(Then it will be said): O ye who disbelieve! Make no excuses for yourselves this day. Ye are only being paid for what ye used to do" (Qur'an, LXVI, 7).

* * *

This world of creation which we observe does not possess an endless and perpetual life. A day will come when the life of this world and its inhabitants will come to an end as confirmed by the Holy Qur'an. God says, "We created not the heavens and the earth and all that is between them save with truth, and for a term appointed," (Qur'an, XIVI, 3).

One could ask if before the creation of this world and the present race of humanity there had been another world and another human race; or, if after the life of this world and its inhabitants terminates, as the Holy Qur'an declares that it will, another world and humanity will be created. The direct response to these questions cannot be found in the Holy Qur'an. There, one can only discover allusions to the continuity and succession of creation. But in the traditions (*rawayat*) of the Imams of the Households of the Prophet transmitted to us it is asserted that creation is not limited to this visible world. Many worlds have existed in the past and will exist in the future. The sixth Imam has said, "Perhaps you think God has not created a humanity other than you. No! I swear to God that He has created thousands upon thousands of mankinds and you are the last among them."

And the fifth Imam has said, "God, the Exalted, since creating the world has created seven kinds none of whom were of the race of Adam. He created them from the surface of the earth and set them being one after another with its kind upon the earth. Then He created Adam, the father of mankind, and brought his children into being from him." And also the sixth Imam has said, "Do not think that after the passing away of the affair of this world and the Day of Judgment and the placing of the virtuous in heaven and the evil in hell there will no longer be anyone to worship God. No, never! Rather, again God will create servants without the marriage of the male and the female to know His Oneness and to worship Him."

Chapter Seventeen

Ijtihad *and* Marja^ciyyat

According to the Shi^cs, the extension and application of Divine Law (Shari^cah) into the Islamic community (ummah) necessitates the full employment of the human rational faculty (ijtihad) by religious scholars (mujtahids). This is the doctrinal basis at the root of ijtihad as a social institution. In the following passages Mahmud Ramyar and Leonard Binder discuss the question of marja^c-i taqlid (the source of immitation) and the functioning of ijtihad. The excerpts are from Alserat, *pages 253-61, and* POI, *pages 122-26 and 132-34.*

Mahmud Ramyar

Ijtihad, literally, means the exerting of one's self to the utmost degree to attain a matter; and according to Shi^ci belief, it is employing all power to reach a presumptive conclusion in a case or in a rule of Divine Law. Therefore, in order to understand the Book and tradition, it is necessary to employ all power, not just a part of it. In such a case an additional term becomes necessary: *Istinbat*, meaning inference or deduction. The original useage of *Istinbat* in Arabic is to mean the drawing of water from underground.

The *mujtahid* is a person who is qualified in terms of moral behaviour and skill in religious principles so that he can exert independent judgement based on the principles of the *Shari^cah*, or give fresh opinions on matters of the *Shari^cah*; in other words, a leading authority in the Divine Law is called in Shi^cism a *mujtahid*. Thus, one who exerts *ijtihad* must be qualified and strive with all his energy to discover the meaning of a passage from its words through inference and deduction.

In Islamic law there is a difference between a jurist (*faqih*) and a transmitter (*muhaddith*). The jurist must discover the commandment from tradition, but the transmitter only quotes. The following story will aptly illustrate the point. In the second century (A.H.) there was a transmitter who asked a jurist for a decision in a certain case. The jurist answered him, but the transmitter asked, "What is your proof for that?" The jurist said: "Because of that tradition which you, yourself quoted earlier". The transmitter after thinking accepted that and said: "That is true, and it is possible to infer this result from the *hadith*." On another occasion the transmitter asked the same jurist another question and received an answer. The transmitter again asked about the proof and received the same reply that he had been given on the previous occasion. The transmitter thought for a while and said: 'That is right. It is logical to take this result from the *hadith*. Do you know? You jurists are just like physicians and we are like pharmacists".

Whereas, the right *ijtihad* had ceased in Sunni Islam, as even the most learned jurist since the third/ninth century has had to base his decisions on the opinions of earlier jurists . . . and the Sunni position has been expressed by saying that "the gate of *ijtihad* was closed"; on the contrary, "the gate of *ijtihad*" has always been open in Shi^ci Islam.

The Shi^ci Ijtihad

Traces of Shi^ci *ijtihad* go back to the period of the Imams. They tried to train some persons and encourage them to pronounce and reply to the cases of people. As Imam Baqir said to Aban ibn Taghlib: "Sit down at the door of the mosque and pronounce *fatwa* (judgement) to the people. I would like to see many person like you among my people". Ibn Idris quotes from Imam Sadiq that he said: "It is our duty to pronounce the principles, but you must detail them". Another time, Imam Sadiq sent Shu^cayb to Abu Basir al-Asadi to ask him some religious questions that Shu^cayb had had, and also Imam ^cAli al-Rida sent ^cAli ibn Musayyab to Zakariyya ibn Adam for the same purpose. There is another *hadith* in *al-Kafi* and *Wasa'il* which is related by ^cUmar ibn Hanzala and the Shi^ci ^culama' accepted it. In this *hadith*, Imam Sadiq said:

> Look to the person who relates our *hadith*, knows what is forbidden or permitted, and recognizes our rules, then accept him as a jurist, because I made him your jurist.

Tabarsi quotes from Imam Hasan al-Askari in his *Ihtijaj* that the Imam said:

> It is obligatory upon the common people to follow the jurist who could prevent himself (from doing wrong), support his religion, oppose carnal desire, and obey his master (*mawla*).

Replying to Ishaq ibn Ya^cqub, the twelfth Imam wrote in a command (*tawqi^c*):

> In every event, refer to our relaters. They are my proof of God.

In this manner, the traces of Shi^ci *ijtihad* date to the time of Imams, and it is clear that the Shi^cis were spread all over the Islamic cities, and being under government pressure, or long distances, made access to the Imams very difficult or impossible. But, from day to day, there were some new cases which needed new replies. There must be, necessarily, someone to reply to these new questions. As among the companions of the Imams there were some well-known persons such as Zurara, a companion of Imam Baqir, Jumayl ibn Darraj, a companion of Imam al-Sadiq, Yunus ibn ^cAbd al-Rahman and Safwan ibn Yahya, companions of Imam ^cAli al-Rida who replied to the questions. Also, Imam al-Sadiq referred someone to Al-Asadi to reply to his questions and Imam cAli al-Rida did the same to Zakariyya ibn Adam.

After the Greater Occultation, there were two Shici jurists who were well-known:

The first one was Ibn cAqil al-cUmani (Hasan ibn cAli, in the first half the fourth century), who refined Shici jurisprudence, used some new opinions, and separated the discussions about principles from subordinates. He was the teacher of Ibn Qawlawayh al-Qumi and wrote *Al-Tamassuk bi Habl al-Rasul*, and *Al-Karr wa'l-Farr*. He was the first one who resorted to the root of jurisprudence and had intellectual reasoning. Afterwards, Ibn Iskafi (Abu cAli Muhammad ibn Ahmad ibn Junayd, d. 381/991) continued this method. He wrote some books, among them are: *Mukhtasar al-Ahmadi, Tazhib al-Shici, al-Asfar*. But, his books were abandoned, since he used *qiyas* in his deduction. There two jurists are called the two ancients (*Qadimayn*).

In spite of that, their method was not popular and had no adherents until Tusi gave a definite shape to the Shici *ijtihad*.

The movements and qualitative changes of Shici jurisprudence, since jurists (*fuqaha'*) have undertaken *ijtihad*, should be considered in three stages:

First of all, the positive statement of Shici *ijtihad* by Tusi.

Secondly, the root of the Shici jurisprudence took definite shape at the hands of Muhaqqiq Hilli (676/1227) and cAllamah Hilli (726/1325), and the weak *hadith* became separated from the sound. The book of Muhaqqiq (*Sharaci*) is still a textbook. At the end of this period Muhammad Amin al-Astarabadi (1034/1624):

> is held to be the leader of the attack on the *mujtahids* and those who believed in *ijtihad*, and the founder of a subdivision of the Imamites known as Akhbarites ("*traditionists*"). Their view was that legal opinions should be based on tradition (*akhbar*) only, and not derived from general principles (*usul*) by analogical reasoning or otherwise.

This discussion went on until the period of Wahid Bihbahani (1117-1205/ 1705-1790) who attacked the *Akhbaris* in his debates and books (like *al-Ijtihad wa'l-Akhbar*, and *Fawa'id al-Ha'iriyyah*), and, finally, the method of the Akhbarites was abandoned by the Shici.

In the third stage, the Shici *ijtihad* reached its climax through Shaykh Murtada al-Ansari (1281/1864).

The Main Differences

Tusi, like the ^culama', founded his *ijtihad* on four bases: the Book, the tradition, consensus, and reason. Mention should be made here of two main differences in *ijtihad* between the Shi^ci and Sunnites. 1. *Qiyas* (analogy): Literally, it means "to measure", "to compare" and "to weigh up". It might have been derived from the word *qaws* (bow) used for measurement in Arabia. *Qiyas* in the root of jurisprudence is a *tamthil* in the *Organum*. It must be noted that *qiyas* in the Aristotelian *Organum* was syllogism. It is comprised of the major and minor premiss, the middle terms, and the result. But, *tamthil* is to carry a matter out in analogous cases, and *qiyas* in jurisprudence is the same. It means, while there is a rule on a subject, it could occur in similar cases. For example, wine is forbidden in the Qur'an, because it causes drunkenness. Beer is intoxicating and makes one drunk. Drunkenness is a common factor between these two similar matters. Thus, beer must be forbidden. In this case, the *ratio legis* (^cilla) (drunkenness) is explicated, and the majority of Shi^cis are inclined to accept it. But, the *ratio legis* (^cilla) (the common factor between two similar matters), is not always clear, and the most difficult question is to distinguish this ^cilla. *Qiyas*, among the Sunnites, came into being as a systemmatizing legal principle of individual reasoning because the use of arbitrary personal opinion (*ra'y*) resulted in divergence and chaos. But, *qiyas* itself fell a victim to capricious theorization on the part of the common run of jurists.

In any case, this kind of *qiyas* (or, as it is called, deduced *qiyas, mustanbit al-^cilla*), was opposed by the Shi^ci and some other sects and, as we know, logicians do not view *tamthil* as a definite proof nor does it necessitate knowledge.

Mention should be, also, made that Ibn Shubrumah relates a meeting between Imam al-Sadiq and Abu Hanifah, and a debate about *qiyas*:

I and Abu Hanifah once visited Ja^cfar ibn Muhammad al-Sadiq; I introduced my companion as a jurist from Iraq. Then Ja^cfar said: 'Would it be he who in religious matters produced *qiyas* (anaologies) based on his own *ra'y* (*yaqis al-din bi ra'yih*)? Would it be al-Nu'man ibn Thabit? — I myself, adds the informant, learned his name only from this question. — 'Yes,' replied Abu Hanifah, 'that is, I, may god grant me success!' Then Ja^cfar said: 'Fear God and apply no analogy in religious matters based on your arbitrary opinion, for it was Satan (*Iblis*) who established analogical reasoning first'.

Now, remarks follow that purport to show the inadequacy of speculation in jurisprudico-religious matters.

"Just tell me which, in the eyes of God, is the more serious crime, homicide or adultery?"

"No doubt, homicide is a greater crime", replied Abu Hanifah.

"Yet homicide is judged on the basis of two witnesses' evidence while adultery is proven only by statements from four witnesses. How does your analogy apply in this case? And what is more meritorious before God: fasting or praying?"

"Prayer is definitely more meritorious", replied Abu Hanifah.

"Nevertheless, a woman must make up the fast which she misses through menstruation although she does not have to make up the praying which she missed in this state. Fear God, O servant of God, and do not produce arbitrary analogies in religious matters, for we and our opponents may be summoned before God's tribunal tomorrow. Then we on our part shall say: ᶜAllah said: the Prophet of Allah has said'. You and your companions, however, shall say: "We have heard such; we have guessed such'. But Allah shall treat us and you as He wills."

Tusi quotes in *at-Tahzib* from Aban who asked Imam al-Sadiq about the compensation for a woman whose fingers were cut off. He said:

The compensation is fixed at ten camels for one finger, twenty for two, and thirty for three, but twenty for four. It is the command of the Prophet, and you must not make *qiyas*, because *qiyas* destroys the religion.

It should be noted here, that this opposition is not fanaticism or rejecting the right of reason for mere devoutness, because, the Shiᶜis accepted reason, instead of *qiyas*, as a basis of *ijtihad*.

The Shiᶜi opposition, originally, was founded on two bases: *Qiyas* (like *tamthil* in logic) does not necessitate knowledge and is not really a reliable and trusty method.

It served as a precedent in *fiqh* that exerting *qiyas* resulted in exaggeration and chaos. Without opposition to it, Islamic jurisprudence would be entirely changed.

Besides, *qiyas* does not originally accord to the Islamic attitude of mind. The Islamic principles, like worship, morals and social attitudes are described in the Book and tradition. These principles are adaptable to all details. It is *ijtihad* which must draw the subordinate cases from the principles and deduce rules from Islamic principles in association with events. In any case, the Imams, following the Qur'an, knew reason as an esoteric proof and inner prophet.

For example, these *hadiths* are in *Usul al-Kafi, Kitab al-^caql*:

Imam ^cAli ibn Abu Talib, the first Imam, said: "Gabriel came to Adam, and informed him: "O Adam, I have been ordered to let you choose one out of three things. Therefore choose it and leave the other two." Adam asked: "What are the three things, Gabriel?" He replied: "Reason, modesty and religion (*din*)." Then Adam said: "I choose reason." So Gabriel ordered modesty and faith to withdraw and leave reason, but they said: "O Gabriel, we both have been instructed (by God) to remain with reason wherever it may be." Gabriel answered: "Then that is your situation." And then he ascended towards the heaven."

Imam Abu Ja^cfar Muhammad al-Baqir, the first Imam, said: "When almighty God created reason, He tested it. Then he ordered it to come forward and it came forward. Then God ordered it to go back and it went back. On this Almighty said: "I swear by My power and majesty that no creation of Mine is dearer to Me than you are, and I have only made you perfect in those whom I love. Lo! to you, are My orders and prohibitions addressed. And for you, are My rewards and retributions reserved."

Imam Ja^cfar al-Sadiq, the sixth Imam, was asked: "What is reason?" The Imam replied. "Reason is that by which God is worshipped and a place in Paradise earned." The Imam was then asked: "What did Mu^cawiyah have?" The Imam replied: "That was just wickedness and cunning; it seemed like reason, but it was not reason."

* * *

1. *Ijma^c* (consensus): The third base of Islamic law is *ijma^c* or consensus and it is the unanimous opinion of the *mujtahids* on a religious precept (*hukm*). But, there is a difference between the Shi^cis and Sunnites on its source of validity. The Sunnites accept it through transmission and quote many *hadith* about it. The Shi^cis, however, recognize it as a means of discovering the speech of an infallible *imam*, and it must be clear that the speech of an *imam* is among them. Thus, it will be related to the period of the *imams*. But, as an infallible *imam* exists in every era, and because of the grace of God, Who never leaves His servants without guidance, if the *mujtahids* are unanimous on a religious precept and there are no objections, it would be proof that an infallible (*imam*) is satisfied.

According to Tusi's belief, since consensus is a proof, because it includes the speech of an *imam* who is infallible, and this is an intellectual reasoning, then, the method for proving it should be through intellectual reasoning, not transmission. He resorts often to consensus, even on the principal subjects like prophecy and *imamah*, against opponents who believed in consensus, too. However, in the subordinate cases, he sometimes quotes consensus and at other times rejects it. Al-Shahid al-Thani (Shaykh Zayn al-Din) collected thirty-four cases in which he had been contradictory, sometimes he had accepted consensus and at other times refuted it. (This treatise has been published twice: (1) at the end of *Alfiyyah*, which is written by Shahid Awwal, 1308/1890 and (2) in *al-Zikr al-Alfiyyah*, p. 790, Mashhad, 1391).

Tusi's Ijtihad

There were formerly some *mujtahids* like Ibn ᶜAqil al-Umani and Ibn Junayd al-Iskafi. But this was really a primitive stage and because of some exaggerations and deficiencies, their method was abandoned and nobody followed them, until Tusi, who is really the founder of the Shiᶜi *ijtihad*, established the bases of reasoning in Shiᶜi religious law (*fiqh*).

Shaykh Tusi was one of the people who knew that a primitive view and vulgar comprehension are not sufficient to understand the spirit of Islamic instruction, but rather that good understanding of Islamic teaching needs a deep comprehension. He never refrained from declaring free and independent opinions which caused Subki and Hajji Khalifah to call him a Shafiᶜite and say: He was such a qualified lawyer (*mujtahid*) who did not lean on anything but the Book, the tradition, and his understanding. But, he was really, the one who deduced many subordinate cases from *hadiths* and gave many *fatwas*, and his views were undoubtedly absolutely sovereign in Shiᶜi opinion for one hundred years. Afterwards, Ibn Idris started to cricitize him, but Tusi's basis of *ijtihad* is still confirmed.

Although he is a man of principle and has a great respect for Islamic principles, he gives utterance to the right of reason (*ᶜaql*). In spite of the fact that he is a great traditionist (*muhaddith*), his books *Istibsar* and *Tahzib* are evidence that he knows the religious principles within the terms of reason. It means that he is not a fanatic and does not recognize the religious principles as imitative obedience.

He mentions in '*ᶜUddat al-Usul*' some Shiᶜi persons who are not enlightened and criticizes them:

> If you ask them about the unity or justice of God, prophecy, or succession of the Prophet, they will only quote some *hadiths*.

(instead of resorting to intellectual reasoning). He knows very well that the main beliefs should be understood directly and clearly by everyone through reason, and the transmitted works must only have a guiding role. He was involved with some fanatics who did not accept anything, but the *hadith* word for word, and he was obliged for a long time to shape his idea in the form of the words of *hadiths*. He complains in the introduction of *al-Mabsut*:

I heard constantly that the Sunni jurists despised Shi^ci religious law . . . and I wanted to compile a book including subordinate cases, but I was involved, and among other things, which decreased my intention, was that our companions had less liking for this kind of compilation, because they had got used to the text of *hadith* word for word, and did not want to change any word, if one word were used instead of another, they could not understand it . . .

In any case, Tusi compiled a book in this field and established Shi^ci *ijtihad*, *Al-Mabsut* is a book of *ijtihad*, and it is the first Shi^ci law book in which the subordinate cases are drawn from principles. There are certainly many differences between the *Mabsut* and the *Nihayah* which was attacked by Ibn Idris. In *Nihayah*, Tusi has noted legal cases using the *hadith* words, being nor more than the interpretation of *hadiths*. It is a summary of decisions without references and rational outlines of law, but Tusi's method of *Mabsut* was obtained by reasoning and deduction (*ijtihad*) where necessary. Tusi felt in his time a need to change the method, but the solution was not easy and needed bravery and enormous skill. Tusi managed it conscientiously and caused Shi^ci religious law to enter a new period, and besides, proved that Shi^ci *ijtihad* existed (without *qiyas*) and it is enough to draw new cases from the Islamic principles. The main point is that he recognized the needs of the community and at the same time preserved the principles. He solved the problem very well.

His judgement and *fatwa* are still acceptable, although, sometimes he goes so far that it is difficult to reach him, even nowadays.

There are many patterns in his *fatwas*, but as his book, *Mabsut* is full of detailed cases about worship, morals, and social behaviour, here, mention will be made of only a few of his other special opinions.

Tusi sometimes had ideas which those who came after him lacked the courage to hold. One of them in his opinion on painting and statues. In commentary on the Qur'an (II, 51) which is about al-Samiri who produced for the Jews a calf-statue to worship, and consequently they became oppressors. Tusi says that they were oppressors because of idolatry and not the making of a calf-statue. Of course it (statuary) is disapproved of but is not absolutely unlawful. What is quoted from the Prophet that he cursed portraitists, means that the antoropomorphists and those who liken God to a man are the subjects of this curse. Among the Shi^ci scholars, it is only Tabarsi who quotes this opinion in his *tafsir*, but others rejected it entirely.

Another specific opinion is about the single *hadith*, which, although his teachers al-Mufid and al-Murtada rejected it, he sometimes confirmed.

In the fifth/eleventh century, he defended the spherical nature of the earth. Jubba^ci, like Balkhi and some other astronomers, in the commentary of the *Ayah* that says: "Who had spread the earth as a bed for you" (II, 22), say: "The earth is flat like a bed not spherical. A globe cannot be flat, and reason confirms that. There are so many seas and oceans, and water cannot be fixed without two parallel walls . . . if there is a side shorter than another one, of course, water will have a current . . ." But, Tusi refuted him and said: "These are not the proofs. Belief in the globularity of the earth means believing in its globularity in the whole, not in the part of the earth."

Another piece of evidence for his sound judgement is that Tusi accepts that the clouds are produced by vapour, as he says:

> If it is said that clouds are produced by vapours which rise from the earth, it might be true and there is no intellectual reason against it.

He refutes, also, that the sky is something different from firmament. Rummani says that these are two different things because the firmament moves and rotates, but the sky does not. Tusi refutes him saying: "There is no difficulty in the sky and firmament being the same, although, moving and rotating.

Tusi has other interesting ideas about suffering, comman ding the right and forbidding the wrong, the faith and other theological subjects which will be mentioned another time.

Leonard Binder

. . . The Shi^ci *^culama'*, acting as the general agency until the hidden Imam reveals himself, performs the function of the Imam. The Imam is not a prophet, for the Shi^cis too, adhere strictly to the doctrine that Muhammad was the last of the Prophets and that his revelation perfected all earlier ones. The function of the Imam is to interpret the law of the Qur'an and to apply it, even develop it, as new situations arise. Since the Imamate passed, with one exception, by heredity through the eldest male offspring in the line of ^cAli, it follows that a certain charismatic quality is attached to that office. This quality was further enhanced by the assertions made against the Sunni apologists of the ^cAbbasid Caliphate that the Shi^ci Imam was not only eligible under the Sunni rules of the Caliphate, but that he was the best of those qualified and impeccable besides. The infallibility of the Imam is as firmly asserted and, in practice, unequivocally adhered to. The ^{c}*ulama'* who act in the name of the Imam do not share all of this charisma by any means, but some of it does accrue to them. They are not considered infallible nor impeccable, and the most careful ^{c}*ulama'* may sign themselves as criminal and wrong-doer in the humble recognition that they may have judged incorrectly. The Sunni ^{c}*ulama'* enjoy no similar charismatic quality. Neither the Umayyid nor the ^{c}Abbasid Caliphs claimed the legal authority of the Shi^{c}i Imams. The early ^{c}Abbasid era knew a moderate form of inquisition, still a courtier's very early suggestion that the ^{c}Abbasid Caliphs assume the right to settle doctrinal disputes never came to anything. Only a little later we find Sunni apologists asserting that the Caliph need not be the best of those qualified for the job, nor even the most learned. Al-Baqillani was of the opinion that the consensus of the learned should guide the Caliph and even depose him if he stubbornly refused to follow the law. Al-Ghazzali merely asserted that the Caliph could legitimize his position by taking the advice of the ^{c}*ulama'*.

Under these circumstances we find that the Shi^{c}i ^{c}*ulama'* derive their legitimacy largely from the Imam, while the Sunni ^{c}*ulama'* can lend a measure of legitimacy to the Caliph. For centuries, now, we have had neither an Imam nor a Caliph; and in practical terms both bodies of ^{c}*ulama'* have had to contend with political authorities who established themselves without benefit of religious procedure. Both have tried to play the role assigned to the ^{c}*ulama'* by al-Ghazzali. Consequently, a single tradition of the formal relations of the ^{c}*ulama'* and the Sultan or Shah has come to prevail. On the other hand, there is no question but what the doctrinal authority of the Shi^{c}i ^{c}*ulama'* is both more concrete and more prestigeful than that of the Sunni ^{c}*ulama'*. The Sunni ^{c}*ulama'* do not perform the function of the Caliph, but rather assist the Muslim Community to do that which is incumbent upon all. There is no religious office in connection with the function of the Sunni ^{c}*ulama'*.

The superior authority which inheres in the Shi^{c}i ^{c}*ulama'* as a consequence of their relationship to the Imam was further codified as Shi^{c}i legal theory developed. All Muslims believe that the good is that which God wills and the evil that which God forbids. Man's whole duty is to comply with the will of God, for which reason God revealed his will to man through the prophets. After the last revelation, the Sunnis hold that man can be rightly guided if he follows the explicit commands of the Qur'an, if he follows the traditions reporting the sayings and doings of the Prophet himself, if he follows the consensus of the Community which by the higher authority of tradition will never be in error, or if he deduces new applications by strict analogy to known rules. The Shi^{c}i ^{c}*ulama'* believe that more is necessary if

man is to be rightly guided . . . . The Imams are meant by God for this purpose. In the absence of the hidden Imam, the *culama'* must provide for the
divine guidance of the Community. The Shi^ci *culama'*, however, claim no
charismatic quality or inspiration for themselves. In fact they claim no more
than the long years of study which is the qualification of the Sunni *culama'*.
This failing is accounted for by the differences in the *usul* of science of the
roots of the law of the Shi^cis.

Evidently, Shi^cis *usul* were slow in developing. Professor Shahabi explains this late development as the result of the fact that such a science was
unnecessary until after the lesser occultation. Before this, either the Imams
or their deputies interpreted the law. The period of the lesser occultation
lasted from 869 to 940 A.D. Donaldson points out that the Sunni collections
of traditions or *hadith* were compiled about one generation before those of
the Shi^cis. The Shi^ci collections were made during the domination of the
Caliphate of the great occultation. It is these collections of *hadith* to which
Professor Shahabi refers as the first works on jurisprudence, but in point of
fact it would seem that the first major works devoted to the science of jurisprudence were those by ^cAllamah al-Hilli who died in 1325 A.D. Shahabi admits that al-Hilli went beyond his illustrious grandfather, Shaykh Tusi, ad-
mitting *ijtihad* or independent judgement. However the study of *usul* may
have developed in this period, it was not yet accorded the importance of the
study of *hadith* at the end of the Safavid period when the second Majlisi
who died in 1699 A.D., was the outstanding theologian. Furthermore,
Shahabi indicates that the *usulis* overcame the opposition of the *akhbaris*,
or those who preferred *hadith*, in Karbala' as late as the beginning of the
nineteenth century; and we can guess that the *usulis* did not establish themselves and their views until the latter part of the century. Burujirdi, the late
leader of the Shi^ci *culama'* of Iran, was reputed to have followed a
jurisprudential method akin to that of Shaykh Tusi, so that he was by no
means a convinced and thorough *usuli*.

What conclusions can we draw from this controversy between those who
preferred to rely on the traditions reporting the judgments of the infallible
Imams and those who preferred to supply the *culama'* with a jurisprudential
theory that would permit them to make new interpretations as might the living but hidden Imam? This entire subject has not been sufficiently studied,
but I believe it tenable that even today many of the Shi^ci *culama'* fear losing
the authority of the Imams should they venture far beyond their explicitly
recorded statements. The *usulis*, on the other hand, are far more aware of
the pressures of recent social and political change and fear worse the relega-
tion of Islamic law to a relatively minor position. At the present time no influential *calim* rejects the *usuli* position in its entirety; but there are not many

religious revolutionaries among the Shi^ci *^culama'*. The *akhbari* position assures the *^culama'* of the infallible authority of the Imams while the *usuli* position affords the *^culama'* a method of approximating that authority while adapting Islamic law to new situations.

The four sources of Sunni law are the Qur'an, the *hadith*, the consensus of the Community and analogical deduction. In this sytem, there is no room for independent judgment or *ijtihad*, and reason is to be used within the narrow confines of strict analogy. Independent judgment according to the spirit of the explicit law was the prerogative of the early founders of the four orthodox schools alone. The *^culama'* of subsequent ages must accept their authority according to their choice of school. Acceptance of such authority is known as taqlid and its corollary is the closure of the gate of *ijtihad*. The four sources of Shi^ci law are the Qur'an, *hadith* of the Prophet and the Imams, consensus of the Imams, rather than of the Community, and reason. Reason is not the equivalent of *ijtihad* for certain judgments will be found to be logically necessary. For the rest, however, *ijtihad* in one form or another is the expression of this principle. Once again we find the Shi^ci *^culama'* enjoying authority superior to that of the Sunni *^culama'* in that they are either speaking with the infallibility of the Imams or rendering judgments with an authenticity parallel to that of the founders of the Sunni schools.

Historical circumstances as well as both doctrine and jurisprudential theory have served to enhance the position of the Shi^ci *^culama'*. Prior to the establishment of the Safavid empire in 1500 A.D., there was no extensive or long lasting twelver-Shi^ci sovereignty established anywhere in Islam. The other branches of Shi^cism, such as Zaydis in Yemen, the Isma^cilis, or the Fatimid Caliphate of medieval Egypt, all enjoyed the immediate presence of a living Imam which reduced the status of the *^culama'*. The early Safavids also claimed the Imamate according to Professors Minorsky and Lambton, but the former has presented some evidence to show that this view was accepted only by an elite tribal formation. Professor Lambton offers a good deal of evidence to show that under the late Safavids and throughout the Qajar period, the twelver *^culama'* predominated and were able to suppress to some extent the sufi or mystic tendencies which made such extreme claims by the early Safavids possible. In any event, it is obvious that the Shi^ci *^culama'* were well established and identified with the Imam long before there was a political leader who needed to justify his office by reference to Shi^ci doctrines. For the Sunni *^culama'* the opposite was the case.

The Shi^ci *^culama'* of Iran were then built up into an effective organization with the help of the Safavids as part of the latter's campaign to convert the whole of Iran to Shi^cism. To some extent this organization was recognized

and authorized by royal appointment of the *qadis* and of the *sadr* or leading
alim. The breakdown of central authority toward the end of the Safavid
period, and the invasion of the Sunni Afghans which followed, the chaotic
conditions under the short lived Afshar and Zand dynasties, and the foreign
wars of the early Qajars all tended to enhance the position of the *culama'*.
During those times, the *culama'* served as a stabilizing influence in the provincial towns, sometimes even negotiating with attacking warlords, and
they were essential to the mobilization of the Iranian military forces.... .

* * *

. . . Acknowledged patterns of organizations are few. The most significant
relates to the position of the *Ayatullah al-cUzma*. This position is held by
the one who is considered to be the most learned of the age and whose piety
is also above question. In strict accordance with the generally accepted
definition of religious roles, the Ayatullah al-cUzma is the equivalent of any
mujtahid, that is any one whose learning has reached the stage where he is
capable of making independent judgments. Any Muslim seeking guidance
will usually attach himself to a *mujtahid* from whom he will regularly
receive religious advice. A *mujtahid* with such a following is known as *mar-
jac-i taqlid*. A follower is known as a *muqallid*. To have a wider following, a
mujtahid must publish a book expounding his method and views so that
they can be accessible to people in other cities. It is through the *mujtahids*,
referred to in the constitution of Iran as the "proofs of Islam," that the
general agency of the Imam is carried out. While any *mujtahid* may give
guidance on religious problems, it is acknowledged that they differ in learning if not in piety. In accordance with the Shici insistence that the Caliphate
must go to the one who is best qualified rather than to any one of those sufficiently qualified, there is much prejudice in favor of following the one *mujtahid* who is acknowledged as the most learned. Until his recent death,
Ayatollah Burujirdi was acknowledged to be the Ayatullah al-cUzma. This
acknowledgment was not universal, and some tended to recognize him
merely as the head of the *culama'* in an organizational sense. The key question in this regard is whether the *mujtahid* interviewed believes that the
general agency is carried out by all the *culama'* or by the Ayatullah al-
cUzma. Burujirdi's supporters came close to representing him as the sole
spokesman for the hidden Imam.

While not the apex of a hierarchy, this leadership position does rest on a
foundation of subordinate positions. As might be expected from the fact
that learning is the key to this office, the supporting framework of roles is
based on the traditional educational system to some extent. *cUlama'* tend to
be classified in accordance with the stages of learning they have attained,
but not in accordance with the number of years they have spent at a

madrasah. Other offices coincide with the roles of teaching, preaching, reciting stories of the Imams, serving as *pishnamaz* or in other capacities at mosques, and ministering to the religious needs of villagers.

In the category of neutral organizational prerequisites, we find elaborate, if informal patterns of finance, communication, recruitment, succession to leadership and household administration of the Ayatullah al-^cUzma. While all of these present interesting problems, the most significant for our purposes are the financing of the institution and the succession to leadership. The *^culama'* are supported by contributions from the faithful. These contributions are given the names of the canonical payments of *khums* or *zakat*, that is, the share of the Imam or alms. Actually these sums are to be used for general religious purposes including charitable payments to the indigent. In this way, the *^culama'* are the agents for the disposition of these funds, most of which go to support educational institutions, students, teachers, and *^culama'* of all sorts. The local *mujtahid, pishnamaz,* or village *mullah* are supported by their local adherents for the most part. A *wa^ciz* or *rawdah khan* is often paid by the job. Another source of income is from *waqfs* of pious endowments in the profit from land and buildings. These endowments are usually set aside for religious purposes including education, hospitals, charity, and assistance to travellers; but some of these funds are used to help *tullab* (or students), teachers, and other *^culama'*. Each *waqf* is managed by a *mutawalli* who is often a *mullah* . The *mutawalli* receives a share of the income for his own expenses. Often when the *mutawalli* is not a *mullah*, a *nazir* or supervisor is appointed who is a *mullah*. Beyond these sources of income *^culama'* may engage in any economic pursuit quite apart from their calling. There are, however, relatively few in the bazaar, even at Qum; but many more have considerable landholdings acquired by inheritance, marriage, or even the usurpation of *waqfs*.

The most important basis of organizational finance is still the *khums* and *zakat*. Its importance is directly related to the fact that its payment is based upon acknowledgment of the role of the *mujtahids*; that is, the believers pay their religious dues to the *mujtahid* whom they follow or to his representative. Of course, many individuals may give funds to more than one *mujtahid*; but the important thing is that quite substantial sums of money were paid to representatives of Burujirdi. Some of this money is sent to Qum to support that city's scholars and the rest may be spent in the city where it was collected. Even though many ranks of the *^culama'* receive their incomes independently of this *khums-zakat* system, many will make an occasional trip to Qum where they may pay their respects to the Ayatullah al-^cUzma, possibly receiving some subvention if they are in need. Smaller replicas of the same system are built about other important or locally influential *mujtahids*, and many village mullas are dependent upon the important *mu-*

jtahid of the nearest town for financial assistance. The *waqf* system is no longer an organizational basis of finance, though it is the claim of the *culama'* that the most learned or *aclam* ought to have the right to appoint the *mutawalli* whenever there is no specific agent appointed in the *waqfnamih*.

Succession to leadership depends on many factors, but the most important of them all is learning. Still, other qualities are taken into consideration. According to one source, the following are important: *taqwa* (piety), *mardumdari* (knowing how to deal with people), *mudir budan* (administrative ability), *ustad* (be a teacher), *risala* (have written a book), he must be an older man, he must be of Fars and not an Arab or a Turk, in addition to having great erudition. There is no formal method of choosing the Ayatullah al-cUzma, but it would seem that a relatively small group of some thirty or forty persons, most of whom reside at Qum, perform the function of the College of Cardinals by acknowledging the leadership of someone. To the insiders, these are known as *ra'is tarash* (sculptors of the head) or *marja' dorostkun* (creators of the following). This group is partially comprised of *Ayatullahzadegan* or the descendants of once famous and learned *mujtahids* and partially of the leading teachers at Qum Certain merchants are important, as is the influential Ayatollah Bihbahani in Tehran, and a small group of *muballighin* or propagandists who are not *mujtahids* but preachers.

Part IV

Shi*c*i Spirituality
and Piety

Chapter Eighteen

Religious Rites, Prayers, and Supplications

*For the Shi*c*s, the necessary concomitant of professing their faith is the expression of devotion to God. This devotion is manifested in Islam's injunctions concerning worship: the canonical prayer, fasting, pilgrimage, almsgiving, and supplications. Seyyed Hossein Nasr expounds on the general character and some particulars of the Shi*c*i observance of Islamic worship in the following passage. The excerpt is taken from* SI, *pages 231–33.*

Seyyed Hossein Nasr

The religious rites practiced by Twelve-Imam Shiᶜis are essentially the same as those of the Sunnis with certain minor modifications of posture and phrasing which are little more than the differences that are to be found among the Sunni schools (*mazhabs*) themselves, except in the addition of two phrases in the call to prayer. For Shiᶜism, like Sunnism, the major rite consists of the daily prayers (*salat* in Arabic, *namaz* in Persian and Urdu), comprised of the prayers of sunrise, noon, afternoon, evening and night. Altogether they consist of seventeen units (*rakᶜahs*) divided in the ratio of 2, 4, 4, 3 and 4 for the respective five prayers. The only singular quality of Shiᶜi practice in this respect is that instead of performing the five prayers completely separately, usually Shiᶜis say the noon and afternoon prayers together, as well as the evening and the night prayers.

Shiᶜis also perform superogatory prayers and prayers on special occasions such as moments of joy, fear, and thanksgiving, or when visiting a holy place of pilgrimage. In these practices also there is little difference between Shiᶜism and Sunnism. However, we can sense a distinction in the Friday congregational prayers. Of course these prayers are performed in both worlds but they definitely have a greater social and political significance in the Sunni world. In Shiᶜism, although these prayers are performed in at least one mosque in every city and town, in the absence of the Imam, who according to Shiᶜism is the true leader of these prayers, their importance is somewhat diminished and more emphasis is placed upon individual prescribed prayers.

As for the second basic Islamic rite of fasting, it is practiced by Shiᶜis in a manner that is nearly identical with that of Sunnis and differs only in the fact that Shiᶜis break their fast a few minutes later than Sunnis, when the sun has set completely. All those capable of fasting and above the age of puberty must abstain from all drinking and eating during the month of Ramadan from the first moments of dawn until sunset. The moral and inward conditions that accompany the fast are also identical for the two branches of Islam. Likewise, many Shiᶜis, like Sunnis, fast on certain other days during the year, especially at the beginning, middle and end of the lunar month, following the example of the Holy Prophet.

Also, for the pilgrimage (*hajj*), Shiᶜi and Sunni practices have only very minor differences. It is the pilgrimage to other holy places that is emphasized more in Shiᶜism than in Sunnism. The visit to the tombs of Imams and saints play an integral role in the religious life of Shiᶜis . . . Of course these forms of pilgrimage are not obligatory rites such as the prayers, fasting and hajj, but they play such an important religious role that they can hardly be overlooked... .

* * *

The recitation of the Holy Qur'an is [also] rite . . . and it is a basic Shiᶜi practice as much as a Sunni one. The Qur'an is chanted during special occasions such as weddings, funerals and the like, as well as different moments of the day and night during one's daily routine. In addition the Shiᶜis place much emphasis upon the reading of prayers of great beauty in Arabic from the prophetic hadith and from the sayings of Imams as contained in the *Nahj al-balaghah, Sahifah sajjadiyyah, Usul al-kafi*, etc. Some of these prayers, like the *Jawshan-i kabir* and *Kumayl*, are long and take several hours. They are recited only by the especially pious, on certain nights of the week, particularly Thursday night and the nights of Ramadan. . . .

* * *

al-Hysayn, the Third Imam*

Prayer for the Day of ᶜArafah

Praise belongs to God

whose decree none may avert,
    and whose gift none may prevent.
    No fashioner's fashioning is like His fashioning,
    and He is the Generous, the All-embracing.
He brought forth the varieties of unprecedented creatures
    and perfected through His wisdom all He had fashioned.
    Hidden not from Him are harbingers,
    nor lost with Him are deposits.
He repays every fashioner,
    feathers the nest of all who are content
    and has mercy upon all who humble themselves.
He sends down benefits
    and the all-encompassing Book
    in radiant light,

Ed. Note. Devotional prayers and litanies of Shiᶜis come from the works of their saints: Imams, the household of the Prophet, and their disciples. William Chittick has translated some of the most important devotional prayers of Shiᶜism, the supplication of the third Imam, Husayn ibn ᶜAli, the twelfth Imam, Muhammad ibn Husan, and that of Kumayl ibn Ziyad. Excerpts are taken from SA, pages 91–102 and 122–124.

He hears supplications,
    averts afflictions,
    raises up in degrees,
    and knocks down tyrants.
        For there is no god other than He,
        nothing is equal to Him,
        "Like Him there is naught
        and He is the Hearing, the Seeing" (XLII,2),
        the subtle, the Aware,
        and "He is powerful over all things" (V, 120 etc.).

O God, cause me to fear Thee as if I were seeing Thee,
    give me felicity through piety toward Thee,
    make me not wretched by disobedience toward Thee,
    choose the best for me by Thy decree (*qada'*)
    and bless me by Thy determination (*qada'*),
    that I may love not the hastening of what Thou hast delayed,
    nor the delaying of what Thou hast hastened.
O God, appoint for me sufficiency in my soul,
    certainty in my heart,
    sincerity in my action,
    light in my eyes,
    and insight in my religion.
    Give me enjoyment of my bodily members,
    make my hearing and my seeing my two inheritors,
    help me against him who wrongs me,
    show me in him my revenge and my desires,
    and console thereby my eyes.
O God, remove my affliction,
    veil my defects,
    forgive my offence,
    drive away my Satan,
    dissolve my debt,
    and give me, my God, the highest degree
    in the world to come and in this world.
O God, to Thee belongs the praise,
    just as Thou created me and made me to hear and to see;
and to Thee belongs the praise,
    just as Thou created me and made me a creature unimpaired
    as a mercy to me,
    while Thou hadst no need of my creation.
My Lord, since Thou created me

and then made straight my nature;
my Lord, since Thou caused me to grow
and made good my shape;
my Lord, Thou didst good to me
and gavest me well-being in my soul;
my Lord, since Thou preserved me
and gavest me success;
my Lord, since Thou blessed me
and then guided me;
my Lord, since Thou chosest me
and gavest me of every good;
my Lord, since Thou gavest me to eat
and drink;
my Lord, since Thou enriched me
and contented me;
my Lord, since Thou aided me
and exalted me;
my Lord, since Thou clothed me with Thy pure covering
and smoothed the way for me by Thy sufficient fashioning:
Bless Muhammad and the household of Muhammad,
aid me against the misfortunes of time and calamities of nights
and days
deliver me from the terrors of this world and the torments of the
world to come
and spare me from the evil of that which the evildoers do in the
earth... .

* * *

O He who pardons the greatest sins by His clemency!
O He who lavishes blessings by His bounty!
O He who gives abundance by His generosity!
O Sustenance to me in my adversity!
O Companion to me in my solitude!
O Aid to me in my affliction!
O Benefactor to me in my blessing!
O my God
and God of my fathers,
Abraham, Ishmael, Isaac and Jacob!
Lord of Gabriel, Michael and Israfil!
Lord of Muhammad, the Seal of the Prophets,
and his household, the chosen ones!

Revealer of the Torah, the Gospel, the Psalms and the
      Criterion
and Sender down of *Kaf Ha' Ya' ᶜAyn Sad, Ta' Ha', Ya' Sin,*
      and the Wise Qur'an!
Thou art my cave (of refuge) when the roads for all their
      amplitude constrict me
and the land for all its breadth is strait for me.
If not for Thy mercy, I would have been among the perishing,
and Thou annullest my slip.
If not for Thy covering me, I would have been among the
      disgraced,
and Thou confirmest me with help against my enemies.
And if not for Thy helping me, I would have been among
      those overcome.

* * *

Muhammad al-Mahdi, the Twelfth Imam

Prayer for the month of Rajab

*Shaykh al-Tusi has related that this noble writing came out of the Sacred
Precinct on the hand of that great Shaykh, Abu Jaᶜfar Muhammad ibn
ᶜUthman ibn Saᶜid—may God be pleased with him. Recite it on each day of
the month of Rajab.*

In the Name of God, the Merciful, the Compassionate
O God, I ask Thee by the meaning of all that by which Thou art called
      upon by those who govern with Thy authority:
      those who are entrusted with Thy mystery,
      welcome Thy command,
      extol Thy power,
      and proclaim Thy majesty.
I ask Thee by Thy will which speaks within them, for Thou hast
      appointed them
      mines for Thy words,
      and pillars of the profession of Thy Unity, Thy signs and
            Thy stations,
      which are never interrupted in any place.
Through them knows he who knows Thee.
There is no difference between Thee and them,
      save that they are Thy servants and Thy creation,

their doing and undoing is in Thy hand,
their origin is from Thee and their return is to Thee.
They are aides, witnesses, testers, defenders, protectors, and
searchers.
With them Thou filled Thy heaven and Thy earth until it became
manifest that there is no good but Thou.
So I ask Thee by (all of) that,
and by the positions of Thy mercy's might
and by Thy Stations and Marks
that Thou bless Muhammad and His household
and increase me in faith and steadfastness.

O Inward in His outwardness and Outward in His inwardness and
hiddenness!
O Separator of light and darkness!
O described by other than (His) Essence and well-known in other
than (His) likeness!
Delimitator of every delimited thing!
Witness of all that is witnessed!
Bring into existence of every existent!
Counter of everything counted!
Depriver of all that is deprived!
There is none worshipped but Thou,
Possessor of Grandeur and Generosity!
O He who is not conditioned by "how" or determined by "where"!
O veiled from every eye!
O Everlasting!
O eternally Self-subsistent and Knower of all that is known!
Bless Muhammad and his household
and Thy elect servants,
Thy mankind in veils,
Thy angels brought nigh,
and the untold multitudes (of angels) set in ranks and encircling
(the Throne).
And bless us in this our venerated and honored month
and the sacred months that follow it.
In it bestow blessings upon us copiously,
make large our portions,
and fulfill for us (our) oaths,
by Thy most tremendous, most tremendous, greatest and noblest
Name,
which Thou placed upon the day, and it brightened, and upon the
night, and it darkened.

And forgive us that of ourselves which Thou knowest and we know not,
   preserve us from sins with the best of preservations,
   suffice us with the sufficiencies of Thy determination,
   favor us with Thy fair regard,
   leave us not to other than Thee,
   hold us not back from Thy goodness,
   bless us in the lifespans Thou hast written for us,
   set aright for us the inmost center of our hearts,
   give us protection from Thee,
   cause us to act with the fairest of faith,
   and bring us to the month of fasting
   and the days and years that come after it,
   O Lord of Majesty and Splendor!

* * *

The Supplication of Kumayl ibn Ziyad *

Oh God, I ask Thee by Thy mercy,
      which *embraces all things* (VII, 156);
   by Thy strength,
         through which Thou dominatest all things,
         toward which all things are humble
         and before which all things are lowly;
   by Thy invincibility,
         through which Thou overwhelmest all things;
   by Thy might, which nothing can resist;
   by Thy tremendousness, which has filled all things'
   by Thy force, which towers over all things'
   by Thy face, which subsists after the annihilation of all things;
   by Thy Names, which have filled the foundations of all things;
   by Thy Knowledge, which encompasses all things;
   and by the light of Thy face, through which all things are illumined!
Oh Light! Oh All-holy!
Oh First of those who are first and Last of those who are last!
Oh God, forgive me those sins which tear apart safeguards!
   Oh God, forgive me those sins which draw down adversities!
   Oh God, forgive me those sins which alter blessings!
   Oh God, forgive me those sins which hold back supplication!

Ed. Note: The supplication of Kumayl ibn Ziyad (Du^{c}a-i Kumayl) is of particular importance to Shi^{c}i devotional prayer. For originally it belonged to Khidr—ancient/mythical prophet of Muslims who is the subject of much devotional rituals—and was later recited by Imam ^{c}Ali, who taught it to his close companion and disciple, Kumayl. The excerpt is taken from AMS, pages 6–7, 14.

Oh God, forgive me those sins which cut down the hopes!
Oh God, forgive me those sins which draw down tribulation!
Oh God, forgive me every sin I have committed and every mistake
I have made!
Oh God, verily I seek nearness to Thee through remembrance of Thee.
I seek intercession from Thee with Thyself,
and I ask Thee through Thy munificence
to bring me near to Thy proximity,
to provide me with gratitude toward Thee
and to inspire me with Thy remembrance.
Oh God, verily I ask Thee with the asking of a submissive, abased and
lowly man
to show me forbearance, to have mercy on me
and to make me satisfied and content with Thy apportionment and
humble in every state.
Oh God, I ask Thee with the asking of one whose indigence is extreme
who has stated to Thee in difficulties his need
and whose desire for what is with Thee has become great.
Oh God, Thy force is tremendous, Thy place is lofty,
Thy deception is hidden, Thy command is manifest,
Thy domination is overwhelming, Thy power is unhindered
and escape from Thy governance is impossible.
Oh God, I find no forgiver of my sins, no concealer of my ugly acts, no
transformer of any of my ugly acts into good acts
but Thee. There is no god but Thou!
Glory be to Thee, and Thine is the praise!
I have wronged myself, I have been audacious in my ignorance
and I have depended upon Thy ancient remembrance of me and
Thy favor toward me.
Oh God! Oh my Protector!
How many ugly things Thou has concealed!
How many burdensome tribulations Thou hast abolished!
How many stumbles Thou hast prevented!
How many ordeals Thou hast repelled!
And how much beautiful praise, for which I was unworthy, Thou
hast spread abroad!

* * *

My God, my Master and my Lord!
Canst Thou see Thyself tormenting me with Thy fire
after I have professed Thy Unity?

After the knowledge of Thee my heart has embraced,
the remembrance of Thee my tongue has constantly mentioned
and the love of Thee to which my mind has clung?
After the sincerity of my confession and my supplication,
    humble before Thy lordship?
Far be it from Thee!
Thou art more generous than that Thou should squander him
    whom Thou hast nurtured,
    banish him whom Thou has brought nigh.
    drive him away whom Thou hast given an abode
or submit to tribulation him whom Thou has spared and shown
    mercy.
Would that I know, my Master, my God and my Protector,
    whether Thou wilt give the Fire dominion over faces fallen
        down prostrate before Thy Tremendousness,
        tongues voicing sincerely the profession of Thy Unity and
            giving thanks to Thee in praise,
        hearts acknowledging Thy Divinity through verification,
        minds encompassing knowledge of Thee until they have
            become humble
    and bodily members speeding to the places of Thy worship in
        obedience and beckoning for Thy forgiveness in
        submission.
No such opinion is held of Thee!
    Nor has such been reported — thanks to Thy bounty — concerning
    Thee, oh All-generous!

Chapter Nineteen

Diverse Religious Practices

Certain Shiᶜi religious practices must be mentioned because of their wide popularity. These include alms-giving; petitioning God for favors by giving to the poor; arranging special religious tables, the food from which is given to the poor; and many other practices that carry religion to the intimate activities of daily life. Also of importance is religious taxes: Zakat, *promulgated by the* Shariᶜah, *and* Khums, *a tax unique to Shiᶜism.*

Secondly, Shiᶜi religious worship consists of religious processions, conducted mostly during the month of Muharram, on the days of ᶜAshura *and* Tasuᶜa, *marking the martyrdom of Imam Husayn. The day of* ᶜAli's *martyrdom during the month of Ramadan also is an occasion for such processions.*

Religious processions, much like Rawdah-Khani *and* Taᶜziyyah *have their roots in Shiᶜi devotional worship. The dramatic representations that characterize Shiᶜi popular worship evoke devotion to the Saint-Martyr Imam, who in their eyes is more than just a hero, "since his intercession will be accepted by God for his sinful followers even when the intercession of the prophet has failed." "Go thou", says the latter to him (Husayn) on the Resurrection Day, "and decline from the flames everyone who has in his lifetime shed but a single tear for thee, everyone who has in any way helped thee, everyone who has performed a pilgrimage to that shrine, or mourned for thee, and everyone who has written tragic verse for thee, bear each and all with thee to paradise."*

Religious processions, in practice, consist of well-organized groups of men who travel from one religious shrine, across the streets of cities and towns, to mosques or other holy places of popular gathering. Throughout its progress, a procession chants elegies for martyred Imams, which are followed by the sound of self-flagellations and chest-poundings, done with chains or the palm of the hand. The processions draw a large crowd, many of whom may join in or at least walk along with the procession. Shiᶜis believe that even watching religious procession has merit. In the following passage, I. K. A. Howard's translation of Ayatollah Abu'l-Qasim Khu'i's work on Khums *provides a descriptive account of this popular practice of Shiᶜism. The passage is taken from* Alserat, *pages 169–74.*

Ayatollah Abu'l-Qasim Khu'i

The *khums* is one of the established religious duties which is laid down in the Holy Qur'an. Attention to its importance has also been emphasized in many traditions reported from the sinless *ahl al-bayt*. . . .

The *khums* is *wajib* on seven assets, the first being: *Earned Profits*. These are everything which a person acquires by trade, industry, tenure, or any other kind of earning. Included in this is possession by gift and by legacy and (everything) which comes to one's possession through *sadaqa* (prescribed or recommended alms) and the *khums* and *zakat* (alms). However, the *khums* is not liable on inheritance except when (the inheritor) is not one of the people entitled (by Islamic law). It would be no abandoning of proper care for such a man to pay the *khums* on it.

The *khums* is *wajib* on profits after the deduction of expenditure to cover (commercial production) costs and what exceeds the household expenses of oneself and one's family. Food, drink, accommodation, transport and household furniture come within the meaning of "household expenses" as does expenditure on marriage of oneself or someone connected with one. In addition, the term "household expenses" include payment of *sadaqah* (prescribed alms), religious pilgrimages, (offering of) gifts and food to relatives and friends, and such like. All this differs from person to person. The consideration of the manner and amount of the expenditure will be according to the circumstances of the person himself. If his circumstances require him to spend 100 dinars on his annual household expenses, but he exceeds this and spends 200, he must pay the *khums* on everything over the 100. However, if he lives meagerly and only spends 50 dinars he must pay the *khums* on everything over 50.

When a man's profit only equals the amount of his annual household expenses or less than that, he may use it as capital to trade with or buy the necessary means for his industry. At such a time the *khums* is not levied on him. However, if he makes additional (wealth) over and above his annual household expenses, and he uses it as capital or spends it for the means of his industry, then the *khums* is levied on that amount which is greater than his annual household expenses. . . .

When a man buys a commodity with his profits whose market value increases, or some associated increase occurs in it, the *khums* is not levied on it. However if he sells it and makes a profit, the *khums* is levied specifically on the profit. . . . Isolated increases (in value) are also treated as profits and the *khums* is levied on them provided they are not used up by the annual household expenses. Thus, if a mare gives birth to a foal — to coin an example — the result would be (regarded as) profit. Within the same category come: fruit from trees, and their branches and leaves, the wool, fur, and milk of animals, etc.

Whoever uses his capital — in terms of animals or roofed buildlings (*musqafat*) — in order to live on the produce while still keeping the individual (animals and buildings), is not liable to pay the *khums* on any increase in their market price. Any such increase, whether continuous or isolated, comes within (the term) "profits" made out of such assets.

Whoever uses his financial capital to trade, by buying and selling commodities, is liable to pay the *khums* on any increase in their market price, whether such an increase is continuous or isolated.

When a man trades in a variety of commodities, (such as) animals, food and furniture, their profits should be totalled together and the *khums* paid on the total which is over and above the annual household and commercial expenditure. The same condition also applies if he was engaged in industrial production.

The beginning of the year is the earliest time when the profit becomes clear on any given item, in the sense that when there is profit, and that profit is not used up in expenditure on the household or commercial expenses and thus the year ends, the *khums* will be liable to be paid on it.

When it is possible for a man to live without (using) profit, for example, if he has an inheritance from his father, he does not have to use that inherited money for his annual household expenditure. He may spend his profits on his annual household expenditure and if they do not exceed that amount (of his household expenditure) he is not liable to pay the *khums* on them. However, if he (already) has things which make the spending of the profit unnecessary, for example, if he has a house as his residence, he is not allowed to buy another house from his profits and treat it as household expenditure.

If a man buys some household effect with his profit but after some time has no (further) need of it, the *khums* is not liable on it. Similarly if he buys a horse to ride, then he has no need of it because of an illness which prevents him from riding, he is not liable (to pay) the *khums* on it.

* * *

If a man is in profits, and then he dies, the *khums* must be paid (if applicable) without waiting for the year to end.

If a man makes a profit which enables him to undertake the journey to Mecca during that year, he is allowed to spend the profit on the pilgrimage without the *khums* being liable on it. However, if he fails to make the pilgrimage in defiance of the religious command or some such thing, until the year is over, then the *khums* is liable on it.

* * *

The spending of the Imam's share must be authorised by the legally-appointed ruler or handed to himd to be spent according to his views. The most appropriate (thing to do) (where this is not possible) is to ask the advice of someone who is an authority on the customary practice with regard to it, and the (usual) place of its expenditures. All revenue is subject to the consent of the Imam. However, there is no doubt about it being permissible to spend it on the household expenditure of the deserving, whom one knows to be religious, and engaged in the propagation of the laws of religion. There is no difference when it comes to those who defend the faith, between the Hashimites and others. However, when one has to choose between Hashimites and others, and when "the share of the *sayyids*" is insufficient, and when there is no special factor weighing in the non-Hashimite's favour, preference should be given to the Hashimites according to the most careful observance (of the rules).

In the *khums* the intention of sacrifice should be observed, it is not sufficient merely to pay it.

When the *khums* is paid to the religious authority, his agent or a person entitled to it, it is not allowed to ask for it back.

Earlier we have mentioned that it was not permitted that a deserving person receives his share of *zakat* and then returns it to the giver. Nor it is lawful for the recipient to "negotiate" his expected share for a small sum. Same applies to *khums* letter for letter.

If the *khums* is paid to someone whom the giver believes to be entitled to it and then the opposite is discovered, or it is paid to the religious authority who spends it, the same rules apply as were mentioned in *zakat*.

Being descended from Hashim must be established with mental certainty, just evidence, and through the claimant being well-known in his country.

When a man dies while still responsible for (payment) of some of the *khums*, the same legal requirement is followed as with other debts. It is necessary for it to be paid from the original amount left before any bequest or inheritance.

Mahmud Ayoub *

. . . Here again we see a definite tension within the tradition. We are sometimes told that the day of *cAshura* was a day on which God performed special acts of creation, or manifested His mercy and forgiveness to the prophets of old. We shall examine a few examples of this kind of tradition presently. In the tradition just cited, the *Imam* declared that, . . . God in His wisdom created light on Friday, the first of Ramadan, and darkness on Wednesday, the day of *cAshura.* *cAshura* is a day of darkness and disorder in the universe. On it, darkness, the symbol of evil and chaos, was created; on it, after the death of Husayn, the laws of nature were suspended as the sun darkened in mid-day, the stars collided with one another, and the heavens were troubled.

According to a very early tradition already referred to, the Prophet was told that when Husayn died, '. . . The earth shall be shaken from its foundations, the mountains shall quiver and be disturbed, the seas will rise up in furious waves, and the heavens shall quake with their denizens, all in anger and sorrow for thee O Muhammad, and for what thy progeny shall suffer after thee. . . .' These were not simply portents showing the gravity of the event, but a genuine manifestation of the grief and angry vengeance of entire creation. The tradition goes on to assert that all things would then seek permission from God to lend support to the wronged *Imam* and his companions; but God would insist that vengeance is His, and will mete out such terrible torments for these evildoers so as not to be compared with the torments of any other people.

The imams strongly insist that the day of *cAshura* should not be taken as a day of joy and festivity; according to some non-Shic i traditions, it seems that the day was regarded as such. There is a *hadith* reported from cAli, the first Imam, on the authority of Maytham al-Tammar, who told it to a woman, Jabalah al-Makkiyyah. She asked how it should be that people would regard the day of *cAshura'* as a day of joy and blessing. Maytham wept and answered:

Ed. Note: Shic i devotional worship, in general, revolves around the tragic lives of all the Shic i Imams. However, the martyrdom of Imam Husayn forms the crux of Shic i redemptive suffering and, hence, has galvanized popular religious sentiments into devotional rites and practices. The tacziyyah, *for instance, is concerned with the tragedy of Karbala'. Therefore, the day of martyrdom of Husayn,* cAshura, *the tenth day of the month of Muharram, is of particular significance for Shic is, and serves as the single most important occasion for much of their devotional religious practices and redemptive suffering. In the passage, Mahmud Ayoub examines the significance of* cAshura *ceremonies. The passage is taken from* RSISD, *pages 149–51.*

. . . They shall fabricate a *hadith* [prophetic saying] claiming that it was on that day that God forgave Adam, but in fact, He forgave him during the month of Zhu-l Hijjah [i.e., the month of pilgrimage and feast of sacrifice). They shall assert wrongly that it was the day on which God accepted David's repentence, but that also was in Zhu-l Hijjah.

Then Maytham continued to refute the claims that on the tenth of Muharram, Noah's ark rested on dry land, and God split the Red Sea for the children of Israel, assigning different dates to these events.

The day of ʿAshura according to the eighth Imam, must be observed as a day of inactivity, sorrow and total disregard for worldly cares. It may be that the unique character of this day has evolved as a reaction to traditions which sought to assert its sacred and joyous aspects. It may also be that the ancient Jewish ʿAshura observance, characterized by grief, fasting and total inactivity, played a role in the growth of Shiʿi ʿAshura piety. Furthermore, ʿAshura is the only day in the Islamic calendar, to our knowledge, clearly stipulated as a day of total rest. Of course, this injunction has never been taken literally. Rather, the entire period of ʿAshura, the first ten days of Muharram, is full of activity but of a special kind.

It must also be remembered that the month of Muharram, even in pre-Islamic times, was regarded as a sacred month. Let us conclude our remarks by quoting at some length the stipulations of the eighth Imam concerning the observance of the day of ʿAshura.

He who abandons any cares for his needs on the day of ʿAshura, God would fulfill all his needs in this world and the next. He who takes the day of ʿAshura as the day of his afflictions and grief and weeping, God would make the Day of Resurrection a day of his joy and exaltation, and we shall be a comfort and security for him in paradise. But he who calls that day a day of blessing, and on it stores any provisions in his house, these provisions would not be blessed. He would be moreover consigned along with Yazid, ʿUbaydallah ibn Ziyad and ʿUmar ibn Saʿd to the deepest pit of the first.

The manifestation of sorrow and grief by actually weeping for the Holy Family of Muhammad needs an impetus. We have seen that one strong aid for creating the proper atmosphere of sorrow has been to relate one or more of the many traditions attributed to the imams, enjoining their followers to lament Husayn's martyrdom and the sufferings of other members of his family. By emphasizing one or several aspects of the tragedy of Karbala', the devotees are reminded of the object of their sorrow. Soon special memorial services (the *taʿziyyah majalis*) developed, giving this religio-political phenomenon a rich ritualistic character... .

E. G. Browne*

. . . the contemplation of the sufferings and misfortunes of the Imams has inspired a copious literature, both in verse and prose, of a . . . popular kind. The mourning proper to the month of Muharram finds expression not only in the actual dramatic representations of this cycle of tragedies, of which there are at least forty (a few of which, however, are connected with prophets and holy men antecedent to Islam), but in recitations of these melancholy events known as *Rawdah-Khani*. These latter are said to

---

Ed. Note: A number of religious practices and doctrines besides the basic rites, associated with Imam Husayn, are particular to Shīʿism. These practices and doctrines are related closely to the central place that the martyrdom of Imam Husayn occupies in Shīʿism. The Shīʿis regard the martyrdom of Husayn as a cosmic event around which revolves the entire history of the world, prior as well as subsequent. It is a divinely preordained event, one that manifests God's mercy and Justice, and, hence, allows man to achieve redemption, or conversely, condemns him. The redemptive suffering that characterizes the Karbala' tragedy for the Shīʿis has manifested itself in the lives of the believers in two ways:

First, the martyrdom of Husayn has been seen throughout Shīʿi history as a struggle (jihad) in the path of God — the battle for justice and truth against the forces of evil. The martyrdom of Husayn is an inspiring ideal, which they glorify and towards which they strive. The Shīʿi doctrine of martyrdom is the primary example of this form of redemptive suffering in Shīʿism.

Second, the tragedy of Karbala' evokes redemptive suffering among Shīʿis through the participation of the faithful in the sorrows of the martyred Imam and that of his household. In fact, it is not only the Shīʿis, but the whole of mankind, who are enjoined to participate in the suffering of Husayn. The sixth Shīʿi Imam, Jaʿfar al-Sadiq has said: "if it would please you to have the reward (thawab) of those who were martyred with Husayn, say whenever you remember him, "O how I wish I were with them, that I may have achieved that glory." This form of participation is reflected in the Shiʿi practices of rawdah-khani, taʿziyyah, ziyarah (pilgrimage to the shring-tombs of Imams and saints), and Sini-zani (religious processions associated with redemptive suffering.)

The purpose of all these practices is to involve the faithful in the suffering of Husayn and the tragedy of Karbala'. They all strive to arouse the conscience of the Shīʿis, to bring the tragedy to life, and to immerse the believers in the central theme of their faith — the martyrdom of Husayn. Consequently, Shīʿi redemptive suffering enjoins and provokes weeping for and commiserating with the sorrow of the household of Husayn. Imam Husayn himself said, "I am the martyr of tears (qatil al-ʿibrah), no man of faith remembers me but that he weeps. "Go thou [says Muhammad to Husayn on the day of Resurrection], and deliver from the flames everyone who has in his life-time shed but a single tear for thee, . . . everyone who has performed a pilgrimage to thy Shrine, or mourned for thee and everyone who has written a tragic verse for thee. Bear with thee to paradise."

Rawdah-Khani, the first of these practices to be examined here, consists of sermons, recitations from the Qur'an, and lyricized depiction of the tragic life of various Imams, particularly Imam Husayn. This practice often is witnessed during the months of Muharram and Safar, when the tragedy of Karbala' and its aftermath took place. In Browne's conception, rawdah-khani constitutes popular religious poetry (as opposed to Marathi, which were elegies by lyricists).

In the passage, E. G. Browne provides a descriptive summary of rawdah-khani. The excerpt is taken from LHP, Volume IV, pages 181–86.

derive this name from one of the earliest and best-known books of this kind, the *Rawdatu al-Shuhada* ("Garden of the Martyrs") of Husayn Waᶜiz-i Kashifi, so that these functions are called "*rawdah*-readings," whether the readings be taken from this or from some similar work, such as the *Tufanu'l-Buka'* ("Deluge of Weeping") or the *Asrar al-Shahadat* ("Mysteries of Martyrdom"). Such entertainments are commonly given in the month of Muharram by rich notables, nobles, statesmen or merchants, who provide an adequate number of professional rhapsodists or reciters of this class, called *Rawdah-Khans*, and a more or less sumptuous supper to follow. I possess a copy of a curious little poem entitled *Kitab al-Sufra fi Zammi al-Riya* ("the Book of the Table, censuring hypocrisy") in which the ostentation of the host and the greed of the guests is satirized with some pungency. The following lines describe how the word is passed round as to whose entertainment is likely to prove most satisfactory to the guests:

"Now hear from me a story which is more brightly coloured than a garden flower,
Of those who make mourning for Husayn and sit in assemblies in frenzied excitment.

All wear black for Fatimah's darling,
Establish houses of mourning and make lament for the King of Karbala'.
In every corner they prepare a feast and arrange a pleasant assembly;
They carpet court-yard and chamber, they bedeck with inscriptions arch and alcove;
They spread fair carpets, they set out graceful furnishings;
A host of gluttonous men, all beside themselves and intoxicated with the cup of greed,
On whom greed has produced such an effect that, like the stamp on the gold,
It has set its mark on their foreheads, make enquiry about such assemblies.
One of them says, 'O comrades, well-approved friends, versed in affairs,
'I and Hajji ᶜAbbas went yesterday to the entertainment of that green-grocer fellow.
'In that modest entertainment there was nothing but tea and coffee,
'And we saw no one there except the host and one or two *rawdah-khans*.
'To sit in such an assembly is not meet, for without sugar and tea it has no charm.

'God is not pleased with that servant in whose entertainment is neither sherbet nor sugar.

'But, by Him who gives men and *jinn* their daily bread, in such-and-such a place is an entertainment worthy of kings,

'A wonderfully pleasant and comfortable entertainment, which, I am sure, is devoid of hypocrisy.

'There is white tea and sugar-loaf of Yard in place of sugar,

'And crystal *qalyans* with flexible tubes, at the gargle of which the heart rejoices.

'The fragrance of their tobacco spreads for miles, and the first gleams on their heads like [the star] Canopus.

'No water will be drunk there, but draughts of lemon, sugar and snow.

'One of the reciters is Mirza Kashi, who, they say, is the chief of *rawdah-khans*.

'Another of them is the rhapsodist of Rasht, who is like a boat in the ocean of song.

'From Kirman, Yazd and Kirmanshah, from Shiraz, Shushtar and Isfahan,

'All are skilled musicians of melodious and charming voices : they are like the kernel and others like the shell.

'In truth it is a wonderful entertainment, devoid of hypocrisy : by your life it is right to attend it!'

When the friends hear this speech with one accord they assemble at that banquet."

*Peter Chelkowski**

The tragedy of Karbala' is viewed by the Shi^ci as the greatest suffering and redemptive act in history. Actually it transcends history into meta-

---

Ed. Note: Closely connected with rawdah-Khani *is a passion play* ta^cziyyah. *While not a rite in the sense of prayers,* ta^cziyah *is a manifestation of religious life, one that features prominantly the social, artistic, and literary aspects of the Shi^ci life. In the passage, Peter Chelkowski provides an analytical examination of* ta^cziyah *as a dramatic-religious experience. The excerpt is taken from* ASIHCN, *pages 209–26.*

history, having acquired cosmic proportions. This places the passion of the Imam Husayn at Karbala' at a time which is no time and in a space which is no space. In other words, what happened in the year 61 of the Muslim era (680 AD), on the battle field of Karbala' is as if it were taking place now, in the present, in any place where the Shi^{c}i live, and especially wherever they are humilitated, deprived, and abused.

The timeless quality of this tragedy allows the Shi^{c}i communities to measure themselves against the principle and the paradigm of Husayn. They strive to fight against any injustice, tyranny and oppression today. By so doing they hope to be considered worthy of the sacrifice of the 'Prince of the Martyrs' — Husayn.

The commemoration of the Imam Husayn's passion and martyrdom is charged with unusual emotions throughout the Shi^{c}i communities in the world. The belief that participation in the annual observance of his suffering and death will be an aid to salvation of the Day of Judgement is an additional motive to engage in the many mourning rituals. In the words of the Nobel prize winner, Elias Canetti, the suffering of Husayn and its commemmoration 'became the very core of the Shi^{c}i faith . . .', which is 'a religion of lament more concentrated and more extreme than any to be found elsewhere. . . . No faith has ever laid greater emphasis on lament. It is the highest religious duty, land many times more meritorious than any other good work.' So it is not surprising that during the last thirteen hundred years the historical truth has been embellished by myth and legend, especially at the level of popular and emotional expression.

The mourning rituals have developed and are still increasing in various Shi^{c}i communities, and although they may differ in form, the passionate participation is universal. Some of them may even be considered as unlawful or inappropriate by the ^{c}ulama'. Even though some are frowned upon by rigorous theologians, they are nevertheless a true expression of popular beliefs and sincere devotion.

The mourning rituals, divided into ambulatory or stationary ones, have been performed in the open for centuries, be it in the main artery of a town, on a village common, at a major intersection in the bazaar, in the courtyard of a mosque, of a caravanserai, or of a private house. In order to protect the participants from the weather an awning is sometimes spanned, or a tent pitched, over stationary rituals. The solid edifices were not built until the end of the sixteenth century in India and the middle of the eighteenth century in Western Asia. These are *known as Imambaras, ^{c}Ashur-Khanihs, Takiyyah, Husayniyyihs*, and so forth.

The place of Husayn's martyrdom, Karbala', became a venerated spot for pilgrims. There is an extant account of a pilgrimage which occurred some four years after his death. The pilgrims, who were warriors and avengers of Husayn's blood, called themselves penitents (*tawwabun*). They marched against ᶜUbaydullah ibn Ziyad, the man who laid seige to Husayn's camp at Karbala'. During this vengeful military operation, the warriors stopped in order to pay homage to their martyred hero, and as they moaned and wailed day and night they recalled the tragic events of the Karbala' massacre. They wept so much that 'the sand of the desert became soaked, as if by a current of water'. This became the prorotype for subsequent rituals, especially for a ritual known as the *majlis-i ᶜaza*.

In Baghdad, in the fourth Islamic century, during the Buyid reign of Muᶜizz al-Dawlah, on the day of Husayn's martyrdom, known as *ᶜAshura* (10th Muharram), the bazaars closed and the people circumambulated the city, weeping, wailing, striking their heads, the women dishevelled, everyone in torn, black clothing, mourning for Husayn. Such a public display of grief in processions has become the most common form of ritual for Husayn all over the world, in places as distant from Karbala' as Madras in Southern India and Port of Spain in Trinidad.

* * *

Ritual processions are usually held in the month of Muharram and the following month of Safar, especially on the 10th of Muharram (*ᶜAshura*') and the 20th of Safar, known as *Arbaᶜin* or *Chellah*, which is the fortieth day after Husayn's death. The activities among the marchers, their costumes, clothing, the objects carried, and the accompanying music may differ not only from country to country but also from district to district.

In Iran, these processions are called *Dasta-yi ᶜAzadari*, and they take place in the streets and public squares and in the countryside. They can be simple marches or elaborate pageants, with the characters dressed in colourful costumes, either marching or riding on horses or camels and bearing arms. Live tableaux (floats) representing the scene of the tragedy with mutilated bloody bodies are accompanied by dirges, bands, singing and drums. These are interspersed with men flagellating themselves. The fundamental components seem to be the same but the methods of self-mortification differ. Some beat their chests with their hands (*sini-zani*), others beat their backs with chains (*zanjir-zani*), and still another group beat their heads with swords and knives, so that blood streams down their faces, necks and chests (*shamshir-zani*). Some mortify themselves with stones. All this is done to demonstrate their grief for the wounds the martyrs received at Karbala'.

Their self-mortification is an attempt to identify themselves with the suffering of Hysayn as though Karbala' could be reproduced in the present and they could share in the Imam's passion of martyrdom.

The grandest procession always takes place on the day of ^c*Ashura'*. Each district of a town or city usually has its own order of precedence. The processions join in a fore-ordained succession and end in a specified locality.

The most important object always carried in the procession is the ^c*alam*, which signifies the standard of Husayn at Karbala'. This most sacred object gives the participants the feeling that they are actually fighting at Karbala'. In the Indo-Pakistani subcontinent there are special processions where only ^c*alams* are carried. The reverence for them is universal and special edifices have been constructed to house them as sacred reliquaries.

^c*Alams* are generally made of metal standards, elaborately decorated with plumes, sacred objects, colourful brocades and silks. Some are as high as ten feet, but the sizes vary.

As the ^c*alam* is a symbol of fighting for the uncompromising cause of right and justice, so the *nakhl* (date-palm) is the symbol of death for the cause — it represents the bier of Husayn, that is, of Husayn's beheaded corpse, which was carried from the battlefield at Karbala' to his resting place on a stretcher of date-palm wood. Through the centuries the *nakhl* has lost its resemblance to the original stretcher and has become a structure of various sizes, from small to enormous, like a wooden lattice, shaped in the form of a tear drop, reminiscent of the tears of the faithful shed for Husayn. While this permanent structure is left bare during the rest of the year, in Muharram it is decorated with silks, fine carpets, and brocades. These large ones are carried in the processions by many men.

Another symbol of death is the *tabut* — a bier, like the drapery-covered coffin used nowadays throughout the Islamic world in ordinary funerals.

Since Husayn and his followers were cut off from water, suffering from terrible thirst in the sun-scorched sands of the desert, the routes of the Muharram processions and the places of the stationary rituals are provided with portable water containers, shaped like a saint's tomb.

In the maze of small alleys in a traditional Iranian town, or in the labyrinth of the bazaar, one passes by a wall in which there is a niche containing a large brass receptacle with a tap. There are also several brass drinking cups attached to the container by chains. The niche is decorated with wall paintings or tiles showing scenes from Karbala' or symbolic Shi^ci attributes. There is a low grille over which people reach to get water.

On Thursday evening this little *saqqa'-khanih* ('House of the Water-Carrier') is lit by candles and there is an attendant serving the water and singing dirges. He is also responsible for keeping the container filled during the rest of the week. A religious endowment pays him for these duties.

People slake their thirst here all week long. This has been the symbolic meaning of counteracting the thirst of Karbala' and is also a funerary ritual in so far as the receptacle is surmounted by a dome, symbolizing a sepulchre of a martyred saint. In so far as this is so, the water receptacle comes to mean a minor pilgrimage to a tomb, and people tie bits of cloth to the small grille as they would in the case of the real saint's burial site. The most important tomb is that of Husayn, who is perceived by the Shiᶜi as the 'Fountain of Faith'. Therefore the water from the *saqqa'-khanih* is considered to be blessed. Since ᶜAbbas was not only Husayn's standard-bearer but also his water carrier (he was killed while trying to get water from the Euphrates river for Husayn and his family), the *saqqa'-khanih* is often regarded as a shrine to ᶜAbbas.

In the 1960s the *saqqa'-khanih* gave its name to a school of painting in Iran. The new generation of painters, mostly educated in the West, tried to bridge modern modalities with the Shiᶜi popular tradition.

The stationary ritual is called the *majlis* (pl. *majalis*), meaning 'gathering', 'assembly', 'meeting'. The root of this is derived from *jalasa* which means 'to sit'. The overall term should be *majlis-i ᶜaza*, meaning a 'mourning gathering'. On the Indian subcontinent the ᶜaza is usually dropped, while in in Iran *majlis* is dropped, and instead of *majlis-i rawdih-khani* or *majlis-i taᶜziyah* only *rawdih-khani* and *taᶜziyyah* are in common usage.

Rawdih-khani is an Iranian ritual of publicly recited, chanted elegies which concern the suffering of Husayn and the other Shiᶜi martyrs. Together with the passion plays and the Muharram mourning processings, they constitute the tripod of Shiᶜi mourning observances.

The recitation of chanting of eulogies for the Shiᶜi martyrs go back at least to the year 65. Mourning literature, known as *maqatil*, was mainly written in Arabic. Contemporaneous with the establishment of Shiᶜism as the state religion of Iran by the Safavid king in 1501 was the composition of the *maqtal* literary masterpiece by Husayn Waᶜiz Kashifi, written in Persian, but under the Arabic title of *Rawdat al-Shuhada* (*The Garden of the Martyrs*). *Rawdih-khani* derives its name from the above. The second word in the title is replaced by *khani*, meaning 'chanting recitation', from the Persia verb *khandan*, meaning 'to read, recite of chant'.

The public lamentation of *rawdih-khani* is performed particularly during the mourning months of Muharram and the following month of Safar. Such acts of piety may take place during some eighty days of mourning throughout the year of the Shiᶜi calendar, and also upon the recovery of someone's health, the safe return from a pilgrimage, and so on... .

Taᶜziyah-khani, or *shabih-khani*, popularly known as *taᶜziyyah*, is the Shiᶜi passion play performed mainly in Iran. The only indigenous and serious drama in the Islamic world, *taᶜziyyah* describes the death of Husayn and his followers on the plain of Karbala'.

The *ta^cziyyah* drama which emerged in the middle of the eighteenth century was derived from the Muharram parades and the *rawdih-khani* recitations in the form of the *majlis*. While originally performed at cross-roads and in public squares, *ta^cziyyah* performances soon moved first to caravanserais and private houses, and then to specially built theatres called *takiyyahs* or *Husayniyyihs*. Theatres of various size and construction were built, finally reaching enormous proportions in the huge, elaborate structure built by Nasir al-Din Shah in the 1870s called the Takiyyah Dawlat.

All these performance areas or playhouses have in common a raised circular or square platform upon which the main action takes place. This is surrounded by a narrow strip which is circumambulated or ridden about by the performers to indicate the passage of time or a change of place. This space, as well as several entrances and exits, extends into and through the audience-filled pit where people sit on the ground. In large or opulent homes or theatres, the elite sit in elevated boxes or balconies, where they are well served with food and drink. Water and sweetmeats are also distributed among the general audience — an egalitarian rite. Nowadays, *ta^cziyyah* can be performed throughout the year, but originally it was staged only in the month of Muharram and following the month of Safar.

The protagonists dress predominantly in green, and sing their parts, while the villains, who wear red, speak their lines. Symbolic properties, such as a bowl of water to represent a river, are improvised according to need, particularly in the villages where costumes and properties are scarce. The director-producer is omnipresent on the stage as prompter, property man, and regulator of the actors, musicians, and viewers. Villagers and townsmen participate when professional actors are few, but troops of actors travel from plact to place, with men playing the women's roles. Parts are often passed from father to son in family groups: it is a hereditary trade.

Audience participation is so intense that men and women mourn and weep as though the scenes before them were taking place in the immediate present. Remorse that Husayn should have been allowed to die so horrible a death is felt as a personal loss here and now.

The heyday of the *ta^cziyyah* was in the second half of the nineteenth century. In recent years, due to overt westernization on the one hand, and because of socio-political reasons on the other, the *ta^cziyyah*, which had been an urban creation, retreated to the rural areas. The *ta^cziyyah* repertory is enormous. In addition to the Karbala' events, it also deals with martyrdom prior to, and after, the death of Husayn, and Qur'anic stories or simple stories related to a particular locality. Whatever the tale, it is then always related to the martyrs of Karbala'. This juxtaposition in turn amplifies those happenings.

The main part of the repertory consists of plays devoted to Husayn, ^cAbbas, Qasim, ^cAli Akbar, Hurr, Muslim, and the captivity of the related women.

The Shi^ci of the Caucasus (part of Iran until the early nineteenth century) and of Iraq and southern Lebanon perform *ta^cziyyah* passion plays on a more limited scale.

The *Sufrih-i Hadrat-i ^cAbbas* is another type of mourning ritual not directly devoted to the Imam Husayn, but to his half-brother and standard-bearer on the plain of Karbala', ^cAbbas. Thanks to his chivalry, gallantry, and bravery, ^cAbbas enjoys a special place in the Shi^ci communities, particularly among the women. *Sufrih* is a serving cloth upon which they spread food following a vow made by somebody, and during the ensuing feast there are reminiscences and stories told about ^cAbbas and Karbala'. Afterwards, food is distributed among the poor.

The *Shamayil-Gardani,* or *Pardih-Dari* is a one-man show with a backdrop painting depicting the scenes of the battle of Karbala', from left to right, painted in cartoon style. There is a definite sequence of events of the battle. On the right side of the painting there are scenes of the hereafter, which represent the fate of Husayn's supporters in the beautiful vista of paradise, while his opponents are tortured in hell. This oil painting is generally 3½ x 1½ metres, on canvas, and is easily rolled up for transportation. The *Pardih-dar* (singer) goes from one locality to another, hangs the painting and sings the story, using a pointer to elucidate the scenes... .

Mahmud Ayoub *

. . . The chanter begins the *majlis* with the following set formula:

> Peace be upon you, O master, O Apostle of God, the elect of God from among His creatures. Peace be upon you and upon the people of your household, the good and pure ones, the wronged and scattered ones. O Abu ^cAbdullah [Husayn] you who are in a strange land (*gharib*) would that I were with you that I may achieve great victory.

---

*Ed. Note: Mahmud Ayoub provides an example of the proceeding of a ta^cziyyah *ceremony in Lebanon. The passage is from* RSISD, *pages 252–53.*

The *majlis* begins with a moving call for weeping put in the mouth of the
martyred Imam himself, followed by a response of the community (*Shi^cah*)
of the imams affirming its continuous sorrow for the great calamities of *ahl
al-bayt*.

> O my *Shi^cah*, do not abandon the pilgrimage to my tomb, for frequent-
> ing it is the best means of achieving nearness [to God] and the *imams*].
> And, whenever you drink cool water remember me, thirsty at the banks
> of the Euphrates at my death. Pour out for me your tears wherever you
> may be, for I am the one killed for the shedding of tears and emitting
> sighs of grief.

The response follows in very colloquial language.

> Your followers [*Shi^cah*], O Husayn, offer their tears to you. They weep
> with hearts burning as if on coals. Your followers (*Shi^cah*) have aban-
> doned sleep, regarding it as a thing prohibited. How could they sleep on
> those nights which filled for you their cup of afflictions. Your *Shi^cah*, O
> Husayn, have donned for you their clothes of mourning. Instead of
> their garments they rent their hearts. For it was the wish of your *Shi^cfah*,
> O Husayn, to protect you with their hearts [*muhaj*, plural of *muhjah*]
> from the sharp lances.

The *majlis* goes on to relocate Husayn's departure from Mecca in the manner of a colorful traditional Arabian tale. The style is extremely simple and
repetitive in order for the participants to absorb fully the atmosphere. The
point is heavily stressed that Husayn had no choice but to leave Mecca, even
without completing his *hajj*.

> They asked him, saying 'O son of the Apostle of God, what has made
> you leave in such haste before completing your *hajj*?' He answered, 'I
> was afraid that the sanctity of this house [the *Ka^cbah*] may be violated
> through me. For the accused Yazid sent thirty men of satans of the sons
> of Umayyah and said to them "Kill Husayn even if you find him grasp-
> ing the veils (*astar*) of the Ka^cbah."'

The death of Muslim is then narrated by two men who heard it from an eyewitness who saw the corpses of Muslim, and Hani ibn ^cUrwah dragged in the
marketplace and saw a crier announcing, 'This is the punishment of anyone
opposing the Amir ibn Ziyad.' Husayn called Muslim's daughter, seated her
in his lap and began to pass his hand over her head as was the custom to do

with orphans. The narrator adds that the girl, when she heard the news of her father's death, wept not for him but rather for being orphaned yet a second time by the death of Husayn who was like a father to her. The narrator then imagines Sukaynah throwing herself over her father's dead corpse after the battle and crying out, 'O father, when night comes who shall shelter our orphans?' The *majlis* ends with another folk dirge for Husayn, who died thirsty and totally abandoned. The chanter concludes with a few petitions of prayer and salutations of peace to the Imam, and a recitation of the *Fatihah*, the opening *surah* of the Qur'an, on behalf of the departed souls of the faithful... .

Dwight Donaldson *

. . . The significance of the pilgrimage to the tomb of ᶜAli is based on traditions from the other Imams. Typical of these is the saying attributed to the

---

Ed. Note: Ziyarah, *the practice of visiting the tombs of Imams, their offsprings,* Imamzadihs, *and saints constitute a major aspect of Shiᶜi popular worship. The most important sites of the pilgrimage for Shiᶜis are the tombs of the eleven Shiᶜi Imams. The burial grounds of descendents of Imams, and the great men of religion also are objects of popular devotion and veneration. Of the major shrine-cities of Shiᶜism, only Mashhad (Iran), the burial site of the eighth Imam, ᶜAli al-Rida, is located outside of Iraq. The tomb of Imam ᶜAli in Najaf, Imam Husayn in Karbala', as well as the shrines of Kazimayn and Samirrah are all located in modernday Iraq.*

These sites are all the objects of pilgrimage and veneration for the Shiᶜis. The practice of visiting holy shrines in Shiᶜism has its roots in the traditions of Imam: For instance, the fourth Imam has said:

> God made the spot of Karabala' a sacred and safe haram . . . moreover God, exalted be He, shall cause the earth to quake and be melted, it (Karbala') shall be lifted up as it is, illuminous and pure, and place in the highest of the gardens of paradise

The prescriptions of the major Shiᶜi ᶜulama' have transformed the enjoined practice into religious rite however. The most authoritative guidebook for Shiᶜi pilgrims is the Tuhfat al-Za'irin, ("A Present for Pilgrims"), written by Muhammad Baqir Majlisi, in the sixteenth century. This book, or those similar to it, outline the religious significance of the pilgrimage to shrines, point out the miraculous qualities of the various shrines, or the religious merit the pilgrims will gain from their visit, and also provide guidelines that are tantamount to pilgrimage rites. In the passage, Dwight Donaldson provides a descriptive account of a Ziyarah. The excerpt is taken from SR, pages 64–65.

Imam Ja^cfar al-Sadiq "that whoever visits this tomb of his own free will and believing in the right of ^cAli—that he was the Imam to whom obedience was required and the true Caliph—for such a pilgrim the Most High will register merit *equal to one hundred thousand martyrdoms,* and *his sins of the past and the present will be forgiven.*" And when a visitor came in person to visit the Imam al-Sadiq, and remarked that he had neglected to go to the tomb of ^cAli, the Imam rebuked him: "You have done badly, surely, if it were not that you are one of our Shi^ci community, I would certainly not look towards you. Do you neglect to make the pilgrimage to the grave of one whom God and the angels visit, whom the prophets visit, and the believers visit?" The pilgrim replied, "I did not know this." The Imam answered, "Understand that the *Amir al-mu'minin* is in the sight of God better than all the Imams, in addition to which he has the merit of his own works."

Before making the visit to the Shrine, according to the Imam Ja^cfar al-Sadiq, the pilgrim should first bathe and put on clean clothing and afterwards annoint himself with perfume. The formal prayer of salutation that is given by al-Kulayni, and which is very similar to that given by Ibn Babuyah, begins as follows:

> Peace be unto thee, O Friend of God;
> Peace be unto thee, O Proof of God;
> Peace be unto thee, O Caliph of God;
> Peace be unto thee, O Support of Religion;Peace be unto thee, O Heir of the Prophets;
> Peace be unto thee, O Guardian of the Fire and of Paradise;
> Peace be unto thee, O Master of the Cudgel and the Brand-iron;
> Peace be unto thee, O Prince of the Believers.

I TESTIFY that thou art the Word of Piety, the Door of Guidance, the Firm Root, the Solid Mountain, and the Right Road.

I TESTIFY that thou art the Proof of God to His Creation, His Witness to His Servants, His Trustee for His Knowledge, a Repository of His Secrets, the Place of His Wisdom, and a Brother of His Apostle.

I TESTIFY that thou art the First Oppressed and the First whose right was seized by force, so I will be patient and expectant. May God curse whoever oppressed thee and supplanted thee and resisted thee, with a great curse, with which every honoured king, even commissioned prophet, and every true worshipper may curse them. May the favour of God be upon thee, O Prince of the Believers—upon thy Spirit, and upon thy Body... .

Mahmoud Ayoub *

. . . As will be seen, this *ziyarah* tells the whole story of the martyrdom of Imam Husayn, and alludes to most of the important hagiographical biographical interpretations that have grown around it. It seems to be of a late authorship (at least fourth century), as it is not included in the earliest standard collection of *ziyarah* texts by Ibn Qawlawayh (*Kamil al-Ziyarat*), or any other collection before *al-Mazar al-Kabir* of al-Murtada. Majlisi, moreover, hints at the possibility that al-Sayyid al-Murtada may have been responsible for at least some parts of this *ziyarah*. It is more probable that he was responsible for the entire text as we have it, relying on some older rescension or at least a tradition of such a *ziyarah*.

This *ziyarah* shows in a striking way the continuity of the imams with the ancient prophets. While most *ziyarah* texts asserting this continuity begin with the salutation of peace to the imams as heirs of the prophets, this text begins with the prophets, from Adam to Muhammad, and goes on to the *imams*, reciting an epithet for each prophet or imam after the salutation. Each sentence addressing a prophet or *imam* begins with *'al-salamu ᶜalayka ya . . .'*, then the name follows:

> Peace be upon you O Adam, the chosen one (*safwah*) of God from among His creatures . . . Peace be upon Seth the friend (*wali*) of God and his elect one (*khirah*) . . . Peace be upon Idris [Enoch] who rose up to uphold the *hujjah* of God. . . . Peace be upon Hud, who was aided by God with His own power . . . Peace be upon Salih whom God crowned with His favor . . . Peace be upon Abraham who was favored by God with His friendship (*khillah*) . . . Peace be upon Ishmael, whom God ransomed with a great sacrificial victim from His paradise . . . Peace be upon Isaac in whose progeny God continued the prophethood . . . Peace be upon Jacob to whom God returned his sight by His mercy. . . . Peace be upon Joseph whom God saved from the well by His great power . . . Peace be upon Moses for whom God split the sea by His might . . . Peace be upon Aaron whom God favored with the gift of prophethood . . . Peace be upon Jethro (*Shuᶜayb*) whom God rendered victorious over his community . . . Peace be upon David whom God had forgiven his sin . . . Peace be upon Solomon to whose greatness the *jinn* were subjected . . . Peace be upon Job whom God

---

*Ed. Note: Ziyarah, *attributed to the twelfth Imam is an important and elucidating example of* Shiᶜi *devotional worship in general and the practice of* Ziyarah *in particular. It is supposed to be performed at the tomb of Imam Husayn on the day of* ᶜAshura'. *This* Ziyarah *is attributed to the twelfth Imam during his occultation. The excerpt is taken from* RSISD, *pages 254–58.*

healed from his disease . . . Peace be upon Jonah (Yunus), for whome
God fulfilled His promise . . . Peace be upon Ezra (cUzayr) whom God
resuscitated after his long death . . . Peace be upon Zechariah who was
patient with his trials (*mihnah*) . . . Peace be upon John the Baptist
whom God favored with his martyrdom . . . Peace be upon Jesus the
spirit of God and His word . . . Peace be upon Muhammad, the beloved of God and His chosen one (*safwah*).

Then the *ziyarah* addresses the five people of the Holy Family (*ahl al-bayt*):
cAli as the brother of the Prophet, Fatimah, his daughter, Hasan as the
viceregent (*wasi*) of God and His representative (*khalifah*). That at great
length the virtues and sufferings of Husayn are recounted, as well as those
of his family.

Peace be upon Husayn, who willingly sacrificed his life. He obeyed God
in his innermost secret and openly in his actions. Thus God made healing to be in his earth, and the answering of prayers beneath his dome.
Peace be upon him in whose progeny God has deposited the imamate.

The spiritual lineage of the Imam is here presented as coeval with his
physical descent. He is '. . . the son of Fatimah al-Zahra', Khadijah al-
Kubra [the venerable one], the heavenly lote tree (*sidrat fal-muntaha*), the
garden of refuge'. The Imam is then declared to be the son of the holy objects of the *hajj* pilgrimage: the well of Zamzam, Safa and Mina... .

Chapter Twenty

Jihad

Perhaps today no issue concerning Islam in general and Shiᶜism in particular is as sensitive or as widely debated as that of jihad. Although the attention focused on jihad and the understanding of the concept in the West is often a consequence of Shiᶜi political revivalism, jihad is not solely a Shiᶜi doctrine but an article of Islamic faith, accepted by all Muslims. It is even often mentioned as the sixth pillar of the religion.

In the West jihad is often understood as a juridical doctrine with political ramifications. Traditional Islam, however, distinguished between the juridical and the spiritual dimensions of jihad, placing greater importance upon the latter. In the following passages, Seyyed Hossein Nasr's examination of jihad elucidates the doctrine in its general Islamic context. Excerpt is from SSJ, 14–19.

Seyyed Hossein Nasr

. . . To understand the spiritual significance of *jihad* and its wide application to nearly every aspect of human life as understood by Islam, it is
necessary to remember that Islam bases itself upon the idea of establishing
equilibrium within the being of man as well as in the human society where
he functions and fulfills the goals of his earthly life. This equilibrium, which
is the terrestrial reflection of Divine Justice and the necessary condition for
peace in the human domain, is the basis upon which the soul takes its flight
towards that peace which, to use Christian terms, "passeth understanding".
If Christianity sees the aim of the spiritual life and its own morality as being
based up on the vertical flight towards that perfection and ideal which is
embodied in Christ, Islam sees it in the establishment of an equilibrium
both outward and inward as the necessary basis for this vertical ascent. The
very stability of Islamic society over the centuries, the immutability of
Islamic norms embodied in the *Shariᶜah*, and the timeless character of traditional Islamic civilization, which is the consequence of its permanent and
immutable prototype, are all reflections of both the ideal of equilibrium and
its realization as is so evident in the teachings of the *Shariᶜah* (or Divine
Law) as well as works of Islamic art, that equilibrium which is inseparable
from the very nature of *islam* as being realted to *salam* or peace.

The preservation of equilibrium in this world, however, does not mean
simply a static or inactive passivity since life by nature implies movement.
In the face of the contingencies of the world of change, of the withering effects of time, of the vicissitudes of terrestrial existence, to remain in
equilibrium requires continuous exertion. It means carring out *jihad* at
every stage of life. Human nature being what it is, given to forgetfulness
and suffering from the conquest of our immortal soul or passions, the very
process of life on both the individual and the human collectivity implies the
ever-present danger of the loss of equilibrium and in fact of falling into the
state of disequilibrium which if allowed to continue can but lead to
disintegration on the individual level and chaos on the scale of community
life. To avoid this tragic end and to fulfill the entelechy of the human state
which is the realization of unity (*al-tawhid*) or total integration, Muslims as
both individuals and members of Islamic society must carry out *jihad*, that
is, they must exert themselves at all momemts of life to fight a battle both
inward and outward against those forces that if not combatted will destroy
the equilibrium which is the necessary condition for the spiritual life of the

person and the functioning of human society. This fact is especially true if society is seen as a community that bears the imprint of the Divine Norm rather than an antheap of contending and opposing units and forces.

Man is at once a spiritual and a corporeal being, a microcosm complete unto himself; yet he is the member of a society within which alone are certain aspects of his being developed and certain of his needs fulfilled. He possesses at once an intelligence whose substance is ultimately of a divine character and sentiments that can either veil his intelligence of abet his quest for his own origin. In him are found both love and hatred, generosity and covetousness, compassion and aggression. Moreover, there have existed until now not just one but several "humanities" with their own religious and moral norms and national, ethnic and racial groups with their own bonds of affiliation. As a result, the practice of *jihad* as applied to the world of multiplicity and the vicissitudes of human existence in the external world has come to develop numerous ramifications in the fields of political and economic activity and in social life and come to partake on the external level of the complexity which characterizes the human world.

In its most outward sense *jihad* came to mean the defense of *dar al-islam*, that is, the Islamic world, from invasion and intrusion by non-Islamic forces. The earliest wars of Islamic history which threatened the very existence of the young community came to be known as *jihad* par excellence in this outward sense of "holy war". But it was upon returning from one of these early wars, which was of paramount importance in the survival of the newly established religious community and therefore of cosmic significance, that the Blessed Prophet nevertheless said to his companions that they had returned from the lesser holy war to the greater holy war, the greater *jihad* being the inner battle against all the forces that would prevent man from living according to the theomorphic norma that is his primordial and God given nature... .

On the more external level, the lesser *jihad* also includes the socioeconomic domain. It means the reassertion of justice in the external environment of human existence starting with man himself. To defend one's rights and reputation, to defend the honor of oneself and one's family is itself a *jihad* and a religious duty. So is the strengthening of all those social bonds from the family to the whole of the Muslim people (*al-ummah*), which the *Shariᶜah* emphasizes. To see social justice in accordance with the tenets of the Qur'an and of course not in the modern secularist sense is a way of reestablishing equilibrium in human society, that is, of performing *jihad*, as are constructive economic enterprises, provided the well-being of the whole person is kept in mind and material welfare does not become an end in itself; provided one does not lose sight of the Qur'anic verse, "The other world is better for you than this one." To forget the proper relation between the two worlds would itself be instrumental in bringing about disequilibrium and would be a kind of *jihad* in reverse.

All of those external forms of *jihad* would remain incomplete and in fact contribute to an excessive externalization of human beings, if they were not complemented by the greater or inner *jihad* which man must carry out continuously within himself for the nobility of the human state resides in the constant tension between what we appear to be and what we really are and the need to transcend ourselves throughout this journey of earthly life in order to become what we "are". From the spiritual point of view all the "pillars" of Islam can be seen as being related to *jihad*. The fundamental witnesses (*shahadah*), "There is no divinity but Allah" and "Muhammad is the Messenger of Allah", through the utterance of which a person becomes a Muslim are not only statements about the Truth as seen in the Islamic perspective but also weapons for the practice of inner *jihad*. The very form of the first letter of the first witness (*La ilaha illa'llah* in Arabic) when written in Arabic calligraphy is like a bent sword with which all otherness is removed from the Supreme Reality while all that is positive in manifestation is returned to that Reality. The second witness is the blinding assertion of the powerful and majestic descent of all that constitutes in a positive manner the cosmos, man and revelation from that Supreme Reality. To invoke the two witnesses in the form of the sacred language in which they were revealed is to practice the inner *jihad* and to bring about awareness of who we are, from whence we come and where is our ultimate abode... .

The great stations of perfection in the spiritual life can also be seen in the light of the inner *jihad*. To become detached from the impurities of the world in order to repose in the purity of the Divine Presence requires an intense *jihad* for our soul has its roots sunk deeply into the transient world which the soul of fallen man mistakes for reality. To overcome the lethargy, passivity and indifference of the soul, qualities which have become second nature to man as a result of his forgetting who he is constitutes likewise a constant *jihad*. To pull the reigns of the soul from dissipating itself outwardly as a result of its centrifugal tendencies and to bring it back to the center wherein resides Divine Peace and all the beauty which the soul seeks in vain in the domain of multiplicity is again an inner *jihad*. To melt the hardened heart into a flowing stream of love which would embrace the whole of creation in virtue of the love for God is to perform the alchemical process of *solve et coagula* inwardly through a "work" which is none other than an inner struggle and battle against what the soul has become in order to transform it into that which it "is" and has never ceased to be if only it were to become aware of its own nature. Finally, to realize that only the Absolute is absolute and that only the Self can ultimately utter "I" is to perform the supreme *jihad* of awakening the soul from the dream of forgetfulness and enabling it to gain the supreme principal knowledge for the sake of which it was created. The inner *jihad* or warfare seen spiritually and esoterically can be considered therefore as the key for the understanding of the whole spiritual process, and the path for the realization of the One which lies at the heart of the Islamic message seen in its totality. The Islamic path towards perfection can be conceived in the light of the symbolism of the greater *jihad* to which the Prophet of Islam, who founded this path on earth, himself referred.

In the same way that with every breath the principle of life, which functions in us is irrespective of our will and as long as it is willed by Him who created us, exerts itself through *jihad* to instill life within our whole body, at every moment in our conscious life we should seek to perform *jihad* in not only establishing equilibrium in the world about us but also in awakening to that Divine Reality which is the very source of our consciousness. From the spiritual man, every breath is a reminder that he should continue the inner *jihad* until he awakens from all dreaming and until the very rhythm of his heart echoes that primordial sacred Name by which all things were made and through which all things return to their Origin. The Prophet said, "Man is asleep and when he dies he awakens." Through inner *jihad* the spiritual man dies in this life in order to cease all dreaming, in order to awaken to that Reality which is the origin of all realities, in order to behold that Beauty of which all earthly beauty of but a pale reflection, in order to attain that Peace which all men seek but which can in fact be found only through the inner *jihad*.

Part V

The Intellectual and Artistic Life

Chapter Twenty-One

Shi^ci Education

The education of the learned men of religion is of great importance to Shi^cism. Shi^ci jurisconsults, mujtahids, also known as maraji^c-i taqlid *(sources of emulation), are charged with supervising the affairs of the community of the faithful and safe-guarding the Shi^ci faith itself. These* mujtahids, *the highest ranking of which are known as* ayatullahs, *are educated in the traditional institutions of Islamic education known as the* madrasah. *The* madrasahs *are often located in the Shi^ci centers of learning,* Hawzih-yi ^cilmiyyah, *such as Qum or Najaf. However, they may be found in all Shi^ci communities.*

The origin of the Shi^ci madrasahs *can be traced to the educational system established by the Persian vizier of the Seljuqs,* Nizam al-mulk, *in 1066 A.D. These early* madrasahs, *known as Nizamiyyah, spread throughout the Muslim world in the Medieval period and eventually became a part of the state bureaucracy of the Ottoman Empire and the lesser sultanates.*

In the Shi^ci world, madrasahs, *developed independent of the state, under the supervision of* mujtahids, *and with the support of the community. The funding of the* madrasahs *came from the religious taxes,* Sahm-i Imam *and* Khums, *or from voluntary contributions.*

*The curriculum often begins with primary education and the Qur'an. More often, however, it is concerned with advanced studies in theology (*Kalam*), jurisprudence (*fiqh*), and even philosophy (*falsafah*). Over the centuries,* madrasahs *became established as the primary centers of Shi^ci learning, a form of university, where a prominent* mujtahid *would supervise the religious and intellectual activities of an array of scholars, students (*tullab*), and novices. The* madrasah, *in addition to training religious scholars, also created bonds that constitute the foundations of Shi^ci religious institutions. The organizational network created between the* mujtahids-*to-be, blessed with the spiritual authority of the supervising* mujtahid, *makes the* madrasah *a crucial link in the working of Shi^ci clerical hierarchy.*

An important point about the Shi^ci education, on which nearly every student of the subject has remarked, is its all-encompassing nature. The Shi^ci education of the madrasahs *is not merely an inculcation of institutional discipline or the filling of a void with knowledge, rather it is an active engagement. The educational process of the* madrasahs *is above and beyond mere learning and involves the initiation of the* talabah *(religious student) into a way of life, a mode of thought, and an outlook onto the world. This institution not only forms the* ^culama', *but also sets them apart from their intellectual cohorts and molds them into a unique spiritual force. In the following passage, Roy Mottahedeh gives a descriptive account of the origins and operations of* madrasahs. *The excerpt is from* MP, *pages 89–94 and 236–37.*

Roy Mottahedeh

. . . The *madrasahs* made their definitive appearance (after a century of uncertain and largely unsuccessful attempts to appear) in the late eleventh century, at least a hundred years before their western counterparts, the European universities. For the Islamic world *madrasahs* really were something new: schools founded on substantial charitable trusts that had been given in perpetuity for the teaching of a specific kind of curriculum. The founders of these *madrasahs*, often viziers and sultans, by the size of their endowments and the stipulations in their deeds of gift, guaranteed that these new schools would last long and take in a large number of students (often as boarders), whom they would attempt to teach a fairly uniform curriculum under the supervision of paid teachers.

The curricula varied, of course, not only according to the stipulations of the founders but also according to the wishes of the teachers and directors of the *madrasahs*. The *madrasah* was not expected to give its students basic literacy or an elementary knowledge of arithmetic. Either private tutors, such as Avicenna's teachers of Qur'an and literature and the vegetable seller who taught him "Indian calculation," or small, unendowed neighborhood Qur'an schools, which lived on the fees they collected, still provided the very beginnings of education. What the *madrasah* was expected to give was a basic education is Islamic religious law. At the same time, from the very beginning it was intended that the *madrasah* should teach the student the relation of law to its sources, especially to the Qur'an and the accounts of what Muhammad said and did.

Very soon the sciences of language — in particular, grammar and rhetoric — became firmly established in the *madrasah* curriculum. How could one analyze the raw material of the law unless one accurately understood the Qur'an and the accounts of what the perfect Muslim, the Prophet Muhammad, did and said, and knew how to analyze the similes and other figures of speech used in this raw material? But, then, a set of systematic principles for deriving the law from its sources was also needed, a science that would sharpen the ability to make strict and consistent use of such instruments of reasoning as the syllogism and the argument *a fortiori*.

This science was jurisprudence, and its presence in the higher stages of *madrasah* learning encouraged the introduction of treatises on logic at earlier stages in the curriculum. Logic could then be used at the higher level of study, which showed the consistency of the law (at least in its relation to its sources and in the relation of its different parts). And, of course, the full meaning of law could be fully understood only through a systematic study of the Creator's intentions for his creation; so scholastic theology in turn moved into what became its firmly held position in these new fortresses of learning.

The new *madrasahs* in fact were not unlike fortresses. They were great enclosed spaces and became almost as predictable a part of an Islamic town of consequence as were the mosque and bazaar. Like fortresses, they were seen and saw themselves as the primary focus of attempts to preserve learning and defend orthodoxy. In many cases they also became a part of the armamentarium of the government, in that they produced highly literate graduates in numbers large enough to supply the bureaucracies of governments as well as the positions more or less reserved for the religiously learned, the Ꜥulama' or *mullahs*, as the Iranians called them. The patronage of *madrasahs* even provided the government with a vital piece of ideological armor. Although the *mullahs* avoided saying that any specific regime was sanctioned by God, they did say that the populace was well advised to obey any regime that protected true religion, and there was no more eloquent way to protect true religion than to found *madrasahs* and foster their graduates.

For these very reasons, in the first thousand years of Islamic Near Eastern history ShiꜤi learning had a very hard time of it. Most of the regimes in this first thousand years were Sunni, and in the view of Sunni regimes ShiꜤi learning was not "true religion"; only Sunni Islam qualified as "true." There had, in fact, been a few ShiꜤi dynasties a generation before the spread of the *madrasah*, in the time of Avicenna, who had preferred the patronage of ShiꜤi kings (even ones who thought they were cows) to that of the Sunnis. About twenty years after Avicenna's death, when a Sunni dynasty had taken over Baghdad and established a large Sunni *madrasah* there, Tusi, a great ShiꜤi scholar, left Baghdad and moved south to the solidly ShiꜤi town of Najaf. Here he established his own school, which may have been a proper ShiꜤi *madrasah*, on the model of the new Sunni *madrasah* in Baghdad, although we have only a hazy idea of the early history of the Najaf school. It does seem certain, however, that he established a curriculum, in part based on his own texts, and the scholars of the ShiꜤi *madrasahs* of Najaf in our time believe themselves to be descended from Tusi through a continuous line of teachers which stretches from the eleventh century to the twentieth.

Tusi's establishment of a school of ShiꜤi learning in Najaf marks the maturity of ShiꜤism as a developed system of Islamic thought.... .

* * *

In the absence of ShiꜤi dynasties the survival of ShiꜤi learning remained precarious and dependent on the scattered ShiꜤi communities in places such as Najaf, in southern Iraq, until the great religious revolution brought to

Iran by the Safavid dynasty in the early 1500s. Until then Shiᶜism had been a minority belief in Iran, a distinguishing characteristic of a few provincial areas and towns such as Qum. Then, at the beginning of the sixteenth century, the Safavids, drawing their support from the Shiᶜi Turkoman tribes of Azarbaijan, the northwest province of Iran, imposed Shiᶜism on almost all parts of the Iranian nation. Not all Iranians accepted Shiᶜism easily. But the nearly simultaneous rise of two mighty Sunni empires, The Ottomans of Turkey on the West and the Mughals of India on East, along with the continuing threat from Sunnis in Central Asia, seems to have made the imposition of a distinctive official religion somewhat more palatable to Iranians; it gave a religious basis to the desire of Iranians to withstand the rule of these powerful neighbors. Iranians were particularly determined to resist conquest by the Ottoman Turks, even if this meant that the Safavid king, or "Sophi," as Milton called him, could at times carry on such resistance only by scorching the earth of Iran to discourage the Ottomans' advance. In the seventeenth century Milton (who was a contemporary of both the Safavids and the Ottomans) described in *Paradise Lost* how:

> . . . *Bactrian Sophi, from the horns,*
> *Of Turkish crescent, leaves all waste beyond*
> *The realm of Aladuk, in his retreat*
> *To Tauris and Cashbeen.*

* * *

If, to protect the Iranian homeland the Safavid or "Sophi," had to leave the very lands he saved scorched and wasted, he was a nurturing rain for the Shiᶜi learned men, the mullahs. Before the Safavids, the Iranian Shiᶜi had not had a strong tradition of learning, and therefore at the beginning of the sixteenth century there were more Shiᶜi learned men in Iraq and in Lebanon than in Iran. The Safavids founded Shiᶜi *madrasahs* in numbers in which they had never existed before. And the attraction of these *madrasahs* and of royal patronage in general drew a stream of Shiᶜi learned men from other parts of the Islamic world to Iran. Shiᶜism was by no means an "Iranian religion," but Iran was emphatically a Shiᶜi kindgom. And from the sixteenth century to the present the weight of Iran among the Shiᶜi, whether in India, the Arabian Peninsula, Syria, eastern Turkey, or Iraq, has continued to be enormous... .

---

*Ed. Note: Mottahedeh writes further on the contribution of religious taxes and endowments to the madrasah *system.*

These endowments continued to support *madrasahs* such as the Fayziyyah, but the discretionary monies at the disposal of the great jurisconsults came from self-tithing by the ordinary Shiʿi. Through secularism, wars, and disputes over religious leadership, money from self-tithing continued to flow in. Thanks to this money, the important jurisconsults could pay the basic student stipend to the *talabihs* at Qum and other centers and could thereby maintain both the tradition of learning and the network of loyalties that they thought indispensable to their own well-being and the well-being of Islam.

Traditional Sunni higher learning enetered the second half of the twentieth century dramatically changed by its environment and, above all, by the Sunni governments in the Arab world and elsewhere which controlled its institutions. For example, the curriculum of the greatest traditional Sunni university, the al-Azhar, has been revised repeatedly during the last century and a half by the Egyptian government. In contrast, the Shiʿi curriculum of Qum and Najaf has been and is dictated solely by the wishes of the mullahs themselves. *Madrasahs* such as the one in Tehran, for example, where the government has dictated some revisions in the curriculum, have lost their prestige among the mullahs. In their own view the mullahs of Iran have kept a great tradition of learning alive in its pure form; in the view of their Iranian critics they have kept their curriculum hermetically sealed against the modern world.

The transformation of the mullahs into something like a clergy reached its height under the leadership of Burujirdi partly because in his time the accommodation of the government and the mullahs to each other was at its most stable. Under the new shah, mullahs were once again exempted from military service. The number of *talabihs* in Qum, perhaps a thousand toward the end of Ha'iri's life, rose to over five thousand. Also, in the time of Burujirdi there was a forcible accommodation of *madrasah* education to the success of secular education that emphasized how much more the *madrasah* had become like a "professional" school. the Qur'an school had died by the end of the Second World War; all *talabihs* came to Qum with an elementary education from a state school. In the state school even on the elementary level subjects such as mathematics and bits of general science were taught by teachers supposedly expert in these fields (while Islamic law and the Qur'an in the Arabic original were taught by mullahs paid to do so by the Ministry of Education). *Madrasah* learning had formerly been a conspectus of higher learning, with its optional courses in Ptolemaic astronomy, Avicennian medicine, and the algebra of ʿUmar Khayyam. But now that the marvel of Halley's Comet had finally been sighted in the heaven of mullah learning, even the mullahs recognized that their learning really was "religious" learning, and only a few enthusiastis studied the traditiona nonreligious sciences such as the old astronomy in private. Increasingly the mullahs called themselves by the neologism used by government and in tellectuals (in their politer moods): they were *rawhaniyyun* — "specialists in spiritual matters."

Chapter Twenty-Two

Shi^ci Theology

Shi^ci theology was formed over the centuries on the basis of the teachings of the Qur'an, the Prophet, and the Imams and in response to the intellectual movements with which Shi^cism came into contact, such as the Mu^ctazilism, as well as the main events of Shi^ci history, such as the Battle of Karbala' and the occultation of the twelfth Imam. The teachings of the Shi^ci Imams, especilaly Ja^cfar al-Sadiq, and the works of certain scholars such as al-Hilli or al-Kulayni, are particularly significant in the formation of Shi^ci theology.

Early Shi^ci theology was formed during the classical period of Islamic history, from the martyrdom of Imam ^cAli in 661 A.D. W. Montgomery Watt elaborates on the evolution of Shi^ci theology after the death of ^cAli. The excerpt is from IPT, *pages 24–25.*

W. Montgomery Watt

. . . The Shi^cism of the Umayyad period was . . . vaguer and more indefinite than later Shi^cism, and lacked any semblance of a coherent theory. It was the manifestation of a deep unconscious need — a feeling in men's hearts that they would be happier and more satisfied spiritually if they had a charismatic leader to follow. The Imam of whom the Shi^cis dreamed is precisely what is meant by a charismatic leader. The history of early Shi^cism, and indeed of much later Shi^cism also, is that of a pathetic quest for individuals to whom the dignity of imam may be attached. Most of those accepted as Imam belied the hopes set upon them; and yet the quest went on. The persistence of the quest shows the depth of the feeling involved. Men with political ambitions and qualities of leadership, but no shadow of a claim to the charismata of the Hashimites, found a way of using this widespread desire for an imam. Al-Mukhtar, for example, asserted that he was acting as the emissary of a genuine imam, Muhammad ibn al-Hanafiyyah; he may have had the consent of the latter in making this assertion, but it is certain that he received no active help from him. There are several later instances of a similar proceeding, and in some of them the Imam invoked repudiated the self-styled emissary. Others seem to have resigned themselves to political inactivity in the foreseeable future; and they found a theological justification for this attitude in the theory that the Imam was not dead but in concealment and that at an appropriate time he would return as the Mahdi or Guided One (a kind of Messiah) to right all wrongs and establish justice on earth.*

. . . The impression given by Shi^ci writers, and even by Sunnite heresiographers, is that during their lives [the Imams], were recognized by a wide circle of followers, indeed by most of the Shi^ci movement. Scrutiny of the Shi^ci accounts of the Imams, however, makes it clear that most of them were politically insignificant, and were not really recognized by anyone at all. Ja^cfar al-Sadiq (d. 765) may have been dabbling in politics before the fall of the Umayyads, and hoping to gain a position of rule; he doubtless realized that political capital was to be made out of the charisma of being a member of the "family" (*ahl al-bayt*). After the ^cAbbasids had established

---

Ed. Note: After the schism that led to the separation of Zaydi Shi^cis from the main body of Shi^cism during the Umayyad era, the Shi^ci theology gradually consolidated around the person of the twelfth Imam. Watt elaborates on this trend as well as other changes in the Shi^ci theory of the ^cAbbasid era: The excerpt is from IPT, *pages 51–54.*

themselves, however, he saw the obvious dangers for himself of political activity, and refrained. His son Musa took the same line. Another son Ismaʿil, however, went ahead and began the process of fusing together several underground revolutionary movements, with results that will be seen presently.

Musa (d. 799) and his branch of the "family" remained politically quiescent until in 817 the caliph al-Ma'mun married his daughter to Musa's son ʿAli al-Rida and declared him heir to the caliphate. This was part of a policy designed to gain further support for the government from persons of Shiʿi sympathies. Unfortunately ʿAli died in 818. His young son Muhammad continued in favour at the court of al-Ma'mun, but died in 835 soon after the latter's death. his son ʿAli al-Naqi was imprisoned as a consequence of the great change of policy about 849, and remained in prison until his death in 868. In turn his son al-Hasan al-ʿAskari was imprisoned for a time after his father's death, but then set free. Soon after his death in 874 the twelfth Imam, his son Muhammad, either died or disappeared, but the majority of the Shiʿis came to believe that he would one day return as al-Mahdi, the Guided One, a figure roughly corresponding to the Jewish Messiah.

From this brief recital, based on Imamite sources, it is seen that during the lifetime of these men there was no organized movement accepting a member of the "family" as Imam. An otherwise suspicious government was not unduly worried, and may have used the imprisonment, which was far from harsh, as a method of exercising surveillance. It follows from this that during the ninth century up to 874 the main body of Shiʿism—assuming there was such a main body—was not a body of people recognizing the Imams who have been named. The little groups of people professing to follow these Imams, living or dead, or other members of the "family", may be neglected. Apart from these there was a number of respectable theologians, calling themselves Shiʿis (but usually called Rafidites or "deserters" by their opponents), who shared fully in the intellectual life of Baghdad and do not seem to have been politically suspect. The best known was Hisham ibn al-Hakam, who was active from the end of the eighth century until 825 or later. What can the Shiʿism of such a person have amounted to?

The chief doctrine held by these Rafidites, and their successors the Imamites (or Ithnaʿasharites or "Twelvers"), was that ʿAli had been clearly designated Imam or leader of the community by Muhammad in succession to himself. This implied that such designation by the preceding Imam was the proper title to succession. Since the Imam was further held to be divinely preserved from error, Shiʿi doctrine was encouraging a very autocratic form of government. (The word "imam" thus in effect means "caliph" or "rightful caliph", but with the Shiʿis, who favoured it, it had the further connotation of divinely given charismata.) A corollary of the main doctrine was the most of Muhammad's Companions (who have a special place of honor in Islam) had disobeyed his order is not recognizing ^cAli as caliph on his death; and a consequence of this was that they were not fit persons to transmit Traditions about him. In this way the Rafidites were undermining the elaborate structure of Tradition, the basis of the *Shari^cah* or Islamic law, and thereby the power and influence of the growing class of *^culama'* — Traditionists and jurists.

Thus this moderate Shi^cism of the early ninth century can be regarded as the intellectual expression of a widespread mentality or outlook, not sufficiently organized to be called a party. One might perhaps speak of the "autocratic bloc", provided it is understood that the persons included in this are not exactly known. On the religious side it would include those who looked to a charismatic leader for salvation and security, and whose politics were affected by this desire. It would also include groups moved by more strictly political interests, the class of secretaries and all the old Persian nobility now involved in the work of administration, and possibly others also. Opposed to this bloc one will postulate a "constitutional bloc", which will include the *^culama'* and all those whose share in power and influence is linked with the development of the Islamic sciences; they are "constitutionalists" in so far as the autocratic power of the caliph and those who are able to act in his name is diminished by the existence of the *Shari^cah*. On the religious side the need felt is for a charismatic community rather than for a charismatic leader.

At numerous points in the earlier history of Shi^cism the messianic ideas endemic in the Middle East had attached themselves to one or other of the many persons recognized as Imam by some small group. After 874 it occurred to certain political leaders of the autocratic bloc that it would be advantageous to have, instead of a living Imam, one whose whereabouts were unknown and whose reutn, though it would happen eventually, was not expected in the visible future. This satisfied men's religious aspirations and also gave the politicians a free hand. On the basis of the recognition of the Twelve Imams many of the distinct groups with Rafidite sympathies were fused into something like a party; and from this time the party or sect is usually called the Imamites. In this work of organization a prominent part was played by Abu Sahl Isma^cil al-Nawbakhti (d. 923). We also hear of the specifically Imamite form of Islamic law being found about this time. The end of the ninth century is thus the period in which Imamite Shi^cism took definite shape.

In the immediately following period it had some successes. Al-Ash^cari, probably writing about 920, says that it is dominant in the Idrisid state of Morocco and in the towns of Qum and Kufah. Soon afterwards it became dominant in the Hamdanid state in Syria, while in 945 the Shi^ci Buyid warlords became virtual rulers in Baghdad. What exactly lies behind these events is difficult to say, but it would perhaps not be far wrong to say that Shiʿism was closely linked with the desire for a more autocratic form of government. Some insight into the intellectual outlook that went with Shiʿism is provided by the thought of one of the great Arabic-writing philosophers, who spent the last few years of his life under the protection of Sayf al-Dawlah of Aleppo.

ʿAllamah al-Hilli*

. . . And there is no doubt that here (in the universe) there is that which exists of necessity. If this be the necessary in itself, then that was what we were seeking. And if it be the possible, then it would need a bringer-into-existence (*mujid*) which would bring it into existence of necessity. Now if the bringer-into existence be the necessary in itself, then that was what we were seeking. And if it be the possible, then it would need another bringer-into-existence. If it be the first, then it is a circle, and that is a fallacy of necessity. And if it be another possible, then it is an endless chain, and that also is a fallacy. For all the links in this chain which includes all possible existences (*al-mumkinat*) are possible of necessity. Hence they share in the impossibility of existence in themselves. Hence they need some bringer-into-existence necessarily outside of themselves. Then that is the necessary (*al-wajib*) of necessity—which was what we were seeking.

. . . And the meaning of Justice is that the Most High is far removed from every evil act and from being remiss in what is incumbent. And since Justice depends on the knowledge of good and evil as determined by reason, he in-

---

*Ed. Note: The intellectual movements prevalent among the Shiʿis in the ʿAbbasid era combined with important historical events that took place during that period to produce the corpus of Shiʿi theology. In this early form of Shiʿi theology, the fundamental beliefs of the faith were put to the test of reason and then canonized as the foundations of Shiʿism, its theology, and its spirituality. Selections from the works of Nasir al-Din al-Tusi and ʿAllamah al-Hilli on theology provide a cursory review of the basic principles of Shiʿi theology.

ʿAllamah al-Hilli's Al-Babu al-Hadi ʿAshar outlines the basic principles of the Shiʿi theology. The book begins with a chapter concerned with proving the existence of God. "The Proof of Self-Existent." Here al-Hilli argues that "every object of thought is either necessarily existent objectively in itself, or is possible of existence in itself, or else is impossible of existence in itself." The passage is from BHA, pages 11-12.

troduced the discussion of that first. And know that an act the conception of which is necessary (*daruri*) either has a quality in addition to its origination (*huduth*), or it has not. An example of the latter is the movement of one who acts thoughtlessly (*al-sahi*) and of a sleeper. And as for the former, either reason hates that addition or it does not—if it does, than is evil (*al-qabih*), and if reason does not hate it, it is good (*al-hasan*). (That is, an act which one can know of necessity, such as the things we see and hear, either has a moral quality in addition to its occurrence, or it has not. If it has, and reason does not hate it, it is good—otherwise it is evil.)

Either (1) the doing and not doing of an act is equal, and this is *mubah* (indifferent); or (2) it is not equal. And (in this latter case) if the not doing of it is preferable, then if the opposite (namely, the doing of it) is forbidden it is *haram*, otherwise it is *makruh*. And if the doing of it is preferable, then if the leaving it undone is forbidden, it is *wajib*; or if the leaving it undone is permissible it is *mandub* (or *mustahabb*).

(1) Doing and not doing *equal*:   *mubah.*

(2) Doing and not doing *not equal*:

    (a) Not doing preferable:

        (α) Doing it forbidden: *haram.*

        (β) Doing it not forbidden: *makruh.*

    (b) Doing of it preferable:

        (α) Leaving it undone forbidden: *wajib.*

        (β) Leaving it undone permissible: *mandub.*

                                        (*mustahabb*).

Since this is explained, know that *good* and *evil* are used in three senses: (1) First, a thing's being a quality of perfection, such as our saying that knowledge is good; or a quality of imperfection, such as our saying that ignorance is evil. (2) Second, a thing's being agreeable to nature, as pleasures; or disagreeable to is, as pains. (3) Third, good is that the doing of which deserves praise in this world and reward in the world to come; and

---

Ed. Note: Having proven the creator, al-Hilli then examines Allah's positive qualities, that He is powerful and Free, is Knowing, Living, is a Willer and a Disliker, is a Perceiver, is Eternal, is a Speaker, and is Veracious. These positive qualities are complimented with His private qualites. He is not compounded, is not a body, is not a locus for originated things, is not visible, has no partner, ideas, states, or needs.

The qualities of God then lead al-Hilli to the argument concerning Allah's justice. This justice emanates from the aforementioned qualities of God, and in turn necessitate the existence of the Prophecy and the Imamate. Al-Hilli, argues further, that the prophet and the Imams have to possess certain qualities such as immunity to sin or infallibility.

The book ends with a chapter on the doctrine of return, macad. Here, al-Hilli discusses resurrection, reward, punishment, and repentance in the context of Shicism. In order to elucidate al-Hilli's style of argument sections from his chapters on Allah's justice and the Prophecy are included here. The passage is taken from BHA, pages 40–45 and 58–61.

evil is that the doing of which deserves blame in this world and punishment in the world to come.

And there is no difference of opinion as to the first two senses being determined by reason. But the scholastic theologians have differed regarding the third sense. The Ashʿarites say that there is nothing in reason which can guide to (a knowledge of) good and evil in this third sense, but law (must be the guide), and whatever it calls good is good, and whatever it calls evil is evil. and Muʿtazilites and Imamites say that there *is* that in reason which can guide to it, and that good is good in itself, and evil is evil in itself, whether the lawgiver pronounces it so or not. And they reply to them (the Ashʿarites) as follows: (1) First, we know of necessity that some actions are good, such as veracity which is profitable and fairness and doing good and returning a trust and rescuing one who is perishing and other such things, without needing law (to tell us so); and that others are evil, such as an injurious lie and injustice and doing harm to one who does not deserve it and other such things, without having any doubt at all about it. For this judgment is inherent (*markuz*) in human nature. For when we say to a person, "If you speak the truth you will get a dinar," and he be unprejudiced, by reason alone he will recognize the truth and desire to speak it.

(2) Second, if that which recognizes (*mudrik*) good and evil were law and nothing else, it would follow that they could not be known apart from it. But this necessity is false, hence that which necessitates it is false also. And the explanation of the fallacy of the necessity is that those who do not believe in a law, like the *Malahida* and the philosophers of India, do affirm that some actions are good and others evil without hesitating in the matter. For if this (knowledge) consisted in what is learned from law then they would not have pronounced an opinion.

(3) Third, if rational good and evil be denied, then it becomes necessary that legal good and evil be denied also. But all agree that this necessity is false. Hence that which necessitates it is false also. And the reason for this necessity (for the denial of legal good and evil), is the denial, in this case, of the evil of a lie on the part of the lawgiver, when reason does not pronounce it evil, so that he gives the lie to himself. And when the evil of a lie in him is denied, then the trustworthiness of what he tells us regarding good and evil must be denied also. (That is, till reason teaches us that a lie is evil, we cannot trust the lawgiver – for perhaps he is lying to us.)

(2) SECOND, WE ARE FREE AGENTS (*faʿiluna biʾl-ikhti-yar*), AND NECESSITY REQUIRES THIS: (*a*) BECAUSE OF THE NECESSARY DIFFERENCE BETWEEN A MAN'S FALLING FROM THE ROOF AND HIS GOING DOWN FROM IT BY A LADDER – OTHERWISE OUR RESPONSIBILITY (*taklif*) FOR A THING WOULD BE IMPOSSIBLE, AND THEN THERE WOULD BE NO SIN; (*b*) AND BECAUSE OF THE EVIL OF HIS CREATING AN ACT IN US AND THEN PUNISHING US FOR IT; (*c*) AND BECAUSE OF TRADITION.

The belief of Abu'l-Hasan and al-Ash^{c}ari and those who follow him is that all actions take place by the Power of Allah the Most High, and no actions taken place by the Power of Allah the Most High, and no action whatever belongs to the creature. And some of the Ash^{c}arites say that the essence of the act is of Allah, and the creature has *kasb*, which they explain as the action's being obedience or disobedience (that is, the moral quality of the act belongs to man, the act itself is Allah's). And some of them say that its meaning is that when the creature determines to undertake some thing, Allah the Most High creates the act thereupon. And the Mu^{c}tazilites and Zaydites and Imamites say that actions which proceed from the creature, and their qualities, and the *kasb* which they spoke of, *all* take place by the power and choice of the creature; and he is not forced, (*majbur*) to act as he does, but he can act and he can refrain from acting, and this is the reality, for several reasons: (1) First, we find a necessary difference between the issuing from us of an action which results from purpose and motive, like the descent from the roof by a ladder, and the issuing of an action of another sort, like falling from the roof either by constraint or accidentally. For we have power to refrain from the first (action), but not from the second. And if actions were not ours, then they would all be of one uniform kind without any distinction. But a distinction is present. Hence actions are ours, and that is what we sought.

(2) Second, if the creature were not the bringer-into-existence (*mujid*) of his actions, then his *taklif* would be impossible, otherwise he would be responsible for what he is unable to perform. And we say this because in this case he would not have power to do that for which he is responsible. For if he were responsible, the responsibility would be for something which he was unable to perform, and this is false, by the agreement of all. And when he is not responsible (*mukallaf*), he is not disobedient (*^{c}asi*) when he opposes (God's will), but by the agreement of all he *is* disobedient.

(3) Third, if the creature were not a bringer-into-existence of his actions, and did not have power over them, then Allah would be the most unjust of unjust beings. For since the evil action proceeds from the Most High (not from man), it is impossible for the creature to be punished for it, for he has not performed it. But all agree that the Most High punishes. Then He would be unjust—but He is exalted above that!

(4) Fourth, the Mighty Book which is the divider (*furqan*) between true and false teaches everywhere the relation (*idafah*) of the action to the creature and its occurrence by his will, according to the word of the Most High, "Woe to those who with their hands transcribe the Book corruptly, and then say, 'This is from Allah,' that they may sell it for some mean price! Woe to them for that which their hands have written! and Woe to them for the gains which they have made!" (II, 73) ". . . they follow but a conceit"

(VI, 116) ". . . So long as they change not what is in their hearts" (VIII, 55) ". . . He who doeth evil shall be recompensed for it" (IV, 122) ". . . Pledged to Allah is every man for his actions and their desert" (LII, 21). And all the verses of promise and threatening and blame and praise (prove this), and they are more than can be numbered.

(3) THIRD, REGARDING THE IMPOSSIBILITY OF EVIL (*qubh*) IN HIM, BECAUSE HE HAS THAT WHICH DETERS HIM FROM IT, WHICH IS THE KNOWLEDGE (*ʿilm*) OF EVIL; AND HE HAS NO MOTIVE FOR DOING EVIL, BECAUSE THE MOTIVE WOULD BE EITHER NEED, WHICH IS IMPOSSIBLE FOR HIM, OR THE WISDOM (*hikmah*) OF IT, WHICH IS EXCLUDED HERE; AND BECAUSE THE PROOF OF PROPHECY WOULD BE IMPOSSIBLE IF IT WERE POSSIBLE FOR EVIL TO PROCEED FROM HIM.

It is impossible for the Most High to be the doer of evil. This is the belief of the Muʿtazilites. But to the Ashʿarites He is Doer of everything, be it good or evil. And the proof of what we have said is twofold: (1) First, that which would deter him from evil exists, and the motive for doing evil does not exist, and whatever is thus cannot come to pass of necessity. Now as for the existence of a deterrent (*al-sarif*), it is the knowledge of evil, and Allah the Most High knows it; and as for the non-existence of a motive – the motive is either need of it, and this is impossible for Him, because He needs nothing; or it is the wisdom of it, and this also is impossible, because there is no widsom in evil. (2) Second, if evil were possible for Him, then the proof of prophecy would be impossible. But this necessity is false by universal agreement, hence that which necessitates it is false also. And in explanation of this necessity – in case He could do evil, the attesting of a false prophet would not be evil for Him, and in such a case assurance (*jazm*) as to the veracity of prophecy would be impossible, and this is self-evident.

HENCE IN THIS CASE THE WILL TO DO EVIL IS IMPOSSIBLE FOR HIM, FOR IT (that will) IS EVIL.

The Ashʿarites hold that the Most High is the Willer (*murid*) of all contingent existence, be it good or evil, vice or virtue, faith or unbelief, because He is the bringer-into-existence of everything, and is therefore also the willer of it. And the Muʿtazilites hold that it is impossible for Him to will evil and unbelief, and that is the reality. For the will to do evil is itself evil. For we know of necessity that just as rational beings blame the doer of evil so also they blame the willer of it, and the command to do it. So the saying of the author, "in this case," stated the result, namely, that the impossibility of the evil act (in Him) necessitates the impossibility of the will to do it... .

* * *

(2) SECOND, REGARDING HIS IMMUNITY TO SIN (*cisma*) AND IMMUNI-
TY TO SINS IS A HIDDEN KINDNESS (*lutf*) WHICH ALLAH THE MOST HIGH
SHOWS TO (the Prophet) ON WHOM HE HAS LAID THIS TASK (*mukallaf*),
THAT HE MAY HAVE NO INCENTIVE TO FORSAKE OBEDIENCE AND TO COMMIT
SIN (*macsiya*), ALTHOUGH HE HAS THE POWER (*qudrah*) TO DO SO. FOR IF IT
WERE NOT SO ONE COULD HAVE NO CONFIDENCE IN HIS WORD. THEN THE
VALUE OF HIS PROPHETIC MISSION WOULD BE NULLIFIED, AND THAT IS IM-
POSSIBLE.

Know that a person immune to sin (*macsum*) shares with others in
the kindness which bring men near to Allah. And in addition to that,
because of the nature of his soul (*malakah nafsaniyyah*), he enjoys a special
form of kindness which Allah bestows upon him, so that because of that he
does not choose to forsake obedience and to commit sin, although he has
the ability to do so. (An angel does not have that ability.) And some hold
that the *Macsum* cannot commit sin, and this is false, otherwise he would
deserve no praise.

Now that this is settled, know that there is a difference of opinion
regarding the immunity of the prophets to sin. And the Kharijites (al-
Khawarij) held that sins (*zunub*) were possible for them, and according to
them all sin is infidelity. And the Hashwites held that it was possible for
them to commit the great sins. And some of them denied (that they committed them) intentionally but not that they committed them unintentionally,
and they held that the intentional committing of small sins was possible.
And the Ashcarites denied absolutely that they could commit the great sins,
but they allowed the small ones unintentionally committed. And the Imamites have made immunity to all sin, intentional and unintentional, absolutely necessary (*wajib*), and that is the reality, for two reasons: (1) The
first is that to which the author referred, and his explanation is that if the
prophets were not *macsum* the value of their mission would be nullified.
And this necessity is false, hence that which necessitates it is false also. And
the explanation of this necessity is that when disobedience is possible for
them no confidence can be placed in their word, because in this case a lie
would be possible (*ja'iz*) for them. And when no confidence could be placed
in them, then their commands and prohibitions would not be obeyed. Then
the value of their mission would be nullified, and that is impossible. (2) Second, if sin (*zanb*) proceeded from them it would (still) be incumbent to
follow them, because tradition teaches that to follow them is incumbent.
But that would be impossible, for it would be evil to follow a man who is a
sinner). Hence it is impossible for sin to proceed from them, which is what
we sought.

(3) THIRD, HE IS IMMUNE TO SIN FROM THE FIRST OF HIS LIFE TO THE
LAST OF IT, BECAUSE THE HEARTS OF MEN WILL NOT BE BOUND IN
OBEDIENCE TO ONE IN WHOM HAS BEEN OBSERVED DURING HIS PAST
LIFE VARIOUS SINS GREAT AND SMALL AND THAT WHICH THE SOUL
HATES.
Those whom we mentioned (the Ashᶜarites) who assert the immunity of the prophets to sin hold that this applies to them only after their inspiration (*wahy*),though they deny that they were previously guilty of infidelity and repeated sin. And our companions (the Imamites) say that immunity to sin is absolutely necessary (*wajib*) both before inspiration and
after it to the ends of life. And the proof of that is what the author mentioned, and it is self-evident.
And that which is found in the Mighty Book (XLVII, 21), "Ask pardon
for thy sin (*zanb*)!", and in the traditions which might lead one to imagine
that they had been guilty of sin involves (only) their living the better course
(*tarku'l-awla*). Thus what reason teaches us harmonizes with the veracity of
tradition, although all of this which has been mentioned has various aspects
and implications. And thou canst read the book, "The Clearing of the Prophets" (*Tanzihu'l-Anbiya*), which Sayyid Murtada ᶜAlamu'l-Huda al-
Musawi composed, and other book also, and if I did not fear to prolong the
discussion I would quote a sample of it.

(4) FOURTH, IT IS NECESSARY THAT THE PROPHET BE THE BEST (*afdal*) OF
THE PEOPLE OF HIS AGE, BECAUSE IT IS EVIL BOTH BY REASON AND TRADI-
TION FOR AN INFERIOR (*al-mafdul*) TO HAVE PRECEDENCE OVER A SUPERIOR
(*al-fadil*). ALLAH THE MOST HIGH SAYS, "IS HE THEN WHO GUIDETH INTO THE
TRUTH THE MORE WORTHY TO BE FOLLOWED, OR HE WHO GUIDETH NOT
UNLESS HE BE HIMSELF GUIDED? WHAT THEN HATH BEFALLEN YOU THAT YE
SO JUDGE?" (X, 36).
It is necessary (*wajib*) that the Prophet possess all the qualities of
perfection and superiority, and it is necessary that he be in that respect
superior to and more perfect than every individual of the people of his age.
For it is evil, both by reason and tradition, for the Wise and Omniscient
(*Allah*) to give to the inferior who needs perfecting precedence over the
superior and the perfector. (It is evil) by reason, as is evident, since it is evil
in the opinion of authorities to make a beginner in jurisprudence take
precedence over Ibn ᶜAbbas and others like him among the lawyers, or to
make a beginner in logic take precedence over Sibawaihi and al-Khalil, and
so in all the sciences. And (it is evil) by tradition, as the Praised One indicated in the verses quoted and in others... .

*Khwajah Nasir al-Din Tusi**

According to al-Tusi:

"The Imam is a (means of) grace (to mankind) and therefore his appointment is required of God, the Exalted, in order to achieve that purpose (of providing men with grace). The explanation that the appointment of the Imam is a means of providing men with grace is because: "He brings men closer to obedience (of God) and keeps them away from disobedience." It is the Imam's role to be a vehicle for God's grace to men so that men can fulfil God's wishes of obeying him and avoiding sin that requires God to appoint an Imam. For al-Tusi regards: "(The provision of the means of) grace (to men) as required of God, the Exalted." This requirement, then, is a logical requirement. God is conceived as rational and will only subject men to His wishes if He has given them the means of fulfilling them. It is through the Imams that men will fulfill God's wishes.

It follows that: "Rational men recognise that corruptions are removed (through him) and grace is vested in him. His existence constitutes one (form of) grace (to men) and his actions another. The negation (of that grace) is due to ourselves." Thus the Imam's role as teacher and explainer will make clear to men the things that they must avoid and his existence will provide men with the grace to obey God. For by the act of recognising His existence men will become more aware of the requirements of God and thus will be more able to carry them out. In the same way men who, by the use of their reason, have recognised the need for the Imam and the necessity of following his instructions through observing his words and actions, will acquire grace to fulfil God's injunctions. However any rejection of that grace, either by men's failure to follow their reasons and accept the Imam or even though accepting him and not following his instructions, is the responsibility of men.

This appeal to reational men is based on the argument that has been put forward by Shi'i scholars from the earliest times that reason leads men to assume the need for leadership. Men recognise by reason that life can only be properly conducted when society is regulated by authority. For this reason men have always sought to appoint someone as their leader in order that society be properly manager. To fulfil this God-created need in men, it

---

Ed. Note: I. K. A. Howard selected and translated excerpts from al-Tusi's Tajrid al-I'tiqad, *where the medieval scholar presents a rational argument based on historical sources for the doctrine of Imamate and its place in Shī'i theology. The passage is taken from* Alserat, *pages 118–19.*

was God's duty to provide man with the grace to fulfil it. This God did through the institution of the Imamate. Although the need for the Imamate was strictly rational, by means of revelation God made it clear to men who were prepared to use their reasons.

The first quality that al-Tusi maintains that the Imam must have is that of infallibility. He argues: "The need to avoid an argument *ad infinitum* requires his infallibility, and also because he is the one who preserves the revealed divine law, and because of the need to disavow him if he committed any sin. The latter would contradict the injunction to obey (him) and would cause the purpose of his designation to be rendered void by making him in a position lower than the lowest of the vulgar masses."

The argument *ad infinitum* refers to the fact that if the Imam was not infallible, we would need another Imam to guide him and so on. Therefore, if the Imam is to be God's guide on earth, God must protect him from error and thus the endless argument would be avoided. By virtue of his infallibility, it is the Imam who preserves God's revelation from being corrupted. The belief in the Prophet's protection from error in the delivering of the revelation is absolutely essential for the validity of the revelation. This argument calls for the same kind of protection in the maintenance of the revelation. It is an argument that produces two answers from two main wings of the Islamic community. For one group, it is the community which, as preserver of the Qur'an and *sunnah*, is infalliable. Nasir al-Din al-Tusi following the logic of his earlier argument concerning the nature of the Imam requires the Imam to be the preserver of the Qur'an and *sunnah* and therefore infallible. This argument in favour of the Imam's infallibility is further strengthened by the nature of the office of the Imam. For if the leader commits errors, those led will cease to have the confidence in his leadership and thus if one is to have a divinely appointed leader, it follows that God will protect such a leader from error.

However, lest the Imam be regarded as someone more than human whose good actions deserve no praise and reward because he is incapable of anything else, al-Tusi adds: "In fallibility (in the Imam) does not deny the capacity (of committing sin)."

Chapter Twenty-three

Intellectual Sciences
and Philosophy

Shicism has a long tradition of intellectual sciences and philosophy. In fact, Shicism views intellect and philosophy as important aspects of religious thought, which positively confirm the fundamentals of Islamic belief and also guide man along the path of truth. cAllamah Tabataba'i elaborates upon the relevance of intellection to Shicism, the place of reason and philosophy in Shici thought, and the contributions of Shicism and Shici thinkers to Islamic philosophy.

In the following passage Allamah Tabataba'i locates the significance of intellectual sciences in the context of the Shici philosophy of science and epistemology. The passage is taken from SI, *pages 106–11.*

ᶜ*Allamah Tabataba'i*

It has been mentioned before that Islam has legitimized and approved rational thought, which it considers a part of religious thought. Rational thought in its Islamic sense, after confirming the prophecy of the Prophet, provides intellectual demonstrations of the validity of the external aspect of the Qur'an, which is a divine revelation, as well as of the definitely established sayings of the Prophet and his noble Household.

Intellectual proofs, which aid man in finding solutions for these problems through his God-given nature, are of two kinds: demonstration (*burhan*) and dialectic (*jadal*). Demonstration is a proof whose premises are true (accord with reality) even if they be not observable or evident. In other words, it is a proposition which man comprehends and confirms by necessity through his God-given intelligence, as for example when he knows that "the number three is less than four." This type of thought is called rational thought; and in case it concerns universal problems of existence, such as the origin and end of the world and of man, it becomes known as philosophical thought.

Dialectic is a proof all or some of whose premises are based on observable and certain data, as for example the case of believers in a religion for whom the common practice is to prove their religious views within that religion by appealing to its certain and evident principles.

The Holy Qur'an has employed both these methods and there are many verses in the Holy Book attesting to each type of proof. First of all, the Qur'an commands free investigation and meditation upon the universal principles of the world of existence and the general principles of cosmic order, as well as upon more particular orders such as that of the heavens, the stars, day and night, the earth, the plants, animals, men, etc. It praises in the most eloquent language intellectual investigation of these matters.

Secondly, the Qur'an has commanded man to apply dialectical thought, which is usually called theological (*kalami*) discussion, provided it is accomplished in the best manner possible, that is, with the aim of manifesting the truth without contention and by men who possess the necessary moral virtues. It is said in the Qur'an, "Call unto the way of thy Lord with wisdom

and fair exhortation, and reason ["*jadil*," from jadal] with them in the better way" (Qur'an, XVI, 125).

*   *   *

As for theology, *Kalam*, it is clear that from the beginning, when the
Shiᶜis separated from the Sunni majority they began to debate with their opponents concerning their own particular point of view. It is true that a
debate has two sides and that both the opponents share in it. However, the
Shiᶜis were continuously on the offensive, taking the initiative, while the
other side played the defensive role. In the gradual growth of kalam, which
reached its height in the second/eighth and third/ninth centuries with the
spread of the Muᶜtazilite school, Shiᶜi scholars and learned men, who were
students of the school of the Household of the Prophet, became among the
foremost masters of kalam. Furthermore, the chain of theologians of the
Sunni world, whether it be the Ashᶜarites, Muᶜtazilites or others, goes back
to the first Imam of the Shiᶜi ᶜAli.

As for philosophy, those who are acquainted with the sayings and works
of the companions of the Prophet (of which the names of 12,000 have been
recorded and 120,000 are known to exist) know that there is little in them
containing an appreciable discussion of philosophical questions. It is only
ᶜAli whose compelling metaphysical utterances contain the deepest philosophical thought.

The companions and the scholars who followed them, and in fact the
Arabs on that day in general, were not acquainted with free intellectual
discussion. There is no example of philosophical thought in the works of the
scholars of the first two centuries. Only the profound sayings of the Shiᶜi
Imams, particularly first and eighth, contain an inexhaustible treasury of
philosophical meditations in their Islamic context. It is they who acquainted
some of their students with this form of thought.

The Arabs were not familiar with philosophical thought until they saw examples of it during the second/eighth century in the translation of certain
philosophical works into Arabic. Later, during the third/ninth century,
numerous philosophical writings were translated into Arabic from Greek,
Syriac, and other languages and through them the method of philosophical
thought became known to the general public. Nevertheless, most jurists and
theologians did not look upon philosophy and other intellectual sciences,
which were newly arrived guests, with favor. At the beginning, because of
the support of the governmental autohrities for these sciences, their opposition did not have much effect. But conditions soon changed and through
strict orders many philosophical words were destroyed. The *Epistles* of the

Brethren of Purity, which is the work of a group of unknown authors, is a reminder of those days and attests to the unfavorable conditions of that epoch.

After this period of difficulty, philosophy was revived at the beginning of the fourth/tenth century by the famous philosopher Abu Nasr al-Farabi. In the fifth/eleventh century, as a result of the works of the celebrated philosopher Ibn Sina (Avicenna), Peripatetic philosophy reached its full development. In the sixth/twelfth century Shaykh al-Ishraq Shihab al-Din Suhrawardi systematized the philosophy of illumination (*ishraq*) and because of this was executed by the order of Salah al-Din Ayyubi. Thereafter, philosophy ceased to exist among the Muslim majority in the Sunni world. There was no further outstanding philosopher in that part of the Muslim world except in Andalusia at the edge of the Islamic world where at the end of the sixth/twelfth century Ibn Rushd (Averroes) sought to revive the study of philosophy.

* * *

In the same way that from the beginning Shi\^cism played an effective role in the formation of Islamic philosophical thought, it was also a principal factor in the further development and propagation of philosophy and the Islamic sciences. Although after Ibn Rushd philosophy disappeared in the Sunni world, it continued to live in Shi\^cism. After Ibn Rushd there appeared such celebrated philosophers as Khwajah Nasir al-Din Tusi, Mir Damad, and Sadr al-Din Shirazi, who studied, developed and expounded philosophical thought one after another. In the same manner, in the other intellectual sciences, there appeared many outstanding figures such as Nasir al-Din Tusi (who was both philosopher and mathematician) and Birjandi, who was also an outstanding mathematician.

All the sciences, particularly metaphysics or theosophy (*falsafah-i ilahi* or *hikmat-i ilahi*), made major advances thanks to the indefatigable endeavor of Shi\^ci scholars. This fact can be seen if one compares the works of Nasir al-Din Tusi, Shams al-Din Turkah, Mir Damad, and Sadr al-Din Shirzai with the writings of those who came before them.

It is known that the element that was instrumental in the appearance of philosophical and metaphysical thought in Shi\^cism and through Shi\^cism in other Islamic circles was the treasury of knowledge left behind by the Imams. The persistence and continuity of this type of thought in Shi\^cism is due to the existence of this same treasury of knowledge, which Shi\^cism has continued to regard with a sense of reverence and respect.

In order to clarify this situation it is enough to compare the treasury of knowledge left by the Household of the Prophet with the philosophical works written over the course of centuries. In this comparison one can see clealry how each day Islamic philosophy approached this source of knowledge ever more closely, until in the eleventh/seventeenth century Islamic philosophy and this inspired treasure of wisdom converged more or less completely. They were separated only by certain differences of interpretation of some of the principles of philosophy.

* * *

Thiqqat al-islam Muhammad ibn Ya^cqub Kulayni (d. 329/940) is the first person in Shi^cism to have separated the Shi^ci *hadiths* from the book called *Principles* (*usul*) and to have arranged and organized them according to the headings of jurisprudence and articles of faith. (Each one of the Shi^ci scholars of *hadith* had assembled sayings he had collected from the Imams in a book called *Asl*, or *Principle*.) The book of Kulayni known as *Kafi* is divided into three parts: Principles, Branches, and Miscellaneous Articles, and contains 16,199 *hadiths*. It is the most trustworthy and celebrated work of *hadith* known in the Shi^ci world.

Three other works which complement the *Kafi* are the book of the jurist Shaykh-i Sadduq Muhammad ibn Babuyah Qumi (d. 318/991), and *Kitab al-tahzib* and *Kitab al-istibsar*, both by Shaykh Muhammad Tusi (d. 460/1068).

Abu'l-Qasim Ja^cfar ibn Hasan ibn Yahya al-Hilli (d. 676/1277), known as Muhaqqiq, was an outstanding genius in the science of jurisprudence and is considered to be the foremost Shi^ci jurist. Among his masterpieces are *Kitab-i mukhtasar-i nafi^c* amd *Kitab-i sharayi^c*, which have been passed from hand to hand for seven hundred years among Shi^ci jurists and have always been regarded with a sense of awe and wonder.

Following Muhaqqiq, we must cite Shahid-i Awwal (the First Martyr) Shams al-Din Muhammad ibn Makki, who was killed in Damascus in 786/1384 on the accusation of being Shi^ci. Among his juridical masterpieces in this *Lum^cah-i dimashqiyah* which he wrote in prison in a period of seven days. Also we must cite Shaykh Ja^cfar Kashif al-Ghita' Najafi (d. 1327/1909) among whose outstanding juridical works is *Kitab kashf al-ghita'*.

Khwajah Nasir al-Din Tusi (d. 672/1274) is the first to have made kalam a thorough and complete science. Among his masterpieces in this domain in his *Tajrid al-kalam* which has preserved its authority among masters of this discipline for more than seven centuries. Numerous commentaries have been written on it by Shi^{c}is and Sunnis alike. Over and above his genius in the science of kalam, he was one of the outstanding figures of his day in philosophy and mathematics as witnessed by the valuable contributions he had to the intellectual sciences. Moreover, the Maraghah observatory owed its existence to him.

Sadr al-Din Shirazi (d. 1050/1640), known as Mulla Sadra and Sadr al-Muta'allihin, was the philosopher who, after centuries of philosophical development in Islam, brought complete order and harmony into the discussion of philosophical problems for the first time. He organized and systematized them like mathematical problems and at the same time wed philosophy and gnosis, thereby bringing about several important developments. He gave to philosophy new ways to discuss and solve hundreds of problems that could not be solved through Peripatetic philosophy. He made possible the analysis and solution of a series of mystical questions which to that day had been considered as belonging to a domain above that of reason and beyond comprehension through rational thought. He clarified and elucidated the meaning of many treasuries of wisdom, contained in the exoteric sources of religion and in the profound metaphysical utterances of the Imams of the Household of the Prophet, that for centuries had been considered as insoluble riddles and usually believed to be of an allegorical or even unclear nature. In this way gnosis, philosophy and the exoteric aspect of religion were completely harmonized and began to follow a single course.

By following the methods he had developed, Mulla Sadra succeeded in proving "transubstantial motion" (*harakat-i jawhariyyah*, and in discovering the intimate relation of time to the three spatial dimensions in a manner that is similar to the meaning given in modern physics to the "fourth dimension" and which resembles the general principles of the theory of relativity (relativity of course in the corporeal world outside the mind, no in the mind), and many other noteworthy principles. He wrote nearly fifty books and treatises. Among his greatest masterpieces is the four-volume *Asfar*.

It should be noted here that before Mulla Sadra certain sages like Suhrawardi, the sixth/twelfth century philosopher and author of *Hikmat al-ishraq*, and Shams al-Din Turkah, a philosopher of the eighth/fourteenth century, had taken steps toward harmonizing gnosis, philosophy and exoteric religion, but credit for complete success in this undertaking belongs to Mulla Sadra.

Shaykh Murtada Ansari Shushtari (d. 1281/1864) recognized the science of the principles of jurisprudence upon a new foundation and formulated the practical principles of this science. For over a century his school has been followed diligently by Shi^{c}i scholars.

ᶜAbd al-Razzaq Lahiji*

Know that there was a school of philosophers in Islam, headed by Shihab al-Din Yahya Suhrawardi, who was renowned under the title "Master of Oriental Theosophy" (*Shaykh al-Ishraq*) for having created in the Islamic era the corpus of the "theosophy of the Orientals." This school supports the thesis that several of the kings and princes of ancient Persia, such as Kay Khusraw and his peers, were initiates of "Oriental theosophy." The Greek sages prior to Aristotle were likewise adepts of this "theosophy of the Orientals." Aristotle, on the other hand, took up an opposite position and created that aggregate of doctrines designated as the "philosophy of the Peripatetics."

The difference between the theosophy of the Orientals and the philosophy of the Peripatetics can be seen from several angles. As everyone knows, the Orientals, of *Ishraqiyyun*, affirm that wisdom can be attained only through a method of spiritual realization; they emphasize the inner effort of spiritual struggle and mystical experience. They value neither pure rational theory nor dialectics as such; one might even say that they are frankly hostile to them. The Peripatetics, on the other hand, base their philosophy on rational theory and logical reasoning, and concede no value to what cannot be reduced to rational argumentation and logical reasoning. The Orientals, or *Ishraqiyyun*, are related to the Peripatetics as the Sufis to the scholastic theologians of Islam (the *Mutakallimun*). This difference can be verified in the prologue of the book which was mentioned previously.

Briefly, the Oriental theosophies and the Sufis agree in defending in philosophy and mystical theosophy a large number of theorems which the Peripatetics and the scholastic theologians, on the grounds that they do not

---

*Ed. Note: The importance Shiᶜism places on rational thought has, over the centuries, encouraged a plethora of works on philosophy. Although the limited space available here does not allow a complete exposition of the spectrum of philosophical thought in Shiᶜism, excerpts from the works of major Shiᶜi philosophers can shed light on the depth and breadth of rational thought in Shiᶜism. Passages chosen from the works of ᶜAbd al-Razzaq Lahiji and Mulla Muhsin Fayd Kashani, provide a cursory survey of philosophy in Shiᶜism.

In the passage, Lahiji discusses the differences between the philosophy of Shihab al-Din Suhrawardi, known as Hikmat al-Ishraq (Illuminationist Theosophy), and the Aristotelean philosophy of the peripatetic thinkers. The excerpts were selected by Henry Corbin and are from SBCE, pages 171–74.

meet the requirements of rational theory and logical argumentation, reject. These theorems notably include the one affirming the existence of the *mundus archetypus*, the autonomous world of archetypal Images or Forms (*ᶜalam-i mithal*). The Oriental theosophists and the Sufis agree in affirming the following: between the intelligible world, which is the world of entirely immaterial pure Intelligence, and the sensory world, which is the world of purely material realities, there exists another universe. The beings of this intermediary universe possess shape and extent, even though they do not have "material matter." Thus the pure Intelligence are separated both from matter and extent; purely material things are clothed with both matter and extent; the beings of the *mundus archetypus* are separate from matter, but endowed with extent in the same way as the forms of imaginative consciousness. Nevertheless, the reality of the forms which are immanent in imaginative consciousness resides in that consciousness itself, not objectively or extramentally, whereas the reality of the world of archetypal Images is objective and extramental.

Thus this world is intermediate between the two universes: as a result of being separated from matter, it is of the same nature as the world of pure Intelligences; as a result of possessing form and extent, it resembles the world of material things. Every being of the two universes, the intelligible and the sensory, has its archetypal Image to this intermediate universe, a self-subsistent Image with autonomous existence; — every creature and everything, including movement and rest, attitudes and physiognomies, flavors and perfumes, and other accidentals. The mode of existentce assumed in this intermediate world by an essentially immaterial being corresponds for this same being to a kind of descent through which it becomes able to take on extent and shape. On the other hand, the mode of existence assumed in it by a material being, for this same being corresponds to an ascent which strips it of matter and certain things inherent in matter, such as localization.

This universe is also designated as the world of autonomous Images and Imagination, and as the world of the *barzakh*. It may happen that a being of this autonomous world of Images makes himself visible, makes his appearance in our material world, and can be perceived in it by the outer senses. Bodies which are perfectly polished and transparent bodies, such as mirrors, still water, the atmosphere, are the places of the epiphany in our material world of the beings of the world of archetypal Images. In the same way, man's Imagination is also the place of their epiphany. Forms contemplated in mirrors and those manifested in the Imagination both belong to that *mundus archetypus*, which is manifested for us in these "epiphanic places" (*mazahir*), that is, the mirror and the Imagination. In the same way also, the forms one sees in a dream, Angels, genii, and demons, are likewise beings belonging to this same world, who are sometimes manifest to a whole group, in such or such an epiphanic place in Air or Water.

There is, moreover, a tradition dating back to the Sages of antiquity concerning the existence of a universe having extent but different from the sensory world — a universe with infinite wonders and countless cities, among them *Jabalqa* and *Jabalsa*, two immense cities, each having a thousand gates and containing innumerable creatures. This is the universe by which the theosophists of that school (the *Ishraqiyyun* or Orientals) explain and authenticate bodily resurrection; they affirm that Paradise, Hell, and the Earth of Resurrection have their existence in this *mundus archetypus*, the autonomous universe of the archetypal Images. This is the universe in which accidents can acquire substance, in which the acts and works of man can take on consistent form and figure. Among the schools that admit bodily resurrection there is one that professes that the human *pneuma* (the subtle body) continues to exist in this world of autonomous Images during the interval which is also called a *barzakh*, and which extends from the death of the individual to the Great Resurrection. Numerous *hadith* and traditions allude to this and can be quoted in support; these will be analyzed later in this book.

This world of archetypal Images differs from the world of Platonic Ideas — the one which owes its name to Plato — in this sense that the Platonic Ideas designate *universal* forms of knowledge, separate from matter and all materials envelopments, self-subsistent, not subsisting only through the person of the knowing subject or through some other substratum. According to Plato it is through these Ideas that the divine Being has knowledge of that which is other. Here exactly is a third way of conceiving divine knowledge insofar as it differs from two other types of knokwledge: *representative* knowledge and *presential* knowledge. Now, according to the Oriental theosophists, the beings of the world of archetypal Images are *particular* forms that are separate from Matter, but by no means from all material (that is, subtle) envelopes. Of course, the world of Platonic Ideas resembles this world of archetypal Images in the sense that these autonomous imagination Forms are self-subsistent, just as the Ideas or intelligible forms are self-subsistent. In sum, the thesis of the autonomous world of archetypal Images is peculiar to the Oriental theosophists (*Ishraqiyyun*) and to the Sufis, and to support this thesis they refer to mystical experience. . . .

Mulla Muhsin Fayd Kashani*

Because the power to govern bodies has been entrusted to Spirits, and because it is impossible for a direct connection to be established between spirits and bodies on account of their heterogeneous essence, God created the world of the archetypal Images as an intermediary (*barzakh*) linking the world of Spirits and the world of bodies. Hence the connection and articulation of each of the two worlds with the other is assured. The emission and reception of the influx of spiritual entities then becomes conceivable; spirits are able to exercise their regency over bodies and come to their assistance. This archetypal world is a spiritual universe. On the one hand, it symbolizes with material substance in that it can be an object of perception, is endowed with extent, and can manifest in time and in space. On the other hand, it symbolizes with pure intelligible substance, in that it is formed of pure light and is independent of space and time. Thus, it is neither a composite material body, nor a pure intelligible substance completely separated from matter. One might rather describe it as a universe having duality of dimensions through each of which it symbolizes with the universe to which that dimension corresponds. There is no existent thing, whether in the intelligible world or in the sensory world, whose image is not recorded in this intermediate universe. This universe, in the macrocosm, is homologous to the active Imagination in the human microcosm. Indeed, it compromises an aspect the perception of which is dependent upon the faculties having their seat in the brain, this being technically called the contiguous imagination contiguous to the archetypal world, while remaining immanent in man). But it also comprises an aspect not subject to this condition, and which is called the Autonomous Imagination (the world of the *Malakut*).

It is through this world, and through its characteristic property, that spiritual entities are corporealized, are embodied, when they are manifested in the epiphanic forms which are the Images with which they symbolize. This is what is referred to in the verse telling how Gabriel "took on a body (was typified) before Maryam in the form of a human being of perfect beauty" (XIX, 16). The story told about the Samaritan alludes to the same thing: "I

Ed. Note: Kashani's treatise deals more directly with philosophical questions. He addresses the nature of the universe and existence. In Corbins' words, Kashani corporealized the spirits and spiritualized all terestrial bodies in creating his philosophic conception of the universe. The excerpt is taken from SBCE, pages 176-79.

saw what they did not see; I took a handful of earth from under the feet of the Messenger" (XX, 96), that is, from under the feet of the Archangel Gabriel. The same reference is also contained in the tradition which relates that the Prophet saw the Archangel Gabriel in the guise of the adolescent Dahya al-Kalbi and heard him read a discourse clothed in words and letters.

This is the intermediate world to which those who are spiritualized (the "pneumatic ones") are carried off in their spiritual assumptions when they shed their elemental physical forms and when their Spirits put on their epiphanic spiritual form. It is in the intermediate world that perfect Souls put on the apparitional forms in which they are perceived in a place other than the one where they actually are; or else appear to him to whom they wish to appear in a form different form that in which they are perceived by the senses during their earthly sojourn. That very thing can come to pass after their transfer to the other world, for then the psycho-spiritual energy is further increased by the fact that the obstacle of the body has been removed.

In short, this is the world of archetypal Images through and in which *Spirits are corporealized and bodies spiritualized.* Through and in this world, ways of being and moral behaviour are personalized, and supersensory realities are manifested in the forms and figures with which they symbolize. And further, the appearance of figures in mirrors or in any reflecting substance, for instance clear water, likewise takes place in this intermediate world, since all figures reflected by mirrors also belong to this world. Again, all forms and figures immanent in our active Imagination are seen in this intermediate world, whether in dreams or in the waking state, because these forms and figures are contiguous to this archetypal world; they receive its light in the way that a ray of light penetrates into a dwelling place through skylight and lattices.

So, this is an immense world, so vast that it contains not only the Forms of the immaterial substances above it, but also the material realities below it. It is the intermediary, the medium through which the connection is effected. The senses and sensory perceptions rise toward it, as the supersensory realities descend toward it. From the place it occupies it continues to gather in the fruits of each thing. It is through this world that the truth is confirmed of the accounts of the Prophet's assumption to Heaven which mention that, in the manner of an eyewitness, he had a vision of the Angels and prophets. It is in this intermediate world that the Holy Imams are present when they appear before a dying person, as related in so many traditional accounts. This is the world in which the interrogation of the tomb takes place, with its delights and its torments; and it is in this intermediate world also that the faithful believer can visit those near to him after their death. Likewise, this intermediate world accounts for the possibility of scenes alluded to in certain traditions: where the Spirits recognize one another *post mortem*, just as corporeal beings recognize one another, ask questions of one another, and so forth. It would seem that the "descent of Jesus" (at the time of the *parousia* of the hidden Imam) belongs to this category of events. In the words of Shaykh Sadduq: "The descent of Jesus to the Earth is his return to this world after being carried away from this world," because God himself proclaims: "It is I who receive you, who carry you off toward myself, and deliver you from those who deny you . . . until the Resurrection day." (III, 48) In the same way, our traditions deriving from the Holy Imams teach us: "At the time of the *parousia* of the *Mahdi* (the 'Guide'), God will cause to come back a certain number of persons who died before; that is, a certain number from among the Initiates and adepts of the Imam, his Shiᶜis, pure believers with pure faith, so that they may gather with him the fruit of his triumph and his invincible help and taste the joy of the epiphany of his reign. God will likewise cause a certain number of the enemies of the Imam to return, pure infidels with pure impiety, so that they may stand accused and receive the punishment they have deserved. . . ." All of this refers to the return which accompanies the *parousia* and to which the faith of our Imamite coreligionists is particularly attached. And this is the spiritual meaning of certain verses relating to the resurrection, when interpreted according to the teaching of our Imams.

Chapter Twenty-four

Shi^ci Literature

Literature in a religious context refers to that body of prose and poetry that either portrays the main tenets, ethos, and life of a religion or plays a role in the practice of religious rites. The function of literature in Shi^cism mostly is that of promoting the spirit of the faith, and complementing its rituals. In this regard, Shi^ci literature fosters devotional worship and redemptive suffering. It seeks to bring to life the tragedies (especially that of Karbala') that lie at the heart of Shi^cism, and to immerse the faithful in them.

Marthiyyah, or lamentation poetry, as the name implies, strives to provoke the feeling of sorrow weeping for the Shi^ci martyrs in general and the martyrs of Karbala' in particular. Marthiyyah, *therefore lies at the foundation of* rawdah-khani *and* ta^cziyyah *ceremonies. In this section, selections from the writings of Mahmud Ayoub, E. G. Browne, and Peter Chelkowski, describe the history and literary structure of* Marthiyyah *literature and provide exmaples of it from the literature of Iran, and the subcontinent of India. These excerpts are from* RSISD, *pages 158–61, and 250–51; and* Alserat, *pages 151–56.*

Mahmud Ayoub

The purpose of writing and reciting lamentation poetry is not simply to display artistic talent, but more importantly to induce sorrow and weeping. Yet a poem that does not describe in tender and highly artistic language some aspect or episode of the tragedy would not have fulfilled its purpose. This gives the *marthiyyah* genre of poetry a unique character. It is perhaps the most dramatic and epic-like poetry, at least in Arabic.

It may be safely inferred from many reports that the imams especially the sixth Imam, used to gather their followers together to remember the death of Husayn. Poets were often asked to recite their verses of lamentation and grief for the gatherings. Two closely analogous traditions are most often cited by Shi⁽c⁾i scholars, both early and modern ones. One day, the sixth Imam, Ja⁽c⁾far al-Sadiq, asked one of his followers, Abu ⁽c⁾Imarah al-Munshid (the chanter or reciter), to recite some verses about Husayn. The man began to recite his verses, and the Imam and his family began to weep until the wailings of the women could be heard in the street. The verses our chanter recited were not of his own composition; they will be discussed later. The Imam then announced to Abu ⁽c⁾Imarah the great reward he would have in the world to come and continued:

> . . . He who recites poetry about Husayn, causing fifty person to weep and weeps himself, will have a place in paradise.

Then the Imam continued to repeat the same statement, each time reducing the number of people caused to weep: first to thirty, twenty, ten, then even to one. He concluded, '. . . Even if one recites poetry about Husayn and weeps himself alone, or even pretends to weep, his will be paradise on the Day of Resurrection.'

. . . The first poet, according to some reports, to compose an elegy (*marthiyyah*) on Husayn was ⁽c⁾Iqbah ibn ⁽c⁾Amr al-Sahmi. In al-Samhi's *marthiyyah*, we see a kind of warm and simple piety and grief for the death of the Imam and those martyred with him. It is an expression of devotion and reverence, free from the hagiographical and political allusions characteristic of many other poems, especially those belonging to later centuries. The poet, we are told, visited Karbala' either soon after the death of Husayn or later towards the end of the century. There he stopped at the tomb of the Imam and recited his verses. His poem seems to have been composed in Karbala', perhaps extemporized as a sudden expression of deep emotion.

I passed the grave of Husayn in Karbala', and on it my tears flowed copiously.
    I continued to weep and grieve for his suffering, and my eye was well assisted by tears and sobs.
And with him I mourned a group of men whose graves surround his own.
    May the light of an eye, seeking consolation in life when you [Husayn and his followers] were frightened in this world, be darkened.
    Peace be upon the dwellers of these graves in Karbala' . . .May peace be upon them with the setting of the sun and its rising: Peace carried from me by the winds as they blow to and fro.
    Men in troops continue to flock in pilgrimage to his grave, where on them flows its musk and sweet fragrance.

*   *   *

The first *marthiyyah* to be composed for members of the Holy Family (*Ahl al-Bayt*) lamented the death of the Prophet himself. The *marthiyyah* was composed by an otherwise little known Companion called Salim who fell in the Battle of Jalula' in the year 16 A.H. The poet begins by enjoining Fatimah, the daughter of the Prophet, to weep: "O Fatimah, weep tirelessly 'til morning, so long as the stars appear. For when he (Muhammad) was laid to rest, the earth collapsed, and who among men was not distressed?" The poet then reproaches his own eyes for not shedding copious tears: ". . . for who after the Apostle is worthy of being lamented with tears and dirges (*nadb*)?" He then enumerates the virtues of the Prophet, his generosity, truthfulness, kindness and magnanimity, and again calls upon his eyes to shed tears, ". . . for him whom the hard mountains lamented."
    Historians and authors of martyrdom narratives (*maqatil*) are not agreed as to who was the first to lament Husayn and his fellow martyrs. A number of late and popular dirges are put in the mouths of one or another of the imams' womenfolk. It is, however, probable that the two *marthiyyahs* attributed to Husayn's wife al-Rabab and his daughter by her, Sukaynah, are very early, if perhaps not authentic. His wife laments him as a good husband, generous and loving, and kind toward the poor and destitute. Sukaynah vows to weep all her life: "O my eye, occupy yourself in weeping all your life; weep with tears of blood not for a child, family or friends, rather for the son of the Apostle of God. Pour out your tears and blood . . ."
    It is also related that when ᶜAli Zayn al-ᶜAbidin, the only surviving son of Husayn reached Medinah with the women captives, a young maid came out chanting, "A crier brought the news of my master's death, which caused me pain. He brought news which made me sick and distraught with grief. Pour out your tears, therefore, o my eye; pour out tears and blood over him

whose death shook the throne of majesty." Another early and moving poem is attributed to the famous Successor Khalid ibn Mi͑dan. It is said that when he saw the head of Husayn nailed to the gate of Yazid's palace in Damascus, he was so struck with grief that he withdrew from human society for a month. Ibn Mi͑dan begins by depicting the scene of the head of Husayn carried on the head of a spear into the city and bathed in blood. The poem, in simple and direct language, addresses Husayn thus: "They killed you thirsty . . . and in killing you, O son of the daughter of Muhammad, it is as though they intentionally slew an Apostle. They cried, 'God is most great!' as they slew you, but with you they slew the proclamation of *takbir* and *tahlil*."

During the Umayyid and the early ͑Abbasid period, poets and other members of the Shi͑i community gathered in secret in the homes of the *Imams* to commemorate the death of Husayn and his male relatives and friends and the humilialting captivity of his womenfolk. It was in such secret gatherings that the real emphasis and purpose for *marathi* was provided. The sixth imam, Ja͑far al-Sadiq, asked the famous reciter of *marathi* Abu ͑Imarah al-Munshid to recite some verses in memory of the Imam's martyred forbear, promising that, "Whoever recites poetry about Husayn, causing fifty persons to weep, and weeps himself, he shall have Paradise." Then, reducing the number to thirty, then twenty, then ten, and finally to only one person, the Imam concluded, "If one recites poetry about Husayn and weeps himself alone, or even pretends to weep, his shall be Paradise on the Day of Resurrection."

The growth of algaic literature must be viewed as an integral part of the development of the Shi͑i ethos of suffering. The picture which tradition paints of the ever suffering mother of the Imam, Fatimah al-Zahra', whose tears in Paradise have transformed the celestial abode of bliss into a house of sorrows, became the subject of many *marathi*. Her final vindication and the intercession promised her for even the most sinful of the devotees of the Holy Family induced empathy, impatient anger, frustration and hope in the hearts and minds of the faithful. Such themes have provided both the inspiration and content of much *marathi* literatures. Thus, quite early in the history of the Muharram cultus, several important themes crystallized into a more or less definite form.

* * *

The mood and context of the *marathi* poetry have in large measure depended on the fortunes of the Shi͑i community. In times of persecution and stress, the mood was one of grief, helplessness and frustration. In more recent times, when relative stability, a measure of power and general acceptance by other Muslims of the Shiᶜi community, the mood has shifted from grief to exultation and from a limited reference to the Shiᶜi of the imams to a view of the universal relevance of Husayn's sacrifice in defence of truth. This, however, has been only a point of greater emphasis rather than an altogether new development. It was in part this recognition of the moral and spiritual aspects of the tragedy of Karbala', which inspired Sunni Muslims to make their contributions to the *marathi* literature. One of the first to do so was Muhammad ibn Idris al-Shafiᶜi, the founder of the Shafiᶜi school of jurisprudence. In his powerful *marthiyyah*, he repeats all the usual themes and finally declares that, "They (members of the Holy Family) shall be my intercessors on the day of my standing before God when men shall behold great portents."

To the old themes of sorrow and grief, modern poets have added those of passionate love (ᶜ*ishq*), valour and courage. Thus Ibn Hammad (d. towards the end of the ninth century A.H.) begins his *marthiyyah* with these verses, "You have abandoned me, O beautiful one, coyly, and made my body a shadow by your separation. You have given me to drink the bitter cup of separation and withheld from me the sweet springs of your pleasure." Another poet, writing in 1957, Muhammad Jamil al-Hashimi, combines this sentimentalism with a sense of exultation in the courage and dignity of the Imam. He also emphasizes the need to remember him with tears: "History brings you back to me with tears and blood. — Every time the eclipsed moon of Muharram appears / May my soul be a ransom for you; how beautiful a melody of love you are! / For which my heart flutters and my tongue sings / . . . Many were those who said to me / . . . 'Why do you weep for this bright world?' / Another, mocking my sorrow, ignorantly / Disputes with me concerning the death memorial of the great patriarch (*sibt*) saying, / 'It is wrong that Husayn be kept alive through a death memorial. / Were people to accept my suggestion, / I would make Muharram a time of joyous celebration. / A day on which Islam erected its true being. / (It) Should be a day for which every Muslim must be congratulated.'" The author answers that he weeps not for the glory of Muharram but for the sufferings which the Imam endured. He thus goes on to enumerate the sufferings of Husayn and his family and then concludes, "My apology I offer to you, Abu Sajjad (Husayn) / For the ambition of a poet wishing to reach you with a ladder / You are he whose greatness the intellect may seek to fathom / Only to find itself in a sea of your mysteries, unfathomable. / For this reason have I taken tears as the telescope of my verse / That through it I may see the hidden mysteries of this universe / . . . You are indeed a vast world, illuminated by moons and radiant with stars / In vain I tried to come near to its sanctity / But my mind and imagination stood helpless before it / If, O poet, you desire eternal fame and glory / Salute the day of Husayn with prayers and peace salutations."

Perhaps the highest expression of the poetic ethos of the Shi^ci community has been the vivid and dramatic imagery which became an essential characteristic of the *marathi* genre. Thus the well known modern poet, Hashim al-Ka^cbi, paints a moving picture of the suffering women of Husayn crowded around his headless body: "thus came the ladies of rich chambers / In whom aspects of sorrow cannot be detailed by any recounter / One of them falls down, pressing him to her bosom / And another attempts to shade him with her robes / Another one, as his neck overflows with blood, dyes her hair / And still another one cries out 'May my soul be a ransom for you!', and another embraces him."

E.G. Browne* (Tr.)

"When they summoned mankind to the table of sorrow, they first
    issued the summons to the hierarchy of the Prophets.
When it came to the turn of the Saints, Heaven trembled at the blow
    which they smote on the heard of the Lion of God.
Then they kindled a fire from sparks of diamond-dust and cast it on
    Hasan the Chosen one.
Then they tore up from Medinah and pitched at Karbala' those
    pavilions to which even the angels were denied entrance.

*   *   *

Many tall palm-trees from the grove of the 'Family of the Cloak'
    did the people of Kufah fell in that plain with the axe of malice.
Many a blow whereby the heart of Mustafa [Muhammad] was rent
    did they inflict on the thirst throat of Murtada ^cAli's successor,
While his women, with collars torn and hair unloosed, raised their
    laments to the Sanctuary of the Divine Majesty,
And the Trusted Spirit [Gabriel] laid his head in shame on his knees,
    and the eye of the sun was darkened at the sight.

*   *   *

Ed. Note: E. G. Browne provides an example of a marthiyyah *composed in the Safavid era by the celebrated poet Muhtashim. The passage is from* LHP, *pages 175-77.*

When the blood of his thirsty throat fell on the ground, turmoil arose
from the earth to the summon of God's high Throne.
The Temple of Faith came nigh to ruin through the many fractures
inflicted on the Pillars of Religion.
They cast to the ground his tall palm-tree even as the thorn-bush;
a deluge arose from the dust of the earth to heaven.
The breeze carried that dust to the Prophet's Tomb: dust arose from
Madinah to the seventh heaven.
When tidings of this reached Jesus dwelling in the heavenly sphere,
he forthwith plunged his garments in indigo in the vat of heaven.
Heaven was filled with murmuring when the turn to cry out passed
from the Prophets to the presence of the Trusted Spirit.
Mistaken imagination fancied that this dust had [even] reached
the skirts of the Creator's glory,
For although the Essence of the All-glorious is exempt from vexation,
He dwells in the heart, and no heart remains unvexed.

* * *

I am afraid that when they record the punishment of his murderer,
they may forthwith strike the pen through the Book of Mercy.
I am afraid that the Intercessors on the Resurrection Day may be
ashamed, by reason of this sin, to speak of the sins of mankind.
When the People of the House shall lay hands on the People of
Tyranny, the hand of God's reproach shall come forth from its
sleeve.
Alas for the moment when the House of ᶜAli, with blood dripping
from their winding-sheets, shall raise their standards from the
dust like a flame of fire!

Peter Chelkowski*

ᶜAbbas was Husayn's half-brother and his standard-bearer. If Husayn
is the supreme martyr, ᶜAbbas is regarded as the supreme fighter. Tradi-

---

*Ed. Note: Peter Chelkowski provides an interpretive account of the role of marathi in Shīᶜī
literature, and cites the structure of drama in an elegy for Hadrat-i ᶜAbbas. The passage is from
ASIHCN, pages 232–33 and 254–59.

tionally the play devoted to ʿAbbas is enacted on the 9th of Muharram known as Tasuʿa. The strong personality of ʿAbbas is very much admired and venerated in Iran and in Shiʿi communities in other countries. There are many shrines devoted to his name. Many *saqqa'-khanih*, water cisterns and fountains in towns and villages, are dedicated to his bravery on the plain of Karbala' when he tried to fetch water for the thirsty family of the Prophet, and had his hands cut off before being killed by Yazid's men.

Swearing on ʿAbbas is the only truly dependable oath in daily life, whereas in contracts his name is added to those of the partners, 'in absentia', to safeguard against the trespassing of anyone's rights. He is also admired by the women for his particular powers. In Iran a feast, *sufrih hadrat-i ʿAbbas*, may be prepared in his honour, as a vowed thanksgiving for a favour received, at which food is distributed to the people.

Most *taʿziyyah* texts are anonymous since the composition is regarded as an act of piety. The Cerulli 513 manuscript is signed by the scribe, Ghulam Husayn Sabiri, and dated 1331; both the dating and the signing are rather unusual. The text seems to be a mixture of at least two plays on the same subject, which is a very common phenomenon. Most of the *taʿziyyah* manuscripts are collections of pieces of paper, some two inches wide and about eight inches long, written separately for each character in the play. The actors hold these scraps in their palms and read their lines. When the actors from various locations merge in order to perform together, the scripts may also merge. Although the play is devoted to ʿAbbas, it gives an overall picture of the suffering and the death of Husayn, his sons and followers on the plain of Karbala'. In the *taʿziyyah* plays all the characters discuss their pre-determined fate. Despite the fact that the death of ʿAbbas took place before that of Husayn and some other members of his family, on the stage ʿAbbas describes the death of Husayn and his relatives vividly before the fact, thus arousing the emotions of the audience. Both the actors and the spectators know the totality of the tragedy, and therefore they do not need to keep it secret for the sake of suspense, as is the case in Western theatre.

The bulk of this play deals with the attempt by Shimr, the villain, to seduce ʿAbbas away from Husayn in order to become the commander of the enemy's army. This is a potent bribe which ʿAbbas sturdily and repeatedly refuses to accept. Temptation is a device frequently used in the drama of both the East and the West. A second dramatic device is that of deception, questioning the courage of the hero. In this case ʿAbbas covers his face and intercepts ʿAli Akbar who is bringing water, to test him. The unknown author or authors of this play were quite familiar with these devices. Although long soliloquies are customary in the early *taʿziyyah* plays, in this instance a rapid dialogue becomes the main mode of personal interaction.

The language, which is in poetry of varied rhythmic patterns, presents an interesting modification of the Western recitative and musical interpretation, in that the good characters sing their lines and the villains recite them. As for the poetic expression, there is a considerable variation of quality which is not unusual in the *ta^cziyyah* repertory. The several references in the text to the sins of the Shi^ci and the redemptive character of Husayn's death bring the tragedy of Karbala' from the historical time to the present. The actors and spectators feel just as responsible for Husayn's death as those who betrayed and abandoned him in the year 61/680.

* * *

The Martyrdom of the Luminous Leader of Banu Hashim, Hadrat Abu'l-Fadl al-^cAbbas: A Ta^cziyyah

Shimr: I am your slave, ready to sacrifice myself. I have a command from Yazid, my lord. I am the son of Zal, Rustam. I am the warrior Afrasiyab. Like Faramarz, I am the champion of the army. I am a temple, I am a convent, a priest, a monk, a Zangi. I closed the book on ^cUthman, I am a wall of iron. Woe to the time when my horse is saddled and I enter the stage of war. Neither the enemy's horse nor the rider shall last long fighting me. Now, hear more: I am a rogue and a thief. I steal people's collyrium from their eyes. I am Satan's guide and preceptor. I am the teacher of that wicked creature. Seven hundred and seventy followers learned from me. I know the mysteries of all nations. Only one equals me in knowledge, I am the mufti, I am graceful, I am a sage; I may be doomed to burn in hell, but I can raise hell in Karbala'. I am an old dragon, a scorpion, a goat, a snake. Sometimes I am thunder, sometimes lightning, sometimes fire, sometimes soft, sometimes cold, sometimes burning like fire, sometimes fast, sometimes slow, sometimes as black as a snake. At times I am sweet as sugar and at times I am bitter as venom. I am the enemy of God, His Prophet, and Murtada. I am the oppressor. You may think I am a grocer from Damascus or a haberdasher from Zangibar or India or one of those filthy mouse-eating Arabs. I am your enemy, the seed of menses, traitors and adulterers. I have seven breasts just like a dog.

[*The actor tries to protect himself against the audience to prove that he himself is not Shimr, whom he hates.*]

I am the rôle-carrier of Shimr and the invoker of the King of religion, Husayn. I hate Shimr, that son of a bitch.

^cAbbas: O shameless bastard and impudent son of damned Zuljushan, I swear by the great God, His prophet, and by the broken heart of the pure Zahra that no matter what their number, no matter where they come from, even if the sand of the desert or the leaves of the trees turn into armies of the foe, I will not be afraid or alarmed. I will draw my sword, call Haydar's name and attack your armies, O outcast on the Day of Judgement, I swear by the hands of Husayn's standardbearer, which are the hands of ^cAli. Who can equal God's hands? O damned people. When I put my feet in the stirrups and mount my horse, I will not take off my boots nor shall I remove the helmet of bravery and zeal. I shall not unfasten the lion's armour from my back until I have had justice from the people of oppression and evil. Then I shall ride to Syria where I shall unseat the damnable adulterer, the cruel, oppressive son of the cannibal Hind, from his throne. I shall lead him on a leash in public and make him run after a horse. I shall humiliate him to the fullest and bring him to the bench of the honourable judge Husayn ibn ^cAli Abu Talib. All the people shall know that courage such as this is not characteristic of ordinary men except for Abu 'l-Fazl, the standard-bearer, who is the water-carrier of Husayn's orphans. I will be proud of myself before the jinn and angels because of this great achievement. If the purpose were not Husayn's martyrdom I would get permission from him to use my sharp sword to strike terror in Karbala' in such a way that nothing would grow from now to eternity for a friend or foe. But what can I do? If I do not immolate myself for the followers of my father, who will become the intercessor for this poor nation of sinners? I swear by God that I have accepted to die, and have my head raised upon spears. I shall be grateful for God's mercy. Go, O son of Satan. Boasting to ^cAbbas, from now until the day of judgement, will do you no good.

Shimr: [*Text missing, begins* 'From what . . .'.]

^cAbbas: I am a pearl from the sea of *wilayah*, I am a lion and the son of the Lion of God. O inferior oppressor, Karbala' alone can not frighten me. Even if you fill the universe with soldiers I will not fear them. I will fight all of them and corner them. I will erase the name of Yazid, that infidel dog, from the face of the earth. I will throw him in the dust and humiliate him! But what can I do? The Shi^ci are sinners and need Husayn's intercession. O friends of Husayn, cry out 'O ^cAli!'

[*In the encampment of Husayn.*]

^c*Ali Akbar:* O God, what is happening on this plain of calamity? There is turmoil on the plain of Karbala'. This night, the spiteful enemy has launched a surprise attack on us. With no water in my throat, I am going to fight the deceitful foe on this miserable plain. Bless me, should I die, my dear father Husayn.

Qasim: O God, what is happening on this plain of calamity? There is turmoil on the plain of Karbala'. This night the spiteful enemy has launched a surprise attack on us. With no water in my throat, I am going to fight the deceitful foe on this miserable plain. Bless me, should I die, my dear uncle Husayn.

Sakinah: O Lord, has the world come to an end? Have the wheels of the universe stopped turning? O uncle, standard-bearer of Karbala', get up and take a look at us. I see the standard but not the standard-bearer. Aunt Zaynab, homeless Zaynab, wake up, wake up, wake up. The cruel enemy surrounds the camp. Wake up, wake up.

Zaynab: O, sweet singing nightingale, why are you wailing in the middle of the night? Why are you sighing so desperately from your heart? Has fire kindled your soul? Why are you wailing in the middle of the night?

Sakinah: Come, O aunt, observe the turmoil and listen to the enemy's drums beating. I have no desire to live. Wake up my father.

Zaynab: Zaynab is distressed. Has her luck turned away from her? Prepare yourself for captivity. The confusion and uproar is coming from the enemy. Zaynab will certainly be taken prisoner. Wake up brother. Wake up from your restful sleep and look into Zaynab's tearful eyes.

Imam: You interrupted my dream of a musk-scented paradise. You interrupted my conversation with my father and grandfather. I heard my mother's voice saying, 'Husayn will be our guest tomorrow night.' You interrupted my dream about my brother.

Zaynab: O companion of my sad heart, the enemy has penetrated the camp. You can hear the beating of the drums of war by the despicable enemy. Listen, O brother, for I am going to be taken into captivity.

^c*Abbas:* I call upon you, Qasim and Akbar. Roar the thunderous cry ^c*Allahu akbar.*'

Imam: Call ^cAbbas, my close companion and great and gallant warrior.

Zaynab [entering the tent of ^cAbbas]: ^cAbbas, O brother, light of Haydar's eyes, the dearest offspring of the Prophet is calling you. I see the standard, but I do not see the standard-bearer. Maybe he has deserted us.

Imam: Do not wail, dear sister. Hurry, and send ^cAli Akbar to me.

Zaynab: [entering the tent of ^cAli Akbar]: Akbar, my darling, open your eyes. Fear makes my bones tremble. Open your eyes. Alas, O brother, there is no sign of ^cAli Akbar. Where has he gone? My sweet ^cAli Akbar?

Imam: Do not wail, do not weep, do not groan. Go, call the light of Hassan's eyes to my presence.

Zaynab [entering the tent of Qasim]: O tranquillity of my soul, O sweet Qasim is not in his bed either. Fate has turned against us.

Imam: O sister, gather all the children and sit in the tents. I shall look for ^cAbbas and Akbar so that I can thwart the army of darkness. O brave brother ^cAbbas, standard-bearer of my army, and ^cAli Akbar, my son, where have you gone?

[sees ^cAbbas]

O ^cAbbas, where have you been? Without you I am helpless.

^cAbbas: O mighty King, joy of Fatimah, greetings to you. Why do you hang your head? Why are you so sad? Are you thinking about martyrdom?

Imam: O light of my tearful eyes, greetings to you. Joy of my heart and my soul, greetings. Your absence in the encampment distressed me. I had to guard it alone against the infidel villain.

^cAbbas: Know, dear Brother, that in the middle of the night Shimr Zuljushan came to my tent. His words set fire to my heart and finally I chased him away with my sword.

Imam: I have heard that the commander of the enemy gave a written decree of amnesty to Shimr to deliver it to you. Go ahead, deny your brotherhood with the prophet's heir. Tell that helpless Zaynab she is not your sister. You need not help me, the forlorn one. ^cAli Akbar suffers for martyrdom with us. Go and save yourself, and God be with you.

^cAbbas: O friends, what should I do with my shame? Husayn has discharged me from his service. My sword and dagger are useless except in the service of my brother. If you, Husayn, are not my protector I have no use for my helmet. I shall go barefoot to do homage to my father's grave.

Where shall I turn for friends? O people, I am abandoned! Husayn had discharged me from his service—I am abandoned. O cruel Karbala', where is thy hospitality? O earth, I shall bury my head in your bosom for I have no mother to lean on. O Zephyr wind, blow on Medinah and tell my mother that I have been abandoned. I am without friends or family. The forlorn are buried without a shroud or camphor, and they take their dreams and hopes to their graves with them. How awful it is to die in a strange land. O dear Sakina, my niece, be my intercessor with Husayn. Go to your father and implore him on my behalf and tell him, 'O father, my uncle seems abandoned by family and friends. He is alone.'

Sakinah: O matchless uncle, why are you crying? May Sakina be your sacrifice. O uncle, do you want Husayn's head mounted upon a spear? I am distraught. Do you know what you have done? Uncle, you broke your promise to my father. You conversed with the damnable Shimr. You broke my father's back.

ᶜAbbas: Come here, dear niece. Come close, O broken-hearted one. Sit on my lap like a flower. Your sorrow has set me on fire. Your face is pale as the moon from thirst and there are fever blisters upon your lips. I am the water-carrier and it shames me. There is nothing I can do. Blood runs down my eyes from sorrow. Husayn is friendless and weary, a stranger in a sea of infidels. His young men will all die and Qasim shall wear a shroud instead of wedding garments. After I die the spring of our lives will dry up as in autumn and the world will succumb to the terror of our enemies. They will show their wickedness and set fire to our tents. I grieve for you, for they will burn your clothes and chain your arms and laugh at your cries and slap your beautiful face. Where will I be at that hour, to take revenge upon these infidels, to save you from evil?

[*There is a pause.*]

O Husayn, to whose court angels come in need, no one has ever dismissed a servant such as ᶜAbbas from his court. If you are ashamed of me as a brother, take me as a servant, do not thing that I am the darling of Medinah. Don't send me away from your blessed presence. It would be the greatest disloyalty to leave you. Take the standard away from me and give it to ᶜAli Akbar and let him be your standard-bearer instead of me.

Imam: Don't say these words, O ᶜAbbas. You are my most respected brother, O ᶜAbbas. Do you want to make me sad? Go say farewell to the distressed Zaynab.

ᶜAbbas: For the sake of the martyrs, I beg forgiveness from whomever I made unhappy or injured on this journey. Pretend it never happened.

Zaynab: O joy of my youth and the cane of my old age. You're going now, and by God my captivity will come true. My humiliation will be a guarantee of your eternal life.

ᶜAbbas: Alas, from now on it will not be possible for us any more to go from Hijaz to Medinah, in glorious grandeur, so that I could carry the flag in front of your camel all the way to the Prophet's grave.... .

Shaykh al-Mufid*

In the morning, [Imam Husayn] stopped and prayed the morning prayer. Then he hurried to remount and to continue the journey with his followers, veering to the left with the intention of separating from (al-Hurr's men). However al-Hurr ibn Yazid came towards him and stopped him and his followers (from going in that direction) and he began to (exert pressure to) turn them towards Kufah, but they resisted him. So they stopped (doing that) but they still accompanied them in the same way until they reached Ninawa, (which was) the place where al-Husayn, peace be on him, stopped. Suddenly there appeared a rider on a fast mount, bearing weapons and carrying a bow on his shoulder, coming from Kufah. They all stopped and watched him. When he reached them, he greeted al-Hurr and his followers and did not greet al-Husayn and his followers. He handed a letter from ᶜUbaydullah ibn Ziyad to al-Hurr. In it (was the following):

> When this letter reaches you and my messenger comes to you, make al-Husayn come to a halt. But only let him stop in an open place without vegetation. I have ordered my messenger to stay with you and not to leave you until he brings me (news of) your carrying out my instructions. Greetings.

Ed. Note: Other forms of Shiᶜi literature are concerned with historiography and establishing the central position of the Imams in the Shiᶜi life and world-view. They consist of eulogies of Imam Husayn or elaborate accounts of the Battle of Karbala'. Although this form of literature also promotes redemptive suffering, its primary function is to relay the historical facts as understood by the Shiᶜi theology from generation to generation. In this regard, this form of Shiᶜi literature also creates myth, which underlies the identity of every religion. Selections from Shaykh al-Mufid's Kitab al-Irshad *provides an example of historiography in the context of the Shiᶜi literature. The passage is from* KI, *pages 339–43.*

When al-Hurr had read the letter, he told them: "This is a letter from the governor ᶜUbaydullah. He has ordered me to bring you to a halt at a place which his letter suggests. This is his messenger and he has ordered him not to leave me until I carry out the order with regard to you."

Yazid (ibn Ziyad) ibn al-Muhajir al-Kindi who was with al-Hysayn, peace be on him, looked at the messenger of Ibn Ziyad and he recognized him.

"May your mother be deprived of you," he exclaimed, "what a business you have come to!"

"I have obeyed my Imam and remained faithful to my pledge of allegiance," (the other man) answered.

"You have been disobedient to your Lord and have obeyed your Imam in bringing about the destruction of your soul," responded Ibn al-Muhajir. "You have acquired (eternal) shame (for yourself) and (the punishment of) Hell-fire. What a wicked Imam your Imam is! Indeed God has said: *We have made them Imams who summon (people) to Hell-fire and on the Day of Resurrection they will not be helped. (XXVIII, 41)* Your Imam is one of those."

Al-Hurr ibn Yazid began to make the people stop in a place that was without water and where there was no village.

"Shame upon you, let us stop at this village or that one," said al-Husayn, peace be on him. He meant by that, Ninawa and al-Ghadiriyyah, and by that, Shufayyah.

"By God, I cannot do that," replied (al-Hurr), "for this man has been sent to me as a spy."

"Son of the Apostle of God," said Zuhayr ibn al-Qayn, "I can only think that after what you have seen, the situation will get worse than what you have seen. Fighting these people, now, will be easier for us than fighting those who will come against us after them. For by my life, after them will come against us such (a number) as we will not have the power (to fight) against."

"I will not begin to fight against them," answered al-Husayn.

That was Thursday, 2nd of (the month of) Muharram in the year 61 A.H. (680). On the next day, ᶜUmar ibn Saᶜd ibn Abi Waqqas set out from Kufah with four thousand horsemen. He stopped at Ninawa and sent for ᶜUrwa ibn Qays al-Ahmasi and told him: "Go to him (al-Husayn) and ask him: What brought you, and what do you want?"

ᶜUrwa was one of those who had written to al-Husayn, peace be on him, and he was ashamed to do that. The same was the case with all the leaders who had written to him, and all of them refused and were unwilling to do that. Kathir ibn ʿAbdullah al-Shaʿbi stood up—he was a brave knight who never turned his face away from anything—and said: "I will go to him. By God, if you wish, I will rush on him."

"I don't want you to attack him," said ʿUmar, "but go to him and ask him what has brought him."

As Kathir was approaching him, Abu Thumama al-Saʿidi saw him and said to al-Husayn, "May God benefit you. Abu ʿAbdullah, the wickedest man in the land, the one who has shed the most blood and the boldest of them all in attack, is coming towards you."

Then (Abu Thumama) stood facing him and said: "Put down your sword."

"No, by God," he replied, "I am only a messenger. If you will listen to me, I will tell you (the message) which I have been sent to bring to you. If you refuse, I will go away."

"I will take the hilt of your sword," answered (Abu Thumama), "and you can say what you need to."

"No, by God, you will not touch it," he retorted.

"Then tell me what you have brought and I will inform him for you. But I will not let you go near him, for you are a charlatan."

They both (stood there and) cursed each other. Then (Kathir) went back to ʿUmar ibn Saʿd and told him the news (of what had happened). ʿUmar summoned Qurra ibn Qays al-Hanzali and said to him: "Shame upon you Qurra, go and meet al-Husayn and ask him what brought him and what he wants."

Qurra began to approach him. When al-Husayn, peace be on him, saw him approaching, he asked: "Do you know that man?"

"Yes," replied Habib ibn Muzahir, "he is from the Hanzala clan of Tamim. He is the son of our sister. I used to know him as a man of sound judgement. I would not have thought that he would be present at this scene."

He came and greeted al-Husayn, peace be on him. Then he informed him of ʿUmar ibn Saʿd's message.

"The people of this town of yours wrote to me that I should come," answered al-Husayn, peace be on him. "However, if now you have come to dislike me, then I will leave you."

"Shame upon you Qurra," Habib ibn Muzahir said to him, "will you return to those unjust men? Help this man through whose fathers God will grant you (great) favour."

"I will (first) return to my leader with the answer to his message," replied Qurra, "and then I will reflect on my views."

He went back to ᶜUmar ibn Saᶜd and gave him his report.

"I hope that God will spare me from making war on him and fighting against him," said ᶜUmar and then he wrote to ᶜUbaydullah ibn Ziyad:

In the name of God, the Merciful, the Compassionate. I am (writing this from) where I have positioned myself, near al-Husayn, and I have asked him what brought him and what he wants. He answered: 'The people of this land wrote to me and their messengers came to me asking me to come and I have done so. However if (now) they have come to dislike me and (the position) now appears different to them from what their messengers brought to me, I will go away from them.'

[Hassan ibn Qa'id al-ᶜAbsi reported:]
I was with ᶜUbaydullah when this letter came to him, he read it and then he recited:

Now when our claws cling to him, he hopes for escape but he will be prevented (now) from (getting) any refuge.

He wrote to ᶜUmar ibn Saᶜd:

Your letter has reached me and I have understood what you mentioned. Offer al-Husayn (the opportunity) of him and all his followers pledging allegiance to Yazid. If he does that, we will then see what our judgement will be.

When the answer reached ᶜUmar ibn Saᶜd, he said: "I fear that ᶜUbaydullah will not accept that I should be spared (fighting al-Husayn)."

(Almost immediately) after it, there came (another) letter from Ibn Ziyad (in which he said): "Prevent al-Husayn and his followers from (getting) water. Do not let them taste a drop of it just as was done with ᶜUthman ibn ᶜAffan."

At once ᶜUmar ibn Saᶜd sent ᶜAmr ibn al-Hajjaj with five hundred horsemen to occupy the path to the water and prevent al-Husayn and his followers from (getting) water in order that they should (not) drink a drop of it. That was three days before the battle against al-Husayn, peace be on him.

ᶜAbdullah ibn al-Husayn al-Azdi, who was numbered among Bajila, called out at the top of his voice: "Husayn, don't you see that the water is as if in the middle of heaven. By God, you will not taste a drop of it until you die of thirst."

"O God, make him die of thirst and never forgive him," cried al-Husayn, peace be on him.

[Humayd ibn Muslim reported:]
By God, later I visited him when he was ill. By God, other than Whom there is no deity, I saw him drinking water without being able to quench his

thirst, and then vomiting. He would cry out, "The thirst, the thirst!" Again he would drink water without being able to quench his thirst, again he would vomit. He would then burn with thirst. This went on until he died, may God curse him.

When al-Husayn saw the extent of the number of troops encamped with ʿUmar ibn Saʿd, may God curse him, at Ninawa in order to do battle against him, he sent to ʿUmar ibn Saʿd that he wanted to meet him. The two men met at night and talked together for a long time. (When) ʿUmar ibn Saʿd went back to his camp, he wrote to ʿUbaydullah ibn Ziyad, may he be cursed.

> God has put out the fire of hatred, united (the people) in one opinion (lit. word), and set right the affairs of the community. This man, al-Husayn, has given me a promise that he will return to the place which he came from, or he will go to one of the border outposts—he will become like any (other) of the Muslims, with the same rights and duties as them; or he will go to Yazid, the Commander of the faithful, and offer him his hand and see (if the difference) between them (can be reconciled). In this (offer) you have the consent (to what you have demanded) and the community gains benefit... .

Chapter Twenty-five

Shi⁣ᶜism and Art

Although there exists no work on the philosophy of art from the viewpoint of Shiᶜism, the contribution of Shiᶜism to Islamic art and the place that art-forms play in Shiᶜi religious rites are well known. In themselves, they indicate the important place art occupies in Shiᶜi spiritual life. Such religious practices as the taᶜziyyah, *while religious in nature, utilize an array of art-forms and symbolism for conveying their spiritual message. Conversely, important forms of Islamic art has been born of Shiᶜism. Schimmel writes of the origins of Islamic calligraphy:*

> *"Muhammad's cousin and son-in-law, ᶜAli ibn Abi Talib is considered, by later calligraphers, as the first master of calligraphy who developed a certain style of Kufic writing where the tops of the* alifs *were twin-horned." (From Annemarie Schimmel.* Islamic Calligraphy. *Leiden, Netherlands: E.J. Brill, 1970, P.3).*

More evident, Shiᶜism has left an indelible mark upon the aesthetic principle of the Persian art. The influence of Shiᶜism has been manifest in Persian art since the time of the Safavids and even the Timurids and their architectural and artistic achievements, and continues to influence Iranian art to this day.

In the following two passages, first Nader Ardalan writes of the importance of the principle of light in Safavid architecture, then Seyyed Hossein Nasr discusses the significance of sacred art in Persian culture. The passages are from CSA, *pages 168–71, and* SAPC, *pages 6–18.*

Nader Ardalan

. . . Because man's creations are in inverse analogy with the Absolute, that his realizations attempt to create a temporal world of everythingness or saturation which symbolically issues forth the partial images of Absolute Existence. Thus in the world of darkness and shadow, light appears; and in the world of essential nothingness, there is a motivation towards everythingness and a saturation of the senses: visually through illuminated spaces, shapes and colors; audibly in speech, music and divine incantation; tangibly through silken, polished, incised or textured surfaces; odorously in fragrant rose gardens and musk perfumed bodies; and finally in taste, in the saffroned rice offerings (*nazr*) where through invocation one symbolically consumes the Divinity into his very being.

Thus, within the phenomenal world, the positive symbols of the concealed reality are exalted. It is this aspect of the world of symbols which plays a dominant role in the saturated use of colors within the creative expressions of the Safavid era. The world of colors is viewed as a manifest symbol of the concept of multiplicity. Just as multiplicity is emanated from Unity, so colors are viewed as emanations from the light of the Absolute. As Suhrawardi states, "Everything in the world is derived from the light of His Essence." Falling, however, through the colorless prism of the world of archetypes, this light is metaphorically refracted into the spectrum of rainbow colors that ultimately reaches the phenomenal world. Thus for the beholder a dilemma concerning the true essence of light and color occurs, but as al-Ghazzali explains,

> The difficulty of knowing God is therefore due to brightness; He is so bright that men's hearts have not the strength to perceive it. There is nothing brighter than the sun, for through it all things become manifest yet if the sun did not go down by night, or if it were not veiled by reason of the shadow, no one would realize that there is such a thing as light on the face of the earth. Seeing nothing but colors, they would say that nothing more exists. However, they have realized that light is a thing outside colors, the colors becoming manifest through it; they have comprehended light through its opposite. . . . He is hidden by His very brightness.

In the process of determination from the First to the Last, the world of color is made manifest and only by returning from the Last to the First can man find the Absolute Light. Within this traditional conception which can be viewed through the symbol of a triangle, the world of colors is associated with the expansion of the base, symbolizing multiplicity, and becomes clearly situated between the world of light, which descends from Unity, and that of darkness, through which Unity is once again regained.

Many metaphysical schemes have been developed in Islamic Persia that build upon this view, but one—that of the system of *haft rang* (seven colors) —has dominated the world of art and architecture. We shall explore further its particular aspects through the conceptual work of the thirteenth century poet and mystic, Nizami, who brilliantly depicted the essence of this system in his epic poem, the *Haft Paykar* (Seven Portraits). Here Nizami depicts the progress of the Sufi through the seven spiritual stages, symbolized by the seven colors which are metaphorically associated to numerous phenomena, such as the seven visible planets, the seven days of the week, the seven metals, the seven climates, the seven levels of traditional education, the seven parts of the body and the seven Prophets (from Abraham to Muhammad).

In the system of seven colors, white, black and sandalwood are viewed as the fist group of three colors, complemented by red, yellow, green and blue, viewed as the second grouping of four colors. Together they numerically constitute the super groupings of seven colors. This numerical distinction is critical for understanding the traditional color system. Objects or concepts taken in isolation are adverse to the Islamic view. Each phenomenon is viewed as part of a great totality to which, for the sake of intellectual clarity, numerical or geometrical characteristics are assigned. Thus a totality is evoked which is larger and more significant than any of its part.

In the system of three colors, three as number, and as triangle in geometry, reflects the fundamental conception. Viewed alternatively as the three motions of the spirit, it evokes the acts of descent, ascent and horizontal expansion.

White is the integration of all colors, pure and unstained. In its unmanifested state, it is the color of the Absolute before individualization, before the One became the many. Light, symbolically viewed as white, descends from the sun and symbolizes Unity.

As it is through white that color is made manifest, so through black it remains hidden, "hidden by its very brightness." Black is "a bright light in a dark day," as only through this luminous black can one find the hidden aspects of the Divine. Black is the annihilation of self, prerequisite to reintegration. It is the cloak of the Ka°bah, the mystery of Being, the light of Majesty, and the "color of the Divine Essence."

Sandalwood is the color of earth. It is the natural base upon which nature (the system of four colors) and the polar qualities of black and white act.

Symbolically, sandalwood is man to the micro-state, earth in the macro-scale, matter to the artisan, the neutral plane to the geometrician, and the floor to the architect.

In the system of four colors, four as number, and as square in geometry, reflects the conceptual configuration of Universal Soul manifested as the active qualities of nature (hot, cold, wet, dry) and the passive qualities of matter (first, water, air, and earth). The quadrants of the day, the quarters of the moon, the four seasons and the four divisions of man's temporal life are secondary reflections of this system. In vision, the primary colors are red, yellow, green, and blue. Red develops an association with fire. It expresses the vital spirit — active and expansive. Cyclically, it is morning, spring, and childhood. The complement of red is green. It characterizes water, the superior soul, passive and contractive. Cyclically, it is evening, fall and maturity. Yellow is air, contemplative, active, and expansive. It stands for noon, summer, and youth. It complements blue, which represents earth, the inferior soul, passive and contractive while symbolically it represents the end of the cycles, for it is night, winter and old age. Viewed as a movement through the four quadrants of a circle, the descending and ascending motions of these colors describe a full circle; the end of one cycle only signals the beginning of another.

Green is viewed in Islam as the superior of the four colors because it embodies all of the others. Yellow and blue join to form the balanced mixture of green, and its afterimage is red. Green is hope, fertility, and eternity with its two inherent dimension of past (blue) and future (yellow) and its opposite, the present seen as red.

Through the science of alchemy man associates himself with the temporal creative process. Alchemy has a twofold aspect. On the one hand, it is the science of a transformation of the soul of man; on the other, through the traditional arts and crafts, it is a science concernedd with the essences and processes of nature.

Traditional man participates in the creative process through the process of the transmutation of matter, the taking back of matter to its state as "hidden gold," as it were. The miniaturist or glazer of tiles participates in the alchemical process physically as well as spiritually. His choice of color symbolizes a particular state of consciousness. In the same way the mystic seeks the transformation of his soul. The method is one of reaching a state of purity and then internalizing it. Colors become an orientation for the mystic, the means by which he judges his level of realizations. He is beyond time, only the world of color provides for his direction and orientation... .

Seyyed Hossein Nasr

. . . Now, in a traditional view of the universe, reality is multi-structured. It possesses several levels of existence. It issues forth from the Origin or the One, from God, and it consists of many levels which can be summarized as the angelic, psychic and the physical worlds. It is to the metacosmic Source, then to Being, and finally to the three principal worlds mentioned above that the term the "Five Divine Presences' alludes. Man lives in the material world that is at the same time surrounded by all of the higher levels of existence above it. Traditional man lives in the awareness of this reality even if its metaphysical and cosmological exposition is beyond the ken of the 'ordinary believer' and reserved for the intellectual elite.

The sacred marks an eruption of the higher worlds in the psychic and material planes of existence. All that comes directly from the spiritual world — which stands directly above the psychic world and must never be confused with it, the one being *ruh* and the other *nafs* in Islamic parlance — is sacred, as is all that serves as a vehicle for the return of man to the spiritual world. But this second case is inseparable from the first because essentially only that which comes from the spiritual world can act as the vehicle to return to that world. The sacred, then, marks the 'miraculous' presence of the spiritual in the material, of heaven on earth. It is an echo from heaven to remind earthly man of his heavenly origin.

'Traditional' and 'sacred' are inseparable, of course, but not identical. The quality 'traditional' pertains to all the manifestations of a traditional civilization reflecting the spiritual principles of that civilization both directly and indirectly. 'Sacred,' however, especially as used in the case of art, must be reserved for those traditional manifestations which are directly connected with the spiritual principles in question, hence with religious and initiation rites and acts, with a sacred subject and a symbolism of a spiritual character. Opposed to the sacred stands the profane and opposed to the traditional, anti-traditional.

Because a tradition embraces all of man's life and activities, in a traditional society it is possible to have an art that has a quality of apparent 'worldliness' or 'mundaneness' and is yet traditional. But it is not possible to have an example of mundane sacred art. There is finally the possibility of a religious art which is not sacred art because its forms and means of execution are not traditional. Only it has chosen for its subject a religious theme. To such a category belong the religious paintings and architecture of the West since the Renaissance and also some of the popular religious paintings executed in the East during the past century or two under the influence of European art. Such religious art must be clearly distinguished from real sacred art... .

* * *

This universal meaning of art in its traditional sense must not of course obliterate the distinction made earlier between sacred art and that aspect of traditional art which is a less direct reflection of spiritual principles. The life of traditional man in all its aspects, from working to eating and sleeping, has a spiritual significance, but rites and specific religious acts nevertheless exist within the rhythm of daily life and reflect in a more direct fashion the principles which govern all life. In the same manner sacred art is a part of traditional art which is combined with the whole of traditional life, but it is concerned especially with those acts of making and doing that are directly connected with spiritual and religious rites and symbols. And because of this fact it is sacred art that is the most essential aspect of traditional art and the one whose survival is most directly connected with the survival of a religion, even after the structure of traditional society has been weakened or destroyed as we see in so many parts of the globe in modern times.

Before discussing the particular forms of sacred art in Persian culture throughout its history, it is necessary to elucidate further the relation between sacred art and a particular religious form, and the link between art and the initiatory organizations such as the Sufi orders. Because sacred art is the bridge between the material and the spiritual worlds, it is inseparable from the particular religion with which it is connected. There is no sacred or liturgical art possible in a vacuum any more than it is possible to 'write' a sacred scripture without a revelation from Heaven. There is Hindu, Buddhist and Muslim sacred art but not an Indian sacred art if by India we mean a land and a people. It is true that the genius of the ethnic group in question plays a role in the style and manner of execution of sacred art, as we see in the difference between the Buddhist art of Japan and Ceylon, but all these differences are within the limits of the principles established by both the spirit and the form of the religion in question. Sacred art derives from the spirit of a particular religion and shares its genius. It also makes use of a symbolism which is related to the form of the religion in question. And it is these elements that dominate. How different are the Hindu temple of Dasavatara and the Delhi mosque, both of which stand in India, or the naturalistic Roman temples and the other-worldly Romanesque churches, both located in Italy.

It is true that a religion can adopt certain forms and even artistic symbols of a previous religion, but in such a case the forms and symbols are completely transformed by the spirit of the new revelation, which gives a new life to them within its own universe of meaning. The techniques and forms of Roman architecture were adopted by Christian architecture to produce work of a very different spiritual quality. Both Islam and Byzantine Christianity adopted Sassanid techniques of dome construction and produced domed structures which, however, reflect two different types of art. In Persia itself Islamic art adopted many motifs of pre-Islamic Persia with its immensely rich artistic heritage as well as those of Central Asia, but they become transformed by the spirit of Islam and served as building blocks in structures whose design was completely Islamic. The same could be said in fact about the Zoroastrian art of the Achaemenian Period which adopted certain Babylonian and Urartu techniques and forms but certainly transformed them into something distinctly Zoroastrian.

To understand sacred art and its efficacy in any context it is far from sufficient to search out the historical borrowing of forms. What is important is what forms and symbols mean. And this question is unanswerable unless one has recourse to the religion which has brought the traditional civilization and sacred art in question into being. One could not understand, not to speak of create, works of sacred art without penetrating deeply into the religion which has produced these works. The attempt of some modern artists in both East and West to do so can be compared to trying to split the atom by copying the outward forms of the mathematical signs found in books of physics. But as far as the result is concerned, this is the opposite, for attempting to create such a so-called 'sacred art' is as lethal as the fallout from a successful atomic explosion.... .

* * *

The connection between art and spiritual methods is more firmly established and clear during the Islamic period. In the Islamic cities which throughout the ages have produced most of the objects of Islamic art, the craftsmen organized early into guilds (*asnaf* and *futuwwat*), which through their close relation with Sufism and the personality of ᶜAli himself derived direct spiritual inspiration from the very heart of the Islamic message. The famous saying, 'There is no man of chivalry but ᶜAli and no sword but the sword of ᶜAli', bears testimony to the basic link between the *futuwwat* and the Sufi orders, the vast majority of both of which derive their initiatory chain (*silsilah*) from ᶜAli. Through this spiritual and institutional link, which still survives in certain places, the masters of the guilds become initiated into the mysteries of Sufism and learn the metaphysical and cosmological doctrines which underly the symbolism of Islamic art, as of every true traditional art. The rest of the members of the guild in question emulate the methods, techniques and symbols involved without necessarily understanding all of the more profound levels of its meaning, although on their own level of understanding the work does have meaning for them. They can use all their creative energy in making it and are far from mere imitators of something they do not understand. The joy of creation present in authentic traditional works of art is the best proof of the creative joy of the artist. It is, moreover, because of this depth of expression innate to the symbols and images transmitted from the master to the craftsmen who study and work with him that often a work produced by a so-called uneducated craftsman has more profundity and intelligence than what many a so-called educated onlooker has the capability to understand.

This same intimate relationship exists between Islam in general and Sufism in particular and the other forms of art. It is not accidental that the vast majority of the great musicians of Persia were connected in one way or another with Sufism or that the most universal poetry of the Persian language is Sufi poetry. Even in calligraphy the number of men associated in one way or another with the esoteric dimension of Islam who were masters of the art is great indeed.

As far as the plastic arts are concerned, in Persia, as in certain other civilizations such as the Christian West, the Hermetic sciences and particularly alchemy played an intermediary role between the purely metaphysical and cosmological doctrines of Islam and the making of things. Art, according to its Islamic definition, is to ennoble matter. Alchemy likewise is a symbolic science of material objects, of minerals and metals in their connection with the psychic and spiritual worlds. It is not, as so many have thought, a prechemistry. It is basically a science of the transformation of the soul based upon the symbolism of the mineral kingdom. For this very reason it also is a way of ennobling matter, of turning base metal into gold. The relation between alchemy and are in Persia, as in Islamic art in general, has been profound. The colours used in so many works of art, far from being accidental, are related to their alchemical symbolism. Through alchemy and similar cosmological sciences Islam was able to create an ambience that was Islamic in both form and content, one in which the religious and spiritual principles were imprinted on matter, in the world that surrounds man in his daily life and has such a profound effect upon the attitude of his mind and soul.

*   *   *

The sacred art of Islam is related in both form and spirit to the Divine Word as revealed in the Holy Qur'an. The Word having been revealed as a book, rather than as a human being as is the case with Christianity, the sacred art concerns the manifestation of the letters and sounds of the Holy Book rather than the iconography of a man who is himself the Logos. The sacred art of Islam in the domain of the plastic arts is more than anything else mosque architecture and calligraphy. One creates a space in which the Divine Word is echoed and the other lines and letters which can be said to be the external form of the Word in the alphabet in which it was revealed, the alphabet of the Arabic and the Persian languages. There are other important forms of traditional Islamic art, but the sacred art *par excellence* consists of architecture and calligraphy, which moreover are inextricably related to the meaning and form of the Holy Qur'an and may be said to 'flow' from it.

The space created inside a mosque far from being arbitrary and accidental is planned deliberately to remove those coagulations and tensions which would prevent the Word from spreading in an illimitable and harmonious space, a space filled with peace and equilibrium in which the Spirit is everywhere rather than being localised in a particular icon or statue. The iconoclasm of Islam, about which so much has been said, does not mean that Islam is opposed to sacred art, without which no religion can create an appropriate ambience for its earthly manifestations. Rather it means that Islam refuses to imprison the Spirit or the Word in any form which would endanger the freedom innate to the Spirit and kill its reflections through imprisonment in matter. It is also related in a principal manner to the insistence of Islam upon 'Divine Unity' (*tawhid*), which cannot be represented in images, and the spiritual style of Islam, which is 'nomadic' rather than 'sedentary' and hence seeks to avoid coagulation in space.

The architecture of the mosque, therefore, in the aims it seeks to achieve and the spiritual reality it creates, derives from the spirit of the Holy Qur'an, no matter what building techniques Islamic architecture borrowed from Sassanid, Byzantine and other sources. Even the outer forms of mosques soon developed so as to reflect through its symbolism, in a clear manner and with blinding evidence, the different Divine Names and Qualities, the dome corresponding to the Divine Beauty (*jamal*) and the minarets to the Divine Majesty (*jalal*). Many varieties of architectural style were developed, according to the ethnic genius of the people involved, but a profound relationship exists which causes mosques as widely separated as the mosque of Cordova, the Jami͗ mosque of Isfahan and the Delhi mosque be united within a single spiritual universe.

Likewise in calligraphy, the very forms and their symbolism are related to the Holy Qur'an and its manner of expression. Here again, different styles have developed according to the genius of the people concerned. The Persians, for example, have been especially known as masters of the *nasta͗liq* and *shikastih*, while the Turks have always produced excellent masters of the *naskh*. Calligraphy in Islamic art has made possible a most powerful decorative art which, however, far from being just a decoration represents also a spiritual style. In the decorated mosque, architecture so typical of the tiled mosques of Persia, the two basic forms of sacred art, architecture and calligraphy, join hands to create a crystal in which is reflected a ray of the light of heaven amidst the darkness of material existence.

One of the remarkable features of Islamic architecture, almost unique in the history of art, is that it reached a peak early in its career and has preserved it to our own times. A traditional style of architecture results not from the false deity of modern times called 'a period' or 'the times,' but from the encounter of the spiritual style of a particular religion and the ethnic genius of a particular people that embraces that religion. That is why the style remains valid as long as that religion and the people in question survive. Persian Islamic architecture presents a perfect example. From the Damghan mosque to the contemporary traditional mosques there are certainly variations, but always upon the basis of a permanence and continuity that is too evident to need elucidation. Our Persian ancestors were too little concerned with 'their times' to produce a local style that, because of its belonging to a particular date, would also soon become out-of-date. They produced an art that was intemporal, that breathed of the eternal and hence was valid for all ages.

Those modern Persians who want to change the style of sacred art, especially mosque architecture, should ponder over the question as to why their 'times' or 'period' should be any different or more important than any other 'times' or 'period' which continued to propagate the traditional styles of Islamic architecture. A profound analysis would reveal that the desire to change the style of mosque architecture issues in most cases not from the so-called exigencies of 'our times,' but from the fact that most of the people who want to carry out such changes have themselves fallen out of the Islamic tradition and have even become alienated from the ethnic genius of the Persian people. Honesty would demand that one not label one's own shortcomings with such epithets as 'necessities of the times' and that one not have the audacity to seek to create a new form of sacred architecture when one has no notion of either the spirit or the form of the religion which has brought the architecture in question into being, or even of the deeper roots of the culture of one's own people — who have nurtured this architectural style over the centuries. The catastrophe brought about in any religion by the destruction of its sacred art is no less than that brought about by the weakening of its moral and spiritual teachings and the negation of the injunctions contained in its Divine Law.

In the realm of the plastic arts, Islamic Persia created other important forms of traditional art which are connected with the forms of sacred art directly related to its religious rites and doctrines. In the realm of architecture, the traditional Persian home is a kind of extension of the mosque in the sense that it perpetuates its purity and simplicity. The carpets over which one does not walk with shoes, their ritual cleanliness which enables man to pray upon them like the carpets of the mosque, the 'emptiness' of the traditional rooms devoid of furniture, and many other elements connect the house in spirit to the mosque. On a larger scale the whole of city planning is related to the mosque not only through the central role of the mosque in the traditional city, but also in a much more subtle way through the domination of the principle of unity and integration over the whole of the Muslim city, from the private home to the city as a totality. Isfahan and Kashan still afford excellent examples of this principle.

Other traditional plastic arts related to the sacred arts include the so-called 'minor arts,' which are of extreme importance because they surround man in his daily life and hence influence him deeply. In this realm the 'seal of the sacred' is to be seen even in the most common everyday objects. The rugs are a recapitulation of paradise, bound by a frame and looking inward toward the centre like the courtyard and the Persian garden. The traditional dress in all its forms not only facilitates the Islamic rites but also reveals the theomorphic nature of man rather than hiding it.

The miniature, which is intimately bound with book illustrations, is an 'extension' of calligraphy and again a recapitulation of the states of paradise. Based on the wholeness of life which characterizes traditional Persian culture, all of the different forms of art are inter-related through the traditional principles which have introduced into them something of the sacred and of the spiritual principles dominating all aspects of the life of traditional man... .

Chapter Twenty-six

Shi*c*ism and the Natural Sciences and Mathematics

*In Islam there always has been a tradition of scientific inquiry within the framework of religious thought. The synthesis of religion and science in Islam produced a unified system of thought and a philosophy of science that emanated from the fountainhead of religious truth. Shi*c*ism, as Nasr points out, contributed greatly to the fusion of Islam and science throughout Islamic history and was particularly conducive to the study of the early or* awa'il *sciences and their continuation within Islamic intellectual life.*

The passage is from IICD, *pages 14–18.*

Seyyed Hossein Nasr

. . . It may of course be asked why the fourth and fifth centuries were a period of great activity in the sciences. The reason is to be sought partially in the historical circumstances of the time. If we divide the Islamic community into the two categories of the Sunni and the Shi^{c}i, we find that during the period of strength of the Sunni caliphate, both Umayyad and ^{c}Abbasid, there was a different social and political background for the growth of the arts and sciences from that which characterized the period when the central authority had weakened and Shi^{c}i elements had become powerful.

In order to understand the reason for this distinction we must return to the first two centuries of Islamic history. From certain sayings of ^{c}Ali ibn Abu Talib and especially the writings of Imam Ja^{c}far al-Sadiq, the first and sixth Shi^{c}i *imams*, it is quite evident that the Hermetic sciences were early integrated into the Shi^{c}i perspective. One need only remember that Jabir ibn Hayyan, the most celebrated of all Muslim alchemists, was the disciple of Imam Ja^{c}far and considered all of his works to be no more than an account of the teachings of his master. Moreover, the discussions of Imam Rida, the eighth Shi^{c}i *imam*, with Ma'mun and ^{c}Imran al-Sabi, made the intellectual sciences (*al-^{c}ulum al-^{c}aqliyah*) once and for all legitimate in the world of Shi^{c}ism.

The early acceptance of Hermeticism by the Shi^{c}is made them the proponents of a synthetic physics, a "periodic" conception of time as consisting of different cycles, or *adwar* and *akwar*, and the tradition of Hippocratic medicine tied to alchemy. Likewise, it made them opposed to the rationalistic elements of Aristotle's philosophy and many aspects of his physics. Consequently, when philosophy did finally become integrated into the Shi^{c}i perspective, it was not in the form of pure Aristotelianism but as that form of wisdom called *hikmah* in which illuminationist and gnostic doctrines play a central role and in which reason becomes only the first stage and discursive knowledge the most elementary form of knowledge to be followed by the direct contemplation of the intelligible realities.

In the Sunni world, "official" learning did not concern itself so much with either Hermeticism or Peripatetic philosophy, except to the degree that philosophical methods were adopted to theological ends by the great Sunni theologians like Imam al-Ghazzali and Fakhr al-Din al-Razi. In fact, from the beginning the Sunnis displayed a greater hostility toward the philosophers than the Shi^{c}is, as demonstrated by the historical evidence of the surival of philosophy, in its new wedding with illumination and gnosis in the orm of *hikmah*, among the Shiᶜis long after it had ceased to exist as a living radition in the Sunni world.

The opposition of the Sunni doctors of the law to philosophy and most of he pre-Islamic (*awa'il*) sciences became more intense after the destruction of the Muᶜtazilites and the triumph of Ashᶜarite theology during the ourth/tenth and fifth/eleventh centuries. Likewise, the Sunni caliphate usually was more favorable to the purely religious disciplines such as the cience of commentary, *hadith*, and jurisprudence, and supported the other ciences like medicine and astronomy only to the extent that they corresponded to the needs of the community.

When we take into account this difference in attitude of the Sunni and the Shiᶜis toward the arts and sciences, it becomes somewhat easier to discover he causes underlying the great activity in the various sciences during the ourth/tenth and fifth/eleventh centuries, the period which we have chosen o study in this book. For it is during these centuries, that Shiᶜism becomes important politically and socially... .

During the fourth/tenth and fifth/eleventh centuries we have discovered that his period was a period during which the authority of the central Sunni government had weakened and Shiᶜi princes were ruling over a large segment of the slamic world. Considering the more sympathetic attitude of Shiᶜism oward the pre-Islamic sciences and philosophy which we have already mentioned, it is not surprising to discover that this period of Shiᶜi domination coincides with a time of great activity in the various intellectual sciences. In act it may be safely asserted that the rise of Shiᶜis in this period was the chief reason for the greater attention paid to the arts and sciences. The Shiᶜis, both in Persia and Egypt, founded schools in which the sciences were aught and established educational and scientific procedures that were later adopted by the Sunnis themselves, as exemplified by the adoption of al-Azhar — originally founded by the Fatimids — for Sunni learning and the building of the Nizamiyyah school in Baghdad upon earlier Shiᶜi models.

The fourth/tenth and fifth/eleventh centuries constitute, therefore, the period of the formation of the Islamic arts, sciences, and philosophy and he period in which the basis of the Islamic sciences was laid, in such a way as to determine the general contour of these sciences as they have been cultivated in the Muslim world ever since. It may be said, then, that to study he sciences in this period is to study the root and formation of the various Islamic sciences and not just a passing moment in the long centuries of Islamic history... .

Part VI

Shi⁽c⁾i Thought in the Twentieth Century

Chapter Twenty-seven

Continuity and Change in the Intellectual Heritage

Most works on modern Shi^{c}i history have tended to focus on the changes in Shi^{c}i political thought and institutions that became apparent during the Pahlavi era in Iran. Implicit in these works is the belief that traditional Shi^{c}i philosophical thought no longer exists or is of any relevance to the reality of Shi^{c}ism. Shi^{c}i intellectual exercises in modern times, in the aforementioned works, begin and end with the writings of activist ^{c}Ulama', on the one hand, and left-leaning lay thinkers, on the other.

Yet, closer examination of Shi^{c}i thought in twentieth century Iran reveals a picture by far more complex and rich than is suggested by studies that fail to go beyond "Shi^{c}i modernism". To this day, traditional Shi^{c}i thought has continued to persist in the Muslim world, both continuing the heritage of such well-known figures as Mulla Sadra or ^{c}Allamah al-Hilli, and changing with view to the sacrosanct canons of the faith, in order to accommodate Shi^{c}ism to the new world and provide answers for the dilemma posed to the faithful by modernity.

In the following section, first Seyyed Hossein Nasr provides an overview of Shi^{c}i thought in twentieth century Iran. Then, selections from the works of ^{c}Allamah Tabataba'i, Hajj Abu'l-Hasan Husayni Qazwini, Murtada Mutahhari, Sayyid Muhammad Baqir Sadr, shed light on the complexity and the nature of continuity and change in traditional Shi^{c}i thought in modern times. The passages are from IPCP, *pages 5–20;* MSCV, *pages 215–17 and 7–22;* PCIP, *pages 66–82; Shams Inati's forthcoming translation of Sadr's seminal work,* Falsafatuna *(Our Philosophy).*

Seyyed Hossein Nasr

One of the unfortunate shortcomings of modern Western scholarship concerning the Islamic world is that while serious studies are often made of the intellectual and spiritual life of what is usually called the "medieval" period, when it comes to the contemporary era most of the studies are limited to the social, economic and political fields. A picture of the contemporary Islamic world is usually drawn depicting it as if it contained nothing of intellectual interest. Even the studies made in art and literature are usually limited only to those individuals or trends that seek to innovate and break existing traditions while the surviving tradition is laid aside as if it did not exist, no matter how vital and active it might be. The bias inherent in most techniques and methods of current research to measure only change ignores permanence by definition no matter how significant the permanent and continuing traditions may be in reality. This is *a priori* judgement of the significance of change and "evolution" vis-à-vis the permanent background of things, combined with the still widely accepted image of the Islamic intellectual tradition as nothing more than a bridge between the Hellenistic world and medieval Europe, have prevented for the most part serious studies from being made about Islamic intellectual life in its more current phase.

In this survey we wish partially to redress this neglect by describing recent activity in Persia in the domain of Islamic philosophy (*hikmat*), thus drawing the attention of the Western audience to one of the main arenas of Islamic intellectual life which has remained especially neglected until now. There are altogether three groups of people who concern themselves with philosophy in Persia today: the completely traditionally educated men who have kept alive the tradition of Islamic philosophy to this day; the scholars who have had both a traditional and a modern education and who combine often the traditional approach with modern techniques of research and exposition; and finally, those who are primarily concerned with the secular, modern European philosophy. Here we are concerned only with the first two groups and not with the third, whose very subject matter differs completely in character from traditional Islamic philosophy although even among this group a few of the better translators have a firm background in the Islamic sciences.

Among the traditional masters of Islamic philosophy most active during the past two decades may be mentioned ᶜAllamah Sayyid Muhammad Husayn Tabataba'i, who is the author of numerous works including the twenty-volume Qur'anic commentary *al-Mizan*, the *Usul-i falsafah* with the commentary of Murtada Mutahhari, and *cAli wa'l-hikmat al-ilahiyyah*, and who is also responsible for the new edition of the *Asfar* of Mulla Sadra, Sayyid Abu'l-Hasan Rafici Qazwini, the great master of Mulla Sadra's school who has written only a few treatises but has trained many outstanding students such as Sayyid Jalal al-Din Ashtiyani, who has studied with both him and cAllamah Tabataba'i; Sayyid Muhammad Kazim cAssar former professor of Islamic philosophy at Tehran University and the Sipahsalar madrasah and the author of *Thalath rasa'il fi'l-hikmat al islamiyyah*, and numerous scattered works now being printed together under the direction of S. J. Ashtiyani; Mirza Ahmad Ashtiyani, known especially for his mastery of ethics and gnosis and the author of *Namah-rahbaran-i amuzish-i kitab-i takwin*; Mahdi Ilahi Qumsha'i, former professor of Tehran University and author of the well-known two-volume *Hikmat-i ilahi khass wa camm*, which has been printed several times, cAllamah Muhammad Salih Ha'iri Simnani, the most loyal follower of Peripatetic philosophy in Persia today, standing "opposed" to the school of Mulla Sadra and the author of *Hikmat-i Bu cAli*; Hajji Aqa Rahim Arbab the last grand master of the school of Isfahan who, although he has not written much on Islamic philosophy, has trained many fine students; cAbd al-Wahhab Shacrani, the editor of Sabziwari's *Asrar al-hikam*; Jalal Huma'i, one of the most outstanding literary figures and scholars of contemporary Persia who, in addition to his numerous works on Persian literature and the Islamic sciences, has also produced the finest modern study of Ghazzali in Persian, the *Ghazzali Namah*; Mahmud Shahabi, both jurisprudent and traditional philosopher, author of a study of Ibn Sina's *al Isharat wa'l-tanbihat*; Jawad Muslih, known especially for his partial translation of the *Asfar* of Mulla Sadra into Persian as *Falsafah-i cali*; Husayn Quli Rashid, famous Khurasani preacher who has written *Daw filsuf-sharq wa gharb*, comparing Mulla Sadra's theory of motion with Einstein's theory of relativity; Sayyid Muhammad Mishkat, the editor of many important philosophical treatises by al-Hilli, Kashani, Ibn Sina, Qutb al-Din Shirazi and others and the author of several independent treatises written before the period under consideration in this essay; and finally a lady of Isfahan who usually signs her works as "a Persian lady" (*Yak banu-yi irani*) and who has written a dozen works on ethics, gnosis, eschatology and religious sciences including *Macad ya akhirin sayr-i bashar*, and a commentary upon the Qur'an.

The younger traditional scholars who have been most active recently in Islamic philosophy include Mirza Mahdi Ha'iri, the only one of the traditional class of *hakims* with an extensive experience of the West and the author of *cIlm-i kulli*, and *Kawishha-yi caql-i nazari*, which marks an important phase in the encounter of traditional Islamic philosophy and Western thought; Murtada Mutahhari, a prolific author whose philosophical studies include the commentary upon ʿAllamah Tabataba'i's *Usul-i falsafah* and the recent edition of Bahmanyari's *Kitab al-tahsil*; and finally Sayyid Jalal al-Din Ashtiyani, the most prolific of the contemporary traditional philosophers whose incredible output during the past decade includes *Hasti az nazar-i falsafah wa ʿirfan*, an edition of Mulla Sadra's *al-Mazahir al-ilahiyyah*, an edition of Mulla Muhammad Jaʿfar Lahijani's commentary (*Sharh al-mashaʿir*) upon Mulla Sadra's *Mashaʿir*, *Sharh-i hal wa ara-yi falsafi-yi Mulla Sadra*, *Sharh bar muqaddamah-i Qaysari dar tasawwuf-i islami*, an edition of Mulla Sadra's *al-Shawahid al-rububiyyah* with the commentary of Sabziwari, and an edition of Sabziwari's *Majmuʿah-i rasa'il*.

The Scholars with Both Traditional and Modern Training

As for the second group, some of the more active among them are Yahya Mahdawi, Ghulam Husayn Sadiqi, Mahdi Muhaqqiq, Seyyed Hossein Nasr, ʿAli Murad Dawudi, Sayyid Abu'l-Qasim Pur-Husayni, Rida Dawari, Sayyid Jaʿfar Sajjadi, Muhammad Taqi Danechepazhuh, Ahmad Fardid, Muhammad Khwansari, Fathallah Mujtab'i, Hasan Malikshahi, Sayyid ʿAli Musawi Bihbahani, and Ibrahim Dibaji, all of Tehran University; Akbar Danasirisht, an independent scholar of Tehran, Ghulam Husayn Ahani and Ismaʿil Waʿiz Jawadi of Isfahan University, Karamat Raʿna Husayni of the Department of Culture and Fine Arts of Shiraz [University], ʿAbd al-Muhsin Mishkat al-Dini and Zayn al-Din Zahidi (Jurabchi) of Mashhad University (who could also be included in the first group), and Muhammad Jawad Falaturi now teaching at the University of Koln in Germany. To this list must of course be added the scholars in the field of Arabic and Persian such as Zabihullah Safa, Mojtaba Minovi, Ghulam Husayn Yusufi and Sayyid Jaʿfar Shahidi who, although not technically in the field of Islamic philosophy, have made important contributions to it through editorial works and scholarly studies.

Centers for the Study of Islamic Philosophy

Islamic philosophy as taught and studied by the first two groups mentioned above has its center in either the traditional *madrasahs*, especially those of Qum, Tehran, Mashhad, and Isfahan as well as Najaf in Iraq, or in universities and institutes, or finally in private circles where much of traditional philosophical instruction is still carried out. As to universities, by far the most important until now has been Tehran, where in both the Faculty of Theology and the philosophy department of the Faculty of Letters and Humanities many courses are offered in Islamic philosophy, both on the undergraduate and graduate levels. But also of importance are the Faculties of Letters and Humanities of Tabriz and Isfahan Universities. Those Institutes that have played an active role in the publication of Islamic philosophical works include: *Anjuman-i athar-i milli, Bunyad-i farhang-i Iran, Anjuman-i tarjamah wa nashr-i kitab*, and two supported by sources from abroad: the French Institut Franco-Iranian, and the Tehran branch of the McGill Institute. The first, which is more precisely the department of Iranian Studies of the Institut Franco-Iranian, has played a very important role in making works of Islamic philosophy known to both East and West as well as in arousing interest among Persians themselves in their own intellectual tradition. Directed for over twenty years by the celebrated French orientalist and philosopher, Henry Corbin, the Institute has published seventeen works on Islamic Philosophy.

The Institute also possesses one of the best libraries anywhere on Islamic philosophy. Professor Corbin himself has conducted many seminars at Tehran University during this period, the past decade usually in collaboration with Seyyed Hossein Nasr. Corbin has also participated over the years in many private discussions and study groups mostly with ᶜAllamah Sayyid Muhammad Husayn Tabataba'i. These encounters, during which often many other noteworthy scholars such as the late Badiᶜ al-Zaman Furuzanfar and Murtada Mutahhari have been present, represent one of the most interesting intellectual encounters between East and West in recent years. They have influenced the writings of Corbin as well as those of the Persian scholars present. In fact a volume entitled *Musahabah-i ᶜAllamah Tabataba'i ba ustad Corbin* has been produced based upon the discussions which have taken place during these gatherings.

The activities of the second foreign Institute, the Tehran Branch of McGill Institute of Islamic Studies, is of much more recent origin. It began two years ago in 1969 when Professor T. Izutsu came to Tehran to co-direct the Institute with Mahdi Muhaqqiq of Tehran University. Since then many scholars and students have visited it. Despite its short life, however, the Institute has already produced a major work in its "Persian Wisdom Series,' the *Ghurar al-fara'id* or *Sharh-i manzumah* of Sabziwari, with an extensive English analysis of his metaphysics by Izutsu. There have also been regular lectures by eminent scholars at the Institute and the first number of its bulletin, entitled *Collected Papers on Islamic Philosophy and Mysticism*, has just appeared. The scholars in the Institute are now busy with the first critical edition of the *Qabasat* of Mir Damad, the glosses of Mirza Mahdi Ashtiyani upon Sabziwari's *Sharh-i manzumah*, and the *Kashif al-asrar* of Isfara'ini which are all to appear shortly... .

ᶜAllamah Tabataba'i

As can be deduced from his own words, Mulla Sadra, at the end of the first period of his intellectual life, came to realize that one should not limit the path of reaching the truth in the sciences and especially metaphysics to dry and uninspired thought which was the method of the Peripatetics. Rather, human perception and intelligence which are the roots of the universal philosophical ideas can bring forth from themselves not only thoughts based upon logical deductions but also other types which are called intellectual intuition, illumination and revelation. And just as among logical thoughts one arrives at things whose reality and principality one can never deny, so does one reach realities of the same nature in the case of intuition, illumination and revelation.

In other words, after man's capacity to see reality is proven by scientific demonstration and it is shown that man's unquestionable perceptions are externally manifested and tell of an external reality, there is no longer any difference between certain demonstration and decisive intellectual intuition; the realities that are reached by means of contemplation based on certainty are like the realities which have been ascertained through logical thought. Likewise, after definitely ascertained demonstration has acnkowledged the truth and reality of prophecy and revelation, there is no longer any difference among genuine religious subjects which describe the truth about the origin and end of things and between the deductions of logical demonstration and intellectual intuition.

As a result of this mental transformation, Mulla Sadra based his philosophical and scientific arguments upon the harmony between reason, intuition and religion, and to discover the verities of metaphysics, made use of logical foundations, truths discovered through contemplation and definitely established religious verities. Although the root of this point of view is to be found also in the writings of Farabi, Ibn Sina, Shaykh a-Ishraq Shihab al-Din Suhrawardi, Shams al-Din Turkah and Khwajah Nasir al-Din Tusi, it was Sadr al-Muti'allihin who succeeded fully in realizing this idea.

* * *

The complete and thorough investigation of religious truths and verities discovered through intuition and their harmonization with logical demonstration gave Sadr al-Din many new foundations and subjects and many new possibilities for extending philosophical discussions, creating new ones and discovering novel and very profound views which could never have been discovered by pure thought alone. That is why in the school of Mulla Sadra the spirit of philosophy was renewed and a considerable amount of new discussions were added to it.

Sadr al-Muti'allihin inaugurates his philosophy with the question of the principiality and then gradation of being and in every succeeding problem seeks to deduce conclusions from these two ideas and establish the basis of the problem upon them.

In the first question he explains that although in opposition to the Sophists and Sceptics, he accepts Being and Reality and proves existing quiddities (*mahiyyat*) for objects and believes that external species have a quiddity belonging to their species and their being, since there is only one reality for each external object, in this external manifestation either quiddity or being must be principial, the other subsisting as the accident of the first.

Since the intellect considers the being and quiddity or essence of things to be separated from each other and quiddity in itself to be equivalent with respect to being and non-being, while being is identical with the reality of being, it must be principial and identical with reality, and quiddity a kind of mental manifestation and appearance. In reality, quiddities are mental limits that the mind abstracts from the limitations of beings. For example, man is [Mulla Sadra] explains that the being of things which is principial and with respect to which the quiddities are accidental, is of one kind in all objects and all beings. And since principiality belongs to being all that can be imagined outside of it is false and unreal.

In the second problem, i.e., that of the gradation of being, which in reality is divided into two problems, one the unity of the truth of being and the other the difference and distinction of the levels of this single truth, Akhund [Mulla Sadra] explains that the being of things which is principal and with respect to which the quiddities are accidental, is of one kind in all objects and all beings. And since principality belongs to being all that can be imagined outside of it is false and unreal.

All the differences that can be observed in external beings, such as the difference in cause and effect, unity and multiplicity, potentiality and actuality, precedence and antecedence and the like, which are real, all come from and take place in being. As a result, being is a single reality which, without any external addition, has differences and distinctions in itself, i.e., that same reality which the being of two objects share mutually is that through which they are distinct and different from each other.

According to Mulla Sadra, this truth is symbolized by physical light which, as can be seen, in spite of its various degrees of intensity, makes objects apparent through its manifestations. The differences which we can sense in light and its dimness and luminosity is not in that dim light is composed of light and darkness, since darkness is non-existent and has no place in being so that it cannot become a part of dim light. Nor is it in that dim light lacks something of the meaining of light which does not exist in the nature of light or that intense light possesses something in addition to light through which it becomes more luminous. Rather, in reality dim light is weak in the very meaning of light that it possesses and has a specific degree and limit, and the intensity of strong light comes back again to the fact that it is light having a determined degree of intensity. What the two degrees of light share in common is the meaning of light, and that in which they differ is also this meaning of light.

The truth of being also has different degrees in its strength and weakness and perfection and imperfection. Its highest degree is the Necessary Being Who is pure perfection devoid of all limits and imperfections and pure actuality. Its lowest degree is the *materia prima* which is imperfect in every sense and is potentiality, its only actuality being that it is potential. Between these two degrees which are situated at the two ends of the chain there are gradations which from the rational point of view are compoased of perfection and imperfection, potentiality and actuality. The higher we ascent in the scale, the greater is the perfection and actuality and the lower we descend the greater the imperfection and potentiality.

The technical expression for this view is the "graded unity of being" (*wahdat-i tashkiki-i wujud*). The proof of these three basic points, i.e. the principiality, unity and gradation of the truth of being, changes completely the conception of the Universe with all that is in it. What appeared at first through simple perception as a world of beings consisting of a series of quiddities or essences without any relations with one another, and separated and strange to each other, disappears from the mind of the philosopher. In its place there appears the luminous truth of Being which possesses the quality of unity and oneness while at the same time having different stages and degrees which, despite being distinct from one another and yet related together.

The world of being can be symbolized by an unlimited luminous space whose source of light, which exists at the heart of it above time and place, illuminates all things constantly with its irradiations and flashes, and its rays depending upon their distance from their source are manifested in their own place with different degrees of intensity, conditions and effects.

It is, therefore, evident that a philosophy which considers the beings of the world in this light differs completely in its method of discussion from a philosophy that considers the world as a series of separated and scattered quiddities and sees all phenomena as independent of one another. In addition, with this method a series of fundamental and profound questions come into being which cannot be proven or solved by any other irregular and unorderly means of discussion.

It is this philosophical method that brought about a wedding between intuition and reason in the sense that it clarified a series of intuitive questions by logical demonstration and put subjects which can be discovered only through intellectual illumination in a logical dress and placed them among philosophical qeustions which come as a result of logical demonstration. As a result, philosophical questions which in the school of Greece and Alexandria amount to at most two hundred problems through this methods became about seven hundred in number.

Mulla Sadra after discussing fully these three problems and the general principles of being such as its simplicity and other negative principles of being, turns to the general divisions of being which are as follows:

1. The division of being into external (*khariji*) and mental (*zihni*). In this discussion he analyzes the science of notions and judgments and the generation of quiddities and concepts in the mind and their kind of being.

2. The division of being into independent (*mustaqil*) and connective (*rabit*). In this discussion beings are divided into two distinct types, and relative and connective beings which have no independence in either essence or conditions or effects are distinguished and separated from independent beings. From the fruitful effects of this division it can be concluded that possible beings are relative and connective with respect to the Necessary Being and have no independence in their essence or effects, and whatever independence is observed in them comes from the Necessary Being.

3. The division of being into in itself (*li nafsih*) and in other than itself (*li ghayrih*). In this division the truth and meaning of the existence of qualities becomes distinct from non-qualities. A discussion independent of these three divisions did not exist before Mulla Sadra.

4. The division of being into the Necessary (*wajib*) and possible (*mumkin*) in which the characteristics of the Necessary and the possible are discussed in detail.

5. The discussion of quiddities (*mahiyyat*) which is in reality the continuation of the discussion on possible beings. In this discussion the division of quiddities into genus and species and the like and their characteristics are mentioned. As an adjunct to this question Sadr al-Muti'allihin gives a thorough discussion of the question of

the archetypes (*'arbab al-'anwa^c*) or "Platonic ideas" and proves their existence.

6. The division of being into unity (*wahid*) and multiplicity (*kathir*) and their features.

7. The division of being into cause (*^cillah*) and effect (*ma^clul*) and an explanation of their kinds and characteristics.

8. The division of being into potentiality (*quwwah*) and actuality (*fi^cl*). In this division being is separated into two categories: actual being, which is a being complete and perfect in itself and its ontological effects evident and constant like a fully grown human individual who is by necessity human and manifests human effects; and potential being which contains the possibility of particular being and has still not manifested its necessary effects like the being of man in the human sperm. The matter of the sperm is in actuality *sperm* and in potentiality *man* but it does not as yet display the necessary signs of being human.

Previous philosophers considered the going of something from potentiality to actuality to be of two kinds: the first, sudden change, like the transformation of one element into another as in the case of fire becoming air, in which case the elemental form is cast away suddenly and a new elemental form takes its place; the second, gradual change which takes place by means of motion such as the gradual transformation of one quality into another or one quantity into another or one situation into another or one place into another. As a result, they limited motion to the four categories of quality (*kaif*), quantity (*kam*), situation (*wa^cd*) and place (*^cain*).

Mulla Sadra, however, as a result of the dmonstrations that he offers, denies the sudden transformation of material substances from one form to another, i.e., generation and corruption. Rather, he considers this type of transformation as a kind of motion and finally proves motion in the category of substance, or substantial motion.

The consequence of this view is that all material bodies are in motion in their substance as well as accidents and all permanent and unchangeable beings are free from matter and potentiality. And according to this view, the division of being into potential and actual is the same as the division of the world into changing and permanent beings. Each material being that possesses potentiality and possibility is changing and in motion and each immaterial being which has no potentiality or possibility is permanent and without motion. The material world with all its substantial and accidental elements is an immense unit in motion, like a boundless stream of flowing water that is constantly passing and is never the same in two successive moments.

As a consequence Mulla Sadra believes that the individuals of corporeal species are all limited to four dimensions, length, breadth, depth and time, that each of these bodies is divided, segmented and scattered according to dimensions of time and its unity preserved by the separated souls (*nufus-i mujarradih*) or archetypes.

This general motion takes place between the two points of potentiality and actuality, and as a result of it the material world is continually transplanting a part of itself from the region of incompletion and imperfection to the world of catharsis (*tajarrud*) or spiritual substances. The world is in reality a plant for generating catharsis, a plant which by its activity guides its primary matter through motion and flow to reach the spiritual world and after complete catharsis and separation from matter turns once again to the transformation of another set of substances.

In the same manner, Mulla Sadra considers the human soul to have a corporeal origin and spiritual subsistence, i.e., the soul in the beginning is the same as the corporeal body which gradually through substantial motion reaches catharsis and at least becomes separated from the body.

9. The division of being into created (*hadith*) and uncreated (*qadim*). In this discussion various kinds of precedence, antecedence and associations that are to be found in the existing world are investigated and then the meaning of created and uncreated and their various categories are considered.

Since the whole universe is caused by the Source of creation and, as a result, the essence and being of the world depend upon His Being, previous philosophers considered the world to be created in essence and originating from the Necessary Being while they believed time to be endless. According to them, the unlimited nature of time in the case of a possible being does not conflict with its having a cause, for having a cause is due to possibility and need and is not limited to that which is created in time. The philosophers were satisfied with the world being created in essence (*huduth-i Zati*), although some proved also its being "created in eternity" (*huduth-i dahri*). Mulla Sadra as a result of substantial motion succeeded in proving also creation in time (*huduth-i zamani*) for the world, for because of the influence of motion and the gradual change from potentiality to actuality, whatever we assume in the world whether it be the whole or its part, is preceded by non-existence.

10. The discussion of the intellect (*ᶜaqil*) and intelligible (*maᶜqul*). In this question Sadr al-Muti'allihin examines and clarifies all kinds of sensory, imaginative, apprehensive and intellectual perceptions and their characteristics. He divides knowledge into acquired (*husuli*) and innate (*huduri*), and unlike the Peripatetics who limit innate knowledge to the knowledge of a thing of its own essence agrees with the Illuminationists and divides it into three types: the knowledge of a separate substance of its own essence, that of a cause of its effect and that of an effect of its cause.

Also in opposition to all the other Muslim philosophers, he accepts the union of the intellect and the intelligible which Porphyry, one of the disciples of Aristotle's school, had acknowledged in summary fashion Mulla Sadra proves in detail the union of the knower and the known (the union of the sense with what is sensed, imagination with that which is imagined, apprehension with that which is apprehended, the intellect with the intelligible.) In a special fashion he approaches this meaning that when a perception goes from potentiality to act there is a kind of ontological elevation of the person who has the perception. In reality, perception is a kind of transformation in which the perceptor is transferred from his grade of being to the station of that which is perceived.

11. The division of quiddity into substance (*jauhar*) and accidents (*'aᶜrad*) and an explanation of their various genus and species.

12. Discussions concerning the Necessary Being (*Wajib al-wujub*). In this question the proof of the essence of the Source of Creation, His Unity, affirmative and negative qualities, the particular features of His acts, the relation of the world to its Creator, the proper order which governs the world and the arrangement existing between creatures are considered.

As can be seen from a comparison of the order of philosophical discussions of Sadr al-Muti'allihin with others, he does not differ greatly in the arrangement of philosophical questions from them. It is only his penetration and depth of understanding of the fundamental problems of philosophy, i.e., the principality, unity and gradation of being, that is the secret of his success and has enabled him to produce masterpieces in philosophical ideas such as substantial motion and its secondary aspects, the creation of time of the world, the union of the intellect and intelligible, the principle of "the truth in its state of simplicity contains all things" (*basit al-haqiqah kull al-'ashya*), the principle of "the possibility of that which is higher" (*'imkan-i 'ashraf*) and many other points of advantage and benefit which can be gathered from the intricate mesh of his thoughts.

Sayyid Abu'l-Hasan Qazwini

The spiritual sage, metaphysical philosopher, illuminated gnostic and expert jurisprudent, Sadr al-Din Muhammad ibn Ibrahim al-Qazwini Shirazi, is one of the greatest glories of Shi'ism and one of the most outstanding sages of Persia. His birth occurred in the year 979/1571 A.H. (lunar), for in the margin of a manuscript of the *Asfar* in the hand writing of Qawam al-Din Ahmad Walad, the author of the *Asfar* who is Sadr al-Din himself, in the discussion of the union of the intellect and the intelligible in the section on general principles, where the author considers the discovery of the truth of the problem of the union of the intellect and the intelligible as a special illumination received personally from God, writes that this illumination occured on Friday of Jamadi al-'ula in the year 1037/1627 A.H. when fifty-eight years had passed from the author's life. His death occured in the year 1050/1640 A.H.

His father, Mirza Ibrahim was one of the Safavid *wazirs*. Since he did not have a male child he decided to spend a great deal of wealth in the way of God if he were to be granted with a devout and worthy son. Sadr al-Din, after reaching the age of adolescence by which time he had completed his elementary education and certain aspects of jurisprudence *(fiqh)* and its principles (*usul*), journeyed to Isfahan.

In Isfahan he studied first with the Shaykh al-Islam of the time, Baha' al-Din ᶜAmili in jurisprudence and its principles and then through his advise presented himself to the "Seal of the sages and religious authorities" (*Khatam al-hukama' wa'l-mujtahidin*), Sayyid Muhammad Baqir Astirabadi, known as Damad and having the pen name Ishraq. To complete his education Sadr al-Din learned the intellectual sciences in the most complete fashin from the inspired breath of Mir and received the highest religious certificate (*ijazah*) to be able to give rullings of his own or *ijtihad* from both masters as he mentions at the beginning of his commentary upon the *Usul-i kafi* naming the two great sages with the highest respect and admiration.

After returning to Shiraz, he became the object of jealousy of the pretenders to knowledge, as has been the case in the ages past and present, and was so much attacked, threatened and insulted that he left Shiraz and retired to a village near Qum. There, he passed his time in ascetic practices sanctioned by religious law, extra-religious duties, daily fasts and keeping awake at night. According to what we have learned from our masters he marched seven time on foot with the caravan to Mecca, this being certainly the most difficult of ascetic practices.

* * *

In the field of metaphysics, penetration into the difficult metaphysical problems, depth of understanding and excellence of taste he is peerless and without rival and in our opinion is superior and preferrable to Ibn Sina in metaphysics and psychology (*cilm al-nafs*). In the beauty of interpretation, clarity of expression and soundness of logic and explanation no one has been able to equal him.

In the science of jurisprudence also he was an authority as can be seen by the fact that an opinion of Sadr al-Din on intention in making ablutions has been mentioned in the *Hada'iq* that "the master of the moderns " *(Ustaz al-muti'akhkhirin)*, Shaykh Murtada has also cited in his book *Taharah* and in both cases Sadr al-Din has been praised and his opinion accepted. And it seems to us that we have seen this matter ourselves in the *Sharh-i usul-i kafi*.

In the knowledge of the biography of famous men (*cilm al-rijal*) he was unmatched in his day as shown in the *Sharh-i usul* where he gives a detailed discussion of the life of the transmitters of the traditions (*hadiths*) of the book *Kafi*. Sadr al-Din was also well versed in the branches of mathematics like geometry and astronomy as can be seen in his commentary upon the *Hidayah* of Athir al-Din Abhari. However, the greatest virtue of Sadr al-Muti'allihin in the sciences was in his harmonization and coordination of the principles of metaphysics (as derived from ancient philosophy and theosophy) (*hikmat-i ilahi*) with the principles of gnosis (*cirfan*) and the method of the gnostics, whereas before him the differences between the flame of theosophy and the *sapientia* of gnosis was well known.

* * *

He was in general oblivious to worldly things and material objects and never thought to speak in the language of the masses. In a period when the majority of writers named their books after the king or various ministers and dignitaries of the time, Mulla Sadra never adopted such a habit and in none of his numerous writings is there a reference to any of the social and political figures of the time. Yet, despite all these virtues, we think that he was somewhat simple-natured and did not exercise enough discrimination in his writings. Certain realities, although true, should not be expressed in works which become public documents, truths of a metaphysical order which in each age only a few people can understand. And since others do not have the capacity to understand them, they accuse the author of beliefs that are just the reverse of what he intended. And if these people have also evil intentions in their hearts and are afflicted with various sicknesses of the soul then they can cause injury and insult to fall upon the author of the book as was the case with Mulla Sadra... .

* * *

[Features of Mulla Sadra's Philosophy]

One—The problem of principality of Being in clear and perfect analysis and demonstration.

Two—Special Unity (*tawhid-khass*), correctly demonstrated.

Three—Motion in the category of substance in perfection and completion.

Four—Problem of the union of the intellect and the intelligence.

Five—The union of the rational soul (*nafs-i natiqah*) with the active intellect (*ᶜaql-i faᶜᶜal*) in its upward progress toward realization.

Six—The rule that the truth in its state of simplicity contains all things (*basit al-haqiqah kull al-'ashya'*).

Seven—The belief that the soul is brought into being with the body but has spiritual subsistence independent of the body.

Eight—The rule that the soul is one in its many faculties.

Nine—The subsistence and catharsis of the power of imagination in the intermediate world (*barzakh*).

Ten—Complete proof of the truth of the archetypes or "Platonic ideas" and what the ancients meant by them.

Eleven—Inquiry into the intermediate forms (*suwar barzakhiyyah*) and reflected images (*muthul maᶜallaqah*) between the world of the intelligibles and Nature.

Twelve—Inquiry into bodily resurrection in a manner of his own which is not to our satisfaction, and other principles.

And this ends our discussion of Sadr al-Din's life and works, thanks be to God.

* * *

In order to complete this article we thought it appropriate to discuss in brief one of the hights of Mulla Sadra's doctrines so that the reader may come to realize the great power of thought and elevation of metaphysical knowledge of that sage. Since the principle of substantial motion and the demonstrations of its reality is characteristic of his doctrines and many other problems are derived from it we have chosen to explain and prove this principle in greater detail.

* * *

Know that this question is extremely worthy and valuable; it is among the most important in the science of metaphysics. Before beginning the discussion we shall mention two introductions:

First introduction: Know that possible being (*mumkin*) is of two kinds: substance (*jauhar*) and accident (*ᶜarad*). Substance is that which subsists through its own essence, that is, considered in itself it becomes all at once a part of the world of existence, and its existence is not derived from and is not an aspect of another being, such as the natural body, the substance of the soul and the intellect.

By accident is meant that which subsists by other than itself, i.e., it has no independence in existence. Its creator and originator must of necessity create its existence in another being and must therefore be among the qualities and aspects of that other being, whether the accident be sensible like white and black and taste, smell, softness, hardness, roughness and the like, or whether it be non-sensible like knowledge (*ᶜilm*) if we consider knowledge as an accident or perhaps like bravery, generosity, joy and sadness and other accidents of the soul.

Since accident as explained above depends upon the existence of substance and has no independent existence of its own, in strength and weakness also it must follow the strength and weakness of the substance which is its abode (*mahall*). For example, the strength and perfection of the perfume and taste of an apple depends upon the strength of the substantial form of the species (*surat-i nawᶜiyyah-i jauhariyyah*) which is the reality of the apple. And if the smell and taste of the apple are not perfect and complete it is because the apple is not as yet ripe, i.e. its substantial form has not yet become strong and its substance has not as yet reached perfection.

In motion and rest also accident is subservient to substance in the sense that whenever a body undergoes motion in its accidents and qualities, it must be said that the substance of its essence is also in movement, and to whatever degree of its substantial form of species it reaches to the same extent and degree does it attain in its accidents and qualities. And when substance exists in one of its qualities and that which moves is not of the degree of that quality, it becomes evident that it is also unchanging and without movement in its substantial essence. We shall explain this matter fully in the conclusion of these introductory remarks, if God wills.

It must be remembered that this discussion concerns accidents belonging to the essential nature of the substance such as the color red in flowers and the smell of apple in an apple. By that is meant that the law of the subservience of the accident to the substance holds true only in the case of accidents which derive from the substance and the essence of the object itself and not from external accidents which come into being as a result of external causes such as a color that has been painted upon an object from the outside or the heat of water which results from its being near a fire. The reason is that these accidents which come into being as a result of external factors depend in their strength and weakness and duration upon the external cause, as is evident.

The second introduction concerns the fact that motion according to the correct defintion is the becoming actual or that which is potential, gradually. By this is meant that the coming into being of something in this world can be conceived in either of two ways:

One, that it occurs suddenly without taking any time or duration. Such a thing is called having sudden existence (*ani al-wujud*) such as the becoming parallel of two lines which were not parallel before and were approaching to become parallel to each other. In such a case although the two lines are gradually approaching to become parallel this is only an introduction not a being really parallel which becomes a reality all of a sudden.

Second, that a thing come into being gradually, i.e. whenever we consider it from the moment of its coming into being until its perfection, it is like an extended line which can be divided into parts, each of which has come into being at a moment and the totality in a fixed time. Such is the case of the redness of an apple where from the moment that the coloring begins until it is perfected, from the beginning to end, individual instances from the quiddity of red color came into being. Motion is thus the departure of a subject from deficiency of a quality and perfection toward the realization of that perfection gradually and in such a manner that one part follows another. In other words in whatever category motion takes place such as for example quality, one can imagine individual instances, one type of which is the immediate instance realized immediately and the other the temporal instance which becomes realized gradually. This gradual becoming is called motion.

After these two introductions we now say that motion in the four categories of place, position, quality and quantity is accepted by all the philosophers and sages and there is no need to cite an example. What concerns us here is motion in substance and the moving essence of things, and whether according to rational demonstration motion in the substantial form of the species, which is called nature, that is moving at every moment and brings into being a particular instance of the substance of its being and its essence at every instant, is possible.

Ibn Sina, who is the master of the Peripatetics in Islam, denies substantial motion and rejects it vehemently. Some of his followers have also denied motion in the category of substance as for example the astute sage Mawla ʿAbd al-Razzaq Lahiji in his *Gawhar-murad* and other works.

The foremost among the sages, Muhammad Shirazi, the author of the *Asfar*, has proved this point perfectly and has established demonstrations according to it. He points out that the philosophers in the pre-Islamic period had indicated this truth in a symbolic language, but in the Islamic period no one has been able to establish the validity of this principle with such rigor and strength.

Before giving a demonstration to prove this point, know that the form of the species (*surat-i naw*c*iyyah*) is the truth in each body from which derive all the effects that belong particularly to that body, for each body has effects and accidents that are particular to itself and are not to be found in other bodies, as for example the different properties of various stones and jewels and the properties of various drugs and the different conditions of animals. This substantial form of the species which is also called nature is the basic reality of each thing and also the cause of the distinction between various species. By substantial motion is meant that this form of the species of the elemental as well as celestial bodies partake of motion, and a particular limit of this form does not remain fixed in matter for one moment, rather it is always in transformation.

Since the substance of a thing is in change and transformation, its accidents and qualities which come after its essence must be also changing and becoming transformed. Mulla Sadra thinks in fact that the rational soul of man which is like the form of the species of his body also partakes of substantial motion and is changing. Those who hold to this doctrine believe that the rational soul at the beginning when it first joins the body is very weak and only through substantial motion and change does it reach the ultimate degree of strength. For this reason the qualities, acts and states of a child are at first quite weak and only after the strengthening of the substance of the essence of the soul the qualities and acts become also gradually strengthened.

One is thoroughly amazed at Ibn Sina when he says that the rational soul of a learned and astute sage at the age of seventy in its degree of being is the same as when he was a baby, the only difference between the two cases being in the appearance of accidents and perfections which did not exist at the beginning but have been acquired later in maturity through study without there being any differences brought about in the substance of the soul's essence. This saying is opposed to the clear conscience of every intelligent person who refers to his own being.

It is now appropriate to mention the demonstration for the proof of substantial motion with God's aid. Since the demonstrations for the proof and confirmation of this meaning is numerous, in this treatise we have selected two demonstration which we have described in our own manner.

The First demonstration concerns that which went before, i.e., accidents like quality, quantity, position and others which are essential to each body and derive their existence from the very substance and form of the species of that body. In reality the creation of the accidents and qualities of a body comes from the natural substantial form.

Now, we say that it is impossible that cause which has had an influence upon the effect can remain in every way subsistent and unchanging while the effect changes and perishes. Rather, each time the effect changes, the cause which has an influence upon it must also change.

For example, if we suppose that the natural color of an apple in its first degree is created by its substantial nature and that substantial nature is the ontological cause for that color in that degree, then if the color which is under the influence of the substantial nature moves toward perfection by God's will and is transformed into a new degree of color, it must be admitted that the substantial nature has also changed in its substantial existence and has become transformed to a stronger degree of being. It has also moved toward its own essential perfection, and in fact the change of the cause from the first to the second limit is the reason for the change in the color.

Whenever one opposes this view by saying that the cause remains unchanged in its own condition and still the change in the color to the second degree occurs, it becomes necessary for the effect to become actualized without a cause, for that which was the effect was the first degree of the color, and if that nature remains unchanged the color would also have to remain in the first degree, while we have supposed that the color and qualities have been transformed.

The summary of our explanation is this, that for an accident like color, there are different degrees and grades from its origin to perfection, each of which has distinguishing features different from others. Moreover, each of the grades of these accidents such as color with its distinct character is brought into being by the substantial nature. Therefore, in accordance with the grades of the accident we must accept grades in the being of the substantial nature that has produced it in such a manner that each particular limit of the accident is produced by a particular grade of the substance. And just as accident reaches perfection through motion and does not remain in one condition for a moment, substantial nature also travels through its limits by motion and does not rest in each degree of its substance for more than a moment, after which it is transformed to a new degree.

This is the well-established demonstration of substantial motion in the nature of the world of generation and corruption and in souls united with natural bodies. The whole of the corporeal world is in motion and journeying toward an end in a caravan whose leaders in this natural journey are the substantial natures and souls.

The result of our discussion is that our intelligence leads us to the conclusion that the cause of that which changes is changing and the cause of that which is unchanging is permanent and one cannot relate changing things in their aspect of change to a permanent cause considered in its aspect of subsistence and permanence.

Difficulties and their solutions — if someone wants to deny substantial motion and overcome the difficulty of relating a changing effect to a permanent cause he can say that the light of intellectual judgment requires that a changing and moving effect be related to a changing cause, and nothing above that is demanded by reason. We can observe this rational principle in another way which is as follows: A moving object from the beginning of its motion toward a goal, no matter how much it moves and approaches its goal at each stage, moves in such a way that its distance and proximity toward its goal changes also and partakes of degrees. As is evident, when an object moves toward a goal three miles away, after travelling one mile it has a certain proximity toward its goal and after travelling two miles its proximity changes and it moves closer to the goal. The fact that the degrees of proximity are different and nature through the existence that has a particular limit gives form to that limit and does not give form to the next degree or limit is due to that that the proximity and particular distance to the next degree which is part of the cause of that degree has not been provided. Therefore, the cause of the renewal of an accident like color and taste is not the change of nature but the renewal, difference and succession of the various degrees of proximity to the goal. Or this possibility still remains, so that one cannot give the above proof for substantial motion and the demonstration remains incomplete.

The answer to this criticism depends upon a detailed introduction which is useful and beneficial in many problems of metaphysics. So, we say that the ontological cause of an effect is of two kinds:

First, the active cause which is also called the ontological (*mujizah*) cause. This means that whenever a being is issued forth from another being and is like the shadow or emanation of that being, then the first being is called effect and the second the active, effective or ontological cause, like fire for heat and turning and the motion of the hand for the turning of the key.

The second kind is the preparing (*mu^{c}iddah*) cause which plays no part in bringing the effect into being. Rather, its effect is that it prepares matter for accepting the effect of the active and ontological cause, such as the dryness of wood for accepting burning from fire and the womb for preparing the sperm to accept human form from the Giver of Forms (God). Therefore, the preparing cause helps the effect in accepting the divine effusion and does not aid the active cause in giving effusion. Between these two kinds there is a great difference which must not remain hidden to the intelligent observer.

Now, we say that the different degrees of proximity to the goal of the moving object is of the kind of preparing cause, i.e., each degree of motion prepares the subject for the next degree which does not arrive until the first degree has been reached. Therefore, changes and differences in the degrees of proximity have no influence upon the differences that are suitable to the substantial nature in issuing forth various degrees of accidents. Rather, they influence the different degrees of acceptability of the subject. Thus, the difficulty of relating a changing nature to a permanent one remains and there is no way to overcome it save by accepting substantial motion. One must pay much attention to this point, for it is very profound and delicate. The Second Demonstration for the proof of substantial motion is in that which we explained at the beginning of this discussion, i.e., accident in its degrees of existence depends completely upon substance and has not independence of its own. Whenever we imaging that it has become independent in some matter, that is, we consider some judgment to hold true for it without reference to its subject, we have gone outside of the reality of the accident, and there must therefore be a transformation in the quiddity of the accident which itself, rationaly speaking, is impossible.

We thus say that one of the degrees of the existence of accident is motion and rest, these two states belonging to the existence of the accident, just as if we were to say permanent and changing color or taste. According to those who deny substantial motion it is necessary that in the case of motion in the category of quality, quantity, place or position, the quality or quantity of the body, for example, becomes separated from its subject, which is the body, in the process of change and transformation. It must also be continuous in the process of going from potentiality to act, while this type of existence for quality or quantity must be permanent irrespective of the subject. This in turn means that these accidents must change their quiddity and become substance, which, however, is impossible.

According to those who accept substantial motion, however, the change of an accident and its transformation is an aspect of the motion of the subject which is the substance, and the principle that an accident is pure subservience is preserved. And this is the desired end... .

Murtaza Mutahhari

He makes the night enter into the day and makes the day to enter into the night and brings forth the living from the dead and brings forth the dead from the living. (The Holy Qur'an)

Conflict, collision and struggle are some of the fixed characteristics of this world. This condition is clearly percevied through superficial observation and profoundly revealed through scientific and philosophical enquiry. We live in a world full of conflict and interference. This is the world of creation and destruction, making and breaking, weaving and tearing apart, birth and death. Here we see a whole series of opposites paired in an eternal embrace: good and evil, being and non-being, pleasure and pain — these are the stuff of reality. As the Persian poet, Sa°di says:

The treasure and the snake,
The flower and the thorn,
Happiness and sadness are inseparable.

Therefore, in each case, two opposite forces are observed existing side by side. Many people consider this world imperfect because of this duality. They say that this is not the best of all possible worlds, that this is not an ideal world. They wish that it were a world in which there was only light, life, goodness, happiness, peace and tranquility. They wish that sickness, darkness, death, evil, misery and anxiety did never exist. These people are amazed that the Creator did not fashion the world in the image of the idealized notions which they happen to conceive.

The ideal of dualism was born from precisely this perception. It was thought that if the world had one source and was ruled by a single principle, two opposite tendencies would never exist.

The opposite way of interpreting this duality is that evil and non-being are superficial and relative aspects of goodness and perfection. In other words, evil is only superficially bad. Opposition, struggle, and conflict are, if not the basic, at least a necessary condition for all progress and development. All beauty, sublimity, exaltation, perfection, movement and evolution is the outcome of conflict, disharmony and imperfection. Conformity and harmony create peace and stagnation, which are always followed by death and annihilation. Dividing objects into two distinct groups and calling one group good and perfect and the other evil and imperfect, and tracing each group's origin to a separate source is the extremity of superficial thinking. When looked at from a higher perspective, the things which were formerly regarded as evil and imperfect are seen to be good and perfect. All things, irrespective of their designation as good or bad, share equally in the make-up of the perfect order and equally contribute to the beauty and ultimate goodness of the macrocosm. Further, they emanate from a common source and are the manifestations of an invisible witness.

Laughter tells of her benevolence and grace
Lamentation is a complaint of her wrath,

These two opposite songs of the world,
Tell of only one Beloved.

Issues regarding the question of opposition such as the tendency of a pair of opposites to cancel and neutralize each other or to combine and synthesize, the tendency of one to beget the opposite of itself, have always occupied the minds of men, although the intellectual responses to such phenomena have not always been the same, taking sometimes an optimistic view and at other times a pessimistic interpretation has been adopted. At times men were led by this apparent dualism to deny the existence and the unity of God, and at other times to believe in the all-pervading will and power of the Creator. Sometimes it has led to theological dualism and at other times given birth to belief in absolute unity of the Divine attributes.

The Holy Qur'an, that ultimate source of Divine revelation, which has had the most significant role in forming the views of Muslim philosophers and scholars, always speaks of opposition and contrast as the "signs" of God:

> *Why do you not acknowledge the magnificence of your Creator, when he made you in so many different kinds. (LXXI, 14)*

And:

> *Among His signs is the variety (difference) of your languages and colours. (XXX, 32)*

Especially, there are numerous references to one opposite giving birth to its own opposite. The Qur'an also considers this condition to be a sign of the wisdom and craftsmanship of God.

> *He makes the night to enter into the day and makes the day to enter into the night and He brings forth the living from the dead and brings forth the dead from the living. (The Holy Qur'an)*

In the *Nahj al-balaghah* we frequently encounter the combination of the opposites treated as an issue relating to the question of the oneness of God:

> The fact that He has made sense faculties proves that He has no sense faculty; the fact that He has made things which are opposite to each other, proves that He has no opposite; the fact that He has made things similar to each other, proves that there is nothing like Him. He made the light the opposite of darkness, clarity the opposite of ambiguity, solidity the opposite of fluidity, hotness the opposite of coldness. He reconciled the homogeneous things and associated the heterogeneous. Things which were far apart He brought close and things which were close, He made distant from each other.

Modern philosophers have attributed great significance to the question of contradiction, holding the view that contradiction is the cause of every movement and evolution. They believe that evolution is nothing but the synthesis of opposites and contradictories and the replacement of simple pairs of opposites by more complex ones. Some of these thinkers went so far as to deny the oldest law of logic i.e. the Principle of Contradiction, which holds that the contradictories are always mutually exclusive. They removed the distance between being and non-being, existence and non-existence. This distance was believed by the ancient philosophers to be infinite and therefore the greatest of distances.

Hegel, the famous German philosopher, is the champion of the philosophy of contradiction. It is he who formulated the triad of thesis, antithesis, and synthesis, which was suggested by other philosophers as the description of birth and synthesis of contradictions. Also, it was Hegel who introduced the contradiction into the concept of dialectics and founded the new dialectics.

In his treatise on dialectics, Paul Foulquié says:

> Hegel did not invent the triad of thesis, antithesis, and synthesis, Fichte and Shelling, Hegel's contemporaries, had also based their metaphysical views on these concepts. Hegel, however, made utmost use of this principle and considered it to be the ultimate explanation of reality. He designated it as "Dialectics" which made the theory strange to the minds of his contemporaries, because, up to that time, the term "dialectics" designated the art of proof and disproof, which were both based on the Principle of Contradiction. Hegel's dialectics, however, meant the "synthesis of opposites".

In another part of Foulquié's treatise he says:

> The difference between the old and the new dialectics is in the way they treat the principle of the mutual exclusivity of the opposites. According to the old dialectics, the principle of mutual exclusivity of the opposites is the absolute law of both objects and the mind. A particular entity cannot both exist and not exist at the same time. And if the human mind encounters two contradictory propositions in succession, one of them must necessarily be false. The new dialectics, however, holds the view that contradiction is a quality of the things themselves and that an object "is" and "is not" at the same time. This quality of self-contradiction is the cause of the change and development of things, so the new dialectics believes, and without it, they would be fixed and unchanging. Therefore, if man is forced to accept two contradictory statements, it is wrong to believe that he is making a mistake. Of course, it is necessary to resolve the contradiction, but neither of the contradictories should be denied.

Also, Foulquié says that, "the reconciliation and synthesis of contradictions in things and in the mind is called dialectics by Hegel. The dialectical method consists of three stages which are usually called 'thesis', 'antithesis', and 'synthesis'. However, Hegel calls these three stages 'affirmation', 'negation', and 'negation of the negation'."

In Hegel's view, *becoming* is neither *being* nor *non-being*. It is the synthesis of both. As Paul Foulquie puts it:

> The first triad of Hegel's philosophy, which is the most famous is this: *Being* "is", i.e. exists. This constitutes the 'affirmation' or the 'thesis' of the triad. But pure unspecified *being* without a particular content of some sort is equivalent to nothing at all. It is the same as *non-being*. Our 'affirmation', therefore, is necessarily followed by its own negation. Therefore, we say that being "is not" or does not exist. Is there a further concept that will overcome this contradiction and prove to be a synthesis of the ideas of *being* and *non-being*? Hegel finds such a concept in that of *becoming*.

We find a view similar to that of Hegel expressed in Islamic philosophy. That is, the state of *becoming*, *being* and *non-being* embrace each other and become one and the same. And that a thing which is *becoming*, both *is* and *is not*. The Islamic philosophers, however, never posited this fact in opposition to the Principle of Contradiction and never believed that it cancels the validity of this principle of logic.

Now, let us take a closer look at what the Islamic philosophers say on the question of contradiction and examine whether it is the same as the views of the Western philosophers; or, if it is not the same, what are the similarities and differences between their views.

Islamic philosophers were well aware of the role of conflict and contradicton in evolution and development, and believed that conflict between creatures is a necessary condition for the continuation of Divine Grace, They have said:

> If there was no conflict, none of the creatures would have emerged.

Or:

> If there were no opposition, the emanation of existence from the First Principle would not have occurred.

That is, no new beings would have been born.

At this point, we should determine whether the Islamic philsophers shared the view of the European philosophers regarding the role of opposition (contradiction) in the process of natural evolution, or if they held a different position. Now, we shall continue our discussion in two parts:

1. The unity of being and non-being in the process of *becoming*.
2. The role of opposition in change, movement and evolution.

* * *

We have already considered Hegel's concept of the reconciliation of the contradictory concepts of *being* and *non-being* in *becoming*. Now, we shall turn our attention to the treatment this subject receives in Islamic philosophy. There are numerous references to this topic by Muslim thinkers.

Fakhr al-Din al-Razi has a famous paradox concerning the problem of becoming. All the things that we think emerge gradually, are in fact born in a sudden manner. The illusion of gradual emergence of a thing is caused by the fact that the object in question is made up of a number of parts. As each part emerges suddenly and these emergences follow one another in succession, we are deluded into thinking that we are witnessing the emergence of one whole object, while in reality we are witnessing the creation of a number of things, each of which is born quite spontaneously; each part being quite separate and independent of the anterior and posterior parts. From this analysis, al-Razi concludes that all movements are in fact a combination of independent parts none of which is a movement and gradual emergence from potentiality into actuality.

Al-Razi defends his position in the following manner. Anything that does not exist and then comes into being, its being must have a *beginning*. Furthermore, this *beginning* is simple and indivisible. It has no beginning, middle, or end. If the *beginning* had a beginning, middle, and end, then the real beginning would be the *beginning* of the *beginning*, and its middle and end would cease to be the part of *beginning*. We apply the same argument to the new *beginning*; if it were not simple the same difficulty would arise. Therefore, we are forced to conclude that *beginning* is simple and indivisible.

Next we say, anything that comes into being, must either be in a state of existence at its *beginning* or in a state of non-existence. If we say that a thing was in the state of non-being at the beginning of its existence, then we cannot say that it was at the beginning of its existence; rather, we must say that it was in the state of non-being and is still in the state of non-being. It would be impossible to say that such an object is in the *beginning* of existence. We are forced to conclude that a thing exists at the *beginning* of its *being*.

Now, either something of that object remains to come into *being* or it does not. If nothing remains to come into *being*, then we have admitted that the thing in question was fully and completely existent at the *beginning* of its *being*. Since the *beginning* is simple and indivisible, the object in question must have come into existence suddenly not gradually. If some of the object still remains, the question arises: is the thing remaining which did not exist at the beginning of the existence of the object, identical with that which existed at the beginning, or, are they two different things? It is impossible for them to be identical because a particular thing cannot both be and not be at one and the same time. If on the other hand, the thing remaining which *is* to come into being is different from that which *has* come into being, then that which came into being in the beginning has come into being fully and instantaneously and nothing of it remains to emerge later. The thing which is yet to come into being, then, is something completely different, distinct and independent of what has already come into being. Gradual emergence and 'becoming,' then, are meaningless notions.

The views expressed by al-Razi caused a great stir among the Muslim thinkers and led to renewed efforts to better understand the nature of movement and time. The theory of time as the fourth dimension of matter, which was forwarded in the Muslim world by Sadr al-Din Shirazi (Mulla Sadra), came in the wake of these intense philosophic efforts.

Mir Damad is the first Muslim thinker to have solved properly the problems raised by Fakhr al-Din al-Razi. Mir Damad first tackles the problem of beginning. He says that when we talk of a gradually emerging object having a beginning, this does not mean that the object in question came into being instantaneously and then continued its existence so that some instant should be taken as the starting point of its being. Such a beginning is appropriate for things which come into existence suddenly and instantaneously, not to gradually emerging things.

Beginning in the gradually emerging things means that since the thing that comes into being has extension and dimensions, which in turn corresponds to a temporal dimension, its *being* possesses the dimension of time, and since its existence is finite, it must have two ends, each end corresponding to a hypothetical point in time. One of these points is its *beginning* and the other is its *end*. Therefore the *beginning* and the *end* of the gradually emerging object both exist in the instant and not in time. The extremities i.e. the *beginning* and the *end* of a continuous entity, whether spatial or temporal, can never be considered as parts of that entity. So the question whether the end points of a continuum are simple or not does not arise. For example, the end point of a line is not part of the line. In fact, the limit of any extended thing has no existence of its own; it is a concept abstracted from the limitation of being. The instant is also nothing but a hypothetical point in time.

Mir Damad then turns his attention to the ontological mode of the temporal and gradually emerging entities and probes into the nature of time itself. He claims that because this kind of objects are existentially weak, the stages of being and non-being are mixed in them. Every stage of their being is associated with the non-being of another stage. Therefore, the answer to the question raised by Fakhr al-Din al-Razi that if a part of a gradually emerging thing becomes existent while another part is still non-existent, does the object in question exist or not, is that every part of that object exists in a particular segment of time. And in another segment of time where another part of the object exists, the first part is non-existent. The totality of the object as a wholly complete unit exists in the totality of time and not in any particular segment of it, and *not* in *any* instant.

In his book *al-Asfar*, Mulla Sadra expresses the same view in a more forceful manner. In the eleventh chapter of his book (the chapter dealing with potentiality and actuality), he says:

> Movement and time are among those things which are existentially weak, i.e. things in which being and non-being are interwoven. Their actuality is associated with their potentiality, and their coming into being is the same as their annihilation. The existence of every part necessitates the annihilation of some other part, or rather, it is none other than the non-being of some other part.

Discussing the relationship of the changing to the unchanging in chapter twenty-one of the discussion on "potentiality and actuality", he first says: "The kinds of actuality and stability that various objects possess are different from one another, and the Ultimate Source has given every object the distinctive form of stability peculiar to itself. And, whenever the stability which an object has is the stability of change, and the actuality of it is the realization of its potentiality and power, inevitably, that would be the sort of stability and actuality which would be granted to it."

Mulla Sadra continues his discussion by saying:

> The thing whose perpetuation or continuity is identical with its becoming ever new is nature. And the thing whose actuality is identical with absolute potentiality, is the primordial, formless matter. And that thing whose unity is identical with its actual multiplicity is the number. And the thing whose actual unity is identical with its potential multiplicity is the body and its physical properties.

In the twenty-eighth chapter of the discussion on potentiality and actuality, Mulla Sadra draws a delicate inference from verse 61 of the sixth chapter of the Holy Qur'an which is as follows:

> *And He is the Supreme, above His servants, and He sends keepers over you; until when death comes to one of you, Our messengers cause him to die, and they are not remiss.*

The inference that Sadr al-Din Shirazi draws from the above quoted verse is this: "A thing, the being and non-being of which are intermixed, and its mere persistence and continuity entails its destruction and annihilation, inevitably, the means of its continued existence are identical with the causes of its destruction and annihilation. Therefore, in the Qur'anic verse the same entities that have the duty of guarding the individual are entrusted with the duty of bringing about his death and oblivion, when the time for it comes. In other words, the agents of survival and preservation of life are trans formed in time into the agents of death and decay."

How is it that such thinkers who so explicitly defend the view that being and non-being are united and intermixed in the natural world, still defend the validity of the Law of Contradiction and call it *umm al-qadaya*, or "the mother of all theorems"?

The fact of the matter is that in the view of these philosophers, the inter wovenness of *being* and *non-being*, which is a necessary characteristic of all changing and transitory things, in no way negates the validity of the Princi ple of Contradiction. In their view, the difficulty has been caused by failing to distinguish between the various ways in which we preceive non-being. In other words, the problem is caused by a failure to adequately understand the mind's tendency to distort and miscomprehend the meaning of non existence.

In order to comprehend this matter properly, two things must be kept in mind:

(a) It is well-known that logicians divide propositions into two general categories of affirmative and negative propositions. In the case of the affir mative propositions, the judgement of the mind is clear: that is, our mind either affirms the existence of the subject of the proposition or its having a particular predicate or property, as, for example, in such statements a "*John is*", or, "*John is standing.*"

Now, how about the negative propositions? For example, if we say "*John is not standing*", what is the purport of this proposition? and what is the mental process involved in reaching a conclusion about it? At first, we might think that the purport of this proposition is that, John is in a non standing position. Such an inference is certainly false. "*John is non standing*" is an affirmative proposition. That is, its essence and nature is af firmative. The negation in the proposition is made a part of the predicate and it is called an 'affirmative proposition with a diverted predicate Whether a proposition is negative or affirmative cannot be determined by its subject or predicate. It is a question the answer to which must be sought beyond the subject and the predicate. Failure to make distinction between these two can cause numerous errors in the reasoning process and in making inferences. Of course, those who are familiar with logic do not mistake these two kinds of propositions with each other and there is no difference of opinion among logicians regarding this matter.

Those who consider the affirmation and negation in propositions to be beyond the scope of the subject and the predicate, belong to two different groups. One group believes that the difference between these two types of propositions is a question of "relationship": affirmative relationship and negative relationship. When we say, "*John is standing*", John and standing are related to each other with a copula which is of the kind that may be designated as "being". And when we say, "John is not standing", the relationship between them is of the "non-being" kind. This group holds the view that the Persian words, *ast* (is) and *nist* (is not) represent the relationship between subject and predicate in a proposition.

However, another group which includes Ibn Sina and Mulla Sadra maintain that the "relationship explanation" is completely erroneous. In their opinion, the same sort of relationship and copula exists in both affirmative and negative propositions. And the kind of copula in both kinds of propositions is affirmative. Such an affirmation, however, is related to concepts (subject-predicate terms) reather than to judgements. The difference between the affirmative and the negative propositions is that in the affirmative proposition the mind judges and affirms the existence of the relationship between the subject and the predicate in the external world, whereas in the negative proposition the existence of such a relationship is denied by the mind.

The purport of the negative proposition, therefore, is not that there exists in the external world a certain thing and that thing is a "relationship of non-being" between the subject and the predicate. What the negative proposition indicates is that the affirmative relationship which exists in the conceptual form in the mind does not exist externally. In other words, what is judged and affirmed in the affirmative propositions is the occurrence of the relationship in the external reality, while in negative propositions what is judged is the non-existence or the non-occurrence of the same relationship. The affirmative proposition tells of the correspondence of the relationship with the external reality, while the negative proposition tells that such a correspondence does not occur. The view that has been expressed while defining declarative statements as opposed to non-declarative ones that "if the truth or the falsehood of the relationship (between the subject and the predicate) can be ascertained through reference to the external reality, the statement is declarative, otherwise it is non-declarative" and that this also applies to the negative propositions, is false.

In the view of these scholars, the content of the negative proposition is *salb al-rabt* (denial of a relation) and not *rabt al-salb* (a negative relation). In other words, the content of the negative proposition is *the negation of the affirmative relation*, not the *affirmation of a negative relation*, which

constitutes the content of an affirmative proposition with a diverted predi
cate (*mujabat ma^cdulat al-muhmul*).

The truly negative proposition is precisely as has just been described, an
this is the only expression for the contradictory of existence. The purport o
the negative proposition is nothing other than the negation of the content o
the affirmative proposition. Furthermore, the negative proposition does no
assign any conditions to the act of negation itself, be they temporal o
spatial. Whatever terms of specifications exist in the negative propositio
are subject to negation and are part of the predicate which is being negated
Only with this consideration could *non-being* be said to exist as a contra
diction and negation of *being*. To put it another way, if we have two prop
ositions one of which negates all the contents of the other and has no othe
function than this, then these two propositions are contradictory. For ex
ample, if we say that "Ahmad is standing at such and such a place at suc
and such a time", its contradictory would be: "It is not the case that Ahma
is standing on such a place at such and such a time." If a thousand condi
tions and terms be added to the first proposition, the second propositio
negates the first proposition with all its myriad of conditions and terms; an
this is the real meaning of the logical axiom that the contradiction of every
thing is its negation (*naqid kull shay' raf^cuh*). Such two propositions, th
real and logical contradictions of each other, are mutually exclusive, an
the law of the mutual exclusivity of the contradictories applies to them.

Non-being, interpreted and used in this way—which is, by the way, th
main interpretation and use of this concept—has no external reality and in
herent existence of its own. It can be neither a subject nor a predicate. The
dimensions of time and space do not apply to it; time and space are not a
vehicle for non-being; they belong to the particular object that it negates.
Therefore, in the sense just mentioned, *non-being* is pure negation. Here
the intellect is taking an overview of the world and concludes that a particu
lar conceptual entity simply does not exist in the external reality, i.e. it ha
no denotation.

There is another interpretation of *non-being* which is in reality a figura
tive one. In this interpretation, *non-being* has a denotation and exists i
time and space. It can be both a subject and a predicate. What we have i
this case is that when the mind surveys the external world and perceives tha
a certain thing is not in it, it supposes that negation has taken the place o
affirmation and that non-being has occupied the place of being. In othe
words, when it perceives the absence of a particular object in a specific loca
tion, our mind imagines that its place is empty and its *non-being* occupies it
Thus interpreted, *non-being* comes to occupy its own space just as *bein*

does. It also comes to possess its own essence and the capacity to be either the subject or the predicate. Therefore, there is a difference between the propositions, "X does not exist in the world", and "X is non-existent in the world". In the second proposition for the "non-existence" of "X" in a particular space in the external world is posited. Of course, we know that *non-being* has no real denotation. Inevitably the existence of other things is figuratively taken to denote the non-existence of the hypothetical object. It is because of this that it is said: every stage of *being* marks the annihilation of another stage.

Now that the two interpretations of *non-being* have been considered, it can be clearly perceived that in its fundamental interpretation and meaning *non-being* has no independent and inherent existence of its own, being purely a negation and denial of *being*. In the second interpretation, *non-being* is granted independent existence metaphorically; however, in the sense it is not the contradictory of *being*.

(b) Now let us consider the question of *becoming*. *Becoming* refers to the continuity, gradualness and the fluidity of *being*. A thing that comes about gradually, possesses a sort of extension and continuity which is parallel to time. In fact, the extension of time is none other than the extension of the continuous and gradual stages of existence which are sequentially related to each other in the relation of potency and act.

A quality of the extended thing is that while it possesses a continuous and actual unity, the intellect is able to divide it into mathematical parts and segments. Since the extension in question is temporal and it has its roots in potentiality and actuality, inevitably, the hypothetical parts and segments precede or succeed one another with no possibility of existing simultaneously. Furthermore, since these segments have no simultaneity, they are devoid of each other, they lack each other. To put it another way, since no two segments can exist in the same time-frame, each part presupposes the non-existence (according to the second interpretation) of the other part. Or we may say that in duration of the preceding part "non-existence" of the succeeding part is true, and in the duration of the following part "non-existence" of the preceding part is true.

On the other hand, we know that these divisions are imaginary and hypothetical ones, not really disconnected and discrete parts. Furthermore, every extended object is infinitely divisible by the mind, and this divisibility does not come to an end. Every segment can be divided into two smaller parts everyone of which is the "non-being" of the other part. Each of these new parts can in turn be divided into smaller parts everyone of which is the "non-being" of all the others. These parts can be divided into even smaller ones,

and so on *ad infinitum.* It is therefore inevitable that segments and stages
are posited on an infinite scale. Furthermore, as degrees and parts are conceived infinitely, it follows that *non-being* is also posited infinitely because
each part implies the *non-being* of all the other parts. Since no end to division can be conceived, being and non-being are so closely interwoven that it
is impossible to imagine any boundary between them.

In objects with a gradual existence, we cannot find any stage in the existence which remains constant in a duration of time irrespective of its
length. We cannot find any stage of the existence of an evolving object remaining fixed in any particular duration of time, irrespective of how small
the duration in question happens to be. Every stage and section of the evolving object can be divided into past and present and into preceding and succeeding parts. Every one of the newly defined stages can in turn be divided
into a preceding and a succeeding section, and this process can be continued
ad infinitum. What cannot be found anywhere here is *now,* that is, the
duration of time lying between the past and the future. The past and the
future are all there is, and every past is a combination of a past and a future.
Whatever exist is either preceding something or following something, and
everything which is preceding is itself a combination of a preceding thing
and a following thing, while everything which is following is itself made up
of something which precedes and something that follows. Everything is
made up of *being* and *non-being.* Anything that exists contains both *being*
and *non-being* within itself, just as everything that does not exist is also
complex, both of being and *non-being.*

Evidently, when we speak of the intermixing of *being* and *non-being,* we
are not talking about the mixing of two real elements. The kind of mixture
we have in mind involves one real element (*being*) and one hypothetical element (*non-being*). Inevitably such a mixture takes place in the mind and the
imagination, not in the external world and the external reality. As far
as the external and the real world is concerned, all there is, is an existence which is slippery and fluid in nature. There is nothing outside of
such existence.

From what has been discussed, it can be clearly understood that *non-
being* taken to mean the negation of *being* has no external reality. Therefore, it would be meaningless to speak of its mixture with existence. On the
other hand, when *non-being* is interpreted as having a sort of hypothetical
existence and reality of its own, and the capacity to mix with *being* it does
not contradict existence. The claim, therefore, that the union of *being* and
non-being in *process* and *becoming* is equivalent to a coupling of contradictions and reconcilement of opposites, and that it negates the Law of Contra-

liction, and furthermore, that Hegelian dialectics has succeeded in disproving the validity of the Law of Contradiction, is caused by not having paid sufficiently close attention to the real meaning of the problem and the different interpretations of the concept of *non-being*.

The truth of the matter is that it is impossible for someone to understand the real meaning of the Law of Contradiction and deny its validity. If someone were to make the sort of claim that has been just mentioned and interpret arbitrary metaphors as contradicting the Law of Contradiction, it must be taken more as a joke than a serious argument. Such claims merely indicate an over-abundant appetite for new ways of philosophizing.

The difference of opininion that prevails between the Islamic philosophers and Western thinkers like Hegel regarding the problem of *becoming* is not limited to the conclusion that Western scholars have tried to draw regarding the union of contradictions. Although both of these modes of thought appear to reach similar conclusions in that they say 'in *becoming*, *being* and *non-being* are in an embrace,' the foundations and roots of these two modes of thought are completely different, and they have emerged from completely different origins.

From the point of view of Hegelian dialectics, "Every conception is a combination of relations. We are able to conceive something only when we can imagine its relationship to some other object and know their similarities and differences. Any conception devoid of relationships would be meaningless. This is what is meant by the dictum 'pure existence is identical with nothingness.' That sort of *being* that is devoid of all attributes and relationships does exist, and is meaningless.'

"The first triad of Hegel's philosophical system, which is also the most famous, is: *being* exists. This is the stage of thesis or affirmation. However *being* which is undefined, and has an unspecified nature so that we cannot say it is this or that, is equal to *non-being* or nothingness. Thus, following our affirmation it becomes necessary to negate it. Therefore, we say: *being* is not. This negation is itself negated, and we reach the third stage: that of synthesis. Thus we say that *being* is *becoming*." (Paul Foulquie's *Treatise on Dialectics*) In Hegel's view, therefore, pure *being* cannot be real, and *being* becomes a reality through synthesis with *non-being*.

In the opinion of the Islamic philosophers, especially Mulla Sadra, what possesses reality is pure *being*, and the determined and manifested beings derive their reality from pure *being*. In the opinion of these thinkers, when *being* reaches its weakest point in the order of its descent, it takes on a fluid quality, mixed with *non-being*, and takes the form of *becoming*. This is precisely the opposite of Hegel's notion of *being*.

Sayyid Muhammad Baqir Sadr

The Principle of Causality

The principle of causality is one of the primary propositions known to people in their ordinary lives. This principle states that for every thing, there is a cause. It is one of the necessary rational principles; for a human being finds at the heart of his nature a motive that causes him to attempt to explain the things he encounters and to justify the existence of such thing by disclosing their causes. This motive is inborn in the human nature. Also it may be present in a number of animals. Thus, such animals instinctively pay attention to the source of motion in order to know its cause. The search for the source of a sound, again in order to know its cause. That is why human beings are always confronted with the question: "Why...?" This question is raised concerning every existence and every phenomenon of which they are aware, so that if they do not find a specific cause of [of such an existence or such a phenomenon], they believe that there is an unknown cause that produced the event in question.

The following things depend on the principle of causality: (1) demonstration of the objective reality of sense perception; (2) all the scientific theories and laws that are based on experimentation; and (3) the possibility of inference and its conclusions in any philosophical or scientific field. Were it not for the principle and laws of causality, it would not be possible to demonstrate the objectivity of sense perception, nor any scientific theory or law. Further, it would not be possible to draw any inference in any field of human knowledge on the basis of any kind of evidence. This point will soon be clarified.

Causality and the Objectivity of Sense Perception

In "The Theory of Knowledge," we pointed out that sense perception is nothing but a form of conception. It is the presence of the form of the sensible thing in the sense faculties. It does not have the character of a true disclosure of an external reality. That is why, in the case of certain illnesses, a human being may have sense perception of certain things, without assenting to the existence of those things. Therefore, sense perception is not a sufficient ground for assent, judgment, or knowledge concerning the objective reality.

As a result of this, the problem we face is that if sense perception is not in itself an evidence for the existence of the sensible thing that lies outside the limits of awareness and knowledge, then how can we assent to the existence of the objective reality? The answer is made ready in light of our study of the theory of knowledge. It is as follows: The assent to the existence of an objective reality of the world is a primary necessary assent. For this reason, it does not require an evidence. However, this necessary assent indicates only the existence of an external reality of the world in general. But the objective reality of every sense perception is now known in a necessary manner. Therefore, we need evidence to prove the objectivity of every specific sense perception. This evidence is the principle and laws of causality. The occurrence [in the senses] of the form of a specific thing under specific circumstances and conditions reveals, in accordance with this principle, the existence of an external cause of that thing. Were it not for this principle, sense perception or the presence of a thing in the senses could not reveal the existence of that thing in another sphere. Due to this, under a specific case of illness, a human being may perceive certain things, or imagine that he sees them, without discovering an objective reality of those things. This is because the principle of causality does not prove the existence of that reality, as long as it is possible to explain a sense perception by the specific case of the illness. Rather, it proves the objective reality of sense perception if there is no explanation of it in light of the principle of causality except by an objective reality that produces the sense perception. From this one can draw the following three propositions: (1) "Sense perception by itself does not disclose the existence of an objective reality, since it is conception, and it is not the task of conception (regardless of its kind) to give a true disclosure." (2) "Knowledge of the existence of a reality of the world in general is a necessary and primary judgment that does not require evidence; that is, it does not require prior knowledge."--this is the point separating idealism from realism. (3) "Knowledge of an objective reality of this or that sense perception is acquired only in light of the principle of causality."

Causality and Scientific Theories

Scientific theories in the various experimental and observational fields are in general primarily dependent on the principle and laws of causality. If causality and its proper order are eliminated from the universe, it becomes very difficult to form a scientific theory in any field. For the clarification of this, we must point out a number of causal laws from the philosophical group [of laws] on which science rests. These laws are the following:

(1) The principle of causality that asserts that every event has a cause; (2) the law of necessity that asserts that every cause necessarily produces its natural effect, and that it is not possible for effects to be separate from their causes; (3) the law of harmony between causes and effects that asserts that every natural group that is essentially in harmony must also be in harmony with respect to [its] causes and effects.

Thus, in light of the principle of causality, we know, for example, that the radiation emitted from the radium atom has a cause, which is the internal division in the content of the atom. Further, in light of the law of necessity, we find that this division necessarily produces the specific radiation when the necessary conditions are fulfilled. The presence of these conditions and the production of this radiation are inseparable. The law of harmony is the basis of our ability to generalize the phenomenon of radiation and its specific explanation to all the radium atoms. Thus, we say that as long as all the atoms of this element are essentially in harmony, they must also be in harmony with respect to their causes and effects. If scientific experimentation discloses radiation in some of the radium atoms, it becomes possible to assert this radiation as a common phenomenon of all similar atoms, given the same specific circumstances.

It is clear that the last two laws, i.e. the law of necessity and the law of harmony, are the result of the principle of causality. If there were no causality in the universe between some things and some other things; [that is], if things happened haphazardly and by chance, it would not be necessary that, when there is a radium atom, radiation exists at a specific degree. Also, it would not be necessary that all the atoms of this element share the specific radiational phenomena. Rather, as long as the principle of causality is excluded from the universe, it would be possible that radiation pertains to one atom and not to another, just because of haphazardness and chance. Thus, both necessity and harmony are attributed to the principle of causality.

After having clarified the three main points, i.e. causality, necessity, and harmony, let us go back to the sciences and scientific theories. We see with clarity that all the theories and laws involved in the sciences are in truth established on the above main points, and depend on the principle and laws of causality. If this principle were not taken as a fixed philosophical truth, it would not be possible to establish a theory and to erect a general and comprehensive scientific law. The reason is that the experiment performed by the natural scientist in his laboratory cannot cover all the parts of nature. Rather, it covers a limited number of parts that are essentially in harmony. Thus, such an experiment discloses that such parts share a specific phenomenon. When the scientist is certain of the soundness, precision, and objectivity of his experiment, he immediately postulates a theory or a general law applicable to all the parts of nature that resemble the subject of his experiment. This generalization, which is a basic condition for establishing a natural science, is not justified except by the laws of causality in general, particularly, the law of harmony which, [as mentioned], asserts that every group that is essentially in harmony must also be in harmony with respect to [its] causes and effects. Therefore, had there not been causes and effects in the universe, and had things occurred by pure chance, it would not have been possible for the natural scientist to say that what is confirmed in his own laboratory is applicable with no restriction to every part of nature. Let us illustrate this by the simple example of the natural scientist who proved by experimentation that bodies expand when heated. Of course, his experiments did not cover all the bodies in the universe. Rather, he performed his experiments on a number of various bodies, such as the wooden car wheels on which iron frames smaller than they are placed when heated. Thus, as soon as these frames cool off, they contract and clasp the wood firmly. Let us suppose that the scientist repeats this experiment on other bodies a number of times. At the end of the experimental course, he can not escape the following question: "Since you have not covered all the particular bodies, how then can you believe that new frames other than those you have tried will also expand by heat?" The only answer to this question is the principle of laws of causality. Since the mind does not accept haphazardness and chance, but explains the universe on the basis of causality and its laws, including those of necessity and harmony, it finds in limited experiments a sufficient ground for accepting the general theory that asserts the expansion of bodies by heat. This expansion that experiments disclosed did not occur haphazardly. Rather, it was the result or effect of heat. Since the law of harmony in causality dictates that a single group in nature is in harmony with respect to its causes and effects, or agents and results, it is no wonder then that all the reasons of securing the applicability of the phenomenon of expansion to all bodies are met.

Thus, we know that the positing of the general theory was not possible without starting from the principle of causation. Hence, this principle is the primary foundation of all the experimental sciences and theories. In short, the experimental theories do not acquire a scientific character, unless they are generalized to cover fields beyond the limits of particular experiments, and are given as a general truth. However, they cannot be given as such except in light of the principle and laws of causality. Therefore, the sciences in general must consider the principle of causality and the closely related laws of necessity and harmony as fundamentally admitted truths, and to accept them prior to all the experimental theories and laws of the sciences.

Causality and Inference

The principle of causality is the foundation on which all attempts of demonstration in all the spheres of human thought rest. This is because demonstration by evidence for a certain thing means that if the evidence is sound, it is a cause of the knowledge of the thing that is the object of demonstration. When we prove a certain truth by a scientific experiment, a philosophical law, or a simple sense perception, we only attempt to have the proof as a cause of the knowledge of that truth. Thus, were it not for the principle of causality and [the law of] necessity, we would not be able to do so. The reason is that if we discounted the laws of causality and did not accept the necessity of the existence of specific causes of every event, there would not be any link between the evidence on which we rely and the truth that we attempt to acquire by virtue of this evidence. Rather, it becomes possible for the evidence to be sound without leading to the required result, since the causal relation between the pieces of evidence and the results, or between the causes and the effects, is broken off.

Thus, it becomes clear that every attempt at demonstration depends on the acceptance of the principle of causality; otherwise, it is a wasteful and useless attempt. Even the demonstration of the disproof of the principle of causality, which is attempted by some philosophers and scientists, also rests on the principle of causality. For those who attempt to deny this principle by resorting to a certain evidence would not make this attempt had they not believed that the evidence on which they rely is a sufficient cause of the knowledge of the falsehood of the principle of causality. But this is in itself a literal application of this principle.

*   *   *

Fluctuation Between Contradiction and Causality

In spite of the fact that Marxism takes the dialectical contradictions as its model in its analytic investigations of the various aspects of the universe, life, and history, still it does not completely escape wavering between the dialectical contradictions and the principle of causality. Since it is dialectical, it emphasizes that growth and development result from the internal contradictions, as was explained in earlier discussions. Thus, the internal contradiction is sufficient as an explanation of every phenomenon in the universe, without need for a higher cause. But, on the other hand, Marxism admits the cause-effect relation, and explains this or that phenomenon by external causes, and not by the contradictions that are stored in the interiority of that phenomenon.

Let us take an example of this waivering from the Marxist historical analysis. On the one hand, Marxism insists that the presence of internal contradictions is the innermost being of the social phenomena is sufficient for the development of such phenomena in a dynamic motion. But it also asserts that the formidable social edifice is established as a whole on one principal, namely the productive forces, and that the intellectual conditions, the political conditions, and the like are nothing but superstructures in that edifice and reflections, in another form, of the productive method on which te edifice is erected. This means that the relation between these super structures and the productive forces is the relation of an effect to a cause. There is no internal contradiction but causality.

It is as if Marxism realized that its position vacillates between internal contradictions and the principle of causality. Thus, it attempted to reconcile both sides. It imposed on the cause and effect a dialectical sense, and rejected its mechanical notion. On the basis of this, it allowed itself to use in its analysis the cause-effect procedure in the Marxist dialectical fashion. Thus, Marxism rejects the causality that takes a straight course in which the cause remains external to its effect, and the effect negative in relation to its cause; for such causality is in conflict with the dialectic, i.e. with the process of essential growth in nature. This is because the effect in accordance with this causality cannot be richer and more developed than its cause, for increase in richness and development would be inexplicable. But what Marxism intends by the cause and effect is this: The effect is the product of its contradictory — thus it develops and grows by an internal motion, in accordance with the contradictions it involves, such that it returns to the contradictory from which it sprang, in order to interact with it and, by means of its union with it, form a new composition more self-sufficient and richer than the cause and effect separately. This notion is in agreement with the dialectic and expresses the dialectical triad, i.e. the thesis, antithesis, and synthesis. The cause is the thesis, the effect is the antithesis, and the union which is a link between the two is the synthesis. Causality here is a process of growth and completion by way of the production of the effect from the cause, i.e. the antithesis from the thesis. The effect in this process is not produced negatively. Rather, it is produced accompanied by its internal contradictions that support its growth and preserve its cause in a loftier and more complete composition.

In our previous discussion of the dialectic, we expressed our view regarding those internal contradictions whose union and struggle in the interiority of a being lead to the growth of that being. In light of the Marxist deeper notion of the cause-effect relation, we can know the error of Marxism in its notion of causality and the growth of the effect to which this form of causality leads, as well as the completion of the cause by union with its effect. Since the effect is a kind of relation and link to its cause, the cause cannot be completed in a loftier composition by means of the effect. In the work, *Our Economy,* p. 23, we discussed some of Marx's applications of his dialectical notion of causality on a historical level, where he tries to prove that the cause is completed by its effect and unites with it in a rich composition. In that discussion of ours, we were able to show that these applications were the product of philosophical inexactitude and lack of precision in defining cause and effect. Two causes and two effects may exist, where each of the two effects completes the cause of the other. When we are not careful in distinguishing the two causes, it will appear as if the effect completes its own cause. Also, the effect becomes a cause of the availability of one of its conditions for existence. But the conditions for existence are other than the cause that produces that existence.

Index

Quraysh Tribe, 87, 134-35, 162, 206
Qurra ibn Qays al-Hanzali, 327
qutb, 106, 179, 202

al-Rabab (Wife of Imam Husayn), 314
Rafidis, 87
Rahman, Fazlur, 98
Ramyar, Mahmud, 5, 227
Ra^cna Husayni, Karamat, 349
Rasa'il of Ikhwan al-Safa, 93, 302-3
Rashid, Husayn Quli, 348
Rashidun Caliphs, 16-18, 67, 71-74,
    77, 88, 158
Rashti, Kazim, 99
Rationalism; Islamic Modernist view
    of, 79-80
rawdih-khani, 254, 260-62, 266, 312
Rawdat al-shuhada, 266
al-Razi, Fakhr al-Din, 67, 342, 371-73
Razi, Najm al-Din (Dayih), 193
Renaissance, 334
Revelation; Shi^ci view of, 127-54
Rida, Muhammad Rashid, 70, 78
Ridwan (the Angel of Paradise), 172
Rightly Guided Caliphs. See Rashidun
    Caliphs
risalah, 155
Risalah fi ma^crifat al-wujud, 190
Ruhban ibn ^cAws, 149
Rukn al-Din Khurshah, 60
Rumi, Mawlana Jalal al-Din, 7
al-Rummani, 236
Rustam, 320

Sa^cadat, Shahriyar, 7
Sabiri, Ghulam Husayn, 319
Sabziwari, Hajj Mulla Hadi, 6, 348-50